T0272147

THE
QUEER
ART
OF
HISTORY

THE
QUEER
ART QUEER
OF KINSHIP
HISTORY
AFTER
FASCISM

Jennifer V. Evans

DUKE UNIVERSITY PRESS
Durham and London
2023

© 2023 DUKE UNIVERSITY PRESS
All rights reserved
Printed in the United States of America on acid-free paper ∞
Designed by A. Mattson Gallagher
Typeset in Untitled Serif and Futura by Westchester
Publishing Services

Library of Congress Cataloging-in-Publication Data
Names: Evans, Jennifer V., [date] author.
Title: The queer art of history : queer kinship after fascism / Jennifer
V. Evans.
Description: Durham : Duke University Press, 2023. | Includes
bibliographical references and index.
Identifiers: LCCN 2022041834 (print)
LCCN 2022041835 (ebook)
ISBN 9781478019794 (paperback)
ISBN 9781478017110 (hardcover)
ISBN 9781478024361 (ebook)
Subjects: LCSH: Sexual minorities—Germany—Historiography. |
Sexual minorities—Civil rights—Germany—History. | Sexual
minorities—Germany—Social conditions. | Queer theory—
Germany. | Intersectionality (Sociology)—Germany. | BISAC:
HISTORY / Europe / Germany | SOCIAL SCIENCE /
LGBTQ Studies / General
Classification: LCC HQ73.3.G3 E93 2023 (print) | LCC HQ73.3.G3
(ebook) | DDC 306.760943—dc23/eng/20221207
LC record available at https://lccn.loc.gov/2022041834
LC ebook record available at https://lccn.loc.gov/2022041835

Cover art: Benny Nemer, video still from *The Rosa Song*, 2011.
Courtesy of the artist.

For Jean, Christine, and Bob.
Gone but not forgotten.

Contents

Illustrations

Figures

Plates

Acknowledgments

This book is a product of the emotional maelstrom that is life in the age of uncertainty. I had been carrying around these ideas for some time. They surfaced periodically, a conference paper here, an article there. Lockdown changed something in me, in all of us too. Along with the sleeplessness and anxiety of those first months, I found solace and not a little escape in writing this book. We all have an account of how we tried to find our way through the pandemic. Mine was by reconnecting with people an ocean away, brought into my orbit through their stories, photographs, and commitments, in some cases generations ago. It was through kinship, in other words, with a past that was not my own that I found the compulsion to write. The ties that bind us emotionally, intellectually, politically—across seemingly insurmountable differences—lent me resilience in the face of adversity, of which there is much, still, today.

There are a great many people whom I call kin, who emboldened me in their different ways to write this book. Some will never know the power of their intervention, although I have tried to show my appreciation through citation in the text itself. Others have given the gift of time, whether in sharing their thoughts on the manuscript as it developed or by checking in to see if I was okay. I treasure these interactions, large and small. They lifted my spirits and helped me in immeasurable ways.

My research into the world of LGBTQIA history in Germany has now encompassed the bulk of my adult life. It came about, in large part, because a host of people opened their hearts and minds to me over the course of many visits. From those early days at the old Landesarchiv Berlin on Kalck-reutstraße, where I first met Andreas Pretzel and he introduced me to the team of citizen researchers doing work on Nazi crimes, I benefited from his enormous generosity of spirit. Through him I met Jens Dobler and Ralf Dose, whose work, friendship, and collegiality has shaped my thinking ever since. This intellectual and friendship network has since broadened to include Martin Lücke and Andrea Rottmann at the Freie Universität Berlin, Benno Gammerl at the European University Institute in Florence, and Katrin Köppert at the Hochschule für Grafik und Buchkunst in Leipzig. I'm especially grateful to be part of an international network of scholars supported by the Deutsche Forschungsgemeinschaft to bring critical queer, lesbian, trans*, and nonbinary history to wider publics. Many thanks to Rüdiger Lautmann and Florian Mildenberger for their deep knowledge of the field and to Micha Eggert for his sweet emails and offer of conversation. Paula Villa Braslavsky has been a kindred spirit since we first met in DC. I cherish her insight into all things and her incredibly sharp wit.

My writing has benefited in untold ways from people who work in precarious positions and on shoestring budgets all in the name of community, art, and history. This has made possible the wonderful collections housed at the Magnus Hirschfeld Foundation, the Spinnboden Lesbenarchiv und Bibliothek, das feministische Archiv FFBIZ, and of course, the Schwules Museum*. I'm especially grateful to Birgit Bosold, Ben Miller, and Peter Rehberg for allowing me into their circle of friends. Activists, artists, and early career scholars have expanded the playing field exponentially and challenged us to rethink what we believe we already know. My deepest appreciation goes out to Bodie Ashton, Katrin Bahr, Ingeborg Boxhammer, Cassils, Nora Eckert, Sanni Est, Kyle Frackman, Christiane Leidinger, Ervin Malakaj, Markues, Adrienne Merritt, Marit Östberg, Jennifer Petzen, Simone Pfleger, Nihad Nino Pušija, Liz Rosenfeld, Tucké Royale, and Jasco Viefhuis and the Autonomous Feminist Women and Lesbians from Germany and Austria. Many thanks too to the anonymous reviewers whose suggestions gave me so much to think about and greatly enhanced this book.

Several people at home and away graciously offered to read early drafts that helped improve the manuscript significantly. At Carleton University,

I could not have hoped for a better group of readers. Ona Bantjes-Ràfols, Dani Carron, Pat Gentile, Laura Horak, Alexis Shotwell, and Christiane Wilke gave the manuscript a trenchant critique with good humor, a few expletives, and tons of support. Katie Sutton gifted me her laser-sharp focus in a rigorous, multipage analysis of the core argument that helped identify inconsistencies and emboldened me to trust myself more. My wonderful student Nicholas Surges created a most usable index. Howard Chiang, Kate Davison, Tiffany Florvil, Craig Griffiths, Anna Hájková, Randal Halle, Lisa Heineman, Sam Clowes Huneke, Erik Huneke, Elissa Mailänder, Laurie Marhoefer, Jake Newsome, Simone Pfleger, Carrie Smith, Helmut Smith, Eliza Steinbock, Bob Tobin, Sébastien Tremblay, and Angela Zimmerman were important interlocutors at crucial points along the way, while Jin Haritaworn was an intellectual lodestar. Monica Black, Laura Madokoro, and Sandra Robinson have brought laughter and joy during difficult times. I'm grateful for the company of these smart women. Finally, Jennifer Adese, Benny Nemer, and Zoe Todd have taught me in very different ways how critical it is that we learn from both the teachings and the mistakes of our ancestors.

This book was written on the unceded, traditional territory of the Algonquin nation. It is a reminder of the responsibility I bear to think about my own implication in the history and legacy of racism and genocide, not as relics of the past but at work today where I live, teach, raise family, and write. This book honors those who labor and struggle to make these stories known.

There are, of course, so many other layers of support that help make books happen. Priya Nelson at Princeton University Press deserves special mention for her help in sparking the idea in the first place, while my former Duke editor, Josh Gutterman Tranen, gave me the gift of freedom to explore. Ken Wissoker and the production team at Duke have been an absolute pleasure to work with, a model for an academic press. The research for this book would not have been possible were it not for research fellowships from Carleton University, the Social Sciences Humanities Research Council of Canada, and the Centre Interdisciplinaire d'Études et de Recherches sur l'Allemagne at Sciences Po. I'm especially grateful for Carleton's Faculty of Arts and Social Sciences and University Research Office and to my dean, Pauline Rankin, who has always been in my corner, even when I was presumptuous as all get out.

I struggle a bit to speak of my immediate kinship circle for—as the kids say—"reasons." The pandemic hit in the middle of already tumultuous teenage years, with a force that was undeniable. There have been transitions big and small. We have survived, sometimes thrived, other times barely held on. We are still here, loving each other, and longing for better days. I know they will come.

ART SAVES ME AND MAKES ME SEE
THE MAGIC. . . . THE MAGIC ALSO
LIES IN THE DESIRE, IN THE EROTIC
ENCOUNTER. UNREPEATABLE,
AND THEREFORE ALWAYS REPEATED,
JUST LIKE PHOTOGRAPHY.

—Krista Beinstein, *Sex Is My Medium*

CRUISING IS HOW YOU TOUCH THE
WORLD, AND THE WORLD TOUCHES
YOU BACK.

—Liz Rosenfeld, "This Should Happen
Here More Often"

INTRODUCTION

When I imagine the stream of my ancestors standing
behind me, I see my adoptive parents, my biological
parents, and I see my queer ancestors.

—Jürgen Baldiga in Jasco Viefhues, *Rettet das Feuer*

ON AN ORDINARY CORNER in West Berlin in the late
1950s, the photographer Herbert Tobias chatted up a
boy. In his late teens or early twenties—it's difficult
to tell from the photographs he'd take over the next
several days—the youth was one of many pickups on
the stroll in the Cold War city. He would be immortalized two decades later, not once, but twice, in the gay
magazine *him applaus*, where readers learned about the
weekend they spent together taking baths, having sex,
and frolicking in the company of an unknown actress,
there along for the ride.[1] The Manfred photo series, as
we'll see in chapter 2, raises a host of questions about
queer life in the aftermath of fascism in a divided city
at the center of the Cold War. But it is instructive in
other ways too for the way it challenges us to think
more capaciously about how people lived, loved, and
lost in the queer past. An association that came quite
naturally for Christopher Isherwood in 1929 when he
wrote "Berlin Meant Boys" is difficult to countenance
today with our heightened sensibilities around consent,

power, and overt expressions of queer desire. It doesn't matter that, at the time these photos were taken, the age of consent was higher for same-sex activity than for straight sex, making boys out of twenty-year-old men.[2] What is interesting is the near unthinkability of intergenerational sex in the gay scene, at least in the main, despite our seemingly prurient age.[3]

This has a history, it turns out, and is central to the story of sexual liberation. But it has also been forgotten. *The Queer Art of History* brings it back into view. Amid the life-altering gains of the second half of the twentieth century, queer claims to the public sphere have papered over the sex of things in favor of a vision of activism and opposition where the messiness of sexual transgression is increasingly written out.[4] It has been sacrificed for several core necessities: an end to illegality and persecution, equal treatment under the law, and unencumbered access to the rights and provisions of citizenship. With the example of Germany, I will show that it is also a response to the institutionalization of LGBTQIA communities generally around the construction of good and bad kin, with some taken up as models of a new civic ideal, while others have been marginalized as a challenge to the norms of respectability. Visibility brought legibility, yet what became legible was not always queer. The gradual embrace of a liberal rights-based framework from the 1970s onward came on the backs of stratifications of race, class, and gender presentation that continue to stigmatize nonnormative kinships today. It traded the radical oppositionality of postwar queerness for a seat at the table. But all is not lost. We can resurrect the potency of these "beautiful inconsistencies" by focusing on queer kinship itself, understood broadly as the coalitions, attachments, hookups, and solidarities of choice and necessity that made up queer life after fascism.[5] The reasons for doing so are not just historiographical; they are urgent.

The memory of the emancipatory projects of the post-1945 period is increasingly under attack, a feature of the deradicalization of social movements generally as well as an organized effort on the part of the populist Right to unmake the gains of the New Left. The two phenomena are not unrelated, and both threaten the democratic aims of social justice, of which queer and trans* worldmaking is a part. This book charts how this has come about and suggests ways that critical historical research and writing can recast the marginalization of transgressive, racialized, and intersectional queer and trans* lives that form part of the contemporary moment. Until we develop methodologies for better understanding the ways in which liberation for some came as violence for others—with race, class, and gender presentation often serving as citizenship's condition of possibility—we overlook the important ways attachments and alliances of kinship provide alternatives to the "markets and morals" sovereignty and subject making of liberal modernity.[6]

To do this, we have to revisit how we write about identity. As LGBTQIA lives have been mainstreamed and protected by legislation in many parts of the world, history writing has moved away from the destabilization of identity and toward embracing it. It wasn't always that way. In the wake of the linguistic and cultural turn, inspired by the work of Judith Butler, Eve Sedgwick, and Michel Foucault, historians called for complex historical explanations of the sexual past to counter the origin stories of social movement–driven histories.[7] Instead of documenting "the evidence of experience" of forebears and ancestors, we were to linger over the conditions that made racialized, queer, and trans* people invisible in the first place.[8] But as Laura Doan and Jin Haritaworn have cautioned in radically different projects, in our quest for queer kin, we have forgotten that the critical work we do is to disturb the practice of essentialism, of seeing queerness unidimensionally, as inherently wed to progressive causes, always on the side of right.[9] Minoritarian impulses are everywhere we look today, and while they help anchor experiences still very much under threat, they can also invoke new universalisms that gloss over the different modalities of situatedness and power that also make up social groups.[10] Not only do we let slip the different inequalities that continue to mark queer and trans* entry into the mainstream—most profoundly around race—but we fail to appreciate what solidarity and coalition building actually looked like when and where it did surface. With queer, feminist, trans*, and intersectional paradigms increasingly up against the wall, it is imperative that we draw lessons from kin formations good and bad to both rediscover and redeploy the radical potential of queer as a politics, analytic, and way of life.

A focus on kinship exposes the power and contradictions of queerness not as an identity category but as a set of relations produced by and through shifting and unequal dynamics of power.[11] Kinship networks and ties, historical affiliations as well as intellectual ones, focus attention on homogenization both within and beyond queer communities, unearthing alternative legacies as a way forward. Thinking about queerness relationally allows us to linger over how certain lives, stories, and ways of being are legitimized while examining what this means for other expressions of solidarity, gender expression, and desire in the past as well as today. If we take a more expansive approach to the range of emotional, political, and intellectual attachments that bind people in opposition to norms, we ask new questions about the successes, failures, and ambivalences of queer activism as we know it.[12]

In Germany, there were countless examples of intersectional queer kinship attachments among gays, lesbians, sexual dissidents, poor and racialized men and women, feminists, and trans* people. There was Elli, the leather-clad butch lesbian bar owner with questionable ties to the Nazis, who sheltered queer and sex worker patrons in 1950s West Berlin. Across the Iron Curtain, East Germany's most famous transvestite (her term), Charlotte von Mahlsdorf, hosted queer dissidents in her suburban villa while sometimes informing on them. Gays and lesbians organized together as well as apart to raise awareness about the persecution of same-sex sexuality in the Third Reich while feminists and lesbian separatists joined forces to lobby for access to abortion and against misogynist media campaigns. Meanwhile, students, artists, and activists tested the boundaries of acceptability within and outside the gay movement, politicizing pedophilia and intergenerational sex and opposing what they saw as assimilation at all costs. That it is hard for us to imagine these entanglements shows how siloed our view of the queer past has become. This book asks: How did we get here? What purpose did these projects once serve? and, critically, Where should we go from here? This last question is all the more imperative as we weather new culture wars that use history as a tool of organized forgetting, separating us from the struggles waged by queer and trans* people and their allies for a more just world.[13]

How might examples from German history aid us in recognizing the problems as well as the possibilities of solidarity building beyond the symbolic purchase of sexology and Nazi persecution, which has a hallowed place in the global queer historical imaginary? Focused around select case studies from East, West, reunited, and contemporary Germany, and the generational changes in German memory culture around race, gender-nonconformity, and sexuality, this book suggests we all fall prey to an orthodoxy of our own when we invoke an identity politics that foregrounds identity but leaves the politics behind.[14]

Between celebrating decriminalization and attaining key social rights, there were and remain fundamental struggles around whose bodies, behaviors, and being belongs in today's Germany, where border policing takes on an entirely new meaning in the era of fortress Europe. A politics of claims making mobilized around siloed identities eschews the transformative power of queer kinship after fascism as queer and trans* people tested out new possibilities for citizenship, love, and public and family life in the decades after World War II. It also fails to address the fundamental inequalities within and among groups themselves. When we layer in race, we see that queer's Other was not always heterosexuality. To get at this, we need a method that coaxes apart the ways our subjects are "differently queered," working against multiple and different forms of pathologization. Using a genealogical approach attuned to the critical interventions of Black feminist, Indigenous, and queer and trans* of color critique around the invisibilization of race, class, and gender presentation in our origin stories is imperative if we are to think anew about intersectional relationalities and the power of diverse and sometimes surprising kinship networks that guided how queer and trans* people lived their lives in turbulent times.[15] It allows us to appreciate the lengths to which people went to make change in both intimate and publicly political ways, and the profound challenges they have faced along the way.

The Intersectionality of Kinship

The main theme that winds through the book is the power of kinship as a way to understand the ambivalences of what David Eng has termed queer liberalism—that is, the empowerment of certain gay, lesbian, and trans* persons through selective rights to privacy, intimacy, and self-determination mediated by race.[16] As an analytic, queer kinship is conceptually nimble. Although it has been used to great effect in gauging filial formations, queer domesticity, and same-sex adoption, scholars of Black feminist and queer and trans* of color critique deploy it to pull apart normative notions of family and nation, placing emphasis on affinities across race and class as well as on the attachments and the affective ties that bind individuals to one another across time.[17] Attention turned to kinship in the 1990s and 2000s, when many Western democracies began debating civil union and gay marriage. Anthropologists and literary and queer theorists asked whether kinship was "always already heterosexual?" Could alternative same-sex and gender-nonconformist community formations retain an element of radicalism or were they destined to mimic reproductive ways of organizing—some would say surveilling—the social?[18] Some, like Lee Edelman and Leo Bersani, jettisoned the filial completely as antithetical to the queer project, while black feminists from Hortense Spillers to Saidiya Hartman and Sharon Patricia Holland pointed instead at kinship's double bind as an institution denied to racialized people through genocide and slavery, opening up new horizons of possibility for relatedness defined differently. These "ethical and sentimental features" that linked diasporic subjects beyond any procreative imperative, in solidarity and salvation, served as a set of relations denied but also as a "technique of renewal." Attachments might serve as acts of resistance and retribution. In this way, kinship is not just biological or even social; it is multidirectional and perspectival. It excavates the past so as to map out new, alternative futures for folks denied the bonds of lineage.[19]

As Elizabeth Freeman contends, drawing on anthropologist David Schneider, these interventions move kinship away from something one *is* to something one *does*.[20] Denaturalizing kinship helps historicize the ties that bind in a broadened sense, facilitating our own entry into the practices and performances of others. It allows us to recognize how kinship networks, allegiances, and affiliations of varying sorts and degrees galvanized a sense of belonging and aided in the formalization of movements and claims making around the removal of antisodomy statutes and discriminatory practices. Unlike identity—tied up in a history of toleration and progress that fails to address the dynamics of exclusion that formed part of this story as well— kinship divulges queer's multiple horizons.[21] But kinship does other work as well. In uniting the stories of disparate people brought together by their shared, though different, experiences of marginalization, it expands queer studies beyond its white, cisgender moorings, providing interpretive space for intersectional critiques of the homologizing force of normativity in late liberalism. Kinship allows us to turn away from a politics of recognition toward the potentiality of the otherwise.[22]

There is a logic to focusing on Germany. Trumpeted as the birthplace of gay identity but also of sexology, its entanglements are part of the warp and weft of queer history and theory.[23] Those entanglements are social, in terms of actors on the ground, but they might also be understood as intellectual in terms of the mythic place of Germany within the global queer imaginary that links us all in kinship with this particular past. Insofar as countless discussions around sexual freedom before and after Nazism were birthed there too, it is the tie that binds us to the perniciousness of twentieth-century ideas around sexuality, taboo, and regulation and also to the different conceptualizations of what forms liberation might take. For some, it is a story that still needs to be told fulsomely, around the eugenic and racial underpinnings of early sexology and the continuation of policies of persecution after 1945. For others, that story has been stylized a certain way, around men's experiences chiefly, and instrumentalized as a success when it might better be viewed as an opportunity to think about continuities of racism, sexism, and transphobia within the German democratic project itself. There is another layer, too, as the narrative of postwar liberalization has become subject to new scrutiny in the era of populism and #MeToo.[24] The need is great for a critical queer history that retains a focus on sexual self-determination, agency, and pleasure amid the possibilities and limits of toleration.

Here, it bears saying that the Right is not alone, or even always the loudest, in miscasting the past to make political points about identity in the present.[25] Laurie Marhoefer has put the lie to the thought that queer politics are always already progressive.[26] And what about gays who could not be properly gay, as Fatima El-Tayeb has stressed, about ethnocentricity in Europe's white queer communities and the outsider status of Muslims?[27] How does it happen that the gains of some come at the expense of others, and what role might our history writing play in changing how that comes about? I argue here that it is owed in part to the way our own histories fall back on certain conventions—conceptual as well as methodological—that cause us to reduce mutable ways of being in the world into hard and fast identities, rigid, legible, uncomplicated, stand-alone, and contained. This inability to see queer and trans* as a series of "perverse assemblages" of productively fraught emotions, stigma, relationships, actions, affiliations, and orientations that are themselves messy, contingent, entangled, and sometimes downright objectionable comes about when we look to the past for histories of confirmation instead of contestations around joy, love, danger, domination, assimilation, and desire.[28] We fall into the trap of telling stories of competing experience instead of commonalities and difference. Most of all, we fail to see queer and trans* lives as associative, as part of elaborate histories of relationality, of kinships bad as well as good, what Sisseton-Wahpeton Oyate professor Kim TallBear calls "all my relations"—that is, the different paths we all take, together and apart, in our search for dignity, resilience, and community in the face of oppression.[29] In order to meet the challenge of backlash and repression, this book provides a tool set for how to think critically about the ties that bind us all to a complicated but no less discernible past as the ground for new sociopolitical futures.

As these chapters show, despite our best efforts to commemorate the victims of National Socialism and Cold War–era persecution to right past wrongs, we have inadvertently reproduced a rigid set of universalist identity categories that have limited whose lives are rendered legible in the past.[30]

This, together with a post-1945 narrative that emphasizes progress over adversity and integration over alterity has glossed over historic and continued tensions within and between queer and trans* communities themselves over the possibilities and boundaries of rights-based legislation and the memories of persecution that buttressed them. In addition to being a narrowed reading of twentieth-century queer sexuality and transgender history more generally, this gloss prevents us from recognizing moments of radical potential in coalition-building practices between and among unlikely groups, like the straight and queer-identified prostitutes huddled together in the ruins of postwar Berlin that sets the stage for the discussion ahead. By looking anew at what happened to the laws and policies regulating same-sex desire after Hitler, and how these have been remembered and re-recast in recent years, *The Queer Art of History* makes a larger argument about what is lost as well as gained by recovering histories of queer persecution, accommodation, resistance, and remembrance without a keener appreciation of the intersectionality of identity.

Kinship as Method

If kinship networks serve as the backbone of this broadened history of nonnormativity after World War II, the book achieves this by interweaving narratives of gender and sexual mutability, bringing together the lives of rent boys and prostitutes, artists and activists, and gender and sexual dissidents to tell an entangled history of same-sex desire, gender nonconformism, persecution and overcoming through the lens of kinship. I submit that existing approaches have produced neat and legible historical subjects at the expense of other, more complex narratives. This periodization, which centers certain experiences as determinative, turns on a teleology of change and progress that reinforces distinct medico-moral, juridical, social justice, racialized, and familial temporalities over the multiple, different, and sometimes problematic ways in which people have led their lives queerly. Looking back over the twentieth century and placing it on a path toward liberalization—one that culminates in the identity, rights, and commemorative movements of the early twenty-first century—is a pattern of argumentation that has coalesced into its own epistemic field, one in which historical actors move from shame to pride, through regulation to decriminalization, and from the margins to the mainstream with little attention to the epistemological and ontological costs of visibility and recognition in the first place. An intersectional analysis of queer kinship shows that this was not the only path available. How we go about recovering this past is, therefore, critical.

But doing so requires drawing a distinction between the politics of visibility as queer genealogy and a genealogical critique of queer visibility. From Karl Ulrichs's definitional approach to naming "urnings" in law, to Magnus Hirschfeld's sexological Third Sex, to the defiance of Charlotte von Mahlsdorf, whose autobiography, *I Am My Own Woman*, brought her life story to the Broadway stage, efforts to address inequality and inclusion revolve around modernity's fixation with seeing, naming, and categorizing the subject. Unlike medievalists and early modernists, whose liturgical, epistolary, literary, and iconographic texts have nudged them to think about sex for the ways it affects a number of knowledge relations—from affective to embodied, relational, cognitive, and physical interactions—modernists seem almost persuaded by the belief that the queer past is somehow fully discernible, a product of modern forms of categorization and display (see fig. I.1).[31] Governmental records, court and medical files, journalistic writing, and photography have afforded us a laser-like focus on what Nikolas Rose has called the politics of life itself—that is, the constitution of queer subject and self-formation through the lens of biopolitics and governmentality.[32] Even when we turn to more subjective sources, so-called ego-documents (photographs, diaries, letters), we still tend to analyze them for how they relate back to the medico-moral logics and temporalities of legal, medical, and state regulation and resistance instead of thinking about them as agents of meaning making in their own right with their own stories to tell about emotional and affective dwelling in history. The "discovery" of queer pasts, then, and their veneration at particular moments in time give us insight into the methods we use to render queer life discernible and our assumptions around what that publicness means in the first place.

But as we'll see with the discussion of photography especially in chapters 2 and 3, sex and gender also comprise bodily experiences, at once deeply subjective and material as well as situational. To get at these several layers, it is useful to think about queerness not just methodologically but conceptually, for what it means as a problem of representation (what aspects of sexuality and gender nonconformism may or may not be rendered or expressed within a given frame), of signification (how something comes to be known in the first place, through the categories at work in a given moment), of materiality (what bodies in fact do), and also of emotion (what it means to want, to desire, and what emotions are deemed valid or peripheral over time).[33] Viewing

FIG. I.1 Charlotte von
Mahlsdorf, *Ich bin
meine eigene Frau /
I Am My Own Woman*
(1992/1995).

queer history more expansively means thinking about how these pasts are
constituted differently than our own as embodied, situated experiences in very
specific conditions that vary, in their construction, across media as well. In
other words, it means paying particular attention to how conceptualizations
of the past are put to use by subsequent generations. Thinking about what
sex, gender, and sexuality mean in their various incarnations requires looking
simultaneously backward and forward chronologically for how queer selves
existed in their own moment, how gay, lesbian, gender-nonconforming, and
trans* people imagined new possibilities in their time, and how both of these
have been drawn from and recast in subsequent iterations. It means turning away from the search for ancestors as coherent exemplars of a simple,

tangible past and thinking instead about identities as constituted sometimes partially, often transiently, as David Halperin once put it, with very little similarity to our own.[34] It also means thinking about how queer subjects and stories are manifested differently through the objects, texts, and visual and emotional traces that help give them shape, including how the sources themselves determine how these pasts are taken up by various audiences. It requires working with and against identity signifiers to see queer and trans* visibility as a complex system of representation—as a social, cultural, and epistemological phenomenon, one caught up in multidirectional forces, in their own time and ours, in each moment seeking definitional appeal. The payoff is not just great, it is essential to envisioning new possible starting points from which to organize a countermovement, sensitive to the fact that exclusions and hierarchies remain a feature of most communal relationships. Retaining a focus on intersectionality allows us to "see outside the presentism of the current emergency [which] can help us see escape routes that others have used in the past and that are still available to us."[35]

Of course, even the search for traces of the queer and trans* past has its own history, the result of profound shifts in historical practice made possible by gay and lesbian organizing, feminist history, the cultural turn, and the rise of queer theory and transgender studies in the 1990s and 2000s.[36] The tendency to use a recuperative lens is part and parcel of the "cultural politics of recognition," a way of politicizing identity against marginalization and forgetting.[37] Yet, as much as it lays a claim to being there and having the permanence of a past, I am not alone in seeing this as sometimes having a neutralizing effect on the power of gender nonconformity and sexuality as categories of analysis.[38] For one thing, it occludes the fact that invisibility itself is a form of representation, as with the illegible legibility of same-sex attraction among women that Carroll Smith-Rosenberg famously described so many years ago.[39] Among the many challenges of recuperative history is that it collapses two modes of being, which might happen coterminously— that of being invisible and also squarely in view. It also valorizes the latter over the former, with the unintended consequence of rerendering certain subjectivities outside history as a strategy with which to narrate power imbalances. The problem with representing lesbianism in this way is that it fails to create a space for "the productive possibilities of . . . derivation."[40] The same might be said for the mainstreaming of transgender studies in the largest sense, which obfuscates the fact that transsexual and transvestite were important signifiers across time, space, and geographies for much of the twentieth century, especially in the non-English-speaking world.[41] In championing visibility uncritically, we fail to appreciate the spectrum of possibilities that variously mark people's lives at a given moment.

Queering Memory

How do we write, then, a history of subtlety and complexity, bearing in mind that our subjects live not just in between but also potentially within multiple coexisting temporalities that, when taken seriously, sometimes challenge the way we have come to periodize LGBTQIA history as moving unilaterally from abjection to acceptance? How might such a critical history help awaken us to the dangers of reproducing this homologized narrative through the very way we render our subjects into history in the first place with paradigms of recognition and representation that deny the larger social systems of power that undergird the conditions of possibility for some identities over others? What of the fraught, maybe even contradictory claims to rhetorical, imagistic, and textual space, the low buzzing hum of those whose presence is inaudible to us because we haven't adequately developed the tools to capture their frequency?[42]

With some thinking, I came to realize that this was partially a historiographical problem, and partially, too, a result of methodology. To some extent, through us, we had let the Gay Liberation movements tell their own history.[43] The result was a rich but protracted focus on social movements at the expense of other stories of being and becoming part of the queer, feminist, antiracist, and sexual avant-garde. For one glaring example, we've only just begun to think through the at times shared homoerotic genealogies that have also led to the New Right.[44] This, combined with the aftermath of the AIDs epidemic and the formulation of rights discourses around struggles for health care and protections under the law, has caused our attention to become even more narrowly focused on the legitimating structures of legal recognition. It was here that scholars like Jasbir Puar noted the emergence of a kind of homonationalism—that is, a hierarchalization of certain queer identities as hallmarks of progressivism.[45] Efforts to gain inclusion for some came at the expense of marginalizing others, positioning certain people as respectable citizens and others—often racialized, gender-fluid, and sexually dissonant people—as monstrous outsiders to the new order. For gender-nonconformity, it is even more complicated, with trans* people often seen as a sign of protolesbianism or protogayness, meaning they are almost included so much as to no longer exist as trans*.[46] In history writing, as in the wider society, the terms of inclusion and exclusion have not simply been imposed from above. They have been perpetuated and affirmed from below as well, through the search for a shared language of affiliation and pathologization between marginalized people and groups and those seeking to tell their stories. This search for a queer sensibility in the past is therefore never fully separable from our own longings for connection to this community, our "impossible desire" to belong to this rich "queer diaspora."[47] We need to be mindful of what it is that draws us to our historical subjects, and how this shapes what we look for in the first place.[48] In this way, a focus on queer kinship brings with it the responsibility to interrogate our own relationship with the past and what we find there.[49]

A truly queered history is a matter not just of selecting better sources, then, but of how we read them in light of contemporary struggles. Our way forward must begin with a history of the present in a Foucauldian sense— that is, with a critical analysis of how the history of queer persecution in Germany has been taken up as a hallmark of white liberal citizenship, which more easily embraces certain victim groups (gay men) over others (lesbians, male prostitutes, trans* people, asocials, habitual criminals, racialized people, etc.). This has led us to write a restorative history, one that circles unendingly around histories of suffering, occlusion, and redemption over other histories, emotions, coalitions, subjectivities, temporalities, and horizons that have marked queer and trans* lives in the latter half of the twentieth century.[50] While history can sometimes be a blunt instrument with which to get at the full spectrum of experience, tapping into more radical and experimental approaches, drawing more extensively on other fields, and queering our own aspirations by being more deliberately self-reflexive is a crucial way forward.

The new universalism at the heart of contemporary discourses of queer citizenship is not just the product of our research methodologies. It is also the result of long-durée tensions within the history of German sexuality generally that hark back to earlier schisms between liberal versus radical elements in pre-Nazi sexology around gender, indeterminacy, immanence, consent, and respectability. As Jonah Garde points out in their essay in *Transgender Studies Quarterly*, the reluctance to question the Eurocentricity of knowledge claims continues to position medical notions of sexual deviance and gender nonconformity as central to modernity.[51] At the same time, this new universalism also echoes some of what legal scholars like Joe Fischel have argued about how even progressive pressure to recognize victimization and redress sometimes inadvertently authorize and enforce new hierarchies that limit our ability to countenance nonpunitive narratives and outcomes.[52] As this book shows, tensions like these have continued to shape the post-1945, post-1989, and post-2001 arenas, enshrining certain groups as acceptable victims while leaving others to fight for their place in the historical register. More important still, the progress narratives have led to siloed histories, with the tale of queer persecution harnessed to a liberalization narrative that fails to account for unanticipated alliances, bad gays, monstrous others, and imperfect heroes.[53] *The Queer Art of History* asks what a queer history of Germany might look like if we were to question the memory of queer history as a story of moving—following Magnus Hirschfeld's dictum—through science (and persecution) to justice? What if we were to adopt an approach that centers our own assumptions over the past as well as our need to see history a certain way, as positivist, linear, uncomplicated, and to a degree unidimensional? If the history of persecution in Germany is not solely wedded to the Nazi past but instead extends backward and forward and into the present day through the persistence of structural racism and discomfort with difference, how might a queer critique of German memory formations aid us in figuring out a more ethical and compassionate way forward?

Kinship and the History of Desire

Kinship allows us to see coalition building in the past, but a focus on desire over regulation makes us revisit how we periodize change over time in the first place. The first three chapters reflect on ambivalences in the representation of deviance for queer and trans* worldmaking in the postwar period in an era marked by ongoing Nazi-era legislation, new sexual science around the frequency of same-sex attraction in adult relationships, decolonization, and a resurgent public sphere that included—for a time—magazines, photographs, sex aids, and print culture emboldening people in their search for gender and sexual self-determination. Instead of relying on the historiographical preoccupation with repression and resistance, these chapters shift the focus to the importance of boundary breaking and cross-group identifications for the unexpected allegiances they helped foster that built a foundation for the social, psychological, and legal changes of the coming decades. They take up the matter of chronology and periodization, specifically how to think about the 1950s as what I call a radical in-between—that is, a moment not just of survival, reaction, and transition but of possibility for those who sought the

promise of the erotic in their everyday lives. We often imagine a more libidinous, free sexual subjectivity as part of the era of post-1960s legal reforms,
with the generational shift that spurred challenges to the status quo. But
by reading our sources for the possibility that the 1940s, 1950s, and 1960s
manifested boundary-breaking queer desire, something else materializes
too: complex and fluid histories of transgression that conjure up a host of
unseemly associations—relationships of trust, kinship, and pleasure alongside shifting affinities that don't quite make sense from our current vantage
point because we have lost touch with how to appreciate them. The question
then becomes How have contemporaries then and now viewed this period
of liminality and autonomy in a different way than we do? And what role
might these simultaneous though different coarticulations play in how we
think about the history of liberalization, emancipation, respectability, and
citizenship as it evolves into the present day? The chapters on photography
take the discussion forward and backward through time, back to the late
war years and through to the 1970s, 1980s, and even the 2000s, to examine
how the period between the war and 1968–69 has been represented and
mobilized to buttress a particular telling of queer emergence that grafts onto
discrete identities that formed the basis of claims making during the sexual
revolution. They posit an alternative way to think about queer subjectivity,
drawing on the insights of trans* and queer of color critique, as heterogeneous
parts of "a shared horizon of struggle" articulated across difference, whose
nonuniversalism has been forgotten in the shadow of its instrumentalization within the politics of gay and lesbian representation in East, West, and
reunified Germany.[54] In chapters 4, 5, and 6 on national and international
kinship networks and memory formations, we will see the way this bears out
in the quest to highlight certain experiences over others in local, national,
and transnational memory communities and art installations. I argue that
kinship allows us to better understand the multiple pathways into the queer
past, while mapping out the tensions around belonging in the queer present.

There is something else at work here that speaks to the larger question
of the place of desire within the history of queer kinship tout court, and the
ways in which we have, to quote Gayle Rubin, "thought about sex" conceptually as well as methodologically to the detriment of writing transgressive
histories of pleasure. As with other chapters in this book, the context may be
Germany, but how we broach the subject of the role of the erotic in shaping
kinship carries import for us all today, in this world of resurgent nationalism,
racial capitalism, and global income disparity.[55] When it came onto the

scene in the 1990s, queer theory was quick to celebrate the powerful place of transgressive desire in thinking about difference. For most adherents, this was never just an intellectual movement, a battle against structuralism and its discontents; it represented the search for a liberation of the senses alongside a wider societal critique. It was a condemnation of institutions of conformity and a hope for something utopian if as yet elusive, just out of reach. But there were already signs of schism, especially around the transgressive power of sexual dissonance and race.

In 1984 Rubin argued that contemporary feminism failed to adequately address the demands of sexual dissidents (prostitutes, "boy-lovers," gays, lesbians, and those who practice S&M), citing the raucous Barnard College conference that was interrupted by antipornography activists, part of the feminist sex wars of the 1980s.[56] Eve Sedgwick took a different tack to advocate for the disarticulation of gender from sexuality and also race in examinations of the unique importance of homosexuality and heterosexuality to the Western canon.[57] Further sedimenting this separationist impulse in queer theory, Michael Warner suggested in his introduction to *Fear of a Queer Planet* that the inherent incommensurability between what he called the "genetic and erotic logics of race and gender" meant "queerness, race, and gender could never be brought into parallel alignment." As queerness is always already subject to moral opprobrium (as opposed to other categories of experience—his thinking), it bears a different and distinct relation "to liberal logics of choice and freedom."[58] Other, more integrationist accounts, like Judith Butler's, saw the cohesiveness of identity itself as the issue, with queer theory serving to break apart any claims to universality or coherence in favor of a more historically and situationally rooted subjectivity. Sexually transgressive desire was not a means to an end of radical worldmaking but it was a start. Yet, despite this openness to a richer analysis of the vicissitudes of difference that mark queer ways of experiencing bodies and pleasures, these approaches have also been taken to task. Critics point especially to their inattentiveness to parallel discussions in Black feminist studies and queer of color critique for how efforts to mark sexual difference often rest on racial markers and uncritical assumptions about transgressing the norms of hegemonic sexual practice and gender identity.[59] One can't think about sexual role play in BDSM, as an example, without recognizing that master/ slave positions carry connotations well beyond the bedroom or play space. As Lorenz Weinberg shows in their fascinating discussion of tensions between lesbians and BDSM practitioners in 1980s and 1990s Germany, this was not lost

FIG. I.2 *Schwule Ladys* (Gay Ladies), 1986. © Krista Beinstein / Schwules Museum*
Berlin.

on German feminists grappling with the boundaries between empowerment
and shame while still very much in the shadow of patriarchy, genocide, and
fascism.[60] This took visual form in the photography of the Austrian enfant
terrible Krista Beinstein, whose sexually charged images of leather women
with penises and shameless embrace of female desire was frequently read
by second-wave feminists as too male-centric for the movement (see figure
I.2).[61] Biddy Martin put it more plainly still in 1996: in queer writing, queer
kinship is often cast as inherently transgressive and norm defying. This has
the effect of not just obscuring how implicated gender and race are in how
people create in-groups and out-groups through claims to representation
and pleasure but suggesting they are "stagnant and ensnaring," propping
up white radical alterity at the expense of exerting any power of their own.[62]

 Still, we can't underestimate the power of the suggestion that to simply
desire queerly was enough to serve as provocation for nonreproductive
kinship.[63] Critics of this formulation, of the inherent radicalism of queer
critique, have come at the question from many different angles. Some have

adopted a more materialist stance. Love—whether emotional or bodily—was not universally accessible to all women or men equally at all times in the past.[64] Others, like Michael Hames-Garcia in the searingly personal "Can Queer Theory Be Critical Theory?" questioned whether privileging queerness as a conduit for freedom smooths over "the collusion of desire with domination and oppression?"[65] All along, he averred, queer theory has struggled to meaningfully integrate race alongside class, gender, and sexuality beyond marginalization, paternalism, and mere tokenism. This disconnect has animated vibrant discussions around how to think about the relationships between categories of experience, with Sharon Patricia Holland endeavoring to bring back into view the legacy of Black women's writing to find points of convergence and divergence around race, the erotic, and "the project of belonging."[66] Let's not forget, too, that queer of color critique draws on woman of color feminism (itself an act of kinship) to explore how racist practice frequently operates as gender and sexual regulation within and beyond the nation state. As Roderick Ferguson reminds us, queer liberalism also buttresses racial capitalism by conjuring up visions of universality in opposition to complex, intersectional affiliations.[67] Finally, as the contributors to the roundtable in *Social Text*'s "Left of Queer" issue argue, we must not forget trans* modalities when approaching kinship in the erotic past. When we deny our own complicity in propping up foreclosed knowledge formations, we neglect valuable opportunities to think anew about the normativizing impulses within queer history writing itself, including assumptions around like-mindedness and homogeneity and also how queer identities and methods can themselves be totalizing and harmful.[68] As Jack Halberstam cheekily put it, "Without a critique of normativity, queer theory may well look a lot like straight thinking."[69]

So just how radical was this radical in-between? These chapters brim with possibility when we learn to read kinship for the particular alongside the universal, the erotic alongside the respectable. Such an approach positions us to view the queer past more suspiciously, as a product of diverse struggles and relations vying for articulation. An approach that views kinships as shifting and porous loosens the reins over history's normativizing impulse. The first three chapters do this by unearthing a myriad of affinities and boundary crossings with unruly teenagers—boys as well as girls, queer and straight—challenging together and sometimes apart hegemonic depictions of sexual propriety and life course as they remove themselves from the grid of maturation, family, and reproduction to find kinships of relationality and choice. The affinities that developed between groups more often relegated to one identity category or another allow us to see the "willfully eccentric modes of being" that emerge beyond the social-sexual frames of the day.[70] There are crossings of other sorts as well, some through space and time. These chapters pick up on the traumas of German history—war, empire, racial aggression, displacement, and genocide—and linger over the way they might enable pleasures both desirable and in excess of community norms. In some instances, they probe the limits of queer organizing around such dissident subjects as the teenager, street youth, sex workers, and leather men for the way they shore up something unassimilable and risqué that deliberately, accidentally, or just by convention challenged the liberationist logics of the nascent gay and lesbian movement. In this sense they are keenly radical, as these examples of sex work, lesbian and queer community making, and fashion and fetish photography often sit together uneasily in the contemporary imagination. But they also might be read in other ways, more critically than I once did, to interrogate whether they also participate in a normativizing violence of their own, at the expense of other tellings and experiences.

In the next three chapters in the book, I ask along with Carolyn Dinshaw What if instead of collapsing time "through affective contact between marginalized people now and then" we might hold on to these tensions and strive instead to touch across temporal boundaries, mindful of our place in the current moment but conscious of the ruptures and disjunctions that mark how our subjects give voice to their predicaments in their own terms as well as ours?[71] Is it possible to foster a new kind of radical relationality, an ongoing sense of kinship and affinity with those in the past, based on difference over homologization, and recognizing—maybe even embracing—the physical, affective, though different ties that bind? This is not a plea for a new ground on which to situate queer history and desire. Rather, it is a call for a model of kinship forged around how we are oriented emotionally as well as intellectually toward the past, and how this search for same-sex desire and gender nonconformity historically might nudge us into remembering a fuller spectrum of queer histories in the present, including those "whose lives and loves make them appear oblique, strange and out of place" today.[72] This form of kinship is not about family formation. Instead, it underscores the enormous potential of a historical practice oriented around relationships of affiliation and encounter, be they intellectual, physical, libidinous, or emotional. It is the kind of caretaking that comes from living in "good relation" with our pasts and futures, with the world around us, beyond the assimilationist scripts of respectability, family, inheritance, and child-rearing.[73] One need not inhabit queer or trans* subject positions to live in good relation to the queer and trans* past.

Ultimately, I argue that such a vision of intersectional queer kinship can only happen through a methodological reworking of how we write the history of nonconformism and desire. This includes ways we conceptualize queer emotions, how we emplot them, and how we think about normative representational models that underwent transformation through a process of disidentification—that is, the way marginalized people disrupt hegemonic categories like persecution in order to make room for pleasure.[74] It requires a "re-wiring of the senses" to harness our own bodies as vehicles of implication and interpretation so as to better appreciate the generative power of the erotic, whether danger or desire, as appreciable through the body as much as imprinted on it.[75] By centering the radical potential of the erotic as an embodied practice and listening to the lessons of women of color feminists, who already in the 1980s had challenged us to see through the allure of respectability and not settle for "the convenient, the shoddy, the conventionally expected, nor the merely safe," we may recognize the ways in which we have colluded with the liberal social contract in how we have imagined queer worldmaking.[76] Remembering in this sense is about orienting ourselves to think about how queer kinships have been recast through memory and memorialization and also in our historical practice itself.

I take up these questions through an exploration of vastly different examples of representation and remembering. While critical queer history has always been a history of the present insofar as contemporary struggles have served as the launchpad for the search for historical antecedents, we have not always written such histories as mindfully as we might. These chapters explore the push to tackle and then commemorate the Nazi persecution of LGBTQIA people in the immediate aftermath of the war, in the 1970s through the work of the gay liberation movement and its erstwhile cis-presenting and lesbian antifascist coagitators, then in different ways in East and West Germany and over the benchmark of 1989. I examine the sometimes incongruent temporal logics around the multiple rememberings of persecution and endeavors to periodize this anew, somewhat more open-endedly, with regard for the different sights, sounds, orientations, and bodily experiences of danger and desire that were produced at different moments and for different audiences. I do this by analyzing the undercommons, those who fail to fit into the dominant representational paradigm, including migrants and refugees, street youth, trans* people, and non-cisgendered academic and radical lesbians who challenge the normative white/cis/male imaginary that has coalesced around the memory of the sex reformer and sexologist Magnus Hirschfeld. I ponder, following Frank Moten and Stefano Harney, the urgency and ambivalences of radical world-building with the hope that a history of queer relationality might allow us to think anew about the ties that bind without simultaneously reproducing new criteria for exclusion.[77] I suggest that we think about positionality in order to expose the logics of middle-class white reproductive temporalities in how queer associations, belonging, futures, and identities are conceptualized at the end of the twentieth century, so as to imagine where we might go in the twenty-first.

A final note on positionality as method: some of these chapters offer deliberate reinterpretations of my earlier writing. Like Kobena Mercer's powerful reworking of his earlier response to Robert Mapplethorpe's photographs of black bodies, they take up the challenge of revision, of historicizing one's own arguments and recasting them in light of changing questions and imperatives. In this regard, they take inspiration directly from antiracist critique, which has sharpened our thinking about the uneasy fit of racialized and otherwise nonnormative subjects in social movements, AIDS activism, and artistic production and representation in these last decades. I aim to bring back into view the idea of queer as provocation while simultaneously demonstrating citational and self-critical practices that serve, themselves, as a model of kinship as relationality, of "finding our way" across time and difference, between those in our midst and those who came before. In this sense, citation is indeed how we acknowledge our debt to our intellectual ancestors; it is how we build and affirm anew queer kinship and memory.[78] As Cathy Cohen puts it in returning to her own iconic article twenty years later, it is an attempt to find ways to think about queer as "a space for agitation across communities defined by 'the other' by the state and/or racial capitalism."[79] In asking us to consider the implications of a historical practice that stresses a particular narrative arc around representation and becoming without adequate consideration of the challenges posed by other forms of experience that might question the teleology of liberalization, the book makes a space for different conditions of possibility between fascism in the past and today, charting in the process alternative kinships, solidarities, and trajectories for collective claims making going forward.

ENTANGLED HISTORIES

1

IN THE EARLY 2000s, when kinship studies met queer theory, new questions surfaced about whether queerness could ever truly encapsulate alternatives to the heteronormative underpinnings of the modern family. Some scholars lauded the creativity of queer communities in seeking to redefine erotic and emotional kin structures and attachments.[1] Others argued that, despite our best attempts at forging queer friendships and families of choice, it was hard to deny the tenacity of kinship's oedipal logics when life course, embodiment, and subculture itself seemed bound to the filial model in a kind of groundhog day of white reproductive cis heteropatriarchy.[2] One answer was to look more closely at queer, queer of color, and transgender bodies, communities, and practices for the way they disrupted totalizing efforts to contain them. As Eve Sedgwick first put it, and Roderick Ferguson and Jack Halberstam fleshed out further, a fundamental feature of queer, queer of color, and trans* possibility was in continually provoking the normativizing power of social formations by failing to live up to temporalities of self-actualization, progress, and identity.[3] Simply put, racialized queer and trans* lives were lived differently. But as we learned too from a host of people working on intersectional methodologies, within differently situated lives there are commonalities of experience, even as those experiences are experienced differently.[4] By broadening the spectrum of relationality and "ideologies of discreteness," queerness might be opened up to "unlikely and unprecedented coalitions."[5] To do so means reminding ourselves that social and political formations, like the memories that undergird them, are never absolute—nor are they always heroic or pretty. We need to remember that amid the quest for longevity, belonging, and outright survival lies the messiness of queer and trans* relations, including their fundamental incoherence and contingency. As Lauren Berlant put it, "Sex is not a thing, it is a relation," but it is also a relation that is unevenly felt and experienced, assigned different meaning over time.[6] To get at these ambivalences means feeling backward through the entanglements of the queer and trans* archive, interrogating what has stuck and what was left behind.[7] Kinship defined robustly opens the door to new possibilities of life lived queerly, at the center of society and within its margins. In this chapter, it guides our way back to postwar Berlin.

When I first wrote *Life among the Ruins*, I knew I wanted to find a way to tell the story of straight and queer sexuality in a single narrative. I didn't realize at the time that there might be an urgency to recall the interconnected ways in which regulation, surveillance, alliances, coalitions, coping strategies, and relationships of convenience as well as purpose manifested kinships of belonging and community in the rubblescape of capitulated Berlin. In reconceptualizing some of this material for this book, I asked myself, What if we focused on common fates and shared experiences that shaped how people lived their lives in the years following the end of the Second World War? What are the advantages of telling the story this way? Without denying hard and fast differences of experience and positionality, how might attention to entanglements reveal parallel logics of assimilation and respectability that challenged dominant notions of gender, sexuality, citizenship and personhood? Such quandaries set up a very different conversation around the interrelated struggles of differently positioned actors within queer history. At the same time that it constructs new frames of reference for how to view allyship, it also points to fundamental tensions within the queer past around whose behaviors, acts, and identities might one day garner the protection of the state. It only makes sense that we begin such an exploration in Berlin, a city renowned for its progressivism in the 1920s, for street fighting in the 1930s, as the seat of a murderous government that brought mass death and destruction on an unimaginable scale. It was also the site of Cold War confrontation for forty years and, after 1989, of German memory culture and national reckoning. As we'll see in chapter 5, the city was important for other reasons too, as National Socialist crimes became a lightning rod for queer and trans* organizing, restitution, and recognition at home and abroad.

Over the course of four years, between 1945 and 1949, Berlin would be occupied by four foreign powers, divided into administrative sectors within zones, before being formally divided between the German Democratic Republic in the East with its pro-Soviet government and the Federal Republic in the West, itself with close connections to the United States. The city destroyed was a palimpsest of past worlds and unknown futures. In May 1945, the guns may have stilled, but Berlin was still very much a conflict zone. Government bodies struggled to rehouse returnees and displaced persons, many of them Jews formerly victimized by these same institutions. Welfare agents and police stared down human privation amplified by devalued currency, a bustling black-market, and an uncommonly cold winter in 1946. All the while, its citizens, many of them women, were preyed on by the occupiers as war booty as they fought to establish a kind of normalcy for themselves and their children in the same streets where they experienced liberation, which for many meant sexual assault.[8] Berlin, in other words, is the perfect setting for a discussion of kinship and the myriad ways in which people found their path through the violent, unnatural, and strange world of early Cold War Germany. Inspired by Susan Stryker's formulation of transness as a way to think about lives lived "across a socially imposed boundary away from an unchosen starting place," be that the gender binary, sexual expression, or boundaries of nationhood, this chapter asks us to consider the entangled relationships that were forged through intersecting moments of transgression and community.[9] In spaces of aftermath, encounter, and survival like the train station, the rubble, and up-market and down-low night life in the city's reconstituted bars and cabarets, forms of comportment document the many different ways people defied the status quo, laying claim to intimacy, companionship, and physical space in forms other than what was intended or desired.

Entanglements

There have been many good reasons why the history of LGBTQIA lives in Germany has been written as separate accounts of persecution and resilience. For one, the sources lend themselves to a focus on siloed categories, with gay men and boys the chief targets of the Nazi and postwar states. But as important as it has been to drill down into extant police and court records to reconstruct the process of targeting so-called other victims of the Third Reich, as a method it is not without reproach. Another reason is that coverage is uneven, with some cities having destroyed records while others were slow in discovering their archival importance.[10] There are other reasons too. As we'll see in the chapter on the Homo-Monument in Berlin, many scholars, activists, and historians have defined persecution discretely, as a juridical category. Claudia Schoppmann, Christiane Leidinger, and Laurie Marhoefer have argued that such a narrow definition fails to appreciate the different barometers of threat and reaction against women involved with other women.[11] Opposition did not just come from within the LGBTQIA scene. Institutional and homophobic barriers to legitimizing this area of research in the German academy have meant that activists were forced to write this history themselves.[12] On the one hand, the extraordinary output of dedicated teams of "quotidian intellectuals" has resulted in what we know today.[13] On the other, together with moments of friction within and among communities, it has meant that historical recovery has been patchy, with some constituents, notably bisexual and trans* people, barely understood at all.[14] Further complicating things, as Corinna Tomberger argues in an edited volume intent on navigating this terrain mindfully, the terms of reference historians use do not always ally well with past subcultural formations.[15] After all, not all people affected by Nazi and postwar persecution understood themselves in the language used then, let alone today. Further still, some may not have viewed who they had sex with and how as the primary mark of identity.[16]

In another corner of the discipline, also coming into its own in the 1990s, entangled history evolved into a vibrant interdisciplinary analysis of interactivity, circulation, overlap, exchange, and transfer.[17] Often employed in the study of state and nonstate actors around relationships of dependence, interference, and flows of knowledge, ideas, institutions, and practices, it promised new ways of thinking about processes of interaction, including border crossing, and categories of reflection between observer and observed, from different angles of perception and debate. While the earliest entangled histories focused on transfers beyond borders in German-French relations, it soon embraced other debates within global and world history, including the criticism of capitalism and commodity consumption, population movement, and even disease.[18] The influx of postcolonial theory shifted the focus once again to transcultural interaction and challenged the primacy of the West while showing the power of common experiences of oppression, survival, and resistance to the construction of subaltern consciousness and subjectivity. Studies of space and spatiality—informed by the work of David Harvey, Henri Lefebvre, and Doreen Massey—introduced ways to think about locatedness, positionality, and time. I drew on this in my own work to analyze the diverse ways in which people might experience a simultaneity of spatial frameworks as reflected through relational processes of social and geographical interaction, with place having its own agentic power to condition social relations.[19]

An entangled history of queer and trans* relationalities in postwar Berlin holds the potential for us to rethink the relationships of bodies, selves, and subjectivities as they developed across local, national, and transnational frames. It also meshes well with trans* methodologies, particularly the way trans* as an analytic highlights the "capillary space of connection and circulation between the macro- and micropolitical registers through which the lives of bodies become enmeshed in the lives of nations, states, and capital-formations."[20] A multiscalar focus on occupied and divided Berlin affords us an opportunity to think about fluid forms of community, subculture, and identity within divergent regulatory schemata in an urban environment steeped in historical significance. Within this is the tension between particularist and universalist notions of sovereignty and the self against the backdrop of authoritarian and pre-Nazi thinking on the role of the family and heteronormativity in the lives of citizens. Thus, an entangled history carves out a space in which to think about kinship as not "merely cultural"—although enculturations, what and how people imagine for themselves, is surely important. But also significant is the way this is imbricated in and shaped by political economies of self and other that reinforced distinct racial, social, and gender hierarchies.[21]

Queer and trans* subjectivities—and the subjectivities of youth especially—are inherently entangled and messy.[22] As Eve Sedgwick put it, they are an "open mesh of possibilities, gaps, overlaps, dissonances and resonances, lapses and excesses of meaning."[23] What is often overlooked is the way that entangled kinships are sometimes enlisted in their multiplicity to reinforce hegemonic discourses of normalization, including normal and perverse medicalized, psychologized, and individuated forms of identity, and how people opt out or try to blunt the forces of co-optation, often in unique ways. In emphasizing transience and flows—whether knowledge transfers, regulatory frameworks, emotional regimes, or actual physical movement through space (what Sara Ahmed calls orientations)—entangled histories can aid us in thinking more carefully about how gendered expectations, self-expression, comportment, and desire help constitute and occasionally disrupt forms of queer relationality, creating unique forms of kinship beyond families of choice or biology. They reveal a kind of queer kinship predicated on shared affinities, experiences, and orientations that mark life outside of the stated norm, which become galvanized in an imaginary of the different if not always the same. As we'll see in later chapters, it is such a vision of kinship—across gender and sexual variability and at multiple levels of transience across space, geography, and time—that holds out the possibility for recognizing more radical forms of coalition building.

Farewell to Berlin?

An entangled history of kinship in a place like Berlin must engage with the presence of the mythic past in the historical present. Unlike Christopher Isherwood's fears that the debauchery of queer Berlin was gone forever with the rise of the Nazis, amid the rubble of 1945, the spirit of the 1920s continued to haunt how people navigated the collapsed city. Indeed, the twilight years between war's end and the building of the Berlin Wall in 1961 saw the city's denizens traversing spaces still bearing the marks of the recent past. More important than the physical renderings of the city were the mental maps of bygone years, as citizen and visitor alike drew on images of the notorious 1920s, which they interpreted in various and contradictory ways. Sometimes the city was cast as a wellspring of dynamism, a symbol of unending modernism, fluidity, and flux. Other times, it was a rogue space of revolution and immorality. For certain, it was a queer space, not a single form of urbanity but multiple experiences pressed together, overlapping, like an onion skin, visible and opaque at the same time. Fundamentally, it was a broken space. Aerial bombing and division altered the physical topography of the city unequivocally; reckoning with genocide would take longer to collectively process. For the better part of the postwar period, the ruined city was a site of "oppositional orientation (and) a delayed search for wholeness."[24]

Despite its scars, or perhaps because of them, Berlin was a honeypot for twentieth-century flaneurs eager to experience the fabled city. In newspaper articles and memoirs, they charted the city's terrain in an archaeology of vice and transgression, drawing points of comparison between the fractious yet exuberant 1920s and the purportedly banal 1940s and 1950s. When combined with police and welfare authority visions of Berlin's trouble spots, they mapped the moral and material state of Berlin's hackneyed reconstruction. They also breathed new life into the rubble, casting its broken spaces as repositories of danger and also desire, creating new frames of reference for the "sexual coding of the city."[25] Far from passive backdrops, these new spaces of contact, entertainment, and frivolity engendered the creation of new social memories that owed much to the changed but still familiar landscape of one of Europe's most vibrant, transgressive cities. The new Berlin emerged out of the confrontation with old ones, with the physical city and the memories it evoked playing a constitutive part not simply in the remembrance of Berlin's gloriously libidinous past but in conceptualizations of its future as well. Central to this story was the intermingling of lives and passions, the importance of gender in thinking about transgression, and the danger posed especially by unattached youths—male and female—to the city's social and political reconstruction, which was viewed by many as intimately connected to the power and permanence of the heteronormative family.

Train Stations

The scale of destruction often had the effect of forcing sympathies with the German population and forgetting Jewish trauma (see figs. 1.1 and 1.2).[26] It also provided cover for the city's clandestine sex trade. Solicitation and its enforcement in the streets surrounding the underground and suburban train network, the U-Bahn and S-Bahn, galvanized a sense of common purpose for state agents seeking an end to teen endangerment. It also created liminal spaces of transit and exchange and was home to time-honored traditions of big city life, which, in Cold War Berlin, represented in microcosm many of the challenges over the form and shape of life after fascism. Just as the mapping of urban spaces like the train station hardened in police procedure and social welfare policy a vision of the endangered boy prostitute and girl streetwalker—dealt with in similar but different ways—it also had the spin-off effect of positioning the hustler at the center of definitions of a more legitimate homosexuality, understood in contradistinction to the effeminacy and debasement of station boys (see fig. 1.3). While poor disaffected teens were similar targets of moral reform in the name of buttressing the family, the demonization of train station youth would play a significant part in the negotiation of homophile kinships and even New Left activism itself in arguments for a radical queer citizenship.[27]

FIG. 1.1 Berlin Friedrichstrasse ruins, 1950. Photographer unknown. © Bundesarchiv
Berlin.

FIG. 1.2 Women on the way to forage for food. Photo by Otto Donath. © Bundesarchiv
Berlin.

FIG. 1.3 Thieves' den
in the underground,
Berlin, March 1949.
Photo by Walter
Heilig. © Bundes-
archiv Berlin.

Although historically associated with working-class districts, prostitution remained a feature of the city's transit network and transcended East
and West Berlin throughout the political conflict of the Berlin Blockade in
1948, the first of several geopolitical confrontations in the city's fraught
history.[28] The gradual stabilization of the economy that had initiated the
standoff between the Soviet and American occupation forces had failed to
eradicate the flesh trade, and although the black market would subside
after the currency reform in June 1948 and the introduction of the deutsche
mark in the western zones, prostitution could be found in every corner of
the city, in central districts as well as at more suburban stops along the far-
flung reaches of the rail network. In other words, despite varying efforts to
combat the structural reasons why people fell into the trade, prostitution
remained a hallmark of city life in early Cold War Berlin. Even after formal
division of the city (and of Germany proper) in the fall of 1949, streetwalking

embodied in flesh and blood the continued disparity of income between those citizens with addresses in the East versus those who settled in the West. It was a constant reminder to German authorities on both sides of the border of the debasement brought about by war, amplified by division, amid the lingering impact of defeat.[29]

If prostitution along the city's transportation corridors belied the permeability of internal boundaries, it also called into question the boundaries of respectability, especially surrounding important social taboos like intergenerational sex and sex between men. But boundary making and the reinforcement of certain social norms also held important spatial-temporal moorings. In the ideological battle to denazify the criminal code, jump-start the economy, and democratize (or socialize) key institutions, loosened sexual mores threatened to uncloak a range of unsavory episodes in the city's recent past, like the Soviet mass rapes or even occasional American transgressions, which, when made public, officials feared might hamper the enlistment of citizens into the Cold War struggle to rebuild Berlin. But the laws themselves, policing procedures, and guiding criminological theories of debasement posed an even more wide-reaching problem insofar as they exposed the extent to which both postwar states continued to rely on pre-1945 maxims and methods of sexual regulation. The policing of street-level sex, in other words, forced an unwilling population to engage the specter of the Nazi past, whether in the form of the 1935 NS law against homosexuality that remained in force until 1968 in the East and 1969 in the West, or more sinisterly, in the words and actions of police and social workers who hoped to stamp out the trade. While the ruins afforded the opportunity of cover, new building projects failed to dislodge the association, now firmly implanted, between transportation nodes and sexual barter and exchange.

During the Cold War the train station took on additional meaning as a gateway to freedom in the West and an access point for cheap goods and services from the East. With the building of the Berlin Wall in 1961 to firm up what was until then a porous inter-German boundary, the sexually delinquent train station youth began to generate fears about national renewal. The police regarded the boys as delinquent homosexuals-in-the-making, the reformers and betrayed clients as blackmailing turncoats, and the criminologists as passive asocials.[30] Girls who actively flaunted their wares belied modesty and respect for the family. Perhaps more than ever before, the train station and its denizens came to symbolize a Germany at a crossroads, still reeling from the recent Nazi past and torn between an emerging Soviet-style dictatorship with its Ten Commandments for Socialist Citizenship (as weird as it sounds), and a consumerist Christian democracy intent on policies of pronatalism and the heteropatriarchal family.[31]

The sex trade refused to recognize administrative boundaries between the four sectors of the city. Male prostitutes frequently traversed internal sector boundaries for evening liaisons, risking possible incarceration under the slow-to-be-reformed, Nazi-era antisodomy legislation, revealing in the process some of the tensions associated with Berlin's homosexual subculture as it evolved after years of Nazi persecution.[32] From archival records, we can map the topography of transgressive sexuality in postwar Berlin, exposing to light the contours of an urban subculture that survived Nazi assaults on same-sex-desiring men. Indeed, despite the concerted efforts of the Gestapo and criminal police to destroy Berlin's reputation as an Eldorado for queer desire, the train station remained an important site of nonnormative sexual expression in the years after the war, a situation that prompted renewed efforts to regulate it.[33] At the same time that unlikely allegiances were forged in and around the city's train stations to combat the threat of homosexuality, haphazard efforts to control transit space afforded boys and men the prospect of mediating their own experience of regulation, providing them with much-needed avenues of resistance while lending insight into the uniqueness of Cold War Berlin.

Catacomb Lives

In the bombed-out bunkers that dotted the city's landscape, in pay-by-the-hour hotels, rented rooms (*Absteigequartiere*), and pungent pissoirs, hustlers turned tricks to help support their liminal existence. Of course, concern about male prostitution was not solely a postwar phenomenon; it had an elaborate history that predated Hitler and the Nazis. Postwar decisions about which version of the law should be upheld broke down along the East/West axis. In the German Democratic Republic, the Supreme Court of Berlin decided on February 21, 1950, that the 1935 variant of Paragraph 175—which expanded the definition of what constituted a homosexual transgression—was an "instrument of power for the Nazi state to prepare for war."[34] Thus, in the emerging GDR, charges that consenting adult men had transgressed Paragraph 175 again required physical proof, which was not the case in the western zone. In West Berlin and the Federal Republic of Germany, the 1935 variant of Paragraph 175 was retained for several more years. However, in considering the second part of the code governing homosexuality—the section that criminalized bought sex and sex with minors (Paragraph 175a)—the Supreme Court of Berlin upheld the Nazi variant since it promoted "sexual integrity and thus the healthy development of the youth." As Günter Grau has argued, when it came to safeguarding the sexual mores of young males, the socialist East and capitalist West upheld similar images of respectability and moral endangerment.[35] While the collapse of the Reich set in motion changes in the process of identifying homosexual transgressions, Nazi-era attitudes about the protection of youth continued to influence the regulation of male prostitution in both Germanys.

If the legislation governing same-sex sexuality was confusing, so too was the prospect of policing a divided cityscape like Berlin, where travel between sectors was relatively unencumbered until the building of the wall. Here, male prostitution flourished. West Berlin's insecure geographical and political status, not to mention the pull of its diverging economic system, made it a particularly alluring site for boys and johns interested in a quick pickup.[36] The stationing of Allied troops in the vicinity also added a sense of allure, with same-sex liaisons often occurring in the bushes near the train stations closest to military bases, belying the suggestion that civilian-military relations were solely heterosexual.[37] Although sector boundaries posed challenges to the enforcement of legal norms, border checks did not hamper same-sex-desiring men from finding available trade. In fact, the vagaries of the legal statutes, together with the mishmash administration of the city's central and suburban train stations, may have actually facilitated contacts.

Added to this was the fact that the homosocial mapping of the city's male sex trade resisted the rigidity of administrative and ideological borders. It was also not unusual for police in the East to ensnare West Berliners buying sex there. Conversely, boys traveled over the sector boundaries frequently in the 1950s to service the needs of gentlemen in the Western half of the city. As late as 1955, the Reinickendorf district welfare agency in northwest Berlin noted it had over fifty boys listed in their register with eastern addresses.[38] Despite the increasingly hostile climate among the Allies and in civic affairs, some degree of cooperation even existed between the eastern and western police. One night in May 1948, for instance, a police task force conducting a raid at Zoo Station in the heart of the British sector asked Horst D., an eighteen-year-old resident of the western district of Neukölln, why he was frequenting this "known hangout for homosexuals and hustlers." Since Horst had "neither identification nor money on him," he had to go to the local police station for questioning, where it was discovered that he was wanted on charges of assault and robbery at two eastern sector precincts.[39] With little fanfare, he was sent eastward for processing. While the police might cooperate in the name of public morals, the general population was less emboldened to act, especially if crossing the border was required for testimony. By 1950, just one year after the establishment of two independent states, the political climate had changed enough so that two West Berlin witnesses refused to cross into East Germany to attend a young man's hearing. Although it might seem like an act of defiance, and perhaps it was, the fact that one of the men was the prosecution's key witness suggests that either he was pressed into making his claim by the police or he had real misgivings about the possibility of leaving East Berlin territory.[40] While Berliners crossed the boundary almost wantonly for work and pleasure, the permeability of the internal border was increasingly called into question in dealings with the regulatory apparatus. Yet the lure for underage, intergenerational kinship was enough to tempt fate even if it couldn't guarantee solidarity after the fact.

Gendering Deviance

If policing behavior was a complicated matter in postwar Berlin, the gendering of deviance further hampered enforcement. As was the case in the pre-Nazi legal code, in 1945 male and female prostitution were understood as different infractions requiring different treatment.[41] We see this in the administrative units assembled to deal with the train station trade. From its headquarters on Dircksenstrasse, steps away from the Alexanderplatz U-Bahn and S-Bahn stops, the police chief Paul Markgraf swiftly reassembled the vice squad to investigate crimes against morality (*Sittlichkeitsdelikte*).[42] Task force MII/4 of the criminal police—staffed with two detectives and a rotating number of lower-ranking officers and the occasional policewoman (*Weibliche Kripo* or WKP)—was charged with investigating cases of seduction, rape, molestation, incest, and same-sex prostitution. Theft, sabotage, youth crime, and female prostitution were left to other units, reflecting the different juridical importance placed on these crimes. This provided a degree of cover for male prostitutes and the johns soliciting their services.

The invisibility of male prostitution is reflected in the historiography, where little exists on the plight of train station boys despite great interest about the impact of the war on women's sexual vulnerability. The diarists whose eyewitness accounts helped define this period as the "hour of the woman" were well aware of the gender imbalance. After all, those raped en masse following the Russian entry into Berlin were women; the faces that Allied authorities saw waiting in line for rations were typically female; the survivors who worked to clear Berlin's debris-congested streets were "rubble women" and girls (*Trümmerfrauen*).[43] And in all four corners of Berlin, it was women who assumed sole responsibility for those under their care. Although male prostitution had a long history in the red-light district of the prewar Friedrichstadt, and cottaging was commonplace in train station urinals before the war, little information has surfaced regarding the plight of young men outside of the narratives of returning soldiers.[44] While part of the oversight is owed to conservativism within the academy where this history was not under the microscope, part, too, is due to the emphasis within the gay and lesbian movement itself in foregrounding the history of activism over the eroticization of the street.[45] Street boys did not easily fit in with activist narratives of queer sociability.

The illegibility of rent boys belies the fact that the streets were a very public space of kinship as male prostitutes stood cheek by jowl with women and girls in the city's solicitation zones, alongside gender nonconformists who might frequent these same strolls. In one case from the pre-1945 period that we'll read about in chapter 3, Fritz Kitzing was picked up while dressed in women's clothes and charged with solicitation under the statute reserved for female prostitution, suggesting that he passed well enough for the charging officer or that in certain city spaces the gay, cisgender, and trans* strolls were in fact mixed.[46] Sometimes, the moral panic surrounding fallen women gave precarious shelter to gender-nonconformist activity, rendering rent boys and transsexuals, the word used at the time, less visible. In a national conference on postwar criminality in 1959, a well-respected West Berlin police officer would go so far as to make the claim that there were few to no hustlers working city streets in the early aftermath of the war.[47] Despite the misgivings of some authorities, trade were very much on the radar of police and welfare workers, even more so when they flaunted gendered notions of deviance and hegemonic masculinity.

While they had not shared the experience of mass rape, there may have been other points of convergence in the kinship between young women and men. Some boys claimed they fell into the trade after being initiated into "abnormal sex" by members of the occupation forces.[48] Rent boys, like female prostitutes, were thought to be attracted to the "easy life" of languishing about, smoking cigarettes, and spending what little money they had on cheap amusements. Because heterosex was an expected norm between cisgendered men and women alongside the necessary power imbalances between the sexes, hustlers presented a different set of paradoxes to the police. Did they choose this life out of necessity or was this a reflection of ingrained desire and orientation?[49] Did they merit society's protection or punishment? Were they victims or agents? In developing a viable policy for the surveillance and arrest of boys suspected of willfully "polluting themselves," the Berlin police navigated a path lined with contradictions.[50] Despite the confusion surrounding a youth's particular predicament, the differential enforcement of moral norms was very visible at the train station.

Since it was commonly accepted that venereal disease originated with women, rent boys were spared the humiliation of health checks, where the mere presence of women congregating at the station could be grounds for forced testing. Of course, not all girls emerging from the underground or chatting on street corners were "on the make," as a raid near the Rathaus Steglitz metro made all too clear when the police forced four fifteen- and sixteen-year-old girls to undergo a mandatory pelvic exam. One of them, it was later confirmed, had never had sex before, while another was a survivor of Soviet rape.[51] These measures may have provoked outrage, but as one police officer was quoted as saying, in the divided city "it is impossible to differentiate between good and bad girls" since even those from good homes have "discovered their bodies as a means by which to live an easy life.[52] While simply being female might be grounds for intervention, hustlers typically had to be caught *in flagrante delicto* or, at the very least, acting in "rent boy–like fashion" (*nach Strichjungenart*). This differential portrayal of debasement owed much to the American command's influence over the West Berlin police force in regulating amoral troop activity. But it also betrays the extent to which train station spaces themselves were imagined, at least by police, as cis-heteronormative places of contact and exchange. Hustlers may have dotted the landscape, but unlike girls, station boys had to go out of their way to arouse suspicion, allowing them to remain hidden in plain sight. The mere presence of women laying claim to public space, unaccompanied or in groups, almost always garnered the immediate response of the police. In postwar Berlin, public space was broken, dangerous, and unruly, especially for girls and women.

A 1946 report of one spot check conducted at the bunker neighboring the Schlesischer station in Berlin's eastern sector provides a case in point. In her log entry, Officer Behr of the WKP noted that the women's detachment had found six youths blocking the entrance to the facility. All were sent to the precinct for processing, but the brothers Georg and Gerhard B. and a friend described only as S. were set free after a short interview. Rolf R., not quite fifteen years old, was transferred to the youth welfare station at Dircksenstrasse since he was homeless, underage, and without a ration card or identification. The two girls in the group, likewise without identification, were sent to police detachment MII/3 where they were held on suspicion of prostitution. One of the pair was forced to undergo a gynecological exam, known to be invasive, embarrassing, and often quite painful.[53]

While women garnered most attention for ambling about along the train station stroll, police also understood boys' endangerment in gendered terms, as symptoms of lapsed masculinity. But concentrating their attention on signs of effeminacy cut two ways. On the one hand, it focused attention on a certain caliber of youth, while shielding those who failed to exhibit signs of "rent boy–like behavior." There was the fact, too, that not all boys on the make performed an effeminate masculinity. In this early part of the postwar scene—as Clayton Whisnant has documented—there was a wide array of gender performances on display, with up-market bar boys sometimes presenting themselves in a more feminine manner, complete with the use of makeup, hair gel, and aggressively feminine gesturing.[54] If they were not obviously effeminate, why did police and social workers pigeonhole hustlers in this way? On one level, if spaces of transit were understood in strictly heteronormative terms, it is not surprising that boy prostitutes might be positioned on par with station girls since they too were part of the economy of barter and exchange that serviced male sexual desire. But there was a material side to the story as well that gets overlooked when we fail to view these experiences as entangled and interconnected. Social service workers and members of the vice squad were motivated to intervene out of fear that station boys had been emasculated not just by the scene itself but by the war, whose impact was felt in the development of a deviant sexual appetite. Simply put, what might appear to be a simple act of quiescence or experimentalism could transform into outright desire for the sinful pleasures of gay sex. In their reports, social workers pointed to a variety of warning signs related to the breakdown of the nuclear family, one of the hallmarks of societal decline in the aftermath of the war. The lack of a fatherly presence or the smothering attention of a doting mother was a recipe for disaster. One mother accused of coddling her son argued in her defense that she had developed a particularly strong bond with him given that "together they had lived through the difficult experience of the Russian invasion." Further hinting at the shared experience of trauma and possibly rape, the boy's father went on record to comment that since that time he had failed to enjoy conjugal relations with his wife, and that this, together with a worsening relationship generally, made it especially difficult to parent their troubled child. Seeking explanations for their son's transgressions, both the boy's parents and the various caseworkers assigned to him forged a link between the emasculating impact of mass violence and the development of healthy adolescent sex drives.[55] The East German endocrinologist Günter Dörner would go so far as to argue that the trauma of the bombing campaign had caused a significant hormonal impact in utero that helped explain the preponderance of effeminate and homosexual youths in the postwar generation.[56] As a cauldron of gender negotiation and trade, the train station was an important locus for the discussion of the lingering impact of past transgressions on postwar lives. More importantly, it positioned gender as a uniquely important category of sociospatial notions of deviance and also of kinship.

Bars

The city inspired kinships of a different sort too, as writers and journalists flocked to Berlin. The relative normalization of daily life by the mid-1950s did little to erase the specter of destruction. As the Scottish correspondent Ewan Butler described in his 1955 book *City Divided*, "behind the front of normality" there often "lurked an uneasiness and a fear, a sense of dark things moving in a half-world."[57] For the *New York Times* foreign correspondent Drew Middleton, divided Berlin was a place where "shots sounded in the night. Dives catering [*sic*] to raw sex, and for those so inclined, every perversion flourished."[58] Although critical of claims of German victimization, correspondents were quick to conjure up images of the city's past as they sought to cement their own authority as tellers of a new round of Berlin stories. These postwar flaneurs had clearly read their Hessel, Isherwood, Benjamin, Kracauer, Roth, and Simmel. But they had also studied the writings of Curt Moreck, whose 1931 text *Führer durch das 'lasterhafte' Berlin* (Guide through Depraved Berlin) mapped the city's underground pleasure spots. Instructing his readers how to "dive into the turbulent whirlpool" that was pre-Nazi Berlin, readers were to romance the shy city by learning the proper way of "coax(ing) it into showing its Janus-face" since "the depths are the more amusing side of life."[59] As David James Prickett argues, Moreck presents the city as a feminized site of congruency, where opposites mix and mingle, and where differences of high and low, day and night, leisure and work are transgressed in the name of pleasure.[60] Its true "intensity is to be experienced only at the vital sites of life, where polar opposites touch, where contradictions become one, where humanity is blended together like a piquant ragout."[61]

Inspired by this instruction, British officer Richard Brett-Smith set about the task of locating the remains of Weimar Berlin (see fig. 1.4). He came up empty-handed. Poorly versed in reading the cues, he lamented that the search for "vice on the scale that had been known before was rather pointless." Dogged in his pursuit, he felt certain that "the same sort of thing went down (on a smaller scale) though it was hard to pin down."[62] The Swiss journalist Manuel Gasser had better luck. He learned from a particularly shifty black marketer that "one can have anything in Berlin, you just have to know the right people."[63] Even if one was lucky, it was clear to most visitors that the late 1940s were not the early 1920s. In his memoir, *Berlin '45: The Grey City*, Brett-Smith lamented that in surveying the landscape "the eye picked out only the Rio Rita and the Femina; the Eldorado, where the clients came dressed as girls, gave way to the postwar Tabasco, and that in time became the Cockatoo (see fig. 1.5); the Silhouette, which used to be attended by a mixture of pansies and Lesbians, the Geisha and the Monocle, both specializing in the latter, Steinmaers, where the dancing partners ogled their customers in bathing-dresses, and the beery, knee-slapping Haus Vaterland—all were gone." In the more upscale dance bars that had survived—like the Roxy, Bobby's, Chez Ronny, and the Rio Rita—"the drinks were expensive and the girls cheap," whereas the Royal Club, on the Kurfürstendamm itself, hosted big shots from the black market, foreign correspondents, and American and British officers. There, "for a change, the girls . . . were beautifully dressed and really lovely." To his mind, it seemed that thirteen years of Hitler's rule, bombing, defeat, and division had forever altered the terrain of the truly transgressive city. In the "mushroom glut of cabarets and Lokale" in the New West, one feature was ubiquitous: the satirical cabarets were often "introduced by a passé showgirl who addressed her victorious patrons in three and sometimes four different languages, making unsubtle and facile digs at Hitler and the Nazis while (for a time) Stalin looked on phlegmatically from a prominent position on the wall."[64] Even the most famous of the gay, lesbian, and trans* bars, the Eldorado, one of the first nightclubs to be targeted by the Nazis upon coming to power, failed to impress. Ewan Butler's

FIG. 1.4 Destroyed Variété Wintergarten. Photographer unknown. © Bundesarchiv Berlin.

boredom was palpable as he described a chanteuse's vain attempt at gender nonconformity. Claiming to be a woman who can't say no ("ich bin eine Frau, die nicht nein sagen kann"), "none of the people sitting round seem to care very much whether the happily married father, who calls himself Dolores, says 'yes' or 'no.'"[65] For many visitors, the prospect of kinship with Berlin's queer past was forever altered by the war's enduring presence.

But all was not lost. Even with the Nazi ban on swing music and its destroyed ballroom, the Femina Palace and dancehall, just to the south of the Kaiser Wilhelm Memorial Church, remained operational throughout the war in one form or another and was quickly called back into action as soon as the guns had stilled. To Brett-Smith, it certainly put on a good cabaret, but their "nauseating bonhomie," "wretched food," and "watered-down red wine" reflected all too well the material realities of the stretched economy.[66] He preferred down-market queer dives like the Robby-Bar on nearby Augsburgerstrasse, which managed to retain its edge, successfully conjuring the abandon of the twenties with boxing nights and members-only gatherings. Brett-Smith barely contained his enthusiasm for this Schöneberg district nightspot that "was still the playground of the pederasts and . . . Lesbians . . . of the latter," he assured, "there were many in Berlin." In the bar's current

FIG. 1.5 Berlin bar, Eldorado. © Bundesarchiv Berlin.

incarnation, "it was genuinely impossible to tell who was a man or a boy and who was a girl. . . . Men danced with men and women with women, and sometimes, oddly enough in that atmosphere, men with women; but it was anybody's guess who was who."[67] Perhaps Brett-Smith's *Grey City* was more colorful than he realized.

New Erotic Centers

The flashy cabarets in the central Berlin districts of Mitte and Schöneberg, near the Friedrichstrasse train station and along the Kurfürstendamm, struggled to rekindle Weimar's lost glory. If police and scene reports were a reliable indication, the remains of a truly transgressive subculture evolved in the twilight spaces along the quickly consolidating border between East and West that became home to the city's entangled gay, lesbian, trans*, and trade scenes. In September 1949, Werner Becker wrote an article in the Swiss homophile magazine, *Der Kreis* (The Circle), telling of the burgeoning nightclub scene where "already in the early days after war's end the first bars and restaurants opened their doors." Not all venues were posh and sophisticated like the supper clubs of the so-called New West. Many were poky backyard bars nestled in the city's various red-light districts like the one surrounding the arches of the Friedrichstrasse train station. Although patrons might be forced to change location due to prying eyes and public opinion, Becker happily reported on the survival of twenty-three men's clubs and fifteen ladies' clubs still in operation. Some, like the Zauberflöte in the Kommandantenstrasse, had attracted an established following in the 1920s through its lesbian nights in which "a wave of light flowed over the mostly young, thin, women's forms, that harmoniously swayed in blithesomeness from mirror dance to waltz."[68] A tad bourgeois with a heady love of schmaltzy music and rigorous entry requirements gendering access along a butch-femme axis, various women's clubs like the Monbijou and Violetta hosted their dances there until the Nazis closed their doors in March 1933, which did little to stifle spirits and only forced a change of venue.[69] As the archivist Jens Dobler pointed out in his book on the history of gays and lesbians in the districts of Kreuzberg and Friedrichshain, on virtually the same spot, the Zauberflöte continued the tradition of irreverence by holding a tongue-in-cheek birthday party "in celebration" of the reopening date—the seventeenth day of the fifth month—a not-so-veiled reference to Paragraph 175 of the Penal Code, which still outlawed sexual relations between men.[70]

While some of these dancehalls were steeped in history and built around prewar kinship networks, others were decidedly more low-key, like the Artistenklause on the Lausitzer Platz in Kreuzberg, housed in a series of simple, spartan gathering rooms tucked into tenement blocks. Here, despite the austere surroundings, patrons were promised a "colorful program" (*buntes Program*) regardless of the fact that few of these establishments held official ordinance or proper licensing given the fears of site inspection and the illegality of gay sociability. In the case of the Artistenklause, the owner experienced the full force of the law's injustice when her husband's wartime homosexuality came to light. In a meeting on November 27, 1951, members of the police licensing committee—which included representatives from the West Berlin youth bureau, select members of the hospitality industry, and, of course, the Allies—determined that in addition to the prior convictions of her husband, the Artistenklause must close shop since it was obviously a meeting place for "known homosexuals." As the police stated in their report, "Nothing about the place inspired confidence" that it would ever be anything but a hookup bar.[71] Despite promising to divorce her husband and secure a temporary license, few of the commission members actually believed she would refrain from holding "dance parties for gays" and allowing "entry to youths." Regardless of these concerns, the bar was allowed to eke out an existence. Taken over by Mamita, West Berlin's famous travesty dance promoter who would soon fall victim to an untimely death in an automotive accident, minigalas continued to be billed for Mondays, Saturdays, and Sundays, and advertisements graced the back pages of the city's newspapers and friendship magazines until anti-smut laws forced them from print.[72]

For the recently decommissioned Wehrmacht soldier Eberhardt Brucks, whose provocative sketches of amorous men adorned the pages of *The Circle*, the parties put on by the newly minted Fine Art Guild of Berlin (Berufsverband Bildender Künstler Berlins, or BBK) in the ball houses surrounding Zoo station were important nodes in the postwar kinship network for contact with like-minded men. Here, the boundary between bohemia and the queer scene was fluid. The Bright Lanterns (Bunte Laterne) Mardi Gras festivals cosponsored by the Association of Handicrafts gave local artists the opportunity to design entire installations in separate chambers within the vast ball houses. These festivals were well attended mostly by the city's more well-heeled gay and lesbian patrons, who, perhaps drawing from prewar experiences and memories of the glory days, "made a great stir" with their creative costuming and disguises.[73] The longest-running drag bar, Cabaret Chez Nous—established as a hole in the wall in 1958 a few blocks away in the neighborhood of Charlottenburg—added a whiff of international glamor with the Algerian-born Ramonita Vargas and by drawing luminaries like Josephine Baker and Hildegard Knef to the revue.[74] Bars, clubs, and cabarets in early Cold War Berlin were transnational spaces of queer kinship that sprang out of the ruins of the city's past.

Such a mix of high and low, of bohemia and the everyday was also palpable in the north of the city, in the working-class district of Wedding, where since 1949 the lesbian actor and sculptor Toni Höyenborg operated Café Münschhausen, which drew a steady business as the preferred gathering place for journalists, writers, and artists in pursuit of the "light and airy frivolity" that Brucks claimed marked the gallery openings, Christmas parties, and Mardi Gras festivities of the divided city's new center.[75] Many of these parties were open affairs, advertised brazenly in newspapers and on the announcement pages of the various friendship magazines that circulated through the hands of bons vivants in the 1950s, before the 1953 Law for the Protection of Youth (which was really a revivified version of the Nazi Anti-Smut Law) outlawed all gay and lesbian periodicals. Informal kinship networks ensured that information was passed to those in the know.[76]

Raids seemed to pick up in frequency in the late 1950s, which mirrored the increase in enforcement in the West. Andrea Rottmann has uncovered that the police force began assembling "pink lists" of known offenders while conducting nightly raids of queer hotspots.[77] It seems plausible that bars like the Artistenklause and Cabaret Chez Nous in West Berlin, Intermezzo in Hamburg, or even Baßgeige in Stuttgart, returned to the elaborately themed parties so prevalent in the 1920s and 1930s to cloak revelers in the security of travesty and masquerade.[78] These were mixed affairs, with cross-dressing an important feature of friendship circles, balls, and ladies' clubs well after Hitler came to power. Since lesbianism was not illegal under Paragraph 175, women's clubs had been somewhat shielded from direct intervention, although many, like the parties organized by members of the Comical Nine (Lustige Neun) had a history of being on the Gestapo's radar as late as 1940.[79] Observation reports from that time note that men in drag also attended, but they were sometimes taken for mannish women and left alone. On the parquet dance floors of Friedrichshain's Residenz-Rooms (Residenz-Säle) and the neighboring Concordia-Festsäle (Concordia Concert Halls), ambiguous sexual performances might also have helped shield partygoers from the prying eyes of the police.[80] Raid reports from 1957 and 1958 suggest that normative gender appearance, upper-class status, and the air of heterosexuality could similarly save patrons from on-the-spot arrest, while "obvious" transgressors, poorly passing transvestites, and street trade were routinely rounded up and placed in paddy wagons for processing.[81] Indeed, class status was an important, if not signature, marker of kinship in vulnerability. More upscale establishments like the Robby-Bar and Kleist-Casino, with their international, tourist, and white-collar clientele, were treated much differently than patrons of Elli's Bier-Bar a few blocks away, who were often jeered at by neighbors happy to see the police force "fight the vice."[82]

Although the gallantry of the ballhouse captivates the imagination, it was the smaller, more ramshackle venues that provided comfort and companionship for the less well connected. In time, it was spaces like these that galvanized the burgeoning scene. Nook-and-cranny bars hidden among the ruins like the Berliner Kind'l-Diele (later called the Schnurrbartdiele and then F13 for its Friesenstrasse 13 address) were simple wood barracks on a piece of abandoned property near the Tempelhof airfield.[83] Like many of the watering holes catering to a predominantly gay male clientele, the F13 came under the scrutiny of the police-directed licensing committee whose primary purpose was to enforce building code and public morals. Faced with the threat of closure, the F13's owner opted to take his case to court and received a verdict in his favor. In his address to the court, the judge evoked the sexologist Magnus Hirschfeld's notion of constitutional homosexuality and questioned whether the committee's energy might be better served in "not prohibiting every men's dance" but by treating "this impossible to eradicate vice" by protecting "normal oriented people" from stumbling into one of these establishments unawares?[84] After the court decision, the bar continued to operate more or less without difficulty, and the new proprietors, Hermann and his partner Werner, held dances complete with a three-piece band. Gottfried Steckers recalled in his memoirs how he frequented the bar after fleeing as a refugee from the East, fending off elder suitors who bowed courteously while asking "May I have this dance?" The older crowd of suited, mustached men danced under the watchful eye of the "boss lady," who took her position at the entrance and decided with a quick "he comes in" who was (and was not) allowed access.[85]

Although Christopher Isherwood's edgy Kit Kat Club and the notorious Eldorado hold court in the Anglo-American imagination as the premier icons of the gay and transvestite scene, if notoriety and rumor are markers of cult status, another bar is arguably more deserving of the moniker. Elli's Bier-Bar in Kreuzberg, housed across from the arches of the Görlitzer train station, was lifted to iconic status after it was portrayed in the activist filmmaker Rosa von Praunheim's 1970 film *It Is Not the Homosexual Who Is Perverse but the Situation in Which He Lives*. Although supposedly a meeting place for such notoriously gay (if politically polarizing) luminaries as Klaus Mann and Ernst Röhm already in the 1920s, it only emerged onto the scene as a gay bar in 1946, when Elisabeth Hartung (Elli for short) resurrected the bomb-damaged space her mother had rented since 1912. Despite her own questionable political status—she was personal friends with the NS–Women's League chairwoman and herself a Nazi party member since 1939, causing delayed denazification by the Allies—Elli built her bar into a central meeting space for the West Berlin gay scene, drawing a cross-border clientele until the building of the Berlin Wall. Beer was hauled by wagon from the neighboring Schultheiss brewery while patrons chatted by candlelight given the short supply of electricity. Prone to embellishment and a big personality, in an interview with a Berlin radio station, Elli took pride in having retrofitted the entrance with a door pilfered from the SS guardhouse in the Behrenstrasse and a chandelier from Joseph Goebbels's propaganda ministry. The fact that the bar was only outfitted with a single toilet for its patrons, forcing women to trek upstairs to use a neighbor's facilities, garnered the attention of the Kreuzberg police who conducted the first of many visits on October 20, 1951.[86]

Despite constant troubles with the police and a nasty dispute with her landlady, resulting in a letter campaign against the establishment, Elli continued to operate the bar, and in 1952, after she added the requisite number of toilets, she was granted an operating license to hold dances. Instead of stemming the tide of surveillance, the raids continued and became more frequent. The bar even made a dent in contemporary criminological literature when Detective Superintendent Schramm reported on it at the April 1959 meeting of the Federal Criminal Authority, which had convened to discuss the ongoing problem of sexual immorality and sex crimes. In a raid conducted on November 10, 1957, over one hundred people were questioned of which thirty-three were forced to give further testimony at the neighboring police precinct. Fourteen were eventually charged, although the specific charges were not discussed in any detail. Schramm told the group that given the general atmosphere of bars like Elli's, "anyone who entered such an establishment had to reckon with police action." The motivation was clear: the police claimed access to bars such as Elli's in order to investigate possible infractions against Paragraphs 175 and 175a, which governed male prostitution. Using a variety of laws on the books, ranging from police procedural articles, health and welfare ordinances, and juvenile law, criminal police conducted raids to regulate the spread of venereal disease, protect the youth, and maintain public order.

While Schramm was well known within the criminal police as overseeing the city's fight against homosexuality, in the 1960s his position was taken over by Dr. Karl Kaiser, affectionately referred to by regulars as "the empress," a pun on his name in German. To protect itself from the raids, Elli's, like many of the gay bars and clubs, installed a doorbell to regulate entry and provide enough time for patrons to "straighten themselves out" in advance of a pending raid. One bar owner at La Bohème actually went so far as to "offer" the police a key to the establishment to mediate the need for raids—but the police turned this down, claiming it took away the element of surprise. Elli didn't need to take such a stance since she had a mole within the police service. Taking kinship in bizarre new directions, Kaiser's son was a regular. With advance warning of a raid guaranteed, Elli could notify preferred guests to vacate to the backyard, sacrificing in the process some of the other patrons. As the writer Peter Jürgen Fabich remembered, the police often stuck the more effeminate gay men or "Tunten" into the paddy wagons, while he escaped out the back. By 1965 Elli had taken a more proactive role in warning her guests not to dance too closely, to refrain from kissing on the mouth, and avoid "grabbing of the sex area" just in case.[87]

The motivation was clear: it was not a crime to be gay per se, or to operate a gay bar, but it was dangerous to flaunt one's masculinity, whether effeminate, tough, leather, or trans*. Other bars managed to escape the kind of scrutiny reserved for Elli's, even though they also hosted masquerade dances and balls for mixed crowds. Elli's was different. The police used a range of laws to claim access to her bar in order to safeguard public morals.

Elli's Bier-Bar was without a doubt one of the most colorful attractions in postwar Kreuzberg. Despite her controversial past, Elli's grew to be a major node in various postwar kinship networks, with New Left student activists rubbing shoulders with sex workers, everyday neighbors ("normalos"), leathermen, and the odd well-known actor or actress.[88] Elli herself made a tidy living from the bar. She drove fancy cars, owned property, and lived out her days as hostess to an increasingly eclectic crowd, which over the course of forty years included actors like Hildegard Knef, the writer Günter Grass, and even musicians like Udo Lindenberg. Before the wall went up, gays and lesbians from the neighboring districts made their way across the sector boundary, including the self-named transvestite Charlotte von Mahlsdorf, proud wearer of traditional German dress. On one occasion Elli personally lifted her up onto the bar and yelled for all to hear, "You are my own ornamental doll."[89] Although, as Mahlsdorf reflected back, in 1961 (the year the Berlin Wall was built) "overnight, it was all over," Elli's continued to draw a mixed crowd from the West Berlin scene until it changed hands in the late 1980s once Elli was forced into a nursing home. In the early 1990s, it shut its doors for good. The business was no longer salvageable, as the building required much more money and attention than the landlord was able to afford.

The Bier-Bar is one of many examples of an entangled queer, lesbian, and trans* kinship network that came into its own despite police regulation and morality enforcement in the 1950s and 1960s. One of many lesbian-owned and operated establishments, it projected an air of tolerance within the community itself, as rent boys, transvestites, "half-naked young men, in fancy evening dresses or in enchanting almost transparent flimsy garments," and mannish women sought sanctuary from prying eyes and judgmental minds. As Charlotte von Mahlsdorf put it in her memoir, "Within this topsy turvy turmoil, there was one stable rock: the hostess, [Elli], wearing a striking motorcycle outfit."[90] As much as she is an example of queer kin, she is also a complex historical figure with an even more complicated past. But she is also fascinating for her strength and business acumen as well as for her bar's role as a place of refuge and revelry in a dark time. Her example showcases the complex overlapping worlds, kinships, and jurisdictions that made up the postwar moment. Harking back to what Richard McCormick has character-ized as the quintessential hallmark of 1920s sexuality, the blurring of the boundaries of identity, the Bier-Bar continued this tradition of mixing high and low; gay, lesbian, and straight worlds; trans* masculinities and femi-ninities; and nationalist, fascist, and postfascist orders and orientations.[91] As Rosa von Praunheim described it in the 1970s, Elli's Bier-Bar was first and always a simple hustler bar (*Stricherkneipe*), where a wide range of people sought refuge — "from intellectuals and train conductors to retirees, transvestites, leather types" — the true heirs of Weimar joie de vivre amid the entanglements of postwar life.[92]

As José Muñoz has suggested elsewhere, when queer is deployed to stabilize an identity, it overlooks points of commonality vital to coalition building and shared imaginaries. In essence, it masks the myriad ways in which minoritarian subjects "disidentify" with hegemonic social structures from binary gender norms to heteronormative racial formations, reconfig-uring themselves and the dominant society's scripts in order to thrive and survive.[93] As this chapter has shown, postwar gender and sexual identi-ties are fluid, multidimensional, and relational; they are also formed amid interlocking—though different—structures of inequality and norm building. What is needed is an approach that speaks not only to the asymmetrical, changing, and unstable forms of identity formation, but also to the way they are lived and experienced and constructed in view of these power imbalances. Intersectional approaches, born of feminist and antiracist interventions in the 1980s and 1990s, help us think through the complex interrelationships that emerge between multiple forms of power. But they have been critiqued for overlooking sexuality as a core category of experience and for not always being suitably attentive to differences of ability, passing, class, and how they, in addition to white normativity, might also occasionally reinforce difference.[94] More assemblage driven, entangled approaches might reconcile these omissions, shifting the emphasis toward becoming over being, and mapping the different ways in which selves surface and coalesce and sometimes disperse again in time and space.[95] Seeing gender and sexuality after fascism as entangled histories, sensitive to both the intersectional ways in which they deconstruct and also, at times, reinforce the hetero/homosexual, trans*/cis binary, encourages us to see divided Germany in a more dynamic way, which opens up new questions about how communities relied on kinships to live, thrive, and survive in the turbulent years after the war.

THE OPTICS OF DESIRE

2

THIS IS MANFRED (see fig. 2.1). I first encountered him on the blanched walls of the Berlinische Galerie during its 2008 retrospective on the photography of Herbert Tobias. He was a rent boy, one of Tobias's many pickups from the bars, train stations, and tearooms of the divided city. First captured in this trophy photo and immortalized in the exhibition as high art, Manfred was a stylized token of an erotic adventure.[1] After some digging, I learned more about who he was, not from Tobias's private papers but out of the pages of a 1970s gay men's magazine published in Hamburg on the heels of the 1969 decriminalization of Paragraph 175 of the German criminal code. The relaxation of censorship statutes allowed the Hamburg chronicler Hans Eppendorfer to publish *him* magazine (later renamed *him applaus*), the self-congratulatory "magazine with the man" which was to serve as a signature "Forum for Culture, Show and Erotic" during the early years of the sexual revolution. Once a bright light of the fashion world whose luster had tarnished in subsequent years due to drug use, Tobias became a house photographer and an occasional columnist. Although he was just starting to enjoy modest success with small gallery exhibitions in West Berlin and Amsterdam before succumbing to AIDS in 1982, it was thanks to his friend's benevolence that his homoerotic art first secured a wide audience.

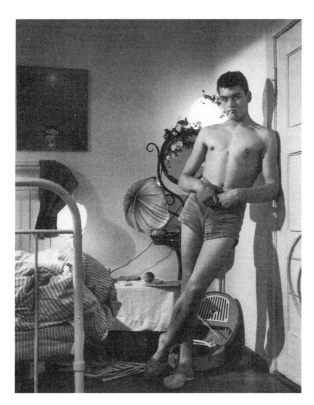

FIG. 2.1 Herbert Tobias, *Manfred Schubert*, West Berlin, 1955. © VG Bild-Kunst, Bonn / SOCAN, Montreal (2023).

I first wrote about Manfred for a conference in London. The three-day gathering, organized by Heike Bauer and Matt Cook, brought together students, scholars, and activists to rethink the 1950s in how we periodize the long era of post–World War II liberalization and reform. Among its many charms, it was a living, breathing exercise in queer kinship. We toured the storied Gay's the Word bookstore, now one of Europe's oldest brick-and-mortar queer bookshops. I had the opportunity to meet (and drink with) icons of the UK feminist and lesbian intellectual world, whose work I had voraciously read as a student. We were treated to a performance by the artist, activist, and feminist Lois Weaver, cofounder of Split Britches and Spiderwoman Theater. Matt Houlbrook and Laura Doan were finishing up what would go on to be signature interventions in queer history, and I crossed swords with an established scholar, then bonded with another who recalled fondly the world I had sketched out in my talk. All the while, a queer elder reminded us that this was not some intellectual dance but a matter of life and death for folks like him, who still lived with the memories of the dark days before legality.

Participants had traveled long hours to attend—some from antipodean former colonies, me from Canada—to establish a new research agenda for how to rethink this much-maligned decade. Although the kinship networks that brought us together reproduced some of the ties of empire, there was a dedicated effort to think about how sexual knowledge traveled locally as well as transnationally, and where resistance and change might and did happen, coalescing, as it often did too, around white, same-sex sexualities. In fact, what the presentations and later chapters in the conference volume had in common was the way they questioned the stability of identity, shifting the focus to the "process by which racialized subjects have been produced as insiders and outsiders to our postwar sexual categorizations."[2] But this was also tricky since only two chapters took up the matter of race explicitly—one veiled somewhat within a postcolonial reading of French cultural imaginaries after the Algerian War and the other centering on African American and Puerto Rican American lesbian teen coming-of-age stories.[3] Despite our very best intentions, the revised 1950s queer subject we conjured through our conference and volume was still forged through hegemonic whiteness.

When I wrote up the Manfred story more fulsomely for the *American Historical Review* in 2013, I came back to this question of how to think about the place of the 1950s both in the context of its time and also as inherited in the social memory of queer activism in the wake of the gay and feminist liberation movements of the 1970s. I was struck, then as now, by the transgressive nature of Tobias's subjective, emotional, and erotic visual sensibilities, how his depiction of intergenerational sex challenged sexological, iconic, and subcultural framings of male same-sexuality. His original and irrepressibly erotic form of claims making resonated with me for its shameless pursuit of pleasure as a fundamental feature of erotic life. My goal was not to recenter the subject. But while I remained convinced that the institutionalization of histories of sexuality—like the rights discourses they helped buttress—had come to emphasize movements over actors, respectability over transgression, and identity as fixed as opposed to radically in-between, something remained elusive still. Like the conference proceedings that explored the intricacies of 1950s kinships amid ambivalences of race and empire, Tobias's world of pickups, rent boys, and underage casual sex at once provided an important revision of postwar imaginaries while trading on mythologies of its own, chiefly iconographies of race, age, and otherness that were central to the production and consumption of pleasure but fundamentally at odds with how we think about good, equitable, consensual relations today. It made me wonder, How should we understand these tensions of queer kinship around age, consent, and generation?

Fortunately for me, I landed on the work of Jennifer Nash, Celine Shimizu, and Eliza Steinbock, which helped me rethink filmic representations of difference beyond presumptions of harm and injury in ways that allowed the subaltern to speak and provided audiences a space to claim difficult desires. I asked myself, How might we interpret the absent presence of racialized and underaged iconographies in Tobias's images for the power of their "productive perversity," how it contests authority while at the same time reinforcing longer-standing tropes within the Western queer imaginary?[4] What might this tell us about queer kinship, both its potential and pitfalls? As I will argue here, these fraught kinships are worth thinking about, especially for the way intergenerational sex disrupted homophile and New Left sensibilities at the same time that it fascinated viewers then and now, not always in the right way. If we label it solely as exploitative, "bad representations" of queer kinship, we neglect the potency of transgression in what Shimizu playfully calls "the bottomless pit of wonder that is sexuality."[5] These ambiguities of fantasy, mutuality, reciprocity, and desire open up the playing field for radical queer subjectivity, or at the very least what Joe Fischel has called ecstatic, exciting, "nonblah sex."[6] At the same time, as much as they are emancipatory they also eroticize social inequalities and taboos, including the racialized imaginaries of empire and the culture of perpetration during World War II. How should we navigate such fraught terrain?

Drawing inspiration from Kobena Mercer's two-time revision of his original reading of Mapplethorpe's photographs of Black male nudes, instead of an analysis of recovery or spectacularization, I propose shifting the focus to eroticism as a practice of the self, which helps us see and feel another kind of kinship, one guided by our own inner complexities and yearnings.[7] This means historicizing Tobias's images in their time and thinking about why transgressions of age, race, and nonmonogamy retain an erotic charge for contemporary audiences while also seeming out of place in today's sexual culture. Mercer's study of photographic emplotment and the way Mapplethorpe's camera fetishized the Black male body highlights the importance of subjective positionings. There is no doubt that photos such as these perpetuate queer kinship around race and youth sexuality, but here too, depending on the viewer's positionality and the context within which one is located, they might also make possible "subversive deconstruction of hidden axioms" of queer culture. To demonize them outright is not only to dehistoricize them (there were reasons why they were deemed luminously transgressive in their time) but also to circumscribe the already tenuous place of marginalized and misrepresented subjects within the dominant culture.[8] Tobias's quiet pleasures thoroughly animated his art, challenging norms in each moment they surfaced while reinforcing at the same time certain assumptions around race and youth, which have been written out of the history of queer kinship after fascism. This chapter brings them back into view.

In doing so, it will do two things. First, it will offer a methodological argument about ways we might draw on photographic evidence in the reconstruction of historical selves and others. Second, in drawing these reflections through a reading of select images from Tobias's rent-boy photos, it will demonstrate the importance of thinking critically about the work of erotic images in queer kinship, shifting our focus ever so slightly away from what photographs document and portray to the emotions they stir, the memories they resurrect or conjure up and possibly even redeem. Finding ways to historicize the productive work of images is all the more prescient for entangled studies of kinship as intimacy, pleasure, and desire for, although these are fundamental elements of experience and personhood, they remain overlooked in most historical analyses.[9] Training ourselves to see the shifting subjectivities of photographic sources, in other words, those they depict and those they actively create, perhaps we might begin to ask new questions of the image both as an object and a text, one that constructs new social realities as much as it also reflects them.[10]

With Tobias's images of his liaisons and pickups in mind, I will explore what erotic photographs such as these can tell us about the changing optics of desire in queer kinship in the second half of the twentieth century. Using his photography as an entry point into the subjective world of human wants and needs—a realm, it bears saying, into which historians still seem reluctant to tread—we see Tobias's work as operating in three ways: as an icon, an object, and a performative practice. These images help cement a place aesthetically for what might be termed "the cruising gaze," leaving material traces of midcentury queer sociability; they also aid in the creation of desiring subjects from among those forced into their trajectory at distinct moments in time.[11] When we open up our reading of photographs to what José Muñoz refers to as frequencies—visual, symbolic, material, and emotional—we recognize that images do not passively mirror historical change but actively constitute claims to representation, "render(ing) specific distillations of lived experience and ground-level history accessible."[12] Remaining open to the profoundly affective dimension of our own kinship encounters with the queer imaginary, perhaps we might also concede that our desire to grasp the alterity of the past says something altogether more profound about our own personal need to know, explore, and acknowledge equally elusive—perhaps even hidden—parts of ourselves.[13]

The Work of Images

Just why do photographs pose such dilemmas for historians? "Photographs flirt," says Julia Adeney Thomas.[14] They tempt us with an immediate sense of knowing and recognition, which veils the work they actually do in constructing particular images of the past. Instead of denying the affective allure of our sources, perhaps what is truly needed is to do as Elizabeth Edwards suggests and think beyond the visual for the way photographs enliven a myriad of emotional responses in us as we endeavor to access the past.[15] This should be easy enough to imagine with sexually charged images, since erotic photography's promise, in both its composition and circulation, is to elicit intense and immediate (and sometimes altogether unwanted) responses to that which is surreptitiously on display. Not only do erotic images pose the potential of unveiling the shape and face of moral panic, transgression, and sexual regulation; they also offer unparalleled insight into how, at different moments and in different ways, people have imagined the role of sensuality, the illicit, pleasure, and desire in their own intimate lives.[16] Why should we wish to be removed from this process? Instead of an arm's-length excavation of the past for posterity's sake, Thomas and Edwards open the door to the pursuit of embodied knowledge in historical analyses, with attention to the subjectivities of the subjects under analysis and, by extension, those of the people undertaking the investigation itself—namely us, the practitioners, guardians, and caretakers of history. In this way, we are a very real part of the kinship networks we seek to unveil.

While there is excellent work already out there on how to use photography in history writing, why are more sexually charged images still so peripheral considering the enormous potential of these sources in unveiling not only the shape and face of moral panic but also the more pleasant of human capacities like intimacy, physical and emotional compatibility, attraction, and desire?[17] This oversight is only partly due to the subject matter and has more to do with larger struggles surrounding the place of the subjective in history. Unlike our art historian brothers and sisters, we have struggled to find our footing with forms of nontextual representation. Whether a reluctance to fully embrace the cultural turn and the contingent nature of truth or a preference for "the connoisseurship of evidence" over more theoretical undertakings, this unwillingness to stray far from the supposed reliability of textual sources has led many historians to distrust photography or worse, assume its inherent transparency.[18] Where visual sources are employed as evidence, often they are called on to just illustrate an argument.[19] Rarely is emphasis placed on compositional arrangement, competing iconographies, the role of gesture, staging and lighting, and modes of emplotment. Despite efforts to go "beyond words" and draw on such diverse sources as material culture, soundscapes, photography, and film, logocentrism remains very much at the heart of the discipline.[20]

Whether a gendering of knowledge production or a general fear of the subjective, this hesitance toward the visual poses particular challenges for the writing of same-sex history and desire, despite the fact that for some time now scholars of visual culture have viewed photography and film as playing a privileged part in the social constitution of queer kinships.[21] If a photograph has the power to simultaneously reflect historical precedents *and* construct historical claims to being, then the denial of erotic photography's historicity—especially in relation to those still so disproportionately represented in mainstream historical research—threatens to disavow the real, important, and indeed political role of visual sources in realizing a more broadened vision of kinship itself.

And then there is the sheer problem of navigating the sources. Simply put, photographs are tricky. Not only is their meaning subjective but it also changes over time. Must this be something to fear? In his oft-discussed distinction between a photo's studium and its punctum, that which is rendered the subject of a photograph versus the portion that resides beyond the source that "pricks" or "wounds" a viewer's subjectivity, Roland Barthes provided several strategies for firming up photography's fluid encounters. While a photo's studium depicts "historical scenes," its punctum "shoots out of it like an arrow, and pierces" the viewer like a voice begging to be heard. Images instantiate a kind of physical or emotional response, which in turn spurs the viewer to ponder, through introspection, the meanings behind the otherwise elusive encounter.[22] In other words, a photograph is a material object as much as it is an indexical rendering of past events, personages, scenes, and moments. It is an actor and agent in an evolving series of independent encounters beyond the intentions of the photographer. To draw on photos as historical sources means analyzing these three elements together: the conditions that gave rise to a particular rendering, the techniques of emplotment as actualized on paper, *and* the range of subjective resonances these may have occasioned in particular moments in their viewing history given what we might mindfully reconstruct from the period under investigation.[23] What is needed, in other words, is a way to read photography for both its depiction and constitution of queer kinship beginning with the historically contingent construction of subjective wants and needs.

Of course, there is a reason why historians of twentieth-century Europe chose to emphasize the disciplinary potential of "visual power" to better explain how liberal democratic and totalitarian regimes exploited the scopic to garner and maintain popular sentiment and support.[24] It merits asking What is lost when we privilege social discipline, governmentality, and state violence over photography's more constitutive function in the wider sphere of human experience and interaction? Is photography solely capable of rendering reality, as Susan Sontag would have it, as "an item for exhibition, as a record for scrutiny, [and] as a target for surveillance?"[25] Must questions of beauty, intimacy, lust, and eros necessarily remain the domain of art historians and scholars of visual culture?[26] Or is there indeed a place for an embodied history of desire somewhere between these two poles? If we concede that images are not "well-flagged stakes driven into the ground" but moving objects that constitute a wide assortment of experiences from coercion to impulsiveness, trauma to pleasure—and all points in between—then erotic photographs can create a much-needed space for historicizing the productive role and potential of desire, opening up "new acts of seeing" the past, politically and aesthetically as well as emotionally.[27]

To aid us in historicizing the instantiation of intimacy, subjectivity, and desire in Tobias's photographs, it is useful to pick up on what Allan Sekula long ago termed "the historically grounded sociology of the image"—that is, the multiple genealogies at work inside, outside of, and beyond the frame that contribute to a photo's meaning.[28] When we look at the elements inside the frame, we see that Tobias's images gained their visual power by trading on several time-bound aesthetic norms. The choice and rendering of the subject—including the self-conscious deployment of particular techniques of posture, light, and shadow—tapped into (and frequently extended) earlier conventions for visualizing homoerotic desire photographically. Just as his aesthetic draws on images within the early queer canon, it cannot be divorced entirely from the complex formulation and legacy of Nazi iconographies that similarly venerated the racialized—in this case, white—male body and remained unacknowledged features of the 1960s and 1970s New Left and gay scene.[29] This medley of referents, often coexisting within a single photograph, are essential components of the image's meaning. The trick is to find ways of disarticulating the strands.

To pull apart these entangled inferences, we also need to draw on that which lies outside of and beyond the frame—that is, how the image came into being, where it circulated, and the sociohistorical context that undergirded its travels along the way. Tobias's photos form part of a larger aesthetic history of same-sex desire, but they are also part of the history of criminality and persecution before 1969 and the experimentalism of the early sexual revolution. Moreover, his aesthetic voice was not just something produced through his art; it was something he wielded deliberately as a strategy of self-substantiation, one he used deftly, though not unproblematically, to resist the shame and self-loathing many men felt in the years before decriminalization. Viewing his photography as a practice of reclamation as much as a claim to desire, we see that his contributions both to the history of sexuality and to photography lie in creating an existential and iconographic "archive of feeling" that flew in the face of contemporary and subaltern discourses of abjection in the years before the sexual liberation of the 1970s.[30] In a postwar world marked by Cold-War homophobia, lavender scares, and the aftereffects of Nazi-era jurisprudence (which remained in force in West Germany until 1969), these images were a powerful visual form of erotic self-making and remembering in a still-hostile age.[31] When set against the backdrop of the sexual revolution more broadly and the concomitant growth of international gay rights movements, we see that Tobias's praxis of self-actualization was quite liberatory in ways, providing same-sex-desiring men a kind of aesthetic kinship through visual pleasure, which allowed them ways of animating (and thereby legitimizing) their own fantasies, longings, and desires in the process. However, Tobias's enlistment and war service—to say nothing of the prosex strands of Nazi homoerotic aesthetics in some of his later work—temper this otherwise heroic narrative, forcing us to find new ways of teasing apart the conflicting visual frequencies at work in this photographic kinship.[32] In navigating this terrain mindfully, historicizing Tobias's images as calling into being an unashamed—though complicated—optics of queer desire during this slow and haphazard march toward sexual liberalization, not only do we begin to make good on Dagmar Herzog's assertion that we need to ask new questions about the evolution of the sexual revolution (in both its national and transnational frames) but we also see more clearly the ways in which homoerotic aesthetics and self-actualization took on visual proportions that paralleled the key events of the late 1960s, including the widespread legal reforms that swept much of Western Europe and the complicated nature of New Left discourses of sexual liberalization.[33]

Tobias's visualization of queer affect in his images of pickups and rent boys like Manfred underscores the fact that the construction, production, and consumption of erotic photography played a vital if overlooked part of queer kinship in the late twentieth century, for the men in Tobias's midst, for the photographer himself, for the viewers interacting with his legacy in the gallery hall, and perhaps even for some of the readers of this chapter itself.

The Unapologetic One

Who was Herbert Tobias and how exactly did he come to play such an important role in shaping the form and content of this evolving queer aesthetic? His origins are quite unremarkable. He was born in 1924 in Dessau to a petit bourgeois family and first started experimenting with photography as a child, before being forced to put aside his interests in art and theater in favor of more practical work as a landscape surveyor. As Tobias recounted in the few articles he penned for *him* magazine, both of his parents were strong believers in Hitler, so committed, in fact, that they frequently took their two young sons along with them to party gatherings and on leafleting campaigns.[34] After his father's untimely death in 1936 and his brother's subsequent enlistment, Tobias became the sole breadwinner, before he too was called up in 1942 and deployed, like so many young Germans, to the ravages of the Eastern Front.[35] Trying to make sense of the destruction he helped perpetrate, he took atmospheric—one might even say beautiful—editorial shots of villages and troops infused with pathos, suffering, and empathy.[36] Redeployed westward, he fled his detachment; he was arrested by the Americans and sentenced to time in a POW camp. Released in 1947, he enrolled in a theater course and toured with a small company, before breaking away with a few fellow travelers to form their own act. For the next three years they lived hand to mouth, barely eking out a living in and around Heidelberg. It was there that he met an American civilian, employed by the occupation government, whom he'd characterize as his first great love.

Their passion did not go unnoticed, and neighbors informed on the couple, causing them to flee postwar Germany for Paris, where Tobias practiced his photography from the sanctuary of their room in a cheap hotel. Landing a job at a photography studio, his work piqued interest at *Vogue Paris*, and he was invited to hone his talent under the mentorship of the celebrated German photographer Willy Maywald (see fig. 2.2). Over a series of months he explored themes of intimacy, tenderness, and longing in private photographs of the friends, lovers, and acquaintances he met in the Parisian gay scene. From brazen shots out of doors in the city's known cruising nodes to quiet images of cohabitation and repose, Tobias experimented with a range of styles while documenting defiant claims to self-realization within the still repressive climate of the 1950s.[37] Arrested for cruising, he returned to West Germany, where a fortuitous win in a photo competition with the *Frankfurte Illustrierte* provided him with the means to relocate to the leafy green district of Grunewald in what was now West Berlin. From his parterre apartment, the "crazy half underground l'apres midi d'un faun [*sic*]" as he'd call it in *him* magazine—a reference to the nineteenth-century French symbolist Stéphane Mallarmé's ode to homoerotic desire, which would be obvious to queer kith and kin—he captured images of a series of rent boys like Manfred, including some from the other side of the still permeable Iron Curtain.[38]

While biographical and contextual analysis comes easy to historians, a more systematic analysis of Tobias's work must read for queer kinship within the frame and how it evolves in the relationships between photographer, camera, subject, the image's own stylistic conventions, and its circulation against the backdrop of changing aesthetic practices that saw photography used to communicate a particular vision of male beauty to an intended audience.[39] Viewed from this vantage point, we see that Tobias's celebration of the abject world of cruising and the sex trade placed him in conversation with and separate from other artists working within the evolving queer counterpublic, which had started to carve out a space within turn-of-the-century aesthetics for ever more explicit homoerotic themes.[40] Perhaps the best-known purveyor of early erotic photography in the late nineteenth century, the Prussian photographer Wilhelm von Gloeden took hundreds of Arcadian snaps of the bachelor culture of Taormina, Italy, much to the delight of his closeted fin-de-siècle aristocratic patrons, who paid handsomely for his mail-order trade in images of Sicilian youths. Italy did not criminalize same-sex sexuality and was a welcome destination for northern European travelers who saw in it and the boys who courted them

adventures not allowed at home.[41] Across the Atlantic a few decades later, F. Holland Day would experiment with a similar style in the northeastern United States, testifying to the transfer of conventions and poses and the slow coalescence of a common homoerotic visual language. In von Gloeden's visual imaginary, which almost always included symbols of Homeric antiquity, dark-skinned ephebic boys were adorned with laurel leaves and positioned alone or in groups, en plein air, where they reveled in the beauty of their own bodies. Using this symbology to tap into the classical taste and refinement of his patrons and the sensuous potency of the Hellenistic intergenerational idyll, von Gloeden stylized his subjects in a way that was hidden in plain sight while still utterly recognizable, both constructing and trading on this shared vision of gay desire. In no way were these images authentic stylizations of the Greek past. Even Roland Barthes saw in them the imperfections of Eurocentric taste making, especially around race. These boys, whom Barthes derisively called gigolos given the well-known secret that they sold companionship, were not capable of upholding male beauty, too swarthy was their skin, too dark their complexion.[42] As Javier Samper Vendrell has argued compellingly, however, these highly eroticized images of boys with pan flutes and playful glances served as visual reenactments of a vision of the Greek homoerotic past captured within a European imperial gaze accustomed to looking at and fantasizing about its Others.[43] Although they weren't recognized as such at the time, given governing sensibilities around intergenerational sex in the queer counterpublic, by today's standards, Vendrell suggests these might well be considered examples of sexual coercion if not outright assault.[44] Certainly it is important to view these highly charged images within their different moral and temporal frameworks. But to view them exclusively through the lens of colonial violence might say more about our own contemporary concerns around consent, sexuality, and power than about emotions circulating at the time. This is not to negate the possibility or need for such claims; rather, it is to retain a sense of the different moral economies at work 150 years ago versus today. To view these images of what Kadji Amin has called disturbing attachments as an expression of inegalitarianism and coercion has the unfortunate effect of negating the possibility of agency on the part of the boys themselves. It also denies the transgressive power of bad kinship in queer worldmaking, in this case sex across the age barrier, viewing past erotic transactions through the prism of twenty-first-century respectability.[45] Perhaps a better question, following the work of Todd Shepard, might be to ask about the shifting place of white European gay male fantasies around racialized bodies, then as now, and what this tells us about the changing place of desire in queer subcultures (see figs. 2.3 and 2.4).[46]

Although there is no evidence in his personal papers that he owned any of von Gloeden's images, Tobias's photographs hold distinct visual markers that suggest he was very much cognizant of this earlier aesthetic tradition, whether the nineteenth-century original or the remediated versions that found their way into gay and sex reform magazines of the 1920s, which brought the imperial gaze to an even larger audience.[47] In two images in particular, both of boys from the streets of West Berlin, we see similar use of light and shadow alongside the telltale presence of flora and foliage, a nod to the pastoral, preindustrial tradition, equating the unmitigated honesty of ephebic masculinity with the naturalness of

FIG. 2.3 Wilhelm von Gloeden (1856– 1931), *Italian Boy Posing as Bacchus.*

love unbound (see figs. 2.5 and 2.6). This specific iconography, together with the affinity for lower-class masculinity, may be read as an effort to wrap the homoerotic urgency of the photograph in a veil of beauty, masking the tawdry as artful if not entirely respectable. These subcultural cues, as many scholars of queer advertising strategies have shown for the later twentieth-century period, would be suitably opaque to those not in the know. A more educated audience, on the other hand, versed in queer kinship's Hellenistic imaginary would handily decode these references as implied inferences of male-male desire.[48]

Just as the Mallarmé citation in *him* magazine testifies to Tobias's knowledge of and participation in same-sex-desiring traditions, so too did his use of these visual cues deepen the queer historicity of the photos. Of course, immanent sexuality had long been a preoccupation of sculptors and image makers well before Tobias emerged on the scene.[49] Tipping his hat to these earlier aesthetic practices, Tobias's 1950s photographs simultaneously build on and transcend them in extending this racialized visualization of queer desire out of the

FIG. 2.4 Wilhelm von Gloeden (1856–1931), *Leaning Nude Boy*.

countryside and into the street. These vestiges of an earlier erotic canon—
including its racial markers—remain patently visible whether through the
use of leaves and lighting; the emphasis on dirty, roughened hands; or the
continued preoccupation with impish beauty. Even the orientalism of von
Gloeden's oeuvre is noticeably present in Tobias's, not in the guise of agrar-
ian eroticism but through Tobias's own colonization of Berlin city streets in
search of working-class trade. The homoerotic gaze of the photographer,
anticipating the tastes and desires of his queer kin, lingers over these youths.
Drawing on earlier notions of mutuality and erotic friendship, it basks in the
visual pleasure of implied intergenerational love, rendering these boys—as
Laura Mulvey has argued for cinematic depictions of women—objects of the
spectator's desire and longing.[50]

Unlike von Gloeden, however, Tobias did not hide his subject's erotic appeal
behind the faux Hellenism of amphoras, lyres, and pan flutes.[51] These are
photos of street boys, and are captioned as such, leaving little to the imagination about the subject's origins in the squares and alleyways of the Cold
War city. Ever the perfectionist, it is telling that Tobias either deliberately
courted imperfection in these photos or at least allowed existing blemishes
to seep into the final prints. The purity of lines and symmetry, which parallel

FIG. 2.5 Herbert Tobias, *The Boy from East Berlin*, 1957. © VG Bild-Kunst, Bonn / SOCAN, Montreal (2023).

the innocent beauty of the sitting subject, is ever so slightly disrupted when our eyes widen to take in the bandaged index finger on the hand of the blonde boy holding the fan. Similarly, the Boy from Reichskanzler Square is posed under the shadow of a crescent moon cast on an apartment wall, perhaps a nod to this earlier orientalist tradition. His pursed-lipped, curly-haired profile is classically rendered (see fig. 2.7). If it were not for his pockmarked skin, protruding Adam's apple, and dirt-caked fingernails, we might overlook the evocation of the imperial gaze amid the obvious transgression of age and class boundaries that made this image possible in the first place.

Although Tobias draws on the visual language of verisimilitude, these "semiotic clashes" between the innocence of youth and their ostensible desperation are anything but transparent renderings of life on the margins. Instead, they are painstakingly crafted meditations on the place of sexual immanence in the queer visual canon. Tobias is not alone playing around with convention. In East Germany, the graphic artist Jürgen Wittdorf was busy crafting woodcuts and paintings of young male athletes, many of which were under contract with the state.[52] But lest we rush in to call this an un-

FIG. 2.6 Herbert
Tobias, *Photograph
of a Young Boy*, West
Berlin, 1950s. © VG
Bild-Kunst, Bonn /
SOCAN, Montreal
(2023).

equivocal abuse of power—which it could very well have been—recalling
Jennifer Nash and Celine Shimizu, these youths are not easily positioned
as victims of their own representation. Despite the relative inactivity of the
poses and staging, Tobias's street boys may evoke bad kinship but they are
most certainly good embodied subjects. They stare back at the lens. They
force an interpretive encounter. One need only take notice of the Boy from
the East's quizzical counterstare, to say nothing of his erect nipples. Perhaps the cause is innocent enough. But when taken together, these codes
and conventions construct for the knowing viewer an optics of anticipation,
enjoyment, mutuality—and possibly even release. While von Gloeden played
with various erotic looks, Tobias's aesthetic conversations, those both within
and beyond the frame, are explicit without being pornographic, extending
these kinships into the street and back home again, eroticizing intergenerational sex and the cruising gaze as elemental features of queer desire.[53]

The Amorous Regard

At the same time that this visualization of queer kinship drew on existing
signifiers in the gay scene, it was also unique. Tobias's optics of desire differed
significantly from the "amorous regard" of the stylized studio images taken

FIG. 2.7 Herbert Tobias, *The Boy from Reichskanzler Square*, 1955.
© VG Bild-Kunst, Bonn / SOCAN, Montreal (2023).

by pictorialist photographers of the so-called glamour generation, those well-heeled gay mandarins like Carl Van Vechten, George Platt Lynes, and George Hoyningen-Huene who worked within the fashion, film, and literary establishments on both sides of the Atlantic in the 1930s.[54] Tobias's images certainly drew on elements of modernist iconography, but they extended these photographic kinships away from the rarefied world of the movie studio and salon into the street, literally and figuratively. Taking inspiration from the flesh trade directly, Tobias mixed styles and visual metaphors along his own personal axis of high and low, queering the homoerotic gaze and the elements that helped hold it together. Placing these dialectics of transgression front and center stage—at great peril had these images fallen into the wrong hands—his work presaged the autobiographic irreverence and self-referentiality of postmodernist photographers Nan Goldin and Cindy Sherman, who would go on to immortalize street and subculture in the 1970s and 1980s.[55]

Nowhere are the differences in Tobias's aesthetics of queer kinship more discernible than when we compare his 1950s photographs to those of his contemporary Minor White. One of the cofounders of *Aperture* magazine who refused to have his own homoerotic archive exhibited until after his death, White transformed images of the profane into the sacred by shrouding his subjects in shadow and fragmenting their bodies within the frame, using his camera as a surrogate for what he called the search for "intimacy without embarrassment."[56] Unlike White, Tobias allowed his subjects to speak through the lens in a language of unmitigated longing. Of course, Tobias had less to lose as someone living off contracts in fashion photography. But even when compared to the mass-produced images circulating in the beefcake magazines from the Los Angeles–based bodybuilding scene, or the photographs and sketches in so-called friendship magazines like *Der Kreis* (The Circle), symbol of the 1950s international homophile movement, Tobias's vision of queer erotic kinship diverged significantly from the smooth-skinned athletes and classical near-nudes that surveys indicated the readers of these men's magazines preferred.[57]

Looking outside the frame to consider the photograph's movement and migration as a physical object, we see other ways in which we might historicize the role and resonance of the image in constructing queer erotic kinship as a structure of feeling.[58] The Manfred photo had come a long way from the gutter and street, circulating briefly—though not insignificantly—among the photographer's closest friends before being taken out of the confines of vernacular subalternity and into the public sphere in *him* magazine. But this does not mean it was truly hidden. Given his previous interactions with the law, it is fair to assume that Tobias was fully cognizant of the fact that its mere possession might be dangerously incriminating.[59] In light of possible persecution—and according to the rules of evidence in operation in 1950s West Germany, images like this one could still be used as proof of transgression—it is even more astounding that he took no fewer than eight different images of Manfred from quirky close-ups to mise-en-scènes. Whether a twist of archival fate or a testament to Manfred's enduring erotic effect on the photographer, of all the images housed among the Tobias papers at the Berlinische Galerie, Manfred is the most photographed of all his liaisons. Further proof of the artistic and libidinous appeal of this subject, selections of the Manfred photos would surface in no fewer than two different photo essays in *him* magazine once the 1969 decriminalization of homosexuality meant that Tobias no longer had cause to fear arrest or censure.

Folding Tobias's photography into the social history of 1950s and 1960s West Germany, we see his choice of subject was troubling in other ways, especially in contravening the efforts of progressive sexologists intent on reforming the pernicious antisodomy legislation through the promotion of gay respectability. The vision of sexual sobriety cultivated by the homophile lobby—and promoted internationally in the pages of the *Der Kreis*—turned on the disavowal of cruising and male prostitution.[60] This was not a new position in the struggle to eradicate laws against same-sex sexual expression. The Weimar Republic's most strident voice for the repeal of the antisodomy legislation, Magnus Hirschfeld, likewise characterized the boy prostitute as a blight on the gay scene, or worse as a "pseudohomosexual" who challenged sexological discourses of inversion.[61] In West Germany, where a wave of arrests had led to a rash of suicides of young men accused of homosexuality, a progressive jurist warned against the malevolence of the rent boy since it was feared that these arrests originated in the hands of a blackmailing hustler.[62] Armed with the latest studies on sexual deviance from Frankfurt's renowned Institute for Sexual Studies, in 1954 Botho Laserstein wrote *Rent Boy Karl* (*Strichjunge Karl*) as a primer for gay men on how to navigate the homophobic criminal justice system. Laserstein—a Jewish German attorney who had lost his wife in Auschwitz and was hounded out of the profession for his defense of gay clients, actions that brought on a severe depression and suicide—made the case that as long as consensual sex among adult men was criminalized, male prostitution put honest and otherwise law-abiding citizens in harm's way.[63] His view was by no means in the minority even among well-intentioned progressives; far into the 1970s, activists like the filmmaker Rosa von Praunheim and the student movement leaders Martin Dannecker and Reimut Reiche, responsible for some of the most important studies of sexual marginalization during the sexual revolution, criticized cruising as a holdover of illegality and crass capitalism that prevented gay men from lending their energy to organizing for change.[64] Indeed, it wasn't until some years later that a more humanistic light was directed toward the plight of the hustler in a series of sociological studies of boys working in the scene. Even here, the authors struggled to find a press willing to publish their findings, highlighting the continued marginality of street youth in contemporary legal, sexological, and activist discourses.[65] In claiming street-level sex as a fundamental feature of queer desire, Tobias's photography flew in the face of both the visual and social politics of the homophile lobby and progressive networks by articulating a vision of queer kinship that was more reflective of actual practices within the gay scene—because, of course, men continued to cruise other men for sex. Tobias's photographs of a casual connection may be read as a strident affront to the official morality of postwar West Germany, to the elite aesthetics of early queer cosmopolitans, and to the unfortunate hypocrisy of the reform movement that drew on a history of sexology to demonize the passions of the street as antithetical to the politics of modern queer kinship.[66] Expanding the boundaries of homoerotic representational style and subjectivity Tobias, via Manfred, laid unbridled claim to both the street and domestic spaces like the home and bedroom as sites of queer self-formation and desire.[67] Willfully recognizing these overtures to same-sex subjectivization as tawdry and transgressive in both an aesthetic and a social sense, Tobias located queer kinship amid a "poetics of living homosexuality," one that eclipsed the fauxclassicism, shame, and theatricality of previous emplotments of desire.[68]

Tracing the aesthetic and social historical conventions at work in Tobias's photographs of rent boys and pickups provides unparalleled insight into post-1945 illegality as icons and emblems of a defiant desire in a deeply homophobic age, something we fail to appreciate if we view them solely as forms of violence and coercion. Viewing these images iconographically and as material things with distinct, though changing, genealogies allows us to discern ways in which Tobias's renderings form both an evolution of and a deviation from previous visualizations of queer desire over the course of the twentieth century. A third and final way to consider these images is for their role in the actual constitution of a more lubricious queer subjectivity, one that began to take shape in the decades before AIDS fundamentally colored same-sex desire in hues of risk, danger, infection, and aversion.[69] Embracing "the cruising gaze" and embodied desire, Tobias sought to free the queer subject from a kind of kinship based around the normativizing impulses of previous claims to assimilation and respectability, even as this hinged on what might, by today's standards, seem purely exploitative.

From the safety of his apartment in the tony neighborhood of Grunewald, against the prying eyes of the state and the disavowal of the scene, Tobias defiantly styled and photographed his pickup (see figs. 2.8–2.10), whom, he describes in the article in *him* magazine from 1974 where the photo in figure 2.10 first surfaced publicly, he had met hanging around outside a

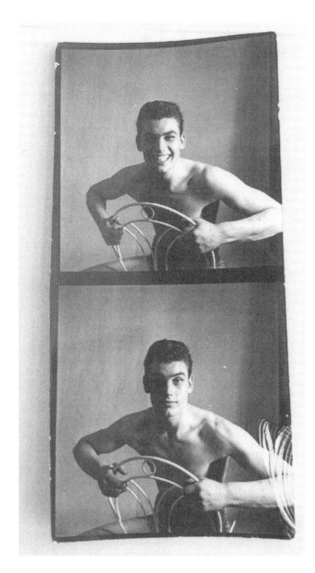

FIG. 2.8 Herbert Tobias, Manfred, seated, undated photo. © VG Bild-Kunst, Bonn / SOCAN, Montreal (2023).

known gay pub in the city center.[70] The composition of the photo, its staging, the narrative scenario presented or hinted at, and Manfred's self-confident counterstare suggests that he was anything but one of the closeted "sad young men" the film historian Richard Dyer has described that surfaced in films of the same era.[71] In this photo of the boy next door, a troubled hood in shorts who'd spent more than his fair share of time in foster care and jail, we are confronted with a gaze that mixes innocence with trust and playfulness with seduction. Tobias pulls back all veneers of respectability

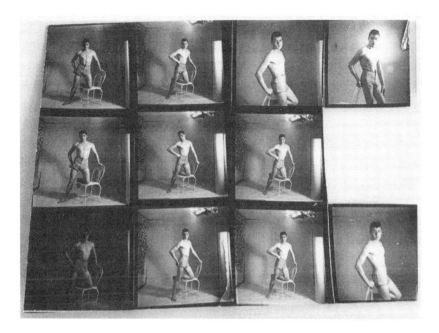

FIG. 2.9 Herbert Tobias, Manfred, standing, undated photo. © VG Bild-Kunst, Bonn / SOCAN, Montreal (2023).

and privacy in this image, implicating the viewer in the construction of an erotic kinship that virtually penetrates the lens.

Visualizing the Sexual Revolution

Let's take another look at this image (fig. 2.10). The Manfred photo, taken in the 1950s, was published in the December 1974 issue of *him*. Despite the obfuscated classical silhouette on the wall in the background—one of Tobias's many self-portraits it just so happens—this photo resonates with the frisson of imminent transgression. For one thing, his form is curiously off-center, nearly inseparable from the hodgepodge of items adorning the scene. The eye has to work hard to focus in on him. Despite the slightly cinematic rendering of his stance, his shoulders, arms, hands, and cigarette all point in the direction of his semi-erect penis, which pushes provocatively against his shorts. Unlike the catalog version, which is more artfully rendered, the magazine image is cropped in such a way as to emphasize his midsection, the focus of allure for *him*'s readership. His cigarette, tousled hair, and rumpled bedsheets

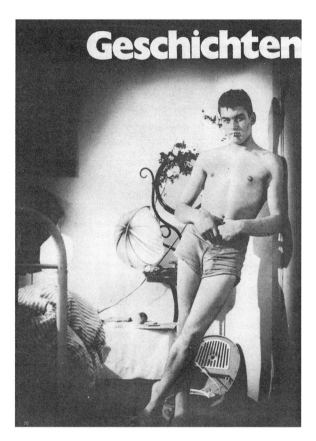

FIG. 2.10 Herbert Tobias, Manfred, "Stories with Manfred," *him*, December 1974. © VG Bild-Kunst, Bonn / SOCAN, Montreal (2023).

further tempt the viewer with suggestions of what was about to transpire (or perhaps already had?). Unlike Minor White's photographs, where the camera captured the subject looking askance—or as a pleasingly rendered (yet fragmented) torso—Manfred's gaze is straight on. Reminiscent of E. J. Bellocq's photographs of prostitutes in the brothels of Louisiana, Manfred stares directly back at his photographer/lover and viewer as an active participant in his own self-narration.[72] While the spectator explores his body with their eyes, Manfred's stance and counterstare invite this action. He is both the subject and object of desire.

If Tobias's 1950s photography turned on the right to desire as an essential element of queer affiliation, how might we understand the role of decriminalization and 1970s gay rights consciousness in this particular visualization of desire? Such an analysis requires that we view the photographic legitimation of abject desire as another feature of the social, aesthetic, and visual history of the sexual revolution. It also means that we consider sexual liberalization to have its roots much earlier. Using pictures such as these as historical sources means subjecting not only their provenance and circulation to analysis but also examining their aesthetic conversation for how, and in what ways, this too has changed and evolved over time. While modernist aesthetics provided some sanctuary for the homoerotic display of male figures as long as they conformed to the image "of the svelte, hairless, well-proportioned body" of the ephebe, athlete, and dancer, in the 1950s Tobias began challenging the gendered implications of this motif in favor of a more complex mix—one might even say jumble—of homoerotic masculinities including those of the impoverished boy prostitutes working the streets.[73] Not only did his photography challenge the classificatory scientific gaze of sexologists and the punitive use of images by the police, but it also built on and transcended the canonical homoeroticism of preceding generations of queer photographers, acting, to use Shawn Michelle Smith's phrasing, as a "counterarchive" to the "counterarchive" by offering a unique visual meditation on erotic friendship, mutuality, and unencumbered homoerotic desire.[74] After the decriminalization of homosexuality in 1969 and the lifting of censorship laws, when more genital and pornographic images gradually penetrated the public sphere, Tobias's work continued to flout convention through the use of nostalgia for the forgotten 1950s when, alongside visual essays on industrial chic and the leather scene, *him* magazine still saved a space for photos of the time when "boys all wanted to look like Elvis" (see fig. 2.11).[75] Indeed, the 1970s iteration of the Manfred photo also includes a story of when the youth came home with him, which turned into a weekend with not just Tobias but also an actress who was crashing at his pad. Playfully hinting at more than just costume play, Tobias challenges the notion that same-sex desire must somehow also be siloed.

Decriminalization had brought the possibility of securing a wider audience for these photos. Yet, just as von Gloeden's portraits had in the late nineteenth century, these images of enraptured male bodies continued to carry complex representational and ontological significance based on the changing contemporary climate. Alongside efforts by academic and self-help organizations to promote visibility and pride as the dual mantra of sexual liberation, in the pages of queer erotic men's magazine, an unabashedly raw sexuality slowly emerged as the symbol of the hard-won right to desire. Although photography had once helped solidify in medical, criminological, and popular discourse the contours of diseased, depraved, effete, and transitional

Herbert Tobias:
Ein nostalgischer Ausflug
in die Vergangenheit

Als die
Jungens
alle wie
Elvis
aussehen
wollten...

24

FIG. 2.11 Herbert Tobias, "A nostalgic trip into the past. When boys all wanted to look like Elvis," *him applaus* 12 (December 1977): 24–25. © VG Bild-Kunst, Bonn / SOCAN, Montreal (2023).

masculinity, in the hands of magazine publishers, collectors, and lay as well as trained photographers of the 1970s it now helped create lasting images of the shamelessly eroticized male body.[76] Tobias's image of nostalgia, longing, and desire—to say nothing of the deeply personal portrayal of Manfred in his many close-ups—helped lend form and contour to this newly emergent embrace of the queer body blemished but beautiful.

If his 1950s photography challenged normative legal and medical discourse as well as the homoerotic canon by advancing the visualization of abjection as elemental to what he himself called "the sensual man," for Tobias the decriminalization of homosexuality did not usher in a dramatic shift away from sensuality toward the explicitly sexual. Indeed, some of his 1970s photographs retained many of the formal conventions of his previous work, as evidenced by figure 2.12, which transgresses racial boundaries instead of intergenerational ones while still drawing on lighting and staging techniques honed during this earlier period. The addition of the Friedrich

FIG. 2.12 Herbert Tobias, "I don't know to whom I belong . . . ," 1972.
© VG Bild-Kunst, Bonn / SOCAN, Montreal (2023).

Holländer lyric made famous by Marlene Dietrich "I don't know to whom I belong" works on several levels, suggesting that he still held a place for homoerotic and subcultural referents in his work despite the passing of time. But its double entendre is inescapable, conjuring images of sexual ownership and even slavery, which may have been mere erotic play but turns on racial fetishism and the spectacularization of the Black male body. For a German navigating the politics of postfascism in the era of civil rights, it appears as sheer ignorance masquerading as sexual and racial liberation, yet another supposedly transgressive fantasy anchored in the objectification of the Black male form based on "unmediated and unilateral control over the other."[77]

Without denying the coercive power of these words, perhaps here too, as with the von Gloeden images, there is another way to view this. Indeed, Mercer's thoughts on Mapplethorpe are instructive here. Taken in 1976 after Tobias had traveled to New York City, and by that time had become an enthusiastic participant in the leather scene, one can't help but wonder whether Tobias crossed paths with Mapplethorpe to talk photography (or not talk at all). The "fantasmic emphasis on mastery" as Mercer puts it in his earlier critique of Mapplethorpe is visible here too, with the camera position angled downward from the spectator's position. Mercer argues in his initial reading of Mapplethorpe's Black male nudes that the colonial gaze of the viewer feminizes the sitting subject, rendering him an object of art and a possession.[78] Although he does create space for the counterstare and its humanizing function, ultimately the use of lighting, staging, and portraiture creates a kind of "juju doll from the dark side of the white man's imaginary."[79] One could certainly argue, as I did in an earlier essay, that this restaging of the Hellenic-inspired Western queer imaginary, with a Black model at its center, simply reinforces the photo's Eurocentrism.

But is there another way to read this image? In "Skin Head Sex Thing"—written in 1994—Mercer returned to his previous renditions, not to debunk his original conclusions but to stress the work of ambivalence and how it lends itself to multiple, coexisting interpretive leanings amid these contradictory structures of feeling. Written in the wake of Mapplethorpe's death from AIDS in 1989, after the artist had endured profound criticism as part of the culture wars, Mercer ceded that he had been perhaps too unequivocal in his judgment of Mapplethorpe. Owning up to his own inner turmoil about the images, he sympathized with the artist, who, as a fellow gay man of a certain age, navigated a kind of hate that transcended race, at least in that instance, creating a kind of kinship across the racial divide. The ambivalences remained, certainly, but the meanings they engendered depended on one's own subjective place as viewer/audience/reader and the space and time of consumption. Although the specific emplotment of the subject seems to reify the colonial gaze, Mercer recognized that there was in fact more going on in the image. These photographs had an agentic quality. They pushed back at the lens, which, as we see in Tobias's 1976 photograph, gives the subject an embodiment of his own. The possibility of mutuality and shared eroticism undercuts the notion that in simply depicting interracial sensuality, the photo is somehow inherently exploitative. Placed within the context of Tobias's long-standing fascination with his own face and self-portrait, there is even the sense that the gaze might be reversible, like the point-of-view shot in pornography. Finally, and with Tobias also succumbing to AIDS, albeit several years earlier than Mapplethorpe, in 1982, this photo becomes a totem of sorts, standing in for the memory of an earlier sexual culture, one imbued with a vision of erotic power and transgression that is difficult to countenance today. As Jennifer Nash reminds us, sometimes agency resides within the exploitative.[80]

Tobias took the opportunity provided by the relaxation of censorship to reflect on his earlier canon, whether in revisiting a particular theme from an earlier series or by returning to the photo of Manfred. The sense of introspection, longing, and existential quandary that animated his earlier images remained very much in evidence in his contributions to the gay magazine, where his pursuit of abjection and the everyday was doubly important in the climate of the 1970s when legality had failed to transcend what he felt was the stultifying conformity, bitterness, and apathy of the slowly commodifying gay scene.[81] What he hoped would awaken the senses to the essence of human existence was more important than ever amid the increasingly youth-obsessed 1970s. Lost in the struggle for greater visibility and acceptance—he argued in a magazine interview in November 1977—was the fact that judgment, criticism, and the inability to countenance beauty remained core features of daily life, and were perhaps even more pronounced in gay subcultures where, as if under a magnifying glass, "life was on display in a much more concentrated form than in wider society."[82] A month after his tell-all interview where he lamented the sexual politics of the scene, Manfred's image was resurrected one last time for this "nostalgic trip into the past."[83] Ironically, in doing so Tobias condemned the youth-obsessed gay scene with his own youthful trophies, simultaneously exposing his existential angst at growing old and his lament that his own queer aesthetic no longer held resonance for the gay community. As we'll see in chapter 4, this coincides with fractures within the German gay rights movement between reformist and radical groups but also among those advocating for the sexual rights of children and youth. Although we have no evidence of Tobias supporting these platforms specifically, his continued interest in images of intergenerational fantasy suggest that cruising and street sex remained a core feature of his art if not also his lived experience. In returning to the Manfred photos later in life, we see Tobias's effort to reclaim himself as a desiring subject (and desirable by extension) at a moment when his ability to express his own erotic subjectivity seemed to be slipping through his fingers, only to be resurrected twenty years later under the auspices of high culture.

By the last decades of the twentieth century, images of queer desire and eroticism had secured a firm place in the photographic register, creating a widening sphere of activity for gay-identified men in fashion, academe, and in the larger art community. Still, slippery obscenity laws and informal practices of self-censorship meant erotically charged photos were rarely curated or on display in museums and galleries.[84] Despite the fact that major artists had traded on homoerotic imagery for some time, the conjoining of intimacy, mutuality, and queer desire was slow to be embraced as high art. Censure in the art world ensured that both explicit and deeply personal depictions of male-male sexuality remained underground until the 1980s. The putatively democratic force of the sexual revolution, together with greater affordability of cameras and film, slowly chipped away at this, creating new agents and conduits of sexual knowledge formation. In West Germany, sex shops flourished, gay-themed magazines were founded, and university students joined New Left activists to press for better information on queer cohabitation, domesticity, aging, and health.[85] Pornographic filmmaking fundamentally changed the playing field creating new modes of self-presentation, and average people began to use the camera in their own erotic play, documenting in the process changing body practices, aesthetics, and subjectivities.[86] Unlike past decades, erotically charged photography literally leapt off the pages of men's magazines into mainstream advertising campaigns, a hallmark of the increasing acceptance of homoerotic imagery and the further commodification of the gay scene. Like never before, men's bodies became "spectacularized" in art and fashion, a consequence of the liberalization of antisodomy laws, the growth of visible urban subcultures, and deliberate attempts by ad executives to harness the potential of this "new male consumer market" without fear of retribution for contravening previously established gender norms.[87]

Placed in this context, Tobias's photos may be understood as a visual marker of changing notions of kinship within both the queer and dominant cultural canons. Going one step further and taking Tobias's erotic archive as a site of self-fashioning as well as a performative practice, we may begin to appreciate more fully the multiple ways in which his mode of visualization served as a living and moving artifact of changing emotional expression. Unfortunately, his pursuit of his art was hampered by his erratic personality and addictions. By the mid-1970s, he had retreated even further from society, turning his back on the fashion industry before being spurned by the nascent gay and lesbian movement that had galvanized on both sides of the Atlantic. Forced back to taking pictures, the changing moral climate of the postdecriminalization years meant he could finally publish his erotic photography publicly and, by the time of his death in 1982, he had begun to taste some artistic success with an exhibition in Amsterdam featuring, among other works, youths like Manfred whom he had first become fascinated with during his time in Berlin.

There is much to be gained by viewing erotic photography as history, especially when we consider the emotional work of images in creating historical subjectivity in the changing places and spaces of viewing and display. Certainly, Tobias's work raises the thorny issue of how historians negotiate the volatility of the image in what Sara Ahmed has referred to as an "affective economy," where emotions like desire, joy, lust, and shame periodize how we understand historical change.[88] How might attention to the affective relationships between subject, photographer, and viewer open up new possibilities for the way we appraise key turning points in the history of postwar liberalism to say nothing of the need for a more nuanced appreciation of queer kinship as both materially grounded and socially constructed? To hazard an answer to this question, let me make four final points regarding the promise of analyzing photography in its iconographic, material, and subjective registers.

First, by attending to an image's aesthetic makeup, we pull out multiple, coexisting meanings that aid us in devising new ways of periodizing queer life after fascism. Recalling that photographs are not only layered aesthetic texts but actual physical entities and things that circulate, are traded, and migrate from their place of creation to new spaces of consumption, we are forced to recognize that they also transcend the boundaries of the local and the national. All images are mobile, but queer erotic photographs are particularly frenetic, trafficked from place to place, circulating in tourist and fine art networks, on the boundary between high and low, and on both sides of the Atlantic as well as along twilight subcultural pathways.

Second, such an emphasis on the social lives of images allows us to better understand the specificities of human experience in the changing sociospatial contexts of viewing. In Tobias's photos of rent boys, we see the aesthetic inheritance of an evolving homoerotic imagination while simultaneously gaining a glimpse into the baleful world of homosexual persecution before the era of decriminalization. They force us to make a space for the sexual and aesthetic avant-garde alongside social movement histories as places of queer politicization and resistance, sometimes against the hegemonic culture but often among subcultures as well, a point we'll return to in the next chapter. Indeed, they surface all sorts of pleasures and anxieties, at the time as well as now, over what constitutes good and bad kinship. In this way, Tobias's photos provide insight into the negotiation of modern sexual subjects in late liberalism as mediated through the realm of desire, ensconcing passion and transgression (over reason and respectability) as elemental to queer personal fulfillment. They do this, in part, by rendering desire visible through the aestheticization (and eroticization) of abject masculinities. Unlike the iconic images of soldiers, sailors, bodybuilders, and wrestlers, or even Robert Mapplethorpe's self-portraiture that brought images of leather men into the gay visual arcana, Tobias combined select elements of turn-of-the-century gay iconography and pictorialism with a fascination with class, race, youth, friendship, and brotherhood to stage a transgressive multivalent gay subjectivity as the cornerstone of queer kinship and identity. His images of street boys reclaimed the gutter, but this in and of itself was not his biggest contribution to the burgeoning gay aesthetic. It is the way these photos helped create a new vision of shared eroticism, one that was neither shrouded in sepia nor graphic in content but that turned on the memory, intimation, or anticipation of lust and desire. In short, it was not the subject matter that was transgressive and new—street sex and intergenerational coupling—but the deeply personal attempt to arrest fleeting moments of longing and desire before they moved into history. In the 1950s, these images portrayed a kinship that was both dangerous and illegal. But they were no more welcome or accepted in the 1970s when queer intimacy struggled to keep pace with more bodily and youth-obsessed depictions of queer desire on the one hand and an increasingly more respectable, assimilationist queer politics on the other. Today, such depictions might be labeled as manipulative and abusive, a product of the time before consent. But here too, we run the risk of oversentimentalizing childhood, of wielding the category too expansively, pathologizing all forms of nonromantic, nonmarital, nonheteronormative sexual encounters as equally manipulative in the same way and in all instances. This all-encompassing approach fails to historicize the role and place of cruising within changing relationships of underground sex over time, which renders unthinkable the fact that these same highly erotic power imbalances might also animate today's scene, both within and alongside marriage equality, civil union, and legalized though not necessarily monogamous sex. That this is so deeply repressed, unacknowledged, or forgotten bears thinking about.

Third, it is undeniable that the creation of what Frank Mort has dubbed the permissive society aided images from the margins to enter into the mainstream. Herbert Tobias's photos of his friends, lovers, and conquests provided insight into the pivotal place of abject desire in this period of transition. His photography bridges the gap between the museum and the street, integrating elements of daily life into the queer visual canon.[89] Although galleries were loath to countenance erotically charged images in the early 1970s, by the late 1980s personal exhibitions of homoerotic images were increasingly published and exhibited, confirming "a real though not unanimous acceptance of homosexuality in cultural milieus, right to the top of the most important museums."[90] The sign of greater acceptance was not the toleration of more explicit imagery but the deliberate targeting of a specific and assumed gay audience, one with its own clearly defined aesthetic tastes.[91] Regardless, the acceptance of the erotically charged male as both a subject and object of art and desire helps periodize this important shift away from the disavowed homoerotic sensuality of pictorialist photography toward a more self-assertive embrace of same-sex desire, mirroring the gains made in the era of decriminalization in the quest for pride over marginality. In other words, by developing ways of reading these images of intimacy and eroticism as lending insight into the era of the sexual revolution, we see that Tobias's photographic practice played an indelible part in challenging the legitimacy of existing sexual practices, social mores, and modes of desire. In this sense, Tobias's visual depiction of queer kinship as pleasure may be said to have a history, one inextricably bound up with and informed by core social, personal, and aesthetic struggles of late twentieth-century liberalism on the West German and increasingly globalized stage. Insofar as his photographs helped construct the history of the age by revealing new visual and social formations, they also serve as evidence of changing historical assumptions and values about the sensual body on display in this widening public sphere, a process that had been underway for the better part of the twentieth century.

But beyond these questions of periodization, what might be gained by viewing erotic photography as an intellectual as well as subjective act of reclamation, kinship, and discovery, a queer art of history? Finding new interpretive strategies to draw out the productive capacity of images along-side their regulative function is essential if we wish to expand the playing field to include sexual self-actualization as a legitimate focus of historical inquiry. Finally, and perhaps most critically, viewing erotic photography itself as history—as an iconography of emotions with time-bound aesthetic trajectories, as a thing eliciting a host of responses filtered through the lens of time and place, and as an agent of self-actualization—we are forced to recognize desire as a fraught site of postwar queer worldmaking. As we'll see in the coming chapters, the politics of representation and desire play a central part in the postwar struggle for queer and trans* rights and kinship.

IMAGINING

TRANS*GRESSION

3

IF YOU WERE IN BERLIN in the summer of 2015, you could not have avoided the marvelously ambiguous torso of a bodybuilder postered all over the city. The body belongs to Cassils, a Canadian performance artist, competitive boxer, former stunt person, and personal trainer (see fig. 3.1). It is the canvas on which they explore the fluidity of gendered norms, how they are constructed and lived. For Cassils, trans* embodiment serves as a form of crossing, "a continual becoming, a process-oriented way of being that works in a space of indeterminacy, spasm and slipperiness."[1] The organizers of an exhibition, shared between Germany's national museum (the Deutsches Historisches Museum) and the Schwules Museum*, could not have picked a better image for their joint endeavor, which was the highlight of the summer exhibition season. From the shiny red lip to the pierced nipples, strong deltoids, and veiny, rigid arms, this photograph of Cassils's flexed body beckons the onlooker to think about the relationship of this extraordinary specimen of whiteness, strength, and beauty to the words etched in a matching red font around their impressive shoulders: *Homosexualität_en* (or "Homosexuality_ies," plural, in English). It is also a curious pairing, because the relationship between gender nonconformism and same-sex sexuality is not and has never been straightforward, whether in the

FIG. 3.1 Homo-
sexualität_en poster,
featuring Cassils,
2015. © Schwules
Museum* Berlin /
chezweitz Berlin.

history of sexology or in the various gay and lesbian rights movements that claimed Berlin as their home. And in a place like Berlin, with all its symbolism and inheritance, the association belies something greater still: the fraught place of trans* bodies, race, and gender variability in an ever more institutionalized if queer-friendly public sphere.

This chapter returns to the role of photography in wedging a space for the historicization of gender-nonconforming bodies and people. In chapter 2, I suggested that photography played an indelible part in white gay male kinship through nostalgia, with the still-taboo depiction of intergenerational sex and racialized desire challenging normative homophile, New Left, and contemporary claims to gay identity. There, the entangled histories of sexual immanence, orientalism, and intergenerational desire were touchstones of a transgressive queer relationality, which, as we'll see, increasingly fell afoul of gay political activism. Here, I shift the focus to trans* visualization to consider whether the normalization of queer history at the beginning of the twenty-first century has in fact resulted in a more fulsome representation and remembrance of gender-atypical lives, loves, leisure, and sexuality. I will argue that it has, but not without consequences. There are two issues at stake. One is that, as with the Manfred images, we need to not just look to the documentary impulse of photographs, the "visual essentialism" of images, but also take seriously the visual, phenomenological, and aesthetic work they do in articulating trans* lives through an alternative optics of kinship. This requires thinking about trans* photographic embodiment beyond scientific, documentary, and social movement frames. The normalization of nonnormative gender and sexuality has been dominated, especially in Germany, by sexology and the way medical narratives have sought to humanize the trans* subject. It has indelibly and productively placed gender variability in the historical register. In order to open up a space for a wider spectrum of bodies and experiences, however, we need to look beyond the sexological for other examples of gender enactment. This chapter will show ways in which high art, scene, and portrait photographs make possible a host of identifications across "differences, genders, sexualities, genres and across 'perversions.'"[2] Photography has the power to actualize a trans*-inclusive queer kinship, but it requires that we ask ourselves, following Eliza Steinbock, What are the conditions of trans* visibility in particular spaces and places in time; what is foregrounded, claimed, and attributed value?[3]

The second issue is the matter of identity. Twentieth-century sexual and gender nonconformism may be described—I suggest here—as marked by a shift away from clinical, regulatory, and scientific visualizations toward subcultural image making as a signature site of self-knowledge and collective curation. This raises several important questions. If photography freezes bodies in time and space, making it possible "to preserve permanent and unmistakable traces of a human being" as Walter Benjamin famously put it, how should we think about bodies that are uneasily anchored or even resistant to static identity frames?[4] Although there is a movement to reclaim transsexuality, the tendency, at least in the mainstream, is to visualize trans* bodies through the legal and medical lens of transition, beginning with gender dysphoria and ending with medical intervention, including hormone therapies and surgery.[5] These "chrononormative temporalities" structure how we view trans* people in the past, as existing as a point on a continuum en route to some utopian place of contentment and legibility within a more authentic self. This trans* temporality not only reproduces strict heteronormative gender binaries but presumes a linear, progressive, and common set of experiences. In this chapter, I ask How does using photography in this way actively impede our efforts to see the past more capaciously for other affinities, kinships, and entanglements?

Finally, I will show that these photos of gender variable bodies create other opportunities as well, especially around possible kinships they may foster between members of the queer and trans* community and past and present interlocutors. One thing images do is allow the contemporary viewer to feel as well as see the instantiation of self and community. As Kaja Silverman argued with analog photography, "The luminous trace of what was in front of the camera at the moment the photograph was made . . . attests to its referent's reality, just as a footprint attests to the reality of the foot that formed it."[6] As we'll see with Benny Nemer's audio guides in chapter 6, a photograph's affective affordances open up the possibility for a relational dialogue with past queer and trans* entanglements as manifested through a complex set of sensory experiences in the present. This form of embodied witnessing puts the viewer in a relationship with trans* ancestors where they reside, holding out the possibility of making new coalitions with those who have been sexed, gendered, racialized, and embodied differently.[7] But trans* visibility as an experience is not the same as its representation. Not only is it not experienced the same way across the board but it is also not a salve against the very real and present danger of antitrans* violence, augmented, worryingly, in times of greater visibility.[8] Still, in the hands of trans* artists, subjects, and photographers, it is a "vital art" and itself a kind of kinship, one that enlists the viewer in an alternative optics against the biomedical and state management of gender nonconformism as deviant, providing critical, life-affirming countervisualizations to necropolitical regimes of classification.[9] At the same time that we hope more and better visualizations of trans* lives will somehow translate into greater acceptance, our cruel optimism can never cut through the fact that trans* visibility is never without its own tensions, as certain bodies are more easily resignified and accepted—like Cassils's—while others retain racialized marks of otherness that fail to mitigate queer and trans* kinship.[10] It bears asking, then, When contemporary trans* aesthetics are drawn upon to help a community constitute and remember itself on a local, national, and transnational scale, when are we truly in kinship with people's subjectivity, even when trans* figurations don't take the shape and form we have come to expect?

A note on language. Throughout the book and especially here I very deliberately use the term *trans** with an asterisk to connote a long and broad history of gender variability.[11] Its usefulness is in signaling that, over the course of the twentieth century and into the twenty-first, there have been many different rubrics for how to categorize, understand, and deploy terms for gender nonconformity. Differences in terminology are notional indices of how law, medicine, and subculture understood, regulated, and lived with and in trans* bodies. But these meanings have changed along with the language used to characterize this experience. The word *trans** as a signifier is truly transitory and constantly on the move. There were sometimes conflicting definitions at play over the course of the twentieth century, but on an existential level there were and remain many ways to understand oneself within these frames and beyond. This chapter explores the term *trans** in its broadest sense, not as an identity frame but as a productively disruptive force that troubles the transparency and naturalness of gender and naming and challenges the disaggregation of complex experiences in the name of authenticity.[12]

In this chapter, I begin with an exploration of the visual history of trans* photography including the way sexologists and National Socialists used images to reinforce their different political aims. I then chart the shift toward portrait and scene photography in the 1980s to better understand the use of the camera in crafting an affective economy of community and difference. Finally, I explore how some of these collections of images, supplemented with others, made their way into a 2015 photography exhibition as part of an effort to move "the enduring and worldwide discourse surrounding equal rights for homosexual approaches to life into the center of society and to position this dialogue in a prominent place"—the city of Berlin.[13]

Sexology's Subalterns

When writing the history of photography, we often land on the coercive role of the police and medical authorities in formalizing iconographies of deviance as forms of discipline, regulation, violence, and control.[14] As we saw in chapter 2, the camera's gaze, fixed on flesh, countenance, body, and gesture eroticizes difference, which some scholars have interpreted as inescapably violent. Others see in it the possibility of resistance.[15] While photography's observational power has pathologized entire communities, it has also unlocked alternative possibilities, whether in legitimizing cultural norms, supporting biological claims to being differently, or creating a sense of kinship and community. Of course, these impulses were often at work simultaneously, and sometimes at cross-purposes. As Katie Sutton points out in her analysis of how Magnus Hirschfeld's Institute for Sexual Science pictured what he labeled transvestite identity in interwar Germany, sexual scientists leaned on personal as well as professional connections to the city's subcultural lesbian, gay, intersex, and trans* communities for images they might use to bolster their quest for legitimacy as a field. Indeed, Hirschfeld could even be quite entrepreneurial. In the preface to his 1912 illustrated addendum to his 1910 book *Die Transvestiten: Eine Untersuchung über den erotischen Verkleidungstrieb* (*Transvestites: The Erotic Drive to Cross-Dress*), he made a direct appeal to readers, urging them to send in their photos, with hopes for future volumes that, for one reason or another, never came to fruition.[16]

Queer and trans* print culture also played a role. Publications like the Berlin-based periodical *Das 3. Geschlecht*, or the Third Sex, which explicitly targeted a trans*-identified audience, published articles drawing on the language of gender fluidity found in sexological discourse (see fig. 3.2).[17] But as Rainer Herrn has shown, the magazine also put out conflicting messages, at once celebrating the eroticism of biological femininity while juxtaposing these same images with sexological portrayals of gender nonconformity as a more earnest expression of otherness, a third sex as the dictum goes.[18] Then there were images that projected the transsexual in the same erotic light as the female nudes, a deviation from the clinical precision of the Hirschfeldian model. Regardless of these inconsistencies, magazines like *Das 3. Geschlecht* helped hone what Jack Halberstam has called a "transgender look" based around competing visual, sexological, and subcultural references and cues.[19] These magazines served a more tangible function too.[20] Inside the pages was advice for how to pass in public and how one might attain a measure of safety and respectability as an upstanding gender-conforming citizen. Publications like these, available by subscription due to relaxed censorship laws, grounded a sense of kinship in still turbulent times.

Early twentieth-century trans* photography instructs us to think more capaciously about the visualization of gender variability and how it was institutionalized in print media and scientific knowledge. It provides instruction into the complex intermingling of visual and sexological cues, which fostered resilience within queer and trans* communities. While medical and

diagnostic imagining reinforced the clinical objectivity of visual evidence, the camera afforded everyday people the opportunity to stage their own self-representations, which often folded back into the sexological gaze. At the same time as the market in trans* images was widening the queer counterpublic sphere, equipping gender-nonconforming people with the tools to navigate daily life, it was reinforcing a class-specific respectability, meaning that even in this early period, trans* visibility hinged on certain styles and embodiments of gender and class over others. While sexology strove to establish itself on the basis of science, it did not entirely jettison the charged erotic and personal registers evoked in and through scene photography. Although sexological and subcultural efforts to construct trans* kinship turned on visual evidence, there was no single archetype amid the countlessly creative bodily interventions.

While there was great fluidity in interwar trans* visuality, during the Nazi period the regime went to great lengths to hammer out a visual vernacular for how to recognize gender nonconformity. But there too, the Nazi visual archive is idiosyncratic and mixed.[21] Photographic depictions of gender fluidity and risk during National Socialism indicate that violence, intimacy, and desire shaped, challenged, and reinforced heteronormative norms during the Third Reich.[22] Any analysis that hinges on a search for intact identity threatens to overlook important ambiguities that have much to tell us about the different ways in which inclusion and exclusion, and stigmatization and appreciation, were experienced in queer and trans* kinship networks.

If studio images and sexological stagings were the mainstay of 1920s queer and trans* photography, during the Third Reich this was supplanted by the police photo and mugshot. Here, the case of Fritz Kitzing is illustrative. Discovered in the archive by Andreas Sternweiler, one of the founders of the Schwules Museum*, the story of Fritz Kitzing's treatment by the Gestapo was one of many to be included in a 1999 book and exhibition on the persecution of gay men in the Sachsenhausen concentration camp (see figs. 3.3 and 3.4).[23] The purpose was clear: to raise awareness around this forgotten victim group, one that would have to wait another twenty years for recognition of wrongdoing. This was pathbreaking, painstaking, and important work at the same time that it made certain assumptions about what exactly was on display, notably that Kitzing was a man dressed as a woman, who cruised men for sex. Clayton Whisnant saw it differently in his 2016 overview of queer identity in pre-1945 Germany (part of the all-too-elusive trans* archive), where he suggests that Kitzing should be known by the pronoun "she."[24] Both accounts give much-needed visibility to critically undertreated subjects. But while we can sympathize with the desire to restore humanity to persons written out of history in the quest for queer and trans* ancestors, what challenge does it open up when we claim Kitzing's identity as bounded in a particular way?[25] Is this perhaps a violence of its own?

When one first encounters Kitzing's Gestapo mugshots, their meaning seems obvious: they show a person posed and humiliated, in women's clothes. As with any image, though, it's not that simple. Like Tobias's Manfred, the Kitzing photo has had many lives.[26] Its first incarnation was in a Gestapo file, where it was stored as evidence. In those pages, we learn that Kitzing was born on December 28, 1905, in Neuruppin, the birthplace of the realist

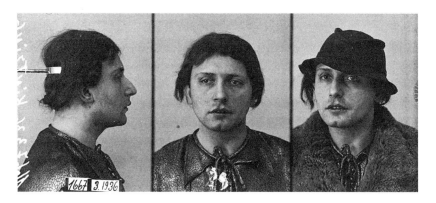

FIG. 3.3 Police mugshot of Fritz Kitzing. © Landesarchiv Berlin.

novelist Theodor Fontane, to the northeast of Berlin. Describing himself with the pronoun "he," whether by force or circumstance, he recounts that he trained as a bookkeeper and moved to the Reich capital in search of work. The city he found was steeped in contradictions. Even as it provided sanctuary to people who transgressed gender norms, provided they had the means, gender variant people still had to navigate a complex and contradictory mix of messages around their way of being in the world. Kinship was not something that could be taken for granted, especially if one didn't have the means.

With the rise of the Nazis, so-called transvestites faced renewed struggles over the administration of gender identity, especially if gender presentation breached convention in obvious ways. Kitzing was no exception. He first became known to the Berlin police force in the final months of 1933, when he was picked up in the street for solicitation. As early as 1931, the police in major Prussian jurisdictions had called for stricter measures to deal with public sex, a response to the growing prostitution rights movement.[27] Their wish was granted in May 1933 in the Law for the Alteration of Criminal Provisions.[28] Unfortunately for Kitzing, this meant that he was charged under Paragraph 361/6, for prostitution, and would serve four weeks in jail and another six months in protective custody.[29]

This is a curious charge, which speaks to the incongruent mechanisms for understanding cross-dressing as a matter of law. In such situations, before 1933, it was quite common to levy a charge under Paragraph 360/11 (mischief) or Paragraph 183 (exhibitionism) for creating a public nuisance.[30] In using Paragraph 361/6, the state seems to have recognized Kitzing's presented gender and not his biological sex, as this article governed women who

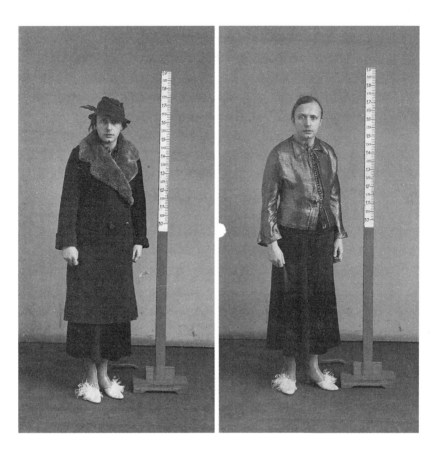

FIG. 3.4 Larger photo of Fritz Kitzing. © Landesarchiv Berlin.

engaged in prostitution, not men.[31] Put more clearly, Kitzing was charged and convicted with a statute typically reserved for the public lasciviousness of women. It is even located in a separate section of the Penal Code from the statute that regulated male prostitution. While it makes little sense to use Paragraph 361/6 against cross-dressing in public, given the tools available to police at the time, this choice sheds light on the changing stakes of moral regulation in the final years of the Weimar Republic into the early Nazi period and the difficult place of gender nonconformists within it.[32]

Kitzing fled protective custody on March 16, 1934.[33] After a strange and circuitous trek to England and back again, he evaded police for a good while before being brought back for questioning in June 1935. Let go with a warning, he was being watched.[34] The police were not the ones to catch him in the act of transgression, however. Reminiscent of the denunciation of Ilse Totzke that Laurie Marhoefer has described so vividly, where Totzke's gender nonconformity was of equal if not more concern than her dalliances with women, it was a neighbor in Kitzing's apartment block who denounced him in mid-July 1935.[35] Ingeborg Boxhammer and Christiane Leidinger have argued that this process of making gender nonconformity visible was an essential feature of lesbian and trans* persecution during the Nazi period, differentiating it somewhat from gay men's experiences because it also lay outside formal police structures and in the hands of different actors.[36]

When officers entered Kitzing's apartment, they discovered what they believed was unequivocal evidence of his wrongdoing: women's stockings, a dress, a wig, and a lady's coat. Purportedly, Kitzing had been going out again, walking the streets, dressed as a woman. And yet, despite this seemingly damning evidence, the Gestapo still let him go. They nevertheless kept in storage a suitcase with his vestments. Forced to respond to new charges three months later, they opened the suitcase, ordered him to dress, and made him pose for the mugshots.[37] On the basis of this new/old evidence, his membership in the trans* community was secured. He was deemed "a transvestite of the worst kind" and sent to Lichtenberg prison where he would spend twelve months in protective custody.

It is worth lingering over these images for the way they sought to produce evidence of transsexuality. The most glaring difference from the interwar photos collated by Hirschfeld is the focus on clothing and not on the body itself. Most famously in *Geschlechtskunde*, which included side-by-side portraits of "female transvestites," one frame with the sitting subject in the clothing of their choice, often suits, the other naked, Hirschfeld displayed his clinical view that gender identity was written on the body.[38] The full-frontal and face portrait in the Gestapo file focuses on Kitzing's countenance and expression, but he does not disrobe. For the police, these photographs alone could provide essential physiognomic data on how to recognize a criminal in their essence. Kitzing's photos were cultural amalgams that helped construct criminality through a typology of a different sort.[39] In the hands of the police, cameras made experts out of beat cops and detectives who recorded what was, for them, the observable truth.[40] When we pull back our own interpretive lens further, we see the artifice with which they constructed idealized and time-specific ways of seeing, bounding, and portraying the cross-dressing transvestite and his kin.

In Kitzing's photos, something else is at play too. In subtle yet distinct ways, the image transcends the intended purpose of the photograph. Even though we know he is being forced against his will, there is something odd about how Kitzing faces down state power. The photos are puzzling, unsettling; like Barthes's punctum, Kitzing's countergaze is what gives the image its meaning. It compels the viewer to look deeper into the photograph, to feel empathy, sympathy, anger, perhaps even remorse.[41] In 1936 the witness was meant to look at a photograph and see confirmation of the criminal within. However, then as now, Kitzing's gaze refuses to yield. It challenges the photograph's intention to visualize a bounded trans* identity. In this way, Kitzing exceeds classification. He remains embodied, complex, human.

The same is true of the full-body portraits. In one frame, the wig is absent, and Kitzing is dressed in a skirt and blouse with a coat. In the other, his stockings and frilly house slippers seem curiously out of place with the outdoor wear, not something one would choose on one's own. His feet are variously positioned pointing both outward and inward, with the same expressionless countenance. When we drop our eyes below the center of the frame, we see something else still: one of Kitzing's hands is semiclenched, a mirror image of the other photo. Only something is different. In the right frame, we see his fingers wound tightly around the cloth of the skirt. It is so tight it tugs at the garment. It leaves wrinkles. If, as Frantz Fanon argued, muscle tension in photos of enslaved people bears witness to the history of enslavement and resistance, we see three things on display here: Nazi and pre–Nazi era criminal biology, the Third Reich's treatment of outsiders, and an expression of refusal, a defiant claim to being in the world differently.[42] Kitzing silently but no less profoundly contested the efforts of police to straitjacket him into a visual admission of guilt. Easily missed, these moments of pushback bear witness to a person in a vulnerable position, trying to blunt the force of state power.

The Kitzing investigation casts light on the changing mechanisms the Nazis used to reveal an essentialized trans* kinship. Unlike Hirschfeld's argument that gender variance was biologically constituted, the Nazis appear more interested in kinship as conduct—what one does, with whom, where and how—which is in keeping with the regime's treatment of gay men. This presents a different symbolic argument about the essence of trans*ness and the challenge it poses to the state. When read queerly, against the grain, these photos reveal the subtle ways in which Kitzing exceeded classification. As Susan Stryker put it in *Signs*, his body "meant otherwise."[43] The quiet violence of the Kitzing photos, together with his subtle yet powerful resistance, sutures the past to the present through the register of suffering, securing our own kinship with him and his gender-nonconforming body.[44] Although the images freeze a moment for posterity, they are not static. While retaining the hallmarks of incommensurability, they surpass what the photograph is meant to document. This raises a host of interesting questions about what it means to picture gender nonconformism on the spectrum between legibility and identity. Claiming him singularly homosexual, transsexual, or as trans* in an identitarian sense fails to appreciate the complex kinships at work for the police, for his neighbors, for friends and family, and for himself, to say nothing of the ambiguous way he lived his life. Reading them as an example of a violent past now overcome belies the fact that displacement and disposition continues to mark insufficiently hetero-, homo-, mis-, and transgender people in today's world.[45]

We don't know what became of Kitzing. What we do know is that his biological kin supported him unequivocally, hinting that they long knew how he was living his life. In a letter to his brother Hans Joachim was emphatic: "I don't know what they are accusing you of, but I will do everything in my power to help you through it." Despite the allusion to past struggles, and the danger of the uncertain times, their bond was uncompromising: "I remain eternally grateful for all the love you've given me."[46] To read Kitzing's file as that of a social outsider transgressing norms of belonging not only adopts the state's gaze but fails to see that Kitzing's complexity was recognized by his family, if not entirely understood.

Mapping Transgression in the Postwar Period

These three genres of images—subcultural, sexological, and police photography—would carry over into the postwar period with continued importance for how we visualize gender variant kinships. Scene and portrait photos were not only evidence of queer and trans* embodiments and networks; they might also have been used in police investigations to support a charge of indecency or homosexuality. Andrea Rottmann's work with the Police Archive in Berlin has revealed that the police made extensive use of photographs to document bar raids, while the East German secret police tended to rely more on testimonials of informants over actual images.[47] Sexological studies in East and West Germany, which were less interested in transsexuality than same-sex desire, similarly neglected the use of photographic evidence in favor of surveys and observation, although the Nazi criminologist Hans von Hentig, who was allowed to return to his position at the University of Bonn after the war, was known to have rather obsessively collected materials related to purported lesbians, which often included actresses, athletes, and wives of prominent politicians.[48] Meanwhile, the German American endocrinologist Harry Benjamin, trained by Eugen Steinach, was purported to have a huge archive of his own, collected from his own patients.[49]

As has already been argued, sexological photographs pictured cross-dressing as evidence not just of passing but of orientation as a bodily construct, an "embodiment of the flesh" that was inborn.[50] The effects of this framing are multiple. Perhaps most significantly, such a vision of the body's agency eschews the act of performance itself, of donning certain clothes, being manipulated by them this way or that. The agentic nature of adornment was not recognized as playing a role in gender identity and expression. An emphasis on flesh also privileges the ethnographic gaze, stressing the lens's mimetic and classificatory power over the inventiveness of the sitting subject. But as we also saw with the Kitzing photographs, photography makes possible ways one might breech categorical confines. Two changes would prove instrumental to the continued development of vernacular modes of nonbinary kinship through images in the postwar period: greater access to cameras, film stock, and development and an expanding art and popular mediascape, which made it possible to picture gender variability for new publics. Why did these parallel modes of visualizing trans* kin not garner a place in Germany's queer imaginary alongside sexology? And what might this tell us about the ambivalent place of trans* kinships in the long history of German liberalism?

When Hirschfeld and Benjamin drew on fine art and scene photography, they did so to document empirically the visualization of trans* embodiment.[51] To bring back Steinbock, the scientific gaze was foregrounded at the expense of more aesthetic interventions.[52] Despite an interest in portraiture and the arts, the genderqueer avant-garde evaded attention even as it was an important site of twentieth-century transing. Perhaps this was owed to its inherent indeterminacy. Surrealism not only defied easy classification, it refused it. When Man Ray and Marcel Duchamp brought their famous New York collaboration to Paris, they introduced to Surrealist and Dada circles the androgynous character of Rrose Sélavy (a play on "Eros, c'est la vie"), portrayed by Duchamp. Rrose is pure performance, juxtaposing artifice (hats and clothes) with the "reality" of the body (Duchamp's chiseled chin and stubble) (see fig. 3.5). Reflecting on Duchamp's alter ego, Gertrude Stein called it "a cessation of resemblances" to maleness or femaleness, a rejection of predictable signs of gender and embrace of the genderqueer

FIG. 3.5 Man Ray, *Por-trait of Rrose Sélavy*, 1921.

performative.[53] Interestingly, the gender play is also rooted in ethnic drag as Duchamp's character was also a stylized meditation on Jewishness with the name Rose, a common diminutive of Ruth, easily identifiable as Jewish in 1920s Paris. Written out as Rose C'est Levy, it also evokes one of France's most recognizable Jewish surnames, Halévy.[54]

There were other Surrealists who similarly experimented with gender ambiguity and performance. In the 1997 Guggenheim exhibition *Rrose Is a Rrose Is a Rrose*, the curator Jennifer Blessing pieced together the social, cultural, and aesthetic entanglements that linked photography across the century, between the multivalent and intersecting genders and sexualities in masquerade, drag, and cross-dressing of the 1920s and 1930s and the emergent genderqueer visual discourses of the 1980s and 1990s.[55] As Vivienne Namaste has argued, the 1990s witnessed a proliferation of interest in cross-dressing, and representations of hypermasculinity and hyperfemininity dovetailed with the advent of queer theory.[56] Yet sexology's omnipresence over the aesthetic register meant that postwar engagements with the ambiguously gendered body were systematically overlooked. The French lovers and resistance fighters Claude Cahun and Marcel Moore remained active, if little known, until their deaths in 1958 and 1972, respectively, while Herbert Tobias took sumptuous black-and-white cross-dressing self-portraits in the 1950s and 1960s.[57] Pierre Molinier's gender fluidity challenged sensibilities in a host of ways, presaging Mapplethorpe's BDSM self-portraiture. The overt eroticism of Tobias's and Molinier's work was out of place in the German and French art scene of the time, and it is not inconsequential that for a variety of reasons, some personal, some aesthetic, all four of these photographers found difficult kinship with the gay liberation movements of the late 1960s and 1970s whose activist agenda embraced Hirschfeld's documentary lens over the embellishments of the avant-garde.[58] For all of these reasons, high-art photography remained a stark alternative to the Hirschfeldian visual archive of before and after images, a key example of what Jay Prosser has called the "transitioning subject; a rewriting of the narrative of transsexuality—and transsexual narratives—as open-ended."[59]

The 1970s Intimate Look

The 1970s saw further changes as new photographic practices and styles came into use in art, pop culture, and everyday life.[60] The representational codes of vérité afforded fine art photographers new ways to present gender nonconformism amid the emergent gay, lesbian, feminist, and cooperative scenes of urban subculture. While feminized and androgynous men were everywhere to be found in the art and music scene, there was less of a place for female masculinity, especially in an art world still intent on viewing women through the heteronormative gaze.[61] But the soil was tilled in a sense; analogies between transgressive and transvestite rock and gender performance percolated into the art world and vice versa, as with the *Transformer* exhibition mounted in Switzerland by Christophe Ammann in 1974, which drew participants from the rock music and art elite. Named after Lou Reed's famous 1972 album that explored similar themes, here, self-portraits became the chosen medium to do the work of destabilizing gender.[62] Women were certainly not absent. The Austrian feminist VALIE EXPORT (as she named herself), already in the *Identity Transfer* photo series from 1968, had teased apart the look and gestures that made up patriarchal conventions within cisgender normativity.[63] The German artist Jürgen Klauke and the Swiss artist Urs Lüthi combined the verve of Actionism with some of the elements of the avant-garde to explore polymorphous gender and sexual forms in their photographic series from the early 1970s. In Klauke's *Physiognomies* from 1972–73, he tempted the viewer to locate in his self-portraits and varied facial expressions an essential identity.[64] Lüthi went a step further in *I'll Be Your Mirror* (1972) using the piercing counterstare while dressed in drag to represent the fact that ambivalence is central to all self-imaginings. In this way, artists resurrected some of the conventions of homoerotic photographic genres and combined them with the Zeitgeist of the 1970s to question the cultural investment in the gender binary. At the same time that they were embraced by the gallery set as normative notions of gender bifurcation, they reinscribed a different form of segregation in the name of integration in the way that they are all white, heteronormative visions of gender play. In an era shaped by Black Power, the absent presence of Black artists, symbols, and aesthetic imaginaries is itself noteworthy.[65]

Behind the Iron Curtain, the situation was quite different. With little to no state support for experimental photography and portraiture, including home-style pornography, queer image making remained more or less a private affair.[66] While on paper at least gay, lesbian, and trans* subculture enjoyed a longer history of legality than in West Germany, nonnormative sexuality was still viewed with skepticism and reproach until the fall of the Berlin Wall.[67] As Josie McLellan has shown convincingly, state photographic practices in East Germany upheld rigid heternormativity as the fulcrum of a prurient socialist citizenship.[68] Where explicit sexuality might be displayed, in the pages of *Das Magazin*, it was framed as straight—with the exception of a landmark series of portraits of gay male life in the late 1980s. But vernacular photos from the collection of the Schwules Museum* provide a glimpse into the lifeworld of people who eschewed traditional notions of masculinity and femininity and queer and straight sexuality to build kinship networks and family away from the eyes of the state. While some of these collections show playful acts of subversion and drag, others hint at more indeterminate visualizations of gender trouble. When strewn together, whether as a personal album or later in the archive or gallery, they help visualize bonds of kinship and belonging at all stages of the photos' existence, through the taking of images, to the act of collection, access, and later display.[69] The question worth asking is How have they been perceived and how might they still be read?

In some instances, these photo collections from the former GDR employed the conventions of studio and portrait photography to try to reframe queer and trans* relationships from heteronormative imaginings. McLellan discusses the stunning couples photo of Rita Thomas and her partner Helli together with their two well-groomed dogs. Thomas, who at the age of fifteen adopted the nickname "Tommy," stands behind her partner, dressed in a vest and cravat, sporting a coiffed hairstyle commonly worn by mods. As with the Kitzing photo, this image may be read in several different ways. Were we to focus solely on the studio shot and not on the other myriad images in the Thomas collection that Rottmann vividly unpacks in her book on queer Berlin, we would have to concede that its staging of a relationship is rather conventional.[70] Taken alongside her stated biography, featured in the 2003 Schwules Museum* exhibition *Mittenmang: Homosexuelle Frauen und Männer in Berlin 1945 bis 1969* (Right in the Middle: Gay Women and Men in Berlin 1945 to 1969), it speaks to the long-term love and partnership of these two women who, over the years, built a business, had a vibrant social life, and became politically active in the early East German gay rights movement, which also included women.[71] But to stop there forecloses other points of entry into the world of nonnormative gender identification, kinship across difference, and sexual expression that likewise animated Tommy's world. For one thing, because of our own fixation with heteronormative timescapes and life course and the homonormative formations that often bear resemblance to them, we might be tempted to view this studio photograph as a portrait of monogamy since it adheres visually at least to a more or less traditional visualization of the couple as an exclusive social norm (even though we know, too, that this is not always a reality). And it is true that Tommy and Helli were longtime loves. To view their relationship solely through this lens neglects the broad circle of friendships, gender play, and nonconformism that also inhabited their world. There was the kinship and activism of the Homosexuelleninterest Berlin or HIB, a haven of gender nonconformity and cross-dressing among male, female, and transsexual activists like Charlotte von Mahlsdorf, who would similarly take photos of parties and gatherings in her Gründerzeitmuseum to the east of the city (see figs. 3.6 and 3.7). As we'll see in chapter 4, in the GDR, their different experiences with state regulation did not preclude some measure of collective mobilization well into the 1980s. Tommy performed in cross-dressing performances with the activist cabaret Hibaré, held wild parties in her house where it's anyone's guess what might have gone down, and as Andrea Rottmann has shown in her work on the queer bar scene, she and Helli frequented all manner of establishments with women who likewise flouted conventional portrayals of femininity.[72] When we view Tommy's photographs as evidence of lesbian subjectivity, we gain access to the world of alternative female intimacies and

FIG. 3.6 Tommy mit Heli und den Pudeln. © Schwules Museum* Berlin.

FIG. 3.6 Tommy mit Heli und den Pudeln. © Schwules Museum* Berlin.

same-sex desire among cis- and alternatively gendered women, a world frequently written out of the history of LGBTQIA life and experience. Yet if we view these photographs flatly as a reflection of static, transparent, and bounded identity categories, we not only neglect the complex web of experiences and subjectivities that may have changed across time as languages for self-actualization have and do but we similarly discount the probability of polyvalent lives percolating in and around Tommy's community.

As essential as it is to listen for the ways in which historical actors characterized their lifeworlds—as in the case of Kitzing—so too is it important to recall the general instability and open-endedness of the categories we use to make sense of the past. As Jack Halberstam has argued, in order to

FIG. 3.7 Faschingsfest im Lichtenberger Krug. © FFBIZ.

be in a position to recognize the insufficiencies of fixed and firm identity classifications, "we need to think in new and different ways about what it means to claim a body."[73] At the same time that Tommy's visual archive is absolutely essential in addressing what is missing in the historical record in terms of female same-sex community and desire, without what Katie Sutton calls "an ethics of attentiveness" to protocols we might use to imagine the possibility that transmasculine and transfeminine bodies also intermixed in this story, we disregard the possibility of transrealities that may have resided beyond the frame.[74] As José Muñoz wrote about the complicated relationship between queer and trans* kinships, sometimes "we may need to squint, to strain our vision and force it to see otherwise, beyond the limited vista of the here and now."[75]

Meanwhile, in West Germany around the same time, Maria Sabine Augstein was undergoing her own existential voyage of self-discovery. Born in 1949, in her words, as an "emerging woman" (*gewordene Frau*), she was the fourth of four siblings of the media mogul Rudolf Augstein, the founder of the political magazine *Der Spiegel*.[76] Maria Sabine realized at a young age that she not only desired women but identified as female as well. She read her way into the feminist and legal literature produced by the student movement, and through conversations with other transsexuals (to use her phrasing), she concretized her desire to begin the process of seeking out medical expertise so as to transition first with hormone treatment and later with surgery in Singapore that her father generously funded. As a trained lawyer, she put her own experience to work to tackle the legal encumbrances faced by gender variant people. And there were many. Although West Germany would be one of the first nations to craft a so-called Transsexual Law in 1980 (which has undergone renewed scrutiny at the time of writing this book as having outlived its utility in helping mitigate the everyday lives of trans* people), there were many examples of discrimination that affected people's lives on the most intimate level, from the inability of the bureaucracy to facilitate a simple change of name and gender to the fact that, legally, a person had to be at least twenty-five years of age to be in a position to claim that new identity (despite the fact that surgery was possible already at age eighteen).[77]

Augstein, a lawyer, earned several important legal victories for trans* rights before the West German Supreme Court, which counted not only for those born in-country but also for persons with long-term residency there.[78] Given that the largest visible minority in the country, Turkish laborers and their families, could not acquire citizenship until the 1990s, this was a huge victory indeed. At important moments, Augstein used her privilege to better the plight of the marginalized, working on some of the major legal victories of the late twentieth century. Her guiding mantra was "The smaller the minority, the more important the opposition." In the exhibition guide to the photographs her life partner took of her over the years, published with the help of her stepmother, Anna Augstein, who supported Maria Sabine's transition and coming out as a lesbian against her uneasy father, she likened being a transsexual to the plight of a refugee. What reads, certainly, as a mark of unequal kinship, privilege, and assumption also speaks to the depths of isolation felt by many transfeminine and transmasculine people in a state that did not move swiftly to bestow full citizenship on trans* people.[79]

But there are other moments in the exhibition catalog that hint at the role of photography in representing the richness of viewing this history through the lens of entanglements, for the way female same-sex companionship, gender nonconformity, and expanded citizenship rights emerged amid tensions surrounding race and racialization. Augstein was deeply enmeshed in the feminist and lesbian scene, and it was there that she met her partner, the photographer Inea Gukema, who at the time of their first encounter in 1978 was one of the editors of the feminist publishing house *Frauenoffensive*. Together they traveled throughout Germany and Europe in search of sites of *herstory*, places of importance to female kinship and legacy, including the graves of Çatalhöyük in Anatolia, where thousands of years ago—it was believed—a matriarchal society once lived and thrived. Seated on the dunes at the burial site, Maria Sabine pondered the absent presence of feminist history here. This dredged up thoughts of her own fraught sense of womanhood, which was captured in the photograph taken by a passerby, where the women are seen smiling. The exhibition guide captioned the photograph with Maria Sabine's reflections, which hint at a return to the centrality of the body in gender expression: "I couldn't win the measure of womanhood I sought out, because I had to realize that it was not something I could will by strength of personality. It is the body that must carry the process of identification."[80] In other portraits in museum spaces, in nature, and in her "her own room" as one taken in 1985 is named, we see her adopt a similar pensive repose. For all the serious images, occasionally she is positioned in deliberately artful poses. Sometimes her entire face is covered, or she wears horns and a mask. At other times, she reclines in the grass in iconic romantic poses.[81] Once, she is pictured sitting on her own bed, flanked with what appear to be photos of an African fertility goddess in the pages of a magazine with a Balinese statue standing over her shoulder (see fig. 3.8). These are deliberately chosen mise-en-scènes, which the accompanying texts explain as affording a glimpse into Augstein's "fighting spirit." As one caption reads: "The impression that she awakens in us is similar to the one we receive when looking at the African mask: petrified horn and hard wood."[82]

It is perhaps not surprising, given the hot-button nature of discussions around race, ethnicity, and migration at the very same time that these legal challenges were making their way through the courts, that this may have given Augstein and her partner a visual and pictorial language with which to imagine the activist's plight. Yet we know too that the world of feminist and lesbian activism in West Germany was not without its tensions, which were felt most perniciously by migrant and Black German women who often felt unwelcome in these same organizations despite their shared goals.[83] This shows that, as important as these legal victories were—and they were vastly significant to the day-to-day lives of gender variant people—these gains were forged in a country wrestling with a host of intersecting, structural challenges around race and ethnicity that meant the bestowal of rights and recognition happened in different measures for different minoritized populations. As Kiliç and Petzen have argued about visual arts, trans* visibility came

FIG. 3.8 Maria Sabine Augstein in her own room. © Inea Gukema-Augstein.

about through certain kinship affiliations, frequently made in the language of progress and humanism, but it all too often coexisted with troubling depictions of institutional violence against racialized populations.[84]

Trans* Portraiture

As I've argued, portrait photography played a heightened role in the historical articulation of trans* visibility. It fixes transience and has the appearance of freezing time.[85] But as we know from Eadweard Muybridge's famous plates on animal locomotion, although individual photographic frames give the appearance of being fixed what is photographed is processual in that what is depicted within a single photograph is part of a larger series of images. The quicker the shutter speed, the more cinematic the process of rendering bodies on paper or, in the digital age, on screen. Walter Benjamin saw in snapshot photography the possibility of subverting bourgeois norms and rules. The split-second rendering of modern photographs cut through the pretension of art's aura. But photographic technology had another power still. It summoned what he called "the optical unconscious," making things visible to the eye that would otherwise be missed.[86] Photography captures life within a series of processes, looking at once forward and backward in time. In this way, image making has the power to make manifest more expansive ways of thinking, remembering, and archiving the world of people and things while commemorating lives already lived.

Nora Eckert began such a journey of self-curation in her autobiography *Like Everyone Else, Only Different* with an image of herself as a boy in her village in 1959 years before she traveled to West Berlin, where she changed her name and gender and lived as a woman before coming out as a transwoman to her coworkers upon her retirement. "Hidden in the photo," as the chapter was titled, was a boy who knew nothing of the road ahead. But "photos tell histories. (And) we attach histories to photos." Looking back on it decades later, Nora realized that that single photograph told both the past and coming future. It is a mark of coexisting temporalities, including a future that might have been, should have been even, had her story and life course played out as her parents imagined. Indeed, there are many images in her autobiography that help picture how she navigated her self and identity in this fascinating yet turbulent time. There are snapshots of her elegantly dressed emerging out of the S-Bahn or smiling wide in the latest fashion at her job as the ticket and cloakroom girl in the legendary Schöneberg underground dance club Chez Romy Haag, which would attract the who's who of 1970s Berlin glitterati including David Bowie, Mick Jaggar, and Freddie Mercury (see fig. 3.9). Romy Haag quickly became her "factory," as she called it, an homage to the diverse cast of characters that made Andy Warhol's warehouse in New York City the stuff of international queer/trans* kinship and legend. The photographs allow Nora to frame herself as she wishes to be seen and remembered. They are liberatory, gorgeous, and present a woman brimming with confidence and thriving among friends and newfound family. They stand in stark contrast, in the memoir, to other ego-documents as they are sometimes called, passports that depict her as a woman with a man's name, medical affidavits to allow her to be able to change her name legally. Both of these texts are conjured up in her story to tell of the pain of occupying that space in between worlds. On a train to visit her mother in the GDR, she is accosted by the conductor who tells every uniformed attendant about "the freak" (her words) in her train car, whose gender doesn't match her stated sex in her personal document. Then there is the story of the medical official whose rubber stamp she requires in order to have the legal registry change her name.[87] Biography and the self-narrating qualities of portrait photography allow Nora to document her life on her own terms. "We trans* people have no history," she writes, "so we celebrate every discovery as proof of our existence" (see fig. 3.10). There are some historical studies, she noted, but "they are all about how we have been viewed by science and society—we the mysterious beings who despite countless sexological, psychological, and medical theories about us remain mysterious beings."[88]

Meanwhile, across the boundary in East Germany, Nadja Schallenberg similarly made use of photography to narrate who she was in a photo album she assembled as a Christmas gift for her family (see fig. 3.11). Calling it her coming-out album, she assembled photos, poems, correspondence, and newspaper clippings to help communicate her sense of self as a lestra (lesbian transsexual), androgynous woman, and punk.[89] Schallenberg helped establish the transsexual counseling service at the Sonntags-Club, an East German gay and lesbian mutual aid center, where she worked to bring folks to the table from gay, lesbian, and trans* circles to gather in each other's differences and find common ground.[90] Photography and life writing gave Nora and Nadja the tools to document their self-discovery, leaving a record that might also lead other queer and trans* persons to the spaces and places of love, compassion, self-help, and kinship.[91]

Scene Photography and Drag

While portrait photography and snapshots provided alternative visualizations of trans*ness than those operating in Hirschfeld's archive, party, drag, and scene photography was a similar locus of experimentation and subjectivity as more and more people used the camera to capture their own stories. But they were equally fraught. As much as they document Berlin's gay, lesbian, and trans* scenes, they are also fundamentally unstable, rendering gender and its relationship to sex and sexuality at once familiar and strange. They serve as a model of disobedience, becoming and unbecoming, of visibility and going stealth, of being on the radar and off it at the same time. In this way, their kinships defy singular narration and identity.

Drag photos from the clubs and stages of East and West Berlin, Hamburg, and Stuttgart were important sites of queer and trans* kinship in still dangerous times, challenging a host of social, gender, and sexual norms.[92]

FIG. 3.9 Chez Romy Haag, 1978.
© Nora Eckert.

FIG. 3.10 Zu Besuch im Martin
Gropius Bau Berlin, 2019. © Nora
Eckert.

FIG. 3.11 Photo of Nadia Schallenberg photo album. © Schwules Museum* Berlin.

Chez Romy Haag and Chez Nous were perhaps the most notorious, emblems of West Berlin fabulousness amid the doom and gloom of the early Cold War. But as the extraordinary collection of Timo/Tina Glamor indicates—which alone includes over twelve thousand photos—drag culture was alive and well in other parts of Germany too, carving out important spaces where nonnormative self-exploration might thrive. "Well into the 1970s," Glamor recalls, "these were some of the only spaces where nonheteronormative bodies might be seen" by a largely straight audience. This visibility was not limited to gender-nonconforming bodies, however. The Berlin-based artist Markues has shown in their interview project "We're All in This Together" that the cabarets challenged all sorts of norms of the time. They were international spaces, some of the first venues in the postwar period to stage French, Spanish, North African, and Black German performers. They expanded other boundaries too, as spaces of encounter between generations of queer- and trans*-identified performers, where "old school transsexuals" and "new women" (gays who dress as women but might not identity as them) redefined what gender nonconformism might mean in both a public and private capacity. As the Black American transsexual and Hamburg club owner Angie Stardust explains to Chez Nous queen Tara in Rosa von Praunheim's 1983 film *City of Lost Souls*, her generation did the heavy lifting in an age before hormones and surgeries (let alone racial sensitivity) to create places for others to thrive. Unlike gay bars, which remained under watch until 1969 and where even going out after hours dressed as a woman might garner the attention of the police, Chez Nous offered a measure of security and respectability. It was different from working regular striptease clubs or the street, where many trans* women struggled to make a living. It was a job, one that paid the bills, but it also housed personal and artistic growth, for performers and audience alike.[93] In this way, drag bars were important sites of all manner of kinship, between and among performers, across generations, in a racially diverse queer/trans* culture of performance and display.

Scene photos in the Schwules Museum* collection show that drag culture was also an East German phenomenon with a similar tradition of using the camera to document friendship, festivity, and club and cabaret life. The Heiner Hilger collection provides a particularly rich portrait of fancy dress preparations for Fasching, the German Mardi Gras. A makeup artist with the East German Berliner Ensemble, Hilger took photos of friends and lovers at home in drag, before going off to parties at the local neighborhood bar Burgfrieden. Peace in the Castle, as it translates—a reference to Kaiser Wilhelm II's promise to overlook class and confessional differences in total war—was an important toehold in the 1960s East Berlin gay scene. But it was not bounded in the way we are accustomed to now. The clientele who frequented Burgfrieden also attended the political cabaret by the cross-dressing Hibaré troup, which poked fun at the social and political sentiments of the day (see fig. 3.12). As Nadja Schellenberg recalled in a 2020 interview, in East Germany there was great fluidity between gay, lesbian, and trans* scenes. All was not perfect, but it was a start.[94]

In the West, the situation was purportedly more siloed, although there is room there too for more research into nonbinary kinships and the way they surfaced within established gay and lesbian scenes. In the 1980s, three photographers were particularly active in capturing the various kinships made possible in this Cold War outpost. Their photographs of Berlin's queer, drag, lesbian, feminist, butch, and sissy (Tunten) scenes would be honored by the Schwules Museum* in the 2000s in a series of exhibitions. Although not without its own challenges, they formed part of the museum's efforts to widen its mandate beyond the history of pink triangle persecution and sexology.

Upon her untimely death in 2012, Petra Gall's collection of photo negatives was secured for the museum by Birgit Bosold, who has taken a keen interest

FIG. 3.12 Cabaret group Hibaré, part of the Berlin HIB. © Hilger Collection / Schwules Museum* Berlin.

in carving out a space for same-sex-desiring women past and present. The well-known historian of feminist and lesbian history Christiane Leidinger set about cataloging the collection with a team of community volunteers. There are in the realm of two hundred thousand objects and images in this single collection, spanning lesbian activism and demonstrations like the Walpurgis Night action against violence against women to the punk and new wave bands that found their way to bars like the lesbian-owned club Risiko, whose logo included a pink triangle with punk typescript signifying that it was open to everyone (see fig. 3.13).[95] A favorite subject of Gall's was the leather jacket butch motorcycle scene, which she documented on frequent trips to East Germany as a journalist for various papers and magazines and through her photo agency, Zebra. Her love of motorcycling would even take her to the former Soviet Union where she took photos of boyish women,

FIG. 3.13 Marina Zustrow. Photo by Petra Gall. © Schwules Museum* Berlin.

Russian "hippies," and motor rockers.[96] These eastern bodies, as Tija Uhlig reminds us, are disruptive bodies. In socialist spaces, the binaries between East and West appear rigid but are at the same time porous. With the fall of the Berlin Wall, and the world turned upside down of the early 1990s, these forms of "dualistic othering" seemed even less certain.[97] Gall's images of female masculinity should be read as equally tenuous. They open up worlds still in need of research for the way they affirmed female desire, community, and kinship and also as possible spaces of gender identification beyond cis/femme and butch lesbianism.

Like Gall, Jürgen Baldiga also came to Cold War Berlin in the 1980s to take advantage of its low rents and free-spirited atmosphere. Before succumbing to AIDS in 1993, he worked alternatively as a barman, a cook, and a sex worker and took hundreds of photos, including poignant self-portraits documenting the advancing virus and male drag culture (see fig. 3.14). In biweekly self-portraits, he even archived his impending death, with a final photograph of himself in a clown nose, taken before he committed suicide. He bequeathed his estate, including over five thousand photographs, to the Schwules Museum*, which mounted an exhibition in 1997. In *Tunten, Queens, Tantes* (Sissies, Queens, Aunties), he took stylized headshots, party photos, and demonstration snapshots of the many different looks in the Tunten scene. As we will see in chapter 4, German Tunten are not simply

FIG. 3.14 Polette.
Photo by Jürgen
Baldiga. © Schwules
Museum* Berlin.

drag queens in the Anglo-American sense. It is an identity unto itself, with
very specific connotations within the history of German gay activism. In the
1970s, Tunten were radical Marxist gay men who took issue with the toxic
cis-masculinity of the early gay rights movement in West Berlin, using effeminate, camp dress as a criticism of what they saw as a homonormative bend
among activists. Discord within these groups between cis and sissy masculinities ultimately fractured the movement into reformist and radical groups,
with those normatively gendered men tending to work within the system,
seeking allies across the labor movement and in political parties, and with
sissies (together with some lesbians) holding firm to this more revolutionary
tradition. Today, Berlin's sissies are a scene unto itself, difficult to situate
on the political or gender/sexuality spectrum. Some notable personalities,
like Patsy l'Amour laLove, hold deeply critical ideas about feminist theory,
queer theory, and the supposed "cultural relativism" of academic writing
that they suggest buttresses a racism of its own against white Germans.[98]

Tunten challenge institutionalization, kinship, and radical embodiment in all sorts of critical (and not always unproblematic) ways.

Annette Frick likewise sought to capture the intimacies of queer and trans* subcultures in post-1989, reunified Berlin. Unlike the detachment of Brassäi, an outsider to the scenes he documented, she trained her eye on the city's subaltern as a participant observer. Photographing from a position of belonging across differences, she occupied a unique position as documentarian and artist, finding ways to intertwine the worlds of these disparate groups. Her photographs of drag queens and kings, transsexuals, lesbians, and feminists gained the support of the Berlin Senate, are recognized in the art world in both Austria and Germany, and have been shown at both the Schwules Museum* and the Märkisches Museum, where a retrospective was held in 2019 featuring performances by some of the same Tunten who were featured in Baldiga's catalog.[99] Hosted by Patsy l'Amour laLove, it was an evening filled with crossings and indeterminacies, from the resurfacing of the 1980s punk scene to the special place of the Tunte in the gay male imaginary. Here too, Berlin's avant-garde played a not insignificant role in her work. As we saw in chapter 1, the broken, changing, and fluid landscapes of Cold War West Berlin created spaces for new kinship entanglements as well as the fault lines that continued to divide communities. Reunification Berlin continued to serve as a backdrop for Frick's photographic depiction of the fluidity of identity. Antifemme impulses were not the sole domain of the gay male subculture. A 2003 photo of the drag king Johnny Kingsize sporting the T-shirt "RESPECT FEMMES" makes a visual argument for the acceptance of femmes, this time in the Lesbian–Inter Trans* communities (see fig. 3.15). As one art magazine noted, Frick's photography helps construct kinships across difference, through the exploration of "new forms of permeability . . . in zones of transition, and with gestures ranging from provocative and extreme to camp, they sensitize the viewer to other, hybrid contexts of perception."[100]

How should we understand these portraits in relation to portraits of trans* women like Maria Sabine Augstein, Nora Eckert, and Nadja Schellenberg? Although some have offered the metaphor of the mask as a way to understand how female impersonators play with identity, it is perhaps better to think of these photographs along the lines already articulated several years ago in *Gender Trouble*, where Judith Butler argued that drag was something else entirely, more in keeping with the more expansive definitional purchase of

FIG. 3.15 Johnny Kingsize. Photo by Annette Frick. © Schwules Museum* Berlin.

trans* outlined in Halberstam and Stryker, as something that critiques the stability of identity itself. As much as drag is transgressive, it brings with it the possibility of affirming hegemonic norms within the queer community, which might include misogyny and white fragility in discussing matters of race. But insofar as drag destabilizes gender by displacing "the entire enactment of gender signification from the discourse of truth or falsity," it questions the firmament on which identity is founded as an external manifestation of internal thoughts or orientation.[101] It stands to reason that Baldiga and Frick's Tunten qualify as trans* enactments insofar as they are, in Eliza Steinbock's terminology, "emergent, affective, and processual" embodiments that go beyond the usual gender scripts and kinships in ways that are not obvious or certain.[102] At the same time, they hold within them the possibility of being reworked in less politically advantageous ways, as we'll see in the book's conclusion.

FIG. 3.16 Cheyane at the Teddy Gala, 1996. From the Photoproject Queens. © Nihad Nino Pušija.

Club Trans*

The 2000s witnessed the emergence of another trans* geography of spectacle, community, and belonging, with roots in the city's underground club scene and the anything goes atmosphere of Berlin after dark. Here we see kinships of a different sort, of race, migration, gender, and sexuality. If Gall, Baldiga, and Frick draw on and transcend the distinct temporalities and affective affordances of lesbian, gay, and trans* traditions, creating a visual vernacular that challenges fixed ideas of identity and community, then the two-decades-old bar and dance club SO36 on Oranienstrasse in the district of Kreuzberg operated a bit differently. The SO36 would go on to play a pivotal role in depictions of the city's postmigrant nightlife in the 1990s onward, with regular parties from "Black Gay Life" to the "Teddy Awards" for queer film, chronicled by the Yugoslavian-born, Berlin-based photographer Nihad Nino Pušija (see fig. 3.16).

Already in the 1970s, SO36 had a loyal following in the punk rock scene, and like many of these Kreuzberg and Schöneberg clubs, it was a transnational space—blocks from the Iron Curtain and in the city's Turkish quarter—and was known in Western Europe for its edginess. In the early 1970s, Türkiyeli migrants were courted vigorously by successive West German governments given the labor shortage amid much-needed infrastructure work.[103] Although the economic turnaround of the lean years of 1973 and 1974 saw efforts to return workers to Turkey, the turbulent political and economic situation there caused many workers to stay and bring their families, turning a migrant worker population into an immigrant one, which, in a country that had no legal parameters for citizenship based on immigration, posed huge problems for Turks who felt the disorienting effects of being in limbo and Germans who did not have a framework for understanding national identity beyond ethnicity. It is common for Türkiyelis to be described as bounded between cultures, but ethnographies of German Turks challenge long-standing assumptions of a bounded culture, pointing, as one might expect, to a wide diversity of experiences and attitudes. As the anthropologist Levent Soysal has pointed out with his study of Berlin youth especially, transnational cultural flows and contemporary discourses around equality, plurality, and human rights complicate easy assumptions around Turkishness and Islam as antithetical to European modernity.[104] For queer Türkiyelis in Berlin, the challenge is further complicated by what one Turkish German activist termed a kind of *Doppeldiskriminierung* or double discrimination—not always feeling welcome in German queer organizations and in wider society in general, with its uneven reckoning with the legacy of structural racism, colonial violence, and the Holocaust (see plates 1 and 2).[105]

Into this mix, the queer Turkish German drag and dance party was born. Beginning as the brainchild of Fatma Souad, Sabuha Salaam, and Cihangir Gümüstürkmen in the late 1990s, for a few hours each weekend the Salon Oriental hosts a cabaret and drag show with themes centered on migration, sexism, and homo- and transphobia. It quickly grew from one to three queer dance parties and a once monthly "Gayhane" event, which combines gay with the Turkish word for home. Here, Turkish music, Arab pop, and Hindi techno are orchestrated at the hands of DJ Ipek Ipekcioglu while collections are taken up in support of a number of Turkish German organizations and initiatives. Ipek calls this genre of music Eklektik BerlinIstan, a product of the unique affordances of the city. The drag and dance parties, including the male belly dancers who perform during the shows, are captured in portrait and occasional scene photography in the work of Nicholas Schmidt and Andrea Saif, who provide rare opportunities to view this unique translocal and transnational space. Souad and DJ Ipek are quite literally the faces of the dance party; their images have been reproduced in newspapers around the globe.[106] Yet, while their faces are very recognizable—in drag or out—the countenances of audience members are less so as vernacular photography is not allowed in the space, given that the club has to guarantee anonymity to people who are potentially still living on the down low. This does not mean that Gayhane is less of a galvanizing site of queer and trans* ways of being in the world. It is transitory, changing from night to night, yet fixed as well to a space that despite gentrification and charges of commercialization remains central to queer Turkish culture and community. While one is tempted to argue that the trade in orientalism runs the risk of fetishizing difference, in SO36, through its diverse audience, the space resists easy classification, creating social, experiential, and affective networks that come close to what Saidiya Hartman describes for New York City, a place of attachment amid "wayward-ness," a "practice of the social otherwise, the insurgent ground that enables new possibilities and new vocabularies," in this instance through the absent presence of scene photography.[107]

Homosexualität_en

Returning to the image at the outset of this chapter of the performance artist Cassils from the joint museum exhibition at Germany's national museum and the Schwules Museum* in 2015, it bears asking what role trans* photography serves in repositioning historical narratives that have previously centered on sexology, the sexual emancipation movement, and persecution of homosexu-als under the Nazis—the three core elements of twentieth-century LGBTQIA history. As we will see in the ensuing chapters, these historical themes have played a pivotal role in undergirding gay and later lesbian activism in the 1960s and 1970s; memory politics in the second half of the twentieth century; and some of the memory wars over who is included and excluded from these narratives, which have by and large centered gay male culture. But outside of the various queer communities, these themes have had little purchase within Germany's national narratives, at least not in terms of how this history has been taken up by universities, art galleries, and museums. Queer history and theory do not have a toehold in German universities—unlike in the UK, Canada, and the United States—despite the high profile of Berlin's iconic permissiveness in the 1920s and the art, theater, social movements, and cultural production it spawned. The curators of the exhibition—Birgit Bosold, Dorothée Brill, and Detlef Weitz—sought new and creative ways to reimagine the exhibition space to address these multiple occlusions in a way that honored the city's diverse communities without imposing a new synthesis. Photography was essential to that undertaking.

The exhibition, which was the biggest draw in the Schwules Museum*'s twenty-year history since being founded by four gay men, provided an opportunity to queer curation through the use of experimental spatial logics and the creative selection and placement of objects, photographs, and ephemera. The aim was not to present a unified narrative but rather to draw on the over seven hundred objects on display at both sites to engineer a series of affective experiences through a scenography of "faggy gestures," as the curators called it in their curatorial statement, an homage to the subtextual referents of gay male knowledge production.[108] The curators sought to move beyond identity, however, in providing windows into the vast and different ways in which people negotiated their experiences of science, law, policing, social movements, and subculture. Such an approach was meant to narrate the city's multiple queer and trans* kinship networks, suturing together communities while still minding the ties that bind—namely, the inescapable place of Nazi persecution and the lack of redress after 1945. But not everyone was satisfied. Some took umbrage at the title of the exhibition itself, seeing in the word *Homosexualität_en* a term long implicated in the medicalization of queer bodies. Others, notably lesbian feminists who have had to wage a long battle for recognition, saw it as reductive, still centering gay men's experiences. It was hoped that the use of the poster of Cassils might open the door to a third way of viewing the images and artifacts on display, beyond the homonormative frame, so as to deconstruct same-sex and gender-nonconforming bodies and kinships from a variety of subject positions, queering nonbinary and trans* embodiments and sexualities and how these have evolved and changed over time.[109]

The constructed nature of identity lies at the core of the exhibition, with the Schwules Museum* explicitly taking the museumgoer into the contemporary moment through diverse examples of work and life beyond the gender binary and heteronormative relationships, families, and communities.[110] The exhibits were designed with the user experience in mind, to give pride of place to certain historical legacies while allowing individuals to make their way according to their own meanderings and interests. The exhibition catalog, on the other hand, is a fundamentally different user experience. One leafs through, page by page, confronted by images in a choreographed succession. Although the curators' intention was not to create a new hegemonic narrative, there is something explicit about how the images line up in the catalog around racialized, nonbinary, and trans*masculine representations of bodies that are still so often marginalized within the queer canon. This mobilizes new ways of seeing and archiving queer/trans* bodies as part of what Jay Prosser has termed "a strategic alliance" between queer and trans* projects, representing a deliberate attempt to expand the German visual archive in important new ways. At the same time, one wonders whether this is held in tension or even possibly negated by the use of the Cassils's cover image, with its marble-like muscularity and alabaster whiteness. Still, that a Canadian body would be called on to represent queer and trans* history in Berlin is itself indicative of the changing entanglements at work among twenty-first-century kin. If we view these tensions as productive, following Prosser, not a queering of trans*ness but the mobilization of alliances, solidarities, and kinships, we recognize incommensurabilities while harnessing the power of queer and trans* fluidity for change.[111]

There are a great many tensions at work in this catalog, and perhaps, on some level, that is the point. While it draws on a visualization of kinships across difference to decenter the hagiography around Magnus Hirschfeld and the hallowed place of Nazi persecution within gay history generally, it both internationalizes and queers the visualization of gender and sexual nonconformism by picturing trans* embodiment, history, and portraiture as performance and physical permanence. It doesn't collapse trans* into queer modes; it keeps them in productive tension, seeing in them parallel, multiple, as well as distinct historical projects.

As I've argued here, both as presences and absences in the queer visual archive, portrait and scene photography were genres of image making that lent themselves well to new articulations of trans* lifeworlds beyond the sexological model. Stylized, black-and-white photography especially provided a visual language and aesthetic vernacular with which diverse communities within the LGBTQIA scenes gave expression to their various forms of *anders Sein* or being different. Buoyed by the cultural avant-garde, from

Surrealism to punk, photography's aesthetic dimensions not only served as counterarchives to the sexological counterarchive; they critiqued the divisions between science and art, archive and gallery, high and low, and queer and trans* representation and embodiment. Keeping trans* open as a category allows us to see the different ways in which gender nonconformism surfaced over the course of the twentieth century as processual, a form of becoming in unbecoming that often eludes classification. At the same time that trans* photography wrests gender nonconformity from the necropolitics of medicalization, the visibility of certain trans* subjects over others suggests that our interpretive lens needs to remain attentive to the ongoing tensions and struggles that continue to surface around trans* kinships especially which subjects are taken up into the mainstream, as part of a transnational politics of remembering.

PATHWAYS TO LIBERATION

4

DRAWING INSIGHT from the preceding chapters on the surprising ways in which queer and trans* kinship is a story of entanglement, sometimes fraught, other times generative, what would happen if we were to apply it to the story of gay liberation? While the tendency has been to disarticulate groups, what if instead we made central the productively charged atmosphere that grows out of the struggle to speak to multiple forms of oppression? Instead of a siloed history of the LGBTQIA quest for recognition or one organized around collectivities of the same, what happens if we stress overlap and interconnectedness amid the disjunct simultaneity of experiences of oppression? Centering kinship allows us to explore new fault lines of difference within collective claims making, a process that might earn some constituents a formal hearing while others still struggle to make their positions known.[1]

An entangled approach to kinships of oppression and liberation in queer history helps us better determine at what cost certain stories, experiences, and identities became palatable both within activist circles and in the wider public consciousness. As Laurie Marhoefer has suggested, the conflation of modern queer historical successes with political liberalism has shrouded the more complex ways in which queer and trans* people have navigated the world, not just as outsiders in a straight society but sometimes within LGBTQIA subcultures themselves.[2] This chapter examines queer activism in the postwar decades as comprising a web of complex social relationships. Despite the centrality of Nazi persecution to the development of gay and lesbian consciousness on both sides of the Cold War divide, challenges both inside and outside of queer activist coalitions inhibited these groups from adhering to more radical efforts to mobilize around gender expression, capitalist exploitation, and sexual freedom. It is here that we begin to see the emergence of a politics of concession to state power, most evident in West Germany. With the onset of the AIDS crisis and abandonment of a multidimensional queer politics, activists crafted kinships that were more palatable to the demands of economic liberalism. This led to what Roderick Ferguson has called the depoliticization of queer politics—that is, a turn away from radical ideological commitments toward what we might call radical interiority.[3] As sexual and gender transgression was gradually mainstreamed, sex became a private matter, part of the sanctity of individual identity, choice, and personhood. What began as coalitional, radical, and intersectional activist kinships gave way to increasingly accommodationist, liberal, rights-based approaches to the sexual compact. This was not neutral or preordained. As this chapter shows, it hinged on a politicization of identity that privileged the white, middle-class, masculinist model it once sought to displace.[4]

Forgetting Fascism

The 2008 unveiling of the Memorial to Homosexuals Persecuted under Nazism (Homo-Monument for short) in the center of Berlin is impossible to imagine without considering the selective moments of remembering and forgetting built into the fabric of German liberal democracy. This had already begun in the early postwar years, when, under the direction of the occupation authorities, judicial officials in East and West Germany combed through their criminal code for traces of Nazi-era jurisprudence.[5] The Nazi version of Paragraph 175 remained in effect after capitulation, and as we've seen, was only repealed in the late 1960s. Because same-sex desire between men was criminalized before the 1935 Nazi legal reform, the antisodomy statute was regarded as having a basis in German legal tradition.[6] Queer kinship after fascism was predicated on the abrogation of responsibility for targeting men as moral and sexual pariahs.

It is not anachronistic to see the continuation of Nazi-era jurisprudence as an abomination. This opinion was even expressed by people at the time, like Curt Röbel, a member of an eastern regional parliament, who wrote a memo to all provincial diets and parties in 1948. Appealing to human decency with a hint of German victimhood, since "over three and a quarter years have passed since the end of the criminal Nazi regime, under which we also suffered especially severely," his expectation was that a new democratic Germany, and by this he meant East Germany, would put an end once and for all to the discrimination against queer men.[7]

There were different public memories of queer persecution and the role it should play in postwar cases. As we read in chapter 1, judges in the western zones of occupation, faced with appeals as early as 1946, reinforced the 1935 version of Paragraphs 175 and 175a, while some magistrates in the Soviet-controlled regions harked back to the law that was in force before the Nazis came to power, which had a different standard of evidence.[8] Some even highlighted the erstwhile efforts of the Social Democratic Party (SPD) and the Communist Party (KPD) in the Weimar Republic to overturn the criminalization of consensual sex between adult men altogether.[9] The tie that bound both countries was homophobia and the limited interest of both states in recognizing queer victimization. In the East, where there were attempts at full decriminalization between 1952 and 1958, this hint of liberalization obfuscated other misgivings. Officials at all levels thought queer sexuality endangered socialist citizenship.[10] Even the simple effort to secure victim recognition for treatment under the Nazis met with blank stares unless someone could prove they were targeted for their communism or Jewishness.[11]

The GDR sexologist Rudolf Klimmer, himself twice jailed under the Nazis, went on record over and over again in hopes of changing public perception of same-sex attraction. Not even his arguments for a biological basis of desire could change the view that there was always something sinister and untrustworthy about queer citizens.[12] In the West, several high-profile suicides in Frankfurt catapulted the story of same-sex sexuality into the headlines, but this failed to bolster sympathy for legal reform. Popular culture proved no refuge as even feature-length films traded on echoes of moral angst.[13] While the story of the Federal Republic is often told as an incremental move away from tyranny toward alignment with the Western liberal tradition, liberalization was not something experienced universally by all citizens.[14]

Throughout the 1950s, the rate of convictions under the Nazi-era statute soared. By 1957, the year the West German Federal Constitutional Court in

Kahlsruhe heard the case of two men seeking to overturn their convictions, there had been an increase of 44 percent over the final years of the Weimar Republic. Worse still, arrests during the Third Reich were used as evidence in postwar trials.[15] The gendered and age-specific dimensions of postwar law meant that the state saw little need to protect women from each other but young men's sexuality was especially concerning, particularly fears of seduction at the hands of "established homosexuals."[16]

Homophobia also meant that kinships among victims were not necessarily guaranteed. In 1950s West Berlin, Martha Mosse—a middle-class, educated woman with legal training and member of the renowned publishing house family—was reproached by a fellow victim of Nazi racial policy for purportedly abusing her position as part of the city liaison service (Reichsvereinigung) to relocate Jews to the so-named Judenhäuser once the order came to evict them from their homes. As Javier Semper Vendrell has noted in his discussion of charges levied against her by a Jewish acquaintance—who survived by passing as Aryan in a mixed marriage—Mosse's unconventional lifestyle (she lived in open partnership with a woman) was a source of scrutiny in the postwar period. Although it was never stated overtly in the charges of crimes against humanity levied against her by Alice Hirschberg (and ultimately deemed unfounded), her class status, comportment, and unconventional living arrangements coded her as a lesbian, making her suspect.[17] Despite their shared experiences as victims of Nazi oppression, class, gender norms, and suspicions of queer sexuality created "economies of domination" instead of kinships of reconciliation.[18]

As also discussed in chapter 1, hustlers were equally unable to secure compassion, either from police and social services, or from homophile groups and the radical gay rights activists who prefaced their own politicization on the need to organize instead of indulging in anonymous sex. The specter of blackmail cast the innocence of trade into doubt. Why such animosity? One way to get at this is to view hustlers, together with women like Martha Mosse, for how they are rendered visible in the first place. To do this, we need to think of their experiences relationally, along a spectrum of queerness instead of in opposition to an absolute queer subjectivity. This reveals the problems and possibilities of queer kinship.

Same-sex-desiring women, youth, and Tunten, or effeminate queer men, occupied similarly liminal positions within the social and legal landscape of the postwar German states. For women, their legibility as desiring subjects both hinged on and was hampered by a gendered sense of their vulnerability and weakness, to such a degree that they were regarded as unequal to men sexually as well as politically. The perception that heterosexuality was under siege meant that young men were similarly disadvantaged, although depending on their class status they might be perceived as potential victims of seduction or aggressive manipulators of men's inborn same-sex desire. And Tunten were disliked across the board, even within parts of the gay subculture itself. According to interviews conducted by Maria Borowski of elder East German lesbians and gay men, all three—in their own way—were affected by corrosive gender norms and encouraged to keep private and out of the public eye.[19] These stories of persecution position women, youth, and gender-nonconforming men in an ambivalent position; they might be subjects of scorn within their own subcultural communities, targets of unbridled intervention, or they were ignored outright. These tropes are themselves marks of visibility in a historical record that often obfuscates their presence.[20] As we'll see in chapter 5, these entangled experiences of oppression surfaced during the debate around the Homo-Monument positioning women's claims as secondary to those of middle-class, cisgendered men. Yet if we widen the lens to view social and cultural forms of aggression more broadly, we see that these experiences surfaced under different conditions of possibility but on a similar spectrum: that of anxiety about nonnormative forms of gender comportment and desire. Postwar jurisprudence and the New Left preoccupation with fascism and National Socialist crimes shaped whose experiences were made meaningful given the legal definition of deviance and its role in determining the discourse of suffering. But these parallel and coterminous experiences of violence, persecution, and homophobia still existed as social and cultural artifacts of illegality and hate. Because they were not interpreted through a legal lens, they fell from view, along with the experiences of trans* persons who were even more marginalized within postwar queer communities. These distinctions, which will matter when memory activists look back on this period to cement claims for a memorial, suggest the usefulness of kinship over identity as a way to historicize the queer past.

Troubling 1968/1969/1989

Thinking about queer and trans* experience relationally as forms of kinship troubles the benchmarks that have come to dominate how we frame this history. Ordinarily, we trace queer visibility back to the decriminalization of the antisodomy statute in 1968 in East Germany and a year later in West

Germany when decriminalization allowed gay-identified men the freedom to live their lives without fear of reproach. The year 1989 is significant, too, because the fall of the wall gave rise to discussions about how to streamline two competing legal systems that regulated sexuality differently, which ultimately led unified Germany to drop the antisodomy statute entirely.[21] And of course, if we seek to situate trans* experience in this timeline, we rub up against other limitations as well. There are, in fact, a number of important qualifiers that question the certitude with which we value legal reforms as markers of progress. There is little doubt that decriminalization had a profound impact on attitudes toward gender nonconformism and sexuality.[22] Still, there are several misconceptions about what these reforms meant in terms of tangible social change. Although same-sex sexual acts were no longer criminal, legality was circumscribed.

These reforms were the result of changes already underway, dating back at least to the 1950s, nudged along by the British Wolfenden Report, which brought together a broad coalition of witnesses, youth leaders, government officials, and clergy to discuss the matter of same-sex attraction.[23] But they also had a longer trajectory still, coming on the heels of decades of social, economic, and generational upheaval. There is no doubt that sexual mores were changing on both sides of the Iron Curtain. In postwar East Germany, as of a 1954 Supreme Court ruling, very few cases met the standard of proof to charge adult men with same-sex activity, although intergenerational sex was still heavily policed, as were depictions of queer sexuality in the public sphere.[24] Meanwhile, reproductive sexuality was lauded as a hallmark of a healthy socialist personhood, and people actively sought out sexual relationships and engaged in sex outside of marriage.[25]

In the West, similar changes were afoot. Consumer desires drove a robust mail-order erotica industry, and many couples increasingly regarded soft pornography and personal sexual aids as important marital agents.[26] Working-class Catholics found little wrong with premarital sex, instructional films emphasized the importance of orgasmic sex to healthy relationships, and by the early 1960s, even the Protestant Church was on board with decriminalizing homosexuality.[27] Changes in heterosexual norms occasioned talk about the need to take on the treatment of same-sex desire. In other words, straight and queer sexual practices were not only enmeshed with one another and intertwined, they might also support the cause for reform, making allies out of unlikely kin. As in the East, fears around heterosexuality continued to drive concern for youth sexuality.[28]

Reforming the antisodomy law was not the same thing as embracing same-sex desire. More than a few social critics supported decriminalization at the same time that they argued that queers were promiscuous, labile, and in need of therapy.[29] Repressed desire was no better. It might be equated with the materialism of bourgeois sensibilities or worse, following the influence of Herbert Marcuse, the cause of fascism itself.[30] Legality certainly did not mean unencumbered sexual self-determination. Sex between men in the FRG was allowable only in pairs of two, provided both were at least twenty-one and it took place in private. In East Germany, although sexual intercourse between men was no longer illegal, Paragraph 151 of the reformed Penal Code now classified sexual activity between an adult and a person under the age of eighteen as a criminal offense and included women in the mix as well. In other words, the liberalization of sexual law meant that, for the first time ever, East German women could be penalized for same-sex sexual activity. Adding insult to injury, the age of consent was set at fourteen for hetero-sexual sexual encounters.[31] These differences in how same-sex activity was regulated would only be rectified after reunification in 1989–90, suggesting that the path toward sexual liberalization was anything but direct.

Within a matter of years, Cold War Germany would wrestle with the im-plications of this newfound liberalization, which created new boundaries of comportment, legality, and behavior.[32] It also gave rise to new queer kinships. Just as some of the differences between heterosexual norms and homosexual practices were eroding, gay- and lesbian-identified men and women began to carve out spaces for themselves in liberation movements designed to break the silence around homophobia.[33] Alongside legal reform, the relaxation of censorship allowed for the efflorescence of gay and lesbian subcultures through print media and film.[34] Suddenly, queer themes were in public cir-culation, providing opportunities for activists to find one another, develop repertoires of contention, and think of ways they might communicate with a variety of publics. The result was a massive memory boom that witnessed a generational rethink of the crimes of their parents' generation as activists turned their attention to the injustices committed under the Nazis.

Postmemory behind the Iron Curtain

In her 2012 book on postmemory, the literary scholar Marianne Hirsch famously inquired how subsequent generations remember the injustices committed by previous ones, thinking specifically about the children of

Holocaust survivors. She asked how they bear witness to the "personal, collective, and cultural trauma of those who came before—to experiences they 'remember' only by means of the stories, images, and behaviors among which they grew up."[35] For queer-identified men and women, this was more complicated because, up until decriminalization, personal stories passed down from kin endangered their personal safety. For many of the queer survivors of the camps, prisons, courts, and jails, silence prevailed. The East German psychiatrist Rudolf Klimmer was jailed twice during the Nazi period and even entered what seems to have been a marriage of self-preservation with Martha Brumecki, purportedly a lesbian, to avoid further persecution. He never went public with his story.[36] It isn't hard to see why. Legal and social stigma continued to dominate well into the era of reform. As late as 1960, Hans Zauner, then mayor of the village of Dachau—home to one of the first concentration camps on German soil—put it bluntly: "Many criminals and homosexuals were in Dachau. Do you want a memorial for such people?"[37]

Despite the continuation of homophobic attitudes, the era of legal reform unleashed activist memory work as younger generations of queers, feminists, and gender nonconforming people were able to meet unencumbered, at times bridging the international boundary separating East and West.[38] From their first encounter underneath the Max Pechstein–designed homoerotic stained-glass window of the Gartenstrasse swimming pool sauna, a known cruising node, Michael Eggert and Peter Rausch went on to host parties and get-togethers with friends and acquaintances out of which they built East Germany's first gay liberation group the HIB (Homosexuelle Interessengemeinschaft, or Homosexual Interest Group).[39] Unlike in the West, gay bars were few in the socialist capital, and the press still embargoed articles that took up explicit gay and lesbian themes. Yet these groups were resourceful. East German activists met their West German brethren in the few establishments that catered to queer people, like the Burgfrieden or Moccabar near the Friedrichstrasse train station, one of the chief entry points for visitors from the West. They even managed to smuggle in copies of the West German gay publication *him*.[40] The American student Jim Steakley would help ensure that the traffic in gay-themed print material traveled in the other direction as well, spiriting out copies of 1920s sex reform magazines across the border to the West (he lived in East Berlin for a time) and copying them with his friends there.[41] At the 1973 World Youth Festival in East Berlin, the Australian Peter Tatchell even smuggled in flyers to distribute at one of the scheduled events.[42] According to Olaf Brühl, they continued to surface for years to come.[43] The border could be permeable, at least in this Cold War city.

The HIB activists forged one of the largest activist networks, utilizing connections with others in their circle to expand to the periphery of the movement. Gatherings at Charlotte von Mahlsdorf's estate on the outskirts of the city were known to attract hundreds. There was filmmaking, costuming, and radical, performative actions including parades tracked by the Stasi. Unlike in the West, however, East German activist kinship networks centered around recent memory—that is, socialist humanism's potential to liberate the soul. The false promises of reform that sprang out of the Prague Spring led otherwise loyal adherents to "drop out of socialism."[44] Some had been Socialist Unity Party (SED) members, like Michael Unger, who believed working with the state might help improve "life for gay men and lesbians." Peter Rausch, the son of a fellow traveler, recalled thinking that the work they were doing was motivated by a sense of queer socialist futurity: "The idea is good. . . . It will just take a few generations."[45] Their worldview was not antithetical to the values propagated by the regime. Rather, activists drew on and extended many of the same ideals in their search for personal fulfillment in the same way that they transposed ideas from West Germany to their own understanding of liberation.[46]

The memory work of East German activists was also palpably different from that on the other side of the Berlin Wall. In the GDR, the lack of a dedicated public sphere meant that activists were most intent on carving out a space for privacy and personhood in an increasingly hostile state. What they created was not the conformist subjectivity of the 1950s homophile movement (see fig. 4.1).[47] As I showed in chapter 3, for them, queerness rested on multiple, intertwined kinships. Parades were mixed affairs, and photographs reveal that cross-dressing and gender nonconformity were steadfast features of HIB cabaret, parties, and dances, harking back to the gay and transvestite ball culture of the Weimar age.[48] Gender play might also have served as a critique of inequalities within the scene itself. Two members of the Gays in the Church group, Ingo Kölsch and Heinrich Vogel, went so far as to provide instruction on the power of gender play in workshops with such provocative titles as "Our Inner Queen" and "I'm a Queen—What Are You?"[49]

All was not perfectly harmonious, of course, but the number of overlapping agendas does raise eyebrows in an era when rendering difference legible often means narrating it discretely or privileging white cisgender gay

FIG. 4.1 Michael Eggert, Charlotte von Mahlsdorf, and Peter Rausch.
© Peter Rausch Collection and Third Generation East.

kinships over more entangled histories.[50] It did not take long before the East German secret police was hot on the HIB's heels, and the group disbanded in 1980. In 1986 Uschi Sillge, a veteran of the original HIB and a lesbian activist, reconstituted the group in a new form from among those who had continued to meet in bars and restaurants on Sundays. Together with members and the interdisciplinary working group Homosexuality at Humboldt University, they organized activities under the moniker "Sonntags im Club," which soon became transmogrified into Sonntags-Club. Part community group, part mutual aid society and self-help association, the Sonntags-Club became a touchstone for queer, lesbian, bisexual, and trans* kinship in the East German capital and beyond.[51] It still exists to this day.

Other queer intersectional kinships began to materialize around this time as well. An agreement between church and state in 1978 afforded a ragtag group of feminists, environmentalists, and peace activists the opportunity to meet on church grounds, though there too the journalist, theologian, and activist Eduard Stapel recalled that the Stasi constantly searched for traitors in their midst.[52] Despite continued attention from the secret police, a multivalent kinship model continued to surface in 1980s activism. As Heidi Müller (a pseudonym) put it in an interview with Josie McLellan in 2010, her home in Prenzlauer Berg was a nexus of queer sociability, "the warmest corner in the East" (warm is a colloquialism for queer). Her circle, explicitly queer, was also unambiguously mixed: "At some point then we set up a gay-lesbian-bi-heterosexual group. . . . We were all mid-twenties and met somewhere, dreamt something up, wrote it down, and went to the *Kirchentag* (Church event), had our own table there."[53]

All was not always harmonious among activists, even among lesbian feminists. Those allied with the formal Lesbians in the Church movement certainly felt part of a larger feminist spirit that was making its way through East German activist organizations (see fig. 4.2). But they also thought their particular experience of homophobia marginalized them from groups like the HIB and the Sonntags-Club.[54] Müller was quick to distinguish her lesbian initiative from what she saw as the factionalism of the explicitly lesbian church groups. She liked it that hers was familiar, informal, and heterogenous.[55] In her interview with Andrea Rottmann, Nadja Schallenberg recalled that there could be tolerance and also hostility in lesbian feminist groups toward transwomen; she experienced both, sometimes within the space of days.[56] These examples tell us three things about queer kinships behind the Iron Curtain: (1) that GDR activists were less preoccupied, initially, with memory and morality after fascism, directing their attention instead to queer sociability and intimacy broadly defined;[57] (2) that the varied, diverse, and heterogenous nature of queer, gender nonconformist, and lesbian activism reflected the convergence of different taxonomies of association, kinship, and organization along with different scales of opposition; and (3) that although there were various mobilizations among women who loved other women, gender was not always a tie that could bind. Despite these tensions, in an era of ongoing surveillance, it is remarkable that activist groups were able to negotiate a means by which to wrest a place for queer kinship in the Workers' and Farmers' State.

Publics and Counterpublics

The politics of visibility took on a different meaning in West Germany, where several important media events in the early 1970s helped concretize the ongoing shift away from homophile respectability. The tactics employed by memory activists are a good indication of the different social and material conditions at work in the West that undergirded the rise of gay, lesbian,

FIG. 4.2 Bettina Dziggel, Group photo of Lesbians in the Church working group at the Erlöserkirche, Ostberlin, 1983. © Robert-Havemann-Gesellschaft Archiv Berlin.

and trans* consciousness around Nazi-era crimes and postwar homophobia. They represent the commingling of efforts to take on structural homophobia through the reminiscences of the victim generation. But as we'll see, there were several snags in how successive groups legitimized their struggle. These would indelibly mar efforts to build kinships of solidarity around queer victimhood.

Two events mark the emergence of the gay liberation movement in West Germany. One was the unprecedented 1971 airing of the filmmaker Rosa von Praunheim and the sociologist Martin Dannecker's film *Nicht die Homosexuelle ist pervers, sondern die Situation in der er lebt* (It's Not the Homosexual Who Is Perverted but the Situation in Which He Lives) on German public television, which motivated hundreds of university students to leave cruising in the toilets for marches in the streets as part of the call to organize.[58] The second event happened the following year with the pseudonymous publication of a concentration camp survivor's account of his life as a man who wore the pink triangle.[59] Whereas East German activism was forged in living rooms and cafés, the West German gay rights movement took place both in the queer counterpublic and in state-sponsored media, and was organized by publicly funded university students and lay activists with strong but different ties to Marxism than their confrères in the GDR.

The leftist students who formed the Homosexual Action Groups in the wake of von Praunheim's call to action took great pains to distinguish themselves from the middle-class homophile activists of the 1950s and 1960s. Like the film's protagonist, who tires of the bourgeois banality of his first big city liaison, gay liberationists saw the politics of the first postwar generation as stultifying and conformist. On one issue there was a curious kinship: queers needed to direct their energy toward radical social change instead of allowing themselves to be bound up with pursuits of the flesh. Just as the conformity, myopia, and materialism of homophiles flew in the face of the issues of the day, so too did the libidinousness of cruising and easy pickups undermine organizing. While this criticism was directed at centrists, as we saw in chapter 1, it also had the unintended effect of demonizing young male trade and anonymous sex as somehow beyond the bounds of politics or the scene.

For all its reticence toward street sex, the film made unambiguous statements linking gay rights with other social justice initiatives, and in its wake, activists joined the various struggles for liberation across the globe, including unionization and women's and minority rights. But there were other interesting, if imperfect, mobilizations and kinships within the amorphous political scene known as the Alternative Left. In 1972, Swiss film student and contributor to the anarchist magazine *Agit 883* Cristina Perincioli founded a women's group under the umbrella of the Homosexual Action Group West Berlin (Homosexuelle Aktion Westberlin, or HAW), out of which sprang several different projects and organizations. Early lesbian activists went on to work with cis-heterosexual feminists in support of the repeal of Paragraph 218, the antiabortion paragraph, while others worked toward the creation of one of the first domestic violence shelters. In 1974, the lesbian activists in the HAW collaborated with Claus Ferdinand Siegfried, who had already filmed a documentary on Paragraph 175 in 1971. Like von Praunheim's film, it brought the issue of homosexuality to West German society. The documentary . . . *And We Take Our Rights* (*Und Wir Nehmen Uns die Rechte*) was shown on the WDR public station during prime time, causing the West Berlin groups to be inundated with letters from women across the Federal Republic. As Perincioli recalled in her memoir, this was the time that "Berlin went feminist."[60] But by the mid-1970s, fissures had emerged in the HAW and in other student groups, leading women's activists to seek out new ways to mobilize around same-sex desire among women.

Frustrations aside, and there were many, Perincioli notes how much these early feminist groups learned from their solidarities with the HAW. They applied many of their tactics.[61] The same was true for groups as far away as Münster who, on April 29, 1973, marched through town in one of the last shows of solidarity between gay men and lesbian women in West Germany.[62] Despite these early successes, Anne Hennscheid, the only woman on the organizational committee of the Münster Homophile Student Group, found it could be challenging to unite the two causes. Unlike in East Germany, intersectional kinships—however fraught—were a hallmark of the movement's solidarity-driven aspirations. In the West, they were increasingly difficult to sustain. From the mid-1970s on, in West Berlin and in other West German cities, men's and women's groups began to walk separate paths, and this schism gave rise to the formal adoption of the term *lesbian* over *gay or homosexual women*, which had been in widespread use.[63]

The early lesbian feminist movement was not alone in struggling with intergroup tensions during the sex wars of the 1970s. The ambivalent view toward cruising's radical potential continued to mark queer politics into the subsequent decades. How West German queers negotiated race also speaks to the limits of liberalization as a paradigm for understanding LGBTQIA organizing across the century. In recent years, race has emerged as a particularly salient touchstone for understanding the normalizing impulses in gay rights activism and the pivot points of histories of emancipation, including the place of the 1969 legal reforms in ushering in a more progressive sexual agenda.[64] If we look at how race surfaced in the radical liberationist movements of the 1970s, we can't help but recognize several contrapuntal features of postwar West German thinking more generally. These contradictions help us understand the different temporalities and turning points in how activists mobilized, remembered, and later commemorated their identities and struggles.

Antiracist Kinship

Defeat ushered in a new language for how to speak about race.[65] An added layer were UN-level conversations around genocide that created new frameworks around persecution and discrimination, which served homophile organizers in the 1950s.[66] Linking their struggle for decriminalization to the plight of racialized minorities persecuted during the Holocaust, homophiles collapsed racial hierarchies and difference, putting the postwar struggle for reform on a similar plane as wartime atrocity. As Christopher Ewing has persuasively argued, this strand of postfascist argumentation was a strategy to appeal to the conservative West German public. And homophiles certainly didn't have it easy with as many as twenty thousand criminal cases filed in the southwest German state of Baden-Württemberg alone, with prosecutors, city officials, and police who had been active during the Nazi years.[67] It is reflective of other elisions as well in terms of how LGBTQIA subjectivities coalesced around particular racial imaginaries and how this has been deployed as a device to secure rights and representation. As homophiles looked for ways to support their claim for sexual dissonance in legal reasoning, they turned to the Arab world and to Asia to showcase the universality of sexual practices and alternative ways of countenancing them. Dotted through issues of *Der Kreis* were references in the 1950s and 1960s to the prevalence of same-sex sexuality in Islamic countries, including arguments that Islam tolerated queerness, even in the face of tightening legal restrictions. Colonial antiliberalism was the true cause of backpedaling.[68] Homophiles linked their own postfascist quest for rights to antiracist, anticolonial kinships that humanized queer sexual desire as a fundamental human right. In West Germany, this early homophile plea for minority rights as human rights opened the door to more expansive engagement with other cultures and their sexual practices.[69] Yet it was not without an orientalism of its own.

As we saw in chapter 2, fantasies about non-European sexualities have a long history, extending back into the nineteenth century, which helped instantiate a new socioscientific lexicon out of which sprang legal and medical efforts to humanize difference.[70] Claims making around queerness was sutured to the notion that it had a biological basis in identity. It also played a vital role in the subcultural identification of queer desire as part of the pornographic imaginary, which eroticized intergenerational sex and the nubile male body. It is curious how both of these aspects of early queer, chiefly male, history played out in the commemorative politics of the post–sexual revolution era. Some of these racial associations were not at all lost on radical gay rights organizers. Rosa von Praunheim drew on homophile fantasies in how he depicted the safe, stay-at-home, bourgeois Carsten, whose flat was festooned with African spears, masks, and tapestries alongside other markers of queer subculture like Oscar Wilde novels and records by the American pop idol Fabian. The New Left criticism of bourgeois queer identity was also a class critique of this postfascist liberal lens. At the same time as it took on the racial shorthand of homophile queerness, it failed to problematize the concomitant fascination with race and racial liberalism that also undergirded New Left notions of desire (see plate 3).

The antiracist kinships of homophiles were problematic in other ways. They could easily give rise to the notion that nonwhite, non-Christian minority cultures in Africa and Asia were more earnest than Europeans. But racialized bodies also retained the original frisson that had attracted queer kin in the first place, and this would prove harder to dislodge. A 1957 survey in *Der Kreis* saw an overwhelming number of respondents answer in the affirmative when asked if they enjoyed the magazine publishing pictures of racialized men, second only to questions about audience interest in semi and full nudes.[71] Although the tenor of gay rights politics changed in the aftermath of decriminalization, as the student movement generation superseded the homophile activism that came before, the exoticization of nonwhite bodies continued to serve as a feature of post-1969 queer print and visual media culture where it percolated back up now and then, unchecked, into the radical agenda of gay liberationists. So, while 1969 represented a break in terms of legality, longer-standing erotic tropes and the power relationships they rested on, drew from older scripts and traditions that continued to define how white, largely cisgender male queers understood their kinships through those of their Others.

This is not dissimilar from the French New Left's engagement with sexual liberty.[72] In the German context, the tensions between a racialized homoeroticism on the one hand and an explicitly antifascist, antiracist agenda on the other continued to percolate into the different strands of 1970s and 1980s gay activism. One thing was certain: bodies were everywhere in 1970s magazines, even if the politics of magazine editors differed from those of the members of the homosexual action groups or the readers newly able to purchase issues at the kiosk.[73] Here, too, politics played out in the world of aesthetics. Emerging on the scene in 1969, *Du & Ich* became a sort of mouthpiece for the old homophile movement, picking up where earlier magazines like *Der Kreis* had left off. In a 1970 editorial, *him* magazine editor Udo Erlenhardt went to great pains to underscore that its purpose was to promote a homophile sensibility over trashy stories of gay sexual escapades with young pickups at train stations.[74] In articles in 1971 and 1972, racialized bodies were put to use to animate homophile antiracist politics, with examples drawn from the civil rights movement.[75] Ewing has shown that Martin Dannecker's view on gay liberation as emancipation over integration trickled into the magazine via a 1971 interview, and the editors seemed to welcome this change in emphasis, perhaps owing in part to fears that it had catered too readily to posthomophile minoritarian views.[76] But it was a struggle to walk the tightrope between radical politics and reader thirst for ever more youthful depictions of boys alongside the overt sexualization of people of color.[77]

The radical gays of the homosexual action groups were not always better at sidestepping the prurience that continued to mark expressions of queer kinship and desire in this period. While the gay press presented a sanitized vision of homosexuality well over the benchmark of 1969, as Craig Griffiths has emphasized, radical and leather subcultures struggled to contain libidinous desires that—when let out of the box—distracted adherents from the work that needed to be done. Still, intergenerational sex remained a core feature of various subcultures—homophile, radical, and unaffiliated alike. Advertisements in *Du & Ich* included fresh-faced boy models with images for purchase in the Netherlands, alongside sketches of Berber, "Sambal," and "Arabian" youths.[78] Martin Dannecker's findings in *Der gewöhnliche Homosexuelle* (The Common Homosexual) confirmed that the erotic aestheticization of young bodies was alive and well in the minds of around seven hundred survey respondents. Writing together with the student leader Reimut Reiche in 1974, Dannecker opined that the object of desire for queer men were partners, long term or occasional, under the age of twenty.[79] Of course, the sex wave of the 1970s unleashed a torrent of images and texts surrounding age, consent, and pubescent desire, not all of it confined to the gay scene. But it also remained a feature of the emancipation movement, such that several action groups even created subsections devoted entirely to pederasty. Over the course of the decade, the inclusion of pederast groups came under criticism from within and without, losing the critical support of some lesbians in advance of a 1980 vote on an antidiscrimination bill that had brought together opposing groups in a moment of solidarity.[80] Intergenerational desire—together with anonymous sex in "discos, orgy bars, and commercial sex"—were hot-button issues throughout the history of gay liberation in West Germany, leading Rosa von Praunheim to condemn the hedonism of the movement in a 1984 article in *Der Spiegel*, the German equivalent of *Time*, going so far as to suggest that uncontained, libidinous queer desire was at least partially responsible for the AIDS plague.[81] This tension between working with the system or against it, working against taboo or embracing and exoticizing it, proved a bitter pill for reformists and radicals alike.

Unlike in the East, where there was more evidence of intersectional kinship, in the West there were other ambivalences that called into question the assumption that from 1969 on, gay liberation marked a seamless march from shame to pride, what Heather Love has called the "affirmative bias" of emancipatory movements.[82] In actual fact, the 1970s and 1980s were a staging ground for contradictory impulses within the various gay, lesbian, pedophile, trans*, and BDSM scenes. Gender presentation and nonconformity were frequently at the center of the debate, especially when they might be connected to the specter of fascism. Same-sex-desiring women and female-presenting camp, trans*, and effeminate men were part of the earliest political movements of the 1970s, yet their position within the groups remained tenuous, especially as cells sought broader coalitional support from the student and labor movements. The HAW had already included a women's section in 1972, and dedicated lesbian movements began to coalesce in some cities in the wake of a scandal in the newspaper *Bild* around the salacious depiction of a lesbian murderer and her lover.[83] Homophobia within the women's movement and frustrations within the HAW led some to form the Lesbisches Aktionzentrum Westberlin (LAZ) while outright conflicts over gender presentation forced other activists to take an even stronger stand with their comrades. This led to fierce quarrels that came to a head in the wake of the Pentecost demonstration in West Berlin in 1973 and continued through 1975. The so-called "fairie, sissy, or drag queens debate" (*Tuntenstreit*) tackled the subject of effeminacy directly. In a series of actions, gender-nonconforming activists questioned whether efforts to secure working-class solidarity had developed into a reverence for a kind of cisgender homonormativity—not unlike bourgeois visions of maleness—that turned on the marginalization of femininity, biological as well as performative.[84] Although von Praunheim's film had originally celebrated the Tunte as a rebellious character who amplified the hypocrisies of normativity, a few years later the exaggerated gestures, hyperbolic drawl, and caricatured movements of the queen seemed out of step with the seriousness of class struggle.[85]

Participants in the *Tuntenstreit* did not understand themselves as trans*.[86] One might certainly consider the Tunte as the embodiment of transing—that is, as a challenge to the supposed rootedness of gender.[87] However, to claim sissies as trans* in an identitarian sense overlooks the complicated place of drag in the homonormative politics of the German gay and labor movements.[88] Recognizing them as kin, as part of different intersecting alliances of oppositionality, affords a new vantage point on gender in radical politics, and possible links between lesbian, feminist, and gender-nonconformist subjectivities. Here, kinship as a category does more interpretive work in laying bare some of the fault lines and fissures in the various intersecting communities of the New Left.

The signature publication to come out of the *Tuntenstreit* points to how the debate was framed in its own time. It sought to reconcile a radical queer agenda with the mainstreaming effect of organizing together with other social movements. Published with the newly minted Verlag rosa Winkel, named for the pink triangle worn in the camps, *Tuntenstreit* explored the role of gender nonconformism within the existential politics of same-sex sexuality and desire. The essays took up the various ways in which the HAW might reconcile the homosexuality of those who aggressively wear their gayness on the outside as queens (men in the HAW called themselves feminists) versus those "who from the outside present as normal gays, whose queerness is lived through declarative statements, or in arguments with heterosexual comrades, or with friends in their specific lifeworld, the gay subculture."[89]

The missive penned by Helmut Ahrens, Volker Bruns, Peter von Hedenström, Gerhard Hoffmann, and Reinhard von der Marwitz entitled "The Gay in Me" is a primer on coming out, living with pride, and navigating the homophobia of postdecriminalization West Germany. It also speaks to gender fluidity and the complicated ways in which people negotiated their sexual selves. Gerhard recalled coming out at fourteen, having many friendships with women and men, before deciding he was attracted to men overwhelmingly. It comes across as an afterthought when he remembers dressing in women's clothes and wearing them out in the street. He calls this moment a period of "gender role trouble" (*Rollenkonflikt*) and leaves the thought open-ended with the use of an ellipsis.[90] Reinhard described his multiyear love affair with a woman, which he finally gave up after his mandatory military service. He fell for a man he met in a gay bar, describing his sexual awakening as an efflorescence, a bodily way of knowing the nature of his desire. Volker recounted how he fantasized about men while masturbating, but still tried to have relationships with women. When he moved home to Celle from boarding school, a cousin told him that queers frequented the Schloßpark after dark, and he gladly went looking for sex, which he dutifully mocked as being somewhat cliché. Helmut told the story of his early coming out and how much he was venerated within the scene, so much so that he pondered working as a rent boy at the train station (but chose not to). He too had relationships with women and pondered why it is that we see homosexuality and heterosexuality as strictly opposite, when clearly, to his mind, they were interrelated phenomena.

This rich discussion of self-discovery reveals the manifold ways in which people voiced their understanding of gender and sexuality. It also reflects the internal pressures within the subculture itself, as each man weighed in on the apolitical nature of the bar scene, how they struggled in the catty and competitive atmosphere of the club, and—considering von Praunheim's film—felt unable to be true to their political, activist selves amid the hedonism of the hookup culture. There is surprising criticism of Hirschfeld's Third Sex model, that sexuality and queerness are beyond majority or minority culture, a true third way of being in the world.[91] This rings strange to our ears given his lionization as the founding father of queer memory today.

Another theme that leaps off the page is the role of race in relation to the queen. The authors describe the challenge posed by the sissy—namely, that as an exaggeration of femaleness, she is the most recognizable stereotype leveled against queers. Her camp troubles normative sexuality because she calls into question the separation of gender roles. In her canonical history of female impersonators, Esther Newton described the camp persona as deeply rooted in the gay scene.[92] Yet, despite being enmeshed in German queer culture, the Tunte was not always readily accepted, especially away from the stage, cabaret, or club. There was the story of Herbert, a member of the HAW who liked to go out wearing makeup and colored hair. He was threatened by the janitor of his building and half of his block after the Pentecost demonstration, having been outed as a queen. In another, we read of a homophile bar, where a sissy coasts in and orders a drink, followed by another, only to have another patron quip, "Is this queen hour or what?" One account outshines all the others. It tells of three heavily made-up Tunten seated on a U-Bahn train together with students. No one bats an eyelash. What happens in a neighborhood "overwhelmingly occupied by guest workers (Kreuzberg)" is most telling. We are told that the three queens are standing on the train station platform. Two "guest workers looking shy but friendly" glance over at them with a "mixture of laughing, smiling, and questioning." Then came the questions:

"Du siehst komisch aus. Macht mir Spaß."—"Nee, nee, nix gut. Du Mann, nich' Frau!"—"Warum Mann immer so (macht, männliche, Körperbewegung) und Frau immer so (macht 'weibliche, Körperbewegung')?"—"Ist richtig."—"Nein, jeder soll so wie er will, wie er ist." "Du schlafen mit Mann, ja? (Lachen) Arschficken, ne".—"Ja." "Na, dann is' gut!"

"You look strange. Makes me laugh"—"No, no, no good. You man, not woman!"—"Why men do this (performs male body movement) and women this (performs female body movement)."—"Right way."—"No, everyone should be who they are." "You sleep with man, yes (laughter) Ass fucker, eh?"—"Yes." "Then that is good."

How should we interpret this exchange, reproduced in a kind of pidgin German? A page later the authors say scenarios like these represent the way queers are welcomed in society, completely ignored on one end of the spectrum and fully embraced on the other. The scenario involving the guest workers, identified ostensibly by the location of the encounter and their manner of speech, is indicative of the overlapping constructions of orientalist sexuality. On the one hand, the "Gay in Me" authors themselves suggest that it exemplifies the quasi-tolerant view in the Muslim world toward same-sex sexuality, provided the roles inhabited conform to heterosexual norms (hence the question of whether one queen would be bottom). On the other, their relationship to the man who sleeps with other men, we are told, "is nothing less than how they understand the oppressed woman, who had no right to orgasm."[93] As with the homophiles before them, the activists who were intent on reforming the HAW during the *Tuntenstreit* challenged gender norms within queer subcultures but did so while perpetuating the eroticized kinships of racialized migrant populations.[94]

At the absolute farthest end of the spectrum was the growing derision among gay liberation activists for the leather and fetish scene which Clayton Whisnant has shown was already a feature in the 1960s.[95] This, too, played out along gendered lines. When a new leather bar opened in West Berlin in 1975, featuring one of the country's first dark rooms, HAW activists grabbed their pens. Darkened cellars, like the one at the *Knolle* bar, gave cover to those who searched out anonymous libidinous adventure, but here too was the suggestion that transgressive bodily desire contained the seeds of the movement's unmaking, especially if associated with "male fascistoid sexuality."[96] The article's author, Claire (a pseudonym), attributed the bar's appeal to the growth of a Nazi aesthetic within the gay scene, only to be called out by a respondent who claimed that the "pink HAW" activists who dominated the West Berlin group needed to stop judging people based on their gender presentation, whether homonormative, queen, or leather man.[97] Gender presentation, performance, and transgression could be searingly revolutionary, pushing the movement forward, but it could also be viewed as destabilizing what little toehold activists felt they had secured within mainstream society. Queer kinship could be fraught indeed.

Fascist Pasts and Fascist Presents

Activists took darkroom masculinities seriously because they believed they were fighting fascism on all fronts both within subcultural circles and in their everyday lives. The antifascism of the Homosexual Action Groups' agenda was more intense than those of other European and American liberationist groups owing to the legacy of National Socialism. The fight against fascism was necessary, activists argued, because of the continuity of Nazi-era legality in Paragraph 175 and the perpetuation of fascist inequalities in liberal democracy. Leftists and liberals were up in arms at the passing of the 1972 antiradical law (*Radicalenerlaß*), which removed civil servants from their positions for belonging to radical causes, and because this was also something that encompassed queers as well—it only served to confirm their suspicions that the Federal Republic was a fascist state.[98] Feminist gender-nonconformist working groups were quick to spring into action.[99] Appeals to memory would be the glue that bound these elements together.

The largest of the action groups, the West Berlin HAW, was also one of its most radical given the sheer number of students, environmentalists, gender nonconformists, lesbians, and antiwar activists in the divided city. Voicing frustration with the cisgendered male leadership, the HAW Feminist Group held its plenum in November 1973 with the stated aim of bringing together the various strands of thought—antifascism, antiracism, and feminist critique of heteropatriarchy—as intersectional elements of the larger revolutionary struggle. Here, they sought to make good on organic fissures within the various radical queer groups while also responding to Black Panther Huey Newton's call to members of the women's and gay movements to unite in their struggle. Newton's letter had recently been translated into German by the Frankfurt group RotZSchwul and was making the rounds of brother and sister organizations in the UK and on the Continent.[100] In a series of addresses following the plenum, the Feminist Group laid out its agenda, which included calling for the adoption of the pink triangle as a symbol of the movement.[101]

Pink triangle consciousness had already been sparked in 1972 with the publication of Joseph Kohout's memoir *The Man with the Pink Triangle*, published under the pseudonym Heinz Heger.[102] Gays, lesbians, and gender nonconformists of all persuasions were encouraged to don the pink triangle as a show of solidarity with those who could not easily hide their sexuality so that "everyone would, as a gay man, be recognized, discovered, discriminated against, and oppressed!"[103] For activists across West Germany, the symbol illustrated that the dangers then continued to exist now. The Homosexual Action Munich (HAM) put an even finer point on it: "Today we wear the Pink Triangle again in order to show that we perceive this society as a new concentration camp."[104] Virtually all the gay publications covered the story of the camps in making parallels to the present, even as far away as Toronto, Canada, where the first historical exposés were written by the American Germanophile Jim Steakley for the *Body Politic*.[105] Taking seriously this call to prevent fascism's reemergence on the basis of memories of fascism's past, a series of activities were organized across West Germany. In April 1974, the HAW mobilized against a planned prayer service organized by neo-Nazis in honor of Rudolf Hess, who was jailed in nearby Spandau Prison. Here, they drew on what Michael Rothberg has called multidirectional memory to link the memory of the Shoah to the struggle for recognition of the persecution of queers.[106] A poster made these linkages plain, reminding the audience that Hess was a participant in the genocidal regime responsible for the deaths of Jews, queers, and other minorities. Reminded of their plight, queers were admonished to "fight the Nazis of today," tying together what Rosa Hamilton has termed "queerphobia" to the machinations of the liberal state since, as the poster said, "For queer people the Third Reich isn't over."[107] In a sense, this was not hyperbole; Germany's complete disregard for pink triangle victims would mean that those affected would have to wait thirty years to receive recompense for their suffering.

The politics of gender nonconformism forced a period of internal searching in the HAW. But it also surfaced how groups dealt with the rise or, some would say, return of fascism both outside and within the scene. As Jake Newsome and Sébastien Tremblay have argued most recently, the Third Reich emerged onto the terrain of memory in the early 1970s as a rallying point in the struggle for continued sexual liberalization for queers.[108] But whereas for a time it helped create coalitions across difference, it also sowed the seeds of factionalism. By the end of the decade, many of the radical action groups would splinter and fall apart completely, effectively divorcing queer liberation from the political struggles around capitalism and racial, class, gender, and transgender equalities, as complicated as they were. Instead, the focus turned toward more single-issue concerns, from coalitional revolutionary politics to a politics of representation within liberal capitalism.

Out of the Closet and into Politics

If the 1970s marked the emergence of brash new radical queer subjectivities, the splintering of the action groups in the early 1980s was a turning point for queer kinship, which ultimately resulted in the mainstreaming of gay liberation as allied with the goals of the liberal democratic project. This marked a shift away from the multidimensional, intersectionally driven politics of coalition building toward a more dedicated embrace of factionalism along the lines of identity. The memory of the pink triangle loomed large here, as activists increasingly allied with the promise of civil liberties put forward by the Federal Liberal Party, or FDP, jettisoning the more utopian, radical politics of the Alternative Left with its full-frontal assault of the bourgeois foundations of the Federal Republic. Instead, the market-driven middle ground of social-liberal consensus would rule the day, and along with it a myopia around the multifaceted origins of the struggle for gay rights, which included fraught though important discussions around race, gender equity, and gender nonconformity.

Long before the AIDS crisis made itself felt, and queers were demonized in the mainstream press for having brought "the homosexual plague to Europe," there was a cultural flourishing on both sides of the Iron Curtain.[109] Gay and lesbian bookstores and presses were founded—like Verlag rosa Winkel in West Berlin, Männerschwarm Verlag in Hamburg, and Verlag Frauenoffensive in Munich (Women's Offensive Publishers)—gay, lesbian, and feminist bars, cafes, and bookstores enjoyed a robust business, and cultural centers sprang up like the Sonntags-Club in East Berlin.[110] Self-help and counseling centers also took root in West Berlin, Hamburg, and Frankfurt and Spinnboden, the archive "for the discovery and movement around lesbian love," was incorporated officially, after having been organized by Gudrun Schwarz out of the earlier activities of the HAW women's section and LAZ.[111] These new brick-and-mortar spaces left an indelible impact on how queer kinships were shaped. They were accompanied by new emotional styles and marked by new forms of intimacy, companionship, and—in the West more so than in the East—consumerism.[112]

Along with this new emotional style came a newfound sense of having a political voice and a purpose. Demonstrations and kiss-ins became highly ritualized parts of public life in most major cities, but by the late 1970s activists began looking for more direct ways of shaping local and national politics.[113] Then just as now, there was no single home for the queer vote. Homophile organizations were believed to be centrists, reflecting their political moorings as socially conservative and assimilationist. The radical vote split in multiple directions. While New Left activists rejected *Modell Deutschland*, the term coined by leftists in 1976 to refer to the technocratic authoritarianism of the Federal Republic, some more strident activists associated with the National Working Group Repression Against Gays saw fascism all around.[114] Centrist gays and lesbians might have found the politics of either of the two major parties, the Social Democratic SPD and the Free Liberal FDP, appealing.[115] As Samuel Clowes Huneke has shown, the national liberal party even went on record with its support for constitutional and minority rights with the 1972 Freiburg Theses; interestingly, it was also the first party to advocate for a complete repeal of Paragraph 175.[116] Martin Dannecker and Reimut Reiche had studied the gay vote and found that a good portion of the queer electorate had already thrown its support behind these same parties in the 1965 and 1969 general elections.[117] By 1979 all but one of the main parties had attended discussions with the organized emancipation movement in West Berlin and Cologne, showcasing how far they had come from the closet to the street and voting booth.[118]

The West Berlin General Homosexual Action Alliance or AHA (Allgemeine Homosexuelle Arbeitsgemeinschaft), which had severed ties with the more radical HAW, was buoyed by this outpouring of support. It made plans for the coming election, targeting the establishment parties with what the gay magazines had called Aktion '80, which included the repeal of Paragraph 175, reparations for victims of fascism, an end to the so-called pink lists of homosexuals on the police watch list, and that an antidiscrimination law be formulated to protect women and sexual as well as ethnic minorities. Crucially, they advocated that same-sex attraction be removed from the World Health Organization's list of illnesses.[119]

Things came to a head at a podium discussion scheduled for July 12, 1980, in the Beethoven Hall in Bonn. In preparation for over a year, the candidates' meeting would include discussion of the Aktion '80 plan in addition to several core issues of relevance to the various groups represented there, including alternative family formation, police targeting of gays and lesbians, and intergenerational sex. The antidiscrimination bill proposed by the AHA included a possible reform of the Basic Law to ensure sexual minorities equal footing in the constitution.[120] In its emphasis on rights-derived solutions to societal problems, it set a course for a different path than the revolutionary Marxism of the action groups, who preferred to emphasize the socioeconomic basis of oppression. The language of human rights, firmed up in the 1975 Helsinki Accords, seeped further into the conversation, providing a wedge between those who turned to law, constitutionality, and ethics as a way to argue for acceptance and those who saw this as simply another form of cultural hegemony that repressed queers.

In Bonn, candidates from all four parties would be in attendance, affirming to organizers that the last several years of organizing at the regional and youth levels had made a dent within the conventional parties. Hundreds of attendees made their way to the Cold War capital from all four corners of West Germany. It was destined to be a momentous occasion, though not for the reasons hoped. Hosted by Radio Luxemburg's chief journalist Reinhard Münchenhagen, who had established himself on television with a sensationalist interview with a coked-up Klaus Kinski, what ensued was nothing short of mayhem.[121] Minutes in, the 800-member audience became agitated. It booed and hissed. Some attendees were angry at the mainstreaming of radical politics; others guffawed at the gumption of propedophilia groups, denied an official platform, who somehow managed to force their way in to speak.[122] Although the entire point of the discussion had been to shine a light on civil liberties, the glue that bound them all in kinship, the event ended with the AHA exercising an ironfisted control over the question of morality.[123]

As the 1986 edited volume *Alle Schwestern werden Brüder* (All Sisters Become Brothers) makes plain, the question about whether there might be a kind of coalition politics across the different spectrums of identity was answered with a stampede exodus from the venue in Bonn. Ultimately, the FDP would go on to squeak out a coalition government together with the SPD, which would not hold past 1982; but the damage had been done to any effort to bring together a queer vote around kinships of radical sexual freedom. Instead, from this moment forward, in West Germany at least, the emphasis would shift from a politics of post-1968-style radical transformation to one of reluctant acclimation to the liberal order via a rights-based approach wedded to the existing political system. The triumph of the Christian

Democratic Union (CDU) under Helmut Kohl and the concomitant memory boom, together with the swelling AIDS crisis, would cast even more light on the history of persecution as a way to cement a national reckoning with Germany's violent past. But as we'll see, the chasms of kinship would make it hard to heal a house so divided.

Queer Memory and the Specter of Persistent Fascism

In the space of a single decade, the majority of West German queers had successfully taken Rosa von Praunheim's advice and moved the fulcrum of their activism, consumption, and socialization out of the gutter and into the street. *Aufklärungsarbeit*, working with the public in the public eye, took on greater importance. Seeing no end to the seemingly indiscriminate police bathroom raids and formally abandoned by the once reform-minded federal liberals, queers turned inward once again, to the community, where they focused on building a vibrant subculture around mutual aid work.[124] Scores of new bars opened up in Hamburg and Berlin and within its pages *Du & Ich* regularly advertised film nights, get-togethers, and AIDS advice centers. Part of a growing spirit of antiquarianism, which saw all federal states adopt legislation to preserve historical sites, these self-help initiatives sprang into full-fledged historical enterprises from the founding at this same time of the aforementioned Spinnboden archive to the creation in 1984 of the Center for Gay History (Centrum schwule Geschichte) in Cologne. Following on the success of the Eldorado exhibition at the Märkisches Museum, which detailed the 100-year history of Berlin's gay and lesbian communities, the Friends of a Gay Museum and Archive founded the Gay Museum (Schwules Museum*) in 1985 and took up residence on Mehringdamm in the district of Kreuzberg.[125]

Despite the fracturing of the movement, the pink triangle persisted as a unifying symbol for various queer communities, and it would go on to assume even greater importance in the 1980s in the so-called memory boom that overtook East and West Germany as Germans looked to their collective past for ways "to mourn and atone for its victims, to emphasize its diversity, and to celebrate its potential for a truly democratic society."[126] For many West Germans, this turn to memory formed part of the Helmut Kohl government's "intellectual, moral turn" ("geistig, morale Wende") away from social experimentation and back to traditional values. In heritage policy, the goal was to set a course for "collective identification with the West and Europeanism."[127] But it was also something queer activists used to refocus attention on systemic mistreatment at the hands of successive West German governments. In his historic speech in 1985 on the fortieth anniversary of the end of the war, Bundespresident Richard von Weizsäcker gave the first public acknowledgment of gays (among others) as victims of the Third Reich, although as much as this was celebrated by activists it failed to translate into tangible reform. Memorial sites still refused to countenance formal discussion of queer victims. It would not be until 1995 that the international committee overseeing the former camp at Dachau would allow Munich queers to lay a commemorative stone. The same challenge faced activists seeking to honor Magnus Hirschfeld in Berlin, which according to the Ministry for Political Education (Bundeszentrale für Politische Bildung), had only materialized that same year.[128]

Meanwhile, in East Germany, activists were similarly hampered from commemorating queer persecution. As Josie McLellan profiled in *Love in the Time of Communism*, after a series of meetings in the Gethsemane Church in East Berlin's Prenzlauerberg neighborhood, in 1984 the Lesbians in the Church group undertook a brazen action to link International Women's Day to the historical oppression of same-sex-desiring women during the Third Reich.[129] This attempt at retooling the history of persecution was aimed at the East German state, which denied any form of victimization except antifascism. But it was also about expanding the scope of history itself and bringing the activism born out of it to the countryside, beyond Berlin. The next year, eleven women made the trek to Ravensbrück, wreath in hand, only they had been informed on, most likely by the florist tasked with the order. They were driven around by a young policeman who threw epithets at them and interrogated them at length. They were ultimately prevented from attending the official commemoration. Refusing to give in, they did what many GDR citizens did for redress: they wrote letters of complaint (*Eingaben*) and sent them to the Ministry of the Interior and the police. They even went so far as to arrange a meeting with Anni Sindermann, the head of the GDR Ravensbrück committee, a survivor of Nazi political persecution herself. Sindermann agreed to meet with three members of the group in May 1985 in her East Berlin apartment, although once there the activists learned she was and would remain unsympathetic to their cause. Her response was both personal and political. As one member of the group recalled, "she explained that our democracy didn't go that far and could not allow that sort of thing," a reference to the idea of citizen-driven action. Then, she outright denied the existence of lesbians in the camps. Finally, she reiterated the importance of the site's dominant narrative: that antifascists—like herself—were the true targets of Nazi oppression. At one point, she even blurted out that the activists should be grateful they hadn't encountered the violence of the true oppressors: "we [the representatives of Lesbians in the Church] would have been treated much worse by the Nazis, after all most of 'these women' had been killed by the Nazis."[130]

As Anna Hájkova's work has made clear, there was great hostility toward women's intimate kinships in the camps during the Third Reich.[131] In this instance, what was most troubling for Sindermann was the fact that the Lesbians in the Church forced a different narrative association between the past and the present; just as the Nazis had targeted women who failed to conform to the dictates of the People's Community (Volksgemeinschaft), so too did East Germany deny them a critical commemorative footing in relation to that past. The activists sought to inject same-sex love and intimate friendship into the commemorative practices of the East German state. They drew simultaneously on local and transnational gay liberation practices of direct action and speaking back to power, especially around the growing symbolism of the pink triangle, and they folded their project into the story of women's emancipation in the GDR more broadly. Finally, in uniting Nazi-era persecution with surveillance and homophobia, they drew on the history and memory of the past to carve out new directions for queer futurities. Curiously, they enjoyed some success. The following year, the women were welcomed to the camp, even given a tour. The director of the facility showed them the pink triangle on prominent display and invited them to sign the guest book. It seemed they had made a difference except that a month later, when someone else had checked, the guest book had been replaced, erasing all evidence of their visit.[132]

As a postscript to this story, opposition did not always come from outside queer circles. When the Autonomous Feminist Women and Lesbians from Germany and Austria collective sought to commemorate lesbian persecution through a ceremonial "memory orb" (Gedenkkügel) in 2016, although it received the support of the International Ravensbrück Committee, several members of the LSVD (the Lesbian and Gay Organization of Germany) opposed it on the grounds that Paragraph 175 was the only prism through which to gauge queer persecution. Alexander Zinn, a sociologist by training, the press speaker for LSVD, and a member of the Advisory Council of the

Foundation for Memorial Sites in Brandenburg, Germany, called organizers of the orb "riotous lesbians" (*Krawallesben*) intent on promoting the "myth of lesbian persecution." As I discuss in chapter 5 on the Berlin Homo-Monument debate, he consistently stonewalled any attempt to expand the definition of victimization to include women.[133] The Gedenkkügel organizers continued their efforts to secure recognition, staging an exhibition on the memorial site itself in 2017 and a conference on memory cultures. The Schwules Museum* went on to display the memorial orb in their permanent collection. In 2021, with the added support of Martin Lücke—the only person to hold a chair in queer history at a German university—the Magnus Hirschfeld Foundation, and a host of feminist, lesbian, and queer civil society groups including this time the LSVD, an application to the Memorial Commission confirming the scholarly basis for lesbian commemoration was accepted and in spring 2022 the Gedenkkügel found a formal place on the grounds of the former camp. Although Zinn claimed in an interview in the *Berliner Zeitung* that this bore a whiff of the antifascist dogmatism of the former East Germany, cross-community activism supported by scholarship suggests a more accurate parallel might be the legacy of intersectional solidarity that has also served as a hallmark of queer kinship (see plate 4).[134]

Memories of Nazi persecution were a salve in the fight against fascism and forgetting on both sides of the Berlin Wall. For queers, who still fought for public acknowledgment of Nazi-era persecution and the structural inheritance of homophobia in the postwar era, activism took on even greater importance as part of the democratic project, however differently understood in the East and the West. Forgetting was, as Theodor Adorno called it in his 1967 lecture on neofascism, "the scars of a democracy that, to this day, has not yet lived up to its own concept."[135]

To meet the challenge, a politics of radical visibility coalesced around the pink triangle, occasioned by a broad coalition of activists from gay men to gender nonconformists, lesbians, and feminists unified in their view that the memory of Nazi persecution might clarify the revolutionary and multipronged direction of the movement. Ultimately, however, these kinships of difference were unable to maintain momentum in the face of a changing queer scene. Importantly, the symbol that recognized the selective treatment of gay men during the Nazi regime was, from the very beginning, expanded to include multiple converging experiences of oppression. In the East, where official homophobia placed tangible limits on working with the state, queers organized intersectionally, both together and apart from other social justice movements, culminating in the mass outpourings in the fall of 1989 which helped bring about the end of the GDR regime. In the West, the pressure to ally with the wider Left and liberal movement was too great, taking the wind out of the sails of these revolutionary groups and focusing attention instead on working with the state. As we'll see in the coming chapter, these tensions between resistance and adaption will come to play determining roles in how groups in unified Germany understood the need for a memorial to LGBTQIA victims of radical nationalism, and the blind spots that entailed.

THE BOUNDARIES
OF TOLERATION

5

IN THE TIERGARTEN PARK in the center of Berlin, among the many memorials to victims of Nazi racial ideology and genocide, there stands a lone gray cube. Not far from the winding trails leading past the Goethe Monument, famous since the nineteenth century as a cruising ground and near the former headquarters of the T-4 program that authorized the forced killing of the sick, diseased, disabled, and dying, the Memorial to Homosexuals Persecuted under Nazism gives solemn remembrance to state-sponsored persecution. As much as it was the culmination of decades of activism, marked by indifference a good part of the way, the Homo-Monument, as it was soon called, was also the source of controversy when design plans were finally unveiled in 2006. Named the 2.712th Stele as a deliberate evocation of Peter Eisenman's Memorial to the Murdered Jews of Europe across the street, it was a concrete example of Michael Rothberg's multidirectional memory, a claim to representation made possible by relating queer persecution to the history of mass violence in the Holocaust.[1] Only instead of an austere concrete mass, the memorial designed by the artist duo Michael Elmgreen and Ingar Dragset would feature a cutout window in the front of the block where a film played, over and again, in an infinite loop. Visitors would watch as two beautiful young men, dressed in crisp white shirts, kissed.

Even before its unveiling, there was opposition.[2] Critics saw the aesthetic similarities to the Eisenman memorial as obscene, forcing the history of the Holocaust into conversation with the persecution of gay men. Women's groups were similarly up in arms: as one magazine put it, once again "women were forgotten."[3] Gay male historians and heritage workers responded by marshalling years of research into the persecution of homosexuals through Paragraph 175 of the German penal code. The controversy raised all sorts of issues about whose experiences should be immortalized in brick and stone in this stretch of land in the center of Berlin, along the former border between East and West that forms part of the city's Memory Mile (Erin-nerungsmeile). In this symbolic cityscape, which includes a rebuilt Prussian palace, the Brandenburg Gate, and the Memorial to the Murdered Jews of Europe, Germans confront their contentious past, including their role and complicity in mass murder. But as chair of the Central Council of Roma and Sinti in Germany Romani Rose commented in 1991 as plans were underway for commemoration of those murdered during the Holocaust, this was not a Jewish or Roma and Sinti space. It was a German one.[4] These memorials mark Germany's genocidal history while heralding a postnationalist future, one built out of the special responsibility Germans bear to right past wrongs.[5] The only problem, as Vanessa Thompson and Veronika Zablonsky point out, was what to do about lingering examples of inequality, violence, and erasure, including the continuation of structural racism.[6] As we'll see here, the debate around the Homo-Monument in the years before it was unveiled in the spring of 2008 surfaced a host of issues around whose lives mattered historically as well as today in how a nation remembers its past, which would say much about how it also conceptualized its present (see plate 5).

I wrote about the memorial debate in 2014 in a contribution to an edited volume I organized together with Birkbeck historian Matt Cook. I was originally interested in how the controversy operated locally, nationally, and internationally given the importance of the Third Reich and Berlin to transnational kinships in the queer imaginary. I argued that although the monument was the culmination of decades of activism, it actually gained gravitas through the controversy, internationalizing the issue of gay and to a lesser extent lesbian persecution, making Berlin—once again—the center of a global queer consciousness with Nazi persecution at its core.[7] Less obvious to me at the time were the homonationalist overtones of the monument's signage, which instructs the visitor that, unlike other nations "where homosexual love remains illegal and a kiss remains dangerous," Germany had succeeded in realizing its special mission to uphold sexual pluralism. Once a model of barbarism, Germany had learned from its past.[8] This statement is problematic in several ways, not least because it glosses over the decades-long struggle to recognize gay persecution in the first place. Something else was afoot here too, something queer and trans* of color antiracist scholars had been pointing out vociferously at the very same time the debate was raging—and which I, and others, had systematically (perhaps willfully?) overlooked: that alongside misogyny, Islamophobia was alive and well within parts of the queer community.[9] Here it was again, the absent presence in official recognition of German queer suffering.

Aided by collaborations between journalists, academics, and some of the very same gay and lesbian organizations that were actively promoting the monument, notions of migrant homophobia began to seep into public discourse in the years following 9/11, helping fuel a moral panic around supposedly unassimilable Muslims, who since the 1970s had formed Germany's largest expat community. It was this realization, that queer groups had not adequately made antiracism a part of their agenda, that led Judith Butler to refuse the 2010 Pride Award for civil courage.[10] Citing growing anti-immigrant and anti-Muslim sentiments within queer organizations themselves, which had moved increasingly from the periphery to the mainstream, the philosopher took a principled stand. On that day in June, looking out at the hundreds who had gathered at the Brandenburg Gate a short block away from the Homo-Monument, Butler took the mic and said that in good conscience they could not accept such an award when "some of the groups [that organize Berlin Pride] have refused to understand antiracist politics as an essential part of their work."[11] In a dramatic display of the politics of refusal, they named the antiracist activists more deserving of such a prize. These included GLADT (Gays und Lesbians aus der Türkei/ Gays and Lesbians from Turkey), LesMigraS (Lesbische Migrantinnen und Schwarze Lesben/Lesbian Migrants and Black Lesbians, an antiviolence antidiscrimination support group for migrant women and Black lesbians), SUSPECT (a queer antiviolence group), and ReachOut (a counseling center for victims of right-wing violence). Recriminations were immediate. One MC even took the stage shouting "You are not the majority!" to those who cheered in support of Butler's actions. Many, including Jan Feddersen, were incensed. Then a journalist with the left-leaning *taz* newspaper and a former organizer of Christopher Street Day (CSD), the name for Germany's Pride, he seized on Butler's star status. CSD was not racist; Butler was dilettantish and way out of line.[12]

Among the many things this event underscored, not two years after the unveiling of the monument, was that the newfound publicness of gay persecution (and the begrudging acceptance that lesbians might be victims too, albeit in different ways) was forged out of siloed kinships, born of suffering. Despite the very public work of antiracist collectives to draw attention to differentiated experiences of marginalization in the past as well as today, there emerged one "fundamental truth," one scholars have seen operating in other parts of Germany's queer imaginary as well: that history's victims, overwhelmingly, are cis, male, and white.[13] In a postunification Berlin that stared down rampant gentrification, skyrocketing incarceration rates for migrant populations, and a resurgent Far Right, the monument debate blurred together Nazi-era hate crimes and Muslim homophobia. Like the antihate initiatives that targeted migrant youth, the real danger to queer acceptance came not from everyday Germans but from racialized and sexualized others.[14] As we saw in chapter 4, as gay liberation was defanged, depoliticized, and mainstreamed, its fraught history was papered over with one of integration, assimilation, and progress. Instead of a radical rethink of social and political formations for the good of all queer kin, it had been supplanted by a longing for an idealized welfare state that "for racialized people was always ambivalent."[15] This chapter pieces together how that came about.

To do this, I would like to return to this question of the place of LGBTQIA visibility, particularly as it presents around the acknowledgment of Nazi persecution (and continued postwar illegality) as a contravention of human rights. I'm interested in one main question: What is lost as well as gained by the recognition of queer commemoration as an expression of the universality of queer rights? If, as it has been argued, the twentieth century has witnessed an ongoing if sometimes haphazard process of liberalization, one in which queer historical actors moved from shame at the hands of society to pride, through processes of regulation to decriminalization, moving from the margins to the mainstream, what are the epistemological and ontological costs of a kinship based around visibility and recognition understood in this way? Who does it serve in particular? As Robert McRuer has argued for disability, "Visibility and invisibility are not, after all, fixed attributes that somehow permanently attach to any identity."[16] What does the legibility of the queer citizen as victim tell us about the intricate as well as explicit social processes at work in shaping kinship, to the benefit of some but to the detriment of others? In short, what does the mainstreaming of gay liberation in queer commemoration tell us about the limits of a politics of toleration, especially around matters of race, gender, and citizenship?

Did the formal recognition of LGBTQIA rights and crimes against the community serve everyone equally at all times? What historical formations are left out of such tellings and how do these arguments come to cohere in the first place? A representation that depicts selective lives as normative is not just ahistorical, it is pyrrhic. But there is more to the story of how queer victimization was conceptualized around particular kinship formations in the memorial space of postunification Berlin. As Christiane Wilke has argued, the monument not only fails to appreciate the complexity of victim experience today but also fails to address the diverse arrays of subjectivities at work in past historical moments. Despite its location within Berlin's memoryfield—with large and smaller-scaled memorials and monuments dotting the landscape between the Reichstag building, Brandenburg Gate, and Potsdamer Platz—the Homo-Monument raises questions about different categories of victimization and by extension perpetration, leaving it to the visitor to parse together how National Socialism was lived and perpetuated as well as resisted. Indeed, there are several moral complexities at work here. One is how to think about a persecuted minority that benefited from race laws that targeted some victims more unequivocally and harshly than others. Another is the challenge of defining queer kinship through victimization, whether to draw on legal terms or societal repression. A third, is how to interpret how the lessons of persecution are framed and deployed today as part of Germany's historic debt to the world to eradicate homophobia, a problem located, the memorial claims, beyond its borders.[17] What the debate around the memorial shows is that when kinship is framed in identitarian terms, it is unable to nurture solidarities around difference.

In what follows, I will map out the foundation for a way to think about queer commemoration less as a project of homogenization and more as opening up the complex, entangled, and sometimes contradictory ways in which queer people in divided and reunited Germany and beyond negotiated what kinship with past violence might look like, and how and in what moments that complexity fell away. This chapter explains what should be self-evident, that not all queers past and present were or are oriented toward progressive politics; that on matters of race, age, immigration status, and gender presentation there were and continue to be contestations over who belongs to the category of victim and hence is kin. This has direct ramifications for who deserves redress, who challenges contemporary norms, and who forms part of the wider LGBTQIA community?[18] If we wish to sediment a more encompassing retributive methodology for remembering victims of violence as the basis for a robust civil society, we must continue unpacking the shortcomings of gay liberation around matters of race and gender nonconformism so as to better understand how queer memory became mainstreamed to serve "properly queer" (and trans*) citizens.[19]

The Limits of Liberalism

In today's Europe, sexuality enjoys a privileged status as a prism through which to gauge all manner of claims around the strengths or weaknesses of democratic pluralism.[20] Yet what the litmus test of progress and enlightenment is for some is society's nadir for others. These contradictory tendencies have always accompanied sexuality as a category of analysis. The current state of play is particularly fractious, with the explicit and organized mobilization of so-called antigender campaigns chipping away at the gains made under the umbrella of sexual citizenship; this includes gender equity laws, family law, reproductive and LGBTQIA rights, and academic feminism. Antigender campaigns are mobilized chiefly on the conservative right as a response to the secularization of European society.[21] They are often supported by the Vatican directly, together with a panoply of Far Right constituents who all agree that women's equality measures, access to abortion, queer workplace protections, so-called gender ideology, civil union, registered partnerships, and queer adoption undermine tradition.[22] Antigender platforms are especially visible in places like Hungary, which has gone so far as to outlaw the teaching of gender studies in universities, and also in Poland where the Law and Justice Party has regularly targeted the abortion law and city councils and school boards have outlawed discussion of LGBTQIA rights.[23]

We would be remiss in thinking this is solely a problem facing Eastern European states with a shallower history of democracy. First, the roots of these campaigns extend back to before 1989, to the 1960s and early 1970s, as a form of retraditionalization that cut across the Iron Curtain in the face of postwar social reforms (to family law, to reproductive rights, to the place of homosexuality in society, and also in response to the growing consumer-oriented dreams and desires of the population).[24] Second, the attack on cosmopolitanism, pluralism, and human rights through a gender and sexuality lens is prevalent in Western Europe as well, in some of Europe's most established democracies, where they are often also caught up in a mix of racial anxieties around migration, religion, and perceived challenges to secular humanism.[25] We see it among populist groups like the Alternative für Deutschland in Germany advocating for a return to family values. We see it in a toxic masculinity that mixes antifeminism, antisemitism, and Islamophobic sentiments like those that motivated the 2019 Halle synagogue shooter, who killed ten people "with migration background" (the problematic German phrasing for people with mixed heritage who might even hold a German passport). And we saw it in the murder of the doctoral student Marwa Ali El-Sherbini—at the hands of a white German—in a court of law in Dresden in 2009 where she sought redress for his racist verbal abuse.

But just as Wendy Brown articulated in *Regulating Aversion* and *The Power of Tolerance*, we would be wrong to see these challenges to privacy, sexuality, and personhood as solely the domain of right-of-center thinking.[26] Brown warns against uncritical celebrations of tolerance as a cornerstone of Western modernity. Anything but a transcendent, universal concept, tolerance must be historicized and placed in its various contexts. Crucially, it must be analyzed for "how it operates normatively, and how its normativity is rendered oblique almost to the point of invisibility."[27] Because liberal ideals of toleration must be conferred on others, those who meet the standards of worthiness however defined, they are always already reflective of power imbalances. These tensions around belonging, identity, and legacies of struggle, understood in different ways, are found across the political spectrum, from the Center Left to the Far Right. While it is obvious that the Far Right's delegitimization of same-sex sexuality is a tactic to win votes, less attention has been given to the way centrists and even progressives have built their argument for inclusion into the family of rights and respectability at the expense of others, and the way race and gender interweave into claims for toleration. With this in mind, it bears asking, then, How did it come to pass that, by 2008, Germany had seen gay and lesbian rights defined as human rights, at precisely the same time that hate-crime activism and integration-related policies targeting the country's Muslim minorities increasingly identified migrants as a danger to this newfound cosmopolitanism? How does the presumption of toleration undermine queer kinship?

The Christopher Street Day organizers cannot be entirely faulted for not understanding how deeply ingrained race is in the movement. Histories of sexology and gay rights rarely explored the ways in which whiteness shaped

the definition of homosexuality and transsexuality by extension, to say nothing of the structural importance of empire to definitions of civilization and
personhood at the turn of the nineteenth century and into the twentieth.
As Laurie Marhoefer puts it, the homosexual was made white insofar as this
legacy has never truly been unpacked, least of all by the activists who have
inherited this mainstreamed version of queer politics after the homogenization of gay liberation in the 1980s.[28] Despite being an opponent of racism
and empire, Magnus Hirschfeld, who helped make Berlin a center of the gay
rights movement, drew on racialized notions of civilization—as did many in
his time—to buttress the call for liberalization of repressive sexual values and
full citizenship for gays and lesbians.[29] One hundred years later, the target
of repressive sexuality was no longer the state, but "persons with migration
background." A series of interventions dotted the landscape of the early
2000s, some from more predictable conservative circles, and others from
more progressive groups. Well before the 2015 Cologne assaults, which
heightened the discourse even more, there was a call for more research
into hate crimes, something notoriously absent from the German arena
given fears around Nazi-era intransigence in matters of policing. Scene
newspapers like *Jungle World*, *Zitty*, and the queer magazine *Siegessäule*
called for more education in neighborhoods thought to harbor "homophobic attitudes" (i.e., where there was a higher population of racialized
inhabitants). Some advocated for ever more police presence in traditional
gay spaces, which, drawing on other cities where this has occurred, is
highly divisive given the historic enmity between LGBTQIA groups and cops.
For a time, the largest national lesbian and gay organization, the LSVD,
threw its support behind a "Muslim Test" linking diversity to citizenship.[30]
While it is perhaps not surprising to hear conservative politicians tout the
cause of "law and order" and coupling it with sexual attitudes, this new
fixation with minoritarian morality gradually informed the position of
the Green Party/Bundnis 90, who in 2009 threw their backing behind
new anti–hate crime measures to combat homophobia as an integration
issue.[31] Meanwhile, the Social Democrats worked together with the Left
Party (the inheritor of the East German Communist Party) and passed
a more progressive city ordinance targeting funds for more education,
youth work, and strengthening civil society institutions along a diversity
model. While this was a step in the right direction, it still lent itself to a
focus on policing instead of prevention, which had the effect of normalizing
revanchist measures against an already overpoliced, racialized population.

Persons with a migration background were presumed to be always already in need of intervention, often at the hands of the state or by arm's-length institutions acting in its name.[32]

While these definitions of endangerment and victimization were percolating in the public eye, the Homo-Monument was undergoing its own scrutiny from within the primarily white gay, lesbian, and feminist scenes. How did the quest for retribution—so hard won—intersect with this other battle being waged over diversity and the politics of integration and kinship? How did it rely on and perpetuate distinct kinship formulations over time, which had the effect of marginalizing certain lives and experiences over others? What might we learn by centering those overlapping, though suppressed, oppressions especially around the linkages between hegemonic memory formations and the pitfalls of toleration at the beginning of the twenty-first century and how they were called on to reinforce a vision of Germany as transcending hate, without recognizing the fictions that perpetuate this telling?

Making Space for Queer Place

Berlin is a city unlike many others, where the specter of history looms particularly large. It is pressed into the landscape, it adorns the buildings, and it is worn on the faces of each generation of city dwellers tasked with finding some way of coming to terms with its heinous past. For the tourist, the city is as fascinating as it is macabre. Along the city's streets and alleyways, copper memorial plaques compete for attention with shiny golden "stumbling stones" (*Stolpersteine*)—small metallic squares hammered into the sidewalk in front of buildings once occupied by those who were rounded up, deported, and killed by the Nazis. The void spaces along the path of the Berlin Wall that once fascinated cultural critics in the early 1990s have long been replaced with several large-scale memorials.[33] Indeed, the entire area along the former death strip between the Reichstag building, the Brandenburg Gate, and Potsdamer Platz has been radically reconstructed as a dedicated space of pilgrimage and introspection, where visitors wander around the concrete stele and reflection ponds in a contemplative fashion, calling to mind—momentarily—the lives, horrors, and fate of the various victims of the Third Reich. As much a transnational space as a German one, each year it plays host to thousands of curious onlookers who make their trek to the capital in pursuit of a personal encounter with Berlin's tragic past.

History is not only manifest in the city's architecture and in its built environment; it comes alive in people's thoughts and minds in the mental maps they draw for themselves based on what they've heard tell of already or read about somewhere. It forms the basis of what they hope to discover and often colors what they find.[34] As the past rubs up against the present, the city's abstract spaces transform into concrete places—of memory, community, even identity. This happens through a range of overlapping interactions "from the global to the intimately tiny."[35] Always evocative, these notions of place are also frenetic, changing, and on the move. They are made and remade through the official meanings envisioned in the grand designs of planners, architects, and government officials, and they are altered, co-opted, and transformed in the everyday tactics of ordinary people forging their own path through the city.[36] What a place represents and means—on an individual or collective level—is imagined and conjured up, experienced and lived, sensed and felt, talked about, fought over, romanticized, and more often than not, rigorously disputed. When the space in question is imbued with national importance, like a memorial site, existing social cleavages become especially apparent; this can be of tremendous help in thinking about how the past is mobilized in how we understand and represent present-day concerns.

The discord generated in 2006 by the proposed plan to commemorate LGBTQIA victims of National Socialism provides an excellent case for analyzing how activists and historians, politicians and city planners—and readers of the international queer media—helped create a space for a queer place in contemporary Berlin.[37] By thinking about efforts to build a national LGBTQIA memorial in Berlin as an exercise in queer place making, I am not suggesting that we imagine it simply as an endeavor by and for queer-identified people.[38] Rather, what was truly queer about the making of this memorial was the unique way in which commemorative strategies unleashed a full-scale crisis of representation, mobilizing in its wake a cacophony of voices that transcended the boundaries of city and nation, lesbian and gay, past and present. Indeed, in considering the transregional ways in which people grappled with National Socialism's enduring legacy when debating the form and function of a simple concrete cuboid in the central Tiergarten park, we are forced to consider aesthetic questions and the debates they engender as critical sites of memory production, social identity, emotions, and community. These debates drew on the history of injury and harm to imagine a future free of homophobia, except the specter of past crimes became transformed into a justification for policing the boundaries of today's imagined community, one

forged around race-blind notions of queer belonging and the marginalization of women's and trans* experience.[39] This debate not only sheds light
on the complicated memorial politics of the early twenty-first century but
also raises important questions about Berlin's contemporary meaning as an
international symbol of human rights triumphs.[40]

Memorials

Ever since the fall of the Berlin Wall, historians and historical geographers
have spilled much ink on the pernicious role of symbolic spaces in creating the
appearance of cohesive identities.[41] Whether triumphalist commemorations
of watershed moments in the birth of a nation or more solemn undertakings, more often than not, memorials are unruly manifestations of intensely
selective memories, representing in concrete and stone the experiences
and desires of particular groups over others. Memorials struggle to capture
multiple and coexisting experiences of marginalization and oppression.[42]
And then there are the complex interactions and entanglements behind the
impulse to commemorate itself, which are often obfuscated by the projection
and appearance of consensus in the rush to unveil a realized design. This is
not to conjure up the specter of overzealous lobby groups; changes to the
built environment are never benign. As Anthony King suggests in his iconic
essay "Architecture, Capital, and the Globalization of Culture," urban forms
"do not just represent, or reflect social order, they actually constitute much
of social and cultural existence."[43] In places like Berlin, with such a highly
fraught and traumatic history, the memorial landscape is particularly tricky.
The intensity of building after the fall of the wall may have created opportunities for large-scale changes to the physical landscape, but it also unleashed
heated debate as Germans contemplated the impact of these alterations on
changing perceptions of past crimes.[44]

The decision to construct several memorial sites in the center of the city
may have appeared as a form of consensus building, but in actuality it was
greeted with skepticism on many sides. At stake was the nature of victimization as the bedrock of queer kinship, and what it meant for the reunified city
to embark on commemoration as official policy. As the historian James Young
put it in his brief to the parliamentary committee on media and culture in
March 1999, "No other nation has ever attempted to re-unite itself on the
bedrock memory of its crimes or to make commemoration of its crimes
the topographical centre of gravity in its capital."[45] With reunification a

not-yet distant memory, there were in fact several concerns percolating about, the largest of which was the problem of different memorial cultures in the former East and West Germanys. In the German Democratic Republic, or GDR, which ceased to exist in 1990, victimization was explicitly linked to ideology, with communists often at the center of memorial campaigns. As we saw in the last chapter, this did not stop East German citizens from trying to expand the definition of victim.[46] State response was often swift and relied on the help of informants. Although the GDR no longer stood by the 1990s, queer activists could not help but wonder what remained of these attitudes.

A team of prominent and largely West German historians, accompanied by the Nobel prize–winning author Günter Grass, took a different tack in a 1998 open letter to then-chancellor Helmut Kohl. Their concern was that the "abstract installation of oppressively gigantic proportions on an area the size of a sports stadium" would not create the "place of quiet mourning and remembrance, of warning or enlightenment" that the promoters envisaged.[47] Despite the appearance of simple contrarianism, the group was among the few to call attention to the need for suitable strategies to mark and remember the experiences of the so-called other victims including the Sinti and Roma, homosexuals, Soviet prisoners of war, and the disabled.

How the newly reunified nation elected to commemorate its past elicited considerable international interest as well.[48] The Berlin memorial debate filled pages of commentary in daily newspapers, garnering the attention of a broad readership. As Jennifer Jordan has argued, Berlin's memorial sites emerged as places of deep significance to European internationalism, especially around the issue of human rights.[49] This opened up a space for minoritarian voices to draw on the legacy of historical injustice to address contemporary inequalities and concerns. The question then became, who would speak for which issue and how?

The LSVD, then overwhelmingly white, cis, and male, would be that lobby. Having made a name for its work on the city's hate-crime initiative, it positioned itself to speak for the queer community despite the fact—it bears remembering—that there were myriad groups of queer, queer of color, lesbian, and trans* activists in Berlin. From the 1990s onward, once it was announced that the city would adopt the New York architect Peter Eisenman's design for the Monument to the Murdered Jews of Europe, each design competition for a new memorial resulted in countless hours of moral and ethical soul searching. After close to a decade of lobbying for national recognition of Nazi crimes and emboldened by Eisenman's memorial, queer activists in Germany felt a glimmer of hope with the 1999 announcement that the Federal Republic was morally obligated "to commemorate the other victims of National Socialism in appropriate ways."[50] Buoyed by this decision, the LSVD built on the actions of earlier initiatives like the Schöneberg district memorial at Nollendorfplatz and submitted a formal petition for a queer monument.[51] The red-green majority in the federal parliament (Bundestag) ensured that in 2003 the request would be honored, and within two years the Berlin Senate Administration for Science, Research, and Culture, Urban, and Architectural Art (Senatsverwaltung für Wissenschaft, Forschung und Kultur Kunst im Stadtraum und am Bau) tendered an open call for design submissions to be vetted first by the LSVD, together with the initiative for the "Commemoration of Homosexual Victims" (Initiative "Der homosexuellen Opfer gedenken"). Of the 127 submissions received from as far away as Tel Aviv, New York, and London, they narrowed the field to 26, to be adjudicated by an 11-member prize committee consisting of the Berlin senator for city development, a prominent art historian, several curators and museum directors, two artists, and Günter Dworek, representing the LSVD.[52]

By 2006 it looked as though the city, state, and nation were well on their way to honoring the homosexual victims of Paragraph 175.[53] The prize committee decided on the submission from the Scandinavian artists and lovers Michael Elmgreen and Ingar Dragset in January 2006 because of the way its innovative minimalist cube design evoked a spectral sense of grief and loss.[54] For many, the simple design bore a striking resemblance to the blocklike stele of the neighboring Holocaust memorial, an aesthetic nod to the pathos of the Eisenman design to solidify an argument about queer suffering as multidirectional memory.[55] It included a single-pane glass window, behind which would screen a continuously running black-and-white film with what one journalist termed "two kissing boys in ironed shirts." Given that, by his estimation, a good portion of the population still found "kissing boys repulsive," this was deemed art "at its most provocative."[56] No doubt the Elmgreen and Dragset design held special resonance with the LSVD, given its own advocacy around contemporary homophobia in the late 2000s. Describing itself as "the biggest civil rights, self-help and welfare organization for gays and lesbians" in Germany, the LSVD adopted the integration of migrants as its main objective after securing the Life Partnership Act in 2001, which paved the way for civil union. With that, it gradually inserted itself into a larger, globalized "integration" discourse, receiving state funds for target initiatives, and rising from a local gay organization to a national presence. By

2006 it had even been granted UN observer status.[57] It is not unimaginable that it would bring this same set of commitments to the memorial debate.

At the same time that they were advocating for a memorial and deciding on the design, LSVD activists were also hard at work crafting education campaigns, conducting surveys, and sponsoring academic initiatives such as the pseudoscientific Simon Study.[58] Defining Germanness as an ethnic category with a definition that was even more strict than contemporary nationality laws, the Simon Study found that homophobia was a concern across milieus. Yet LSVD interventions continued to focus almost exclusively on the Turkish community.[59] Indeed, as Christopher Ewing has argued most compellingly, their own survey results seemed not to dissuade them of their conviction that "Turkish stemming" youth were particularly needy of intervention.[60] Alongside education campaigns, another antiviolence advocacy group, MANEO, which itself had ties to the LSVD, turned to direct action to further address the connections between homophobia and Islam. Mosques became a site of particular interest for white gay activism, with groups of men conducting dramatic kiss-ins in gentrifying neighborhoods with higher than average demographics of working-class and migrant communities.[61] Photos of "public kiss" actions would surface in newspaper stories and poster campaigns alongside headers that pointed in no uncertain terms at the subject of ire ("Muslims against Gays").[62] Unlike the queer kiss-ins of the AIDS era, which took place in front of a hostile public that harbored hopes that the kissers might die, these performances earned the respect of the heteronormative majority population as emblems of Western values and freedom.[63] Although they were formulated with local issues in mind, they were also part of an evolving global queer consciousness with gays and lesbians and to a lesser extent trans* persons demanding rights of sovereignty and sexual citizenship. One kiss-in campaign, held under the mantra "Protect every kiss" (in English), was even staged on May 17 to coincide with International Day against Homophobia. Elmgreen and Dragset's choice of two boys kissing resonated as an emblem of the whiteness of gay identity because it was more than a hallmark of queer survival; it was, as Jin Haritaworn has noted, a response to the particular struggles in Germany over the problem of homophobia— "toleration, privacy, respectability, choice and freedom," framed within "an explicitly racialized iconography and vocabulary."[64] This particular vision of kinship as connected to white European gay vulnerability gained its charge from a narrow view of migrant assimilation.[65]

The Politics of Representation

Despite a few misgivings about the harsh modernism of the cuboid, which differed quite significantly from other monuments in Cologne, Frankfurt, and Amsterdam, the design adjudication committee seemed to have weathered the storm of public opinion in the initial stages, that is until May 2006, when people started to notice there wasn't any sign of women in the monument.[66] Noted feminist editor of *EMMA* magazine Alice Schwarzer mounted a full-scale media attack, opening the floodgates of identity politics. Her argument also focused on the image of the two men kissing, but not because it traded on racialized notions of victim and aggressor. Rather, it was that the design did not just render women invisible, it wrote women out of the history of persecution completely.[67] In a coordinated article in the left-leaning *taz* newspaper, the caberettist Maren Kroymann reiterated many of the same points raised by Schwarzer, most notably that lesbians continued to represent an invisible minority, whose experiences failed then as now to resonate within the majority culture. Using legal persecution as the benchmark of victimization, the whole of women's agency and experience during the Third Reich fell away.[68] Furthermore, she claimed, in framing the memorial, aesthetically, around men's sexuality, Elmgreen and Dragset simply perpetuated the social isolation of lesbians, only they did so both in the name of honoring the victims and in critiquing the here and now. Appealing to them as fellow artists, Kroymann argued that "work with images and symbols" has the potential to make a statement on present injustice as well. The masculine bias was drafted into the very plans themselves. Not only would the proposed memorial fail in its intended purpose of commemorating the dead, if it were built without alteration, it threatened to undercut any meaningful effort to confront present-day homophobia. This action on the part of Schwarzer and Kroymann, and all those signatories who by November 2006 had added their names to the petition "for women in the Homo-Monument," fundamentally changed the terms of engagement. In the following two years, during which time the memorial was reconceived, redesigned, and finally unveiled in the summer of 2008, activists and opponents clashed over the gender of design and history, and despite some tough going, managed to shift the focus firmly away from past injustice to present-day identity politics and all that that entails.

After the *EMMA* action, three things happened: the gender of persecution was debated, the question of collective memory and artistic endeavor was questioned, and finally, a compromise was reached with aspects of the memorial's design being altered. The debate turned on a few core issues. Alongside claims of the historic (and ongoing) occlusion of women from history and history making (two separate but related matters) was the issue of whose task it should be to undertake commemoration generally, whether the LSVD truly spoke for all queer groups or whether the historic enmity toward gays and lesbians was better left to small-scale actions such as those from the decade before, many of which witnessed significant participation of women both separate from and in solidarity with men. Amid all this, the story of discord and rising emotions traveled out of Germany and into the pages of gay and lesbian news media in the UK, the United States, and Canada. So as not to see the project totally derailed, and perhaps to ensure their relevance as the premier gay and lesbian organization, the LSVD orchestrated a series of podium discussions to address the issues swiftly, judiciously, and in public. These, too, were covered extensively by the local Berlin newspapers, by the national media, and, increasingly, by the international queer press. In two of the sessions, the artists were even on hand to defend their design decisions. In a pointed statement later published on the LSVD website entitled "A Portrait Is Not Representative," they systematically addressed the arguments advanced in the *EMMA* article.

They began their commentary by carefully articulating their sympathy for the claim of marginalization, be it in the art world or on the job site. Barely a paragraph in, they dropped this conciliatory tone and turned their sights instead on what they termed the "populist attack unleashed by *EMMA*." "Why on earth would we want to exclude women? Or transsexuals," they exclaimed, exasperated by the campaign. Then something interesting happened. Drawing on aspects of their own aesthetic practice, they put forward a sophisticated discussion of the gender of oppression. "Who has the right to define 'the feminine' and 'the masculine'?" They suggested that, according to the *EMMA* line, "This could be interpreted as a return to traditional and strongly divided depictions of men and women's lives." The decision to fill the memorial's window with a film of two youths kissing was an attempt to portray "a vision of intimacy and tenderness" in the face of rampant homophobia. This image of an "eternal kiss" was to serve as a corrective to the sense of alienation and trauma victims suffer, a sentiment so personal and yet all-encompassing that it "surpasses representation." The pain caused by homophobia exceeds words and images, they argued, and so, the artist is left with only gestures toward lived experience. At the same time that they wished to tackle difficult and ongoing societal problems with their work, theirs was not an experiment in verisimilitude. Indeed, on this they were emphatic, going so far as to say that "a picture or portrait can never be a true representation of something." Accusing the *EMMA* editors of failing to perceive the way they evoked the gender of oppression in their sense of queer kinship—in this case, through the image of youthful and ebullient masculine desire as a salve against a violent and homophobic normative masculinity—Elmgreen and Dragset cheekily claimed that they even failed to recognize the echoes of feminist aesthetic tradition in their plan. In seeking to counter the notion that the film loop made white male sexuality the universal standard for a generalized gay and lesbian experience, rendering men and men's experience the touchstone for all oppression, they returned to this issue of the strengths and limitations of metaphor in renderings of this sort. In a final exasperated outpouring, they further complicated the picture: "We ask ourselves, what kind of depiction of men and masculinity do the editors of *EMMA* expect from us? What if we had two feminine boys that might be easily perceived as girls? What about two masculine girls? Would that be allowed? . . . What counts as sexuality and identity should not be controlled by outmoded markers of what is feminine and masculine."[69] One wonders how the artists would have reacted to the news that surfaced in 2017 that one of the boys in the original film would go on to have a career as a Far Right Danish populist and television personality.[70]

In three single-spaced pages of emotionally inflected prose, in August Elmgreen and Dragset gave voice to their frustration with what they perceived to be the intellectual rigidity of the *EMMA* editorial position. Despite their effort to justify their design choices on the level of aesthetics, it is clear from their exculpatory tone that there was a disconnect between their artistic vision and any sense of responsibility for audience reaction. It is obvious, too, that they were deeply invested in defending their artistic integrity at all costs, which they based around a keenly resonant awareness of the conversations at play between gender, homophobia, and power. While they made some good points about the need to think about degrees of gender variance and possible connections to homophobia, this is not a form of disidentification—of playing off of dominant discourses so as to critique them from within. In disavowing the representational power of their choice of image—an image, it bears saying, with a long aesthetic tradition we will recall that venerates youth, immanence, and beauty as the cornerstone of gay identity—they actually undercut the political power of art.[71] Echoing the language of toleration in the kiss-ins, they underscored that "we are in the end all fighting for a diverse and open society." Yet, as was evident in their statement, they had no trouble foreclosing any suggestion of revisiting their design in response to claims that it had a normativizing effect of its own.[72]

What the artists could not know was that the memorial debate was a replay of debates in the mid-1990s among historians and activist scholars in Germany around lesbians as victims of the regime.[73] The storm had been brewing, in other words, for some time. The memorial brought this out into a broader public. An earlier effort to commemorate NS persecution in Berlin, the "Initiative Gay Monument," had appealed to the Berlin Senate to find suitable ways to articulate gay male suffering under the Nazis. While this centered specifically on men's experiences, historian Ilse Kokula pushed even then for a wider conceptualization of victimization, beyond identity. In her report to the Senate, she noted that such a monument might "cast light on the shared experiences of lesbians and gay men as well as other groups of sexual minorities during National Socialism."[74] Similar sentiments were tabled in 2006, in the aftermath of the *EMMA* action, with the argument that a broadened notion of persecution would enable a richer sense of how different target groups navigated the regime. The backlash was immediate, immense, and sometimes quite juvenile, as in August 2006 when *taz* journalist Jan Feddersen argued in print that "there had been BDM (League of German Girls) lesbian dances well into the 1940s while gay men were persecuted by the Nazis."[75] As long as persecution was defined in identitarian terms, ill-attuned to the broad spectrum of experiences of risk, marginalization, persecution, and social death, kinship on the subject of victimization remained illusory.

A month after Elmgreen and Dragset went public with their position, following a general membership meeting in October 2006, the LSVD posted a resolution on its website calling for much-hoped-for solidarity between gays and lesbians in order to work collectively toward the realization of the memorial's original purpose, to serve as "a visible statement against intolerance, enmity, and isolation." This call for solidarity, however, was premised on the condition that the artists' vision of "an infinite loop of two men kissing" be kept in the final design, both because this was adjudicated by a jury and also because it conformed to the history of persecution more generally, a history that disproportionately affected men. As detailed in her 200-page report on the monument debate, Corinna Tomberger noted that with that slippage, the LSVD failed to ease tensions percolating through the community around how to think more capaciously about the vicissitudes of what Sam Clowes Huneke would acknowledge in 2021 to be lesbians' heterogeneous persecution.[76]

As one might imagine, this action only had the effect of further angering the *EMMA* editorial collective. Under the heading "Stop the Homo-Monument!" Schwarzer and her supporters referenced the "patriarchal dominance of the gay men in the movement and the lack of power of lesbians in positions of leadership."[77] Their voices held resonance beyond the feminist magazine. A special issue of the major LGBTQIA scene newspaper, *Siegessäule*, showcased opposing positions with members of the Schwules Museum*, the initiative "Remember the Homosexual NS Victims," and a former board member of the Foundation for Brandenburg State Memorials represented in the opinion piece alongside a single pro-*EMMA* respondent.[78] Although the question of lesbian marginalization garnered minimal support in the gay press, the position had managed to secure the support of a well-respected member of the European Parliament, who sent a letter to the chair of the Federal Cultural Commission recommending action. Having learned of the artists' reticence to reconceptualize the piece, Lissy Gröner underscored that "there is enough room in the planned memorial site" for both sets of stories. She raised an idea that had long been floating about: the addition of an information sign outlining the shared but different experiences of historical and ongoing persecution, while reminding her federal colleagues that this issue "had awakened European interest." For this reason, she pleaded with them to ensure that "the exclusion of lesbian women" not be allowed to occur.[79] In other words, this issue of what constituted queer kinship within the politics of memory ran parallel to the homophobia debate and had now acquired added international resonance.

Part of the difficulty in expanding the definition of persecution in the spirit of intersectional queer kinship was that Nazi crimes played a signature role in gay identity in the post-1945 period.[80] The Tiergarten itself holds a special place in the story of gay male sociability. Unlike the location of the Eisenman memorial across the street, historian Andreas Pretzel argued, "for homosexuals" the Tiergarten "is a historical and authentic place."[81] Designed in the 1830s by the landscape artist Peter Joseph Lenné as a place of relaxation and respite from the growing city, that the park served as an important node in the city's famously multihued sexual geography was no secret.[82] As criminal case files from the period tell us, in the late 1930s and 1940s it was also a place of persecution, with many men fearing being caught out by so-called stool pigeons (*Lockvögel*)—Hitler Youth specially tasked to lure men with the promise of intergenerational sex only to denounce them later at the nearby Gestapo and criminal police precinct.[83]

This link between sex, space, sociability, and persecution had emerged as a core theme in many of the design submissions, and it also formed a vital part of the lesbian critique of the proposed memorial. Marcel Odenbach had pitched the idea of a so-called warm lake on the proposed site, complete with tropical water lilies—a pun on the notion of "warmer Brüder" or warm brothers in English—the derogatory term for same-sex-desiring men—conjoined with a symbol of immanent sexuality. The submission by Sabrina Cegla, Ingo Vetter, and Amit Epstein proposed a 620-meter labyrinth in artificial baroque style, overlaying the image of cruising, the search for a life partner, and the quest for a way out of persecution. The theme of cruising, landscape, and desire was also taken up by Piotr Nathan, who planned to create a stone lake out of six steel walls. Each would be lined on the outside with vines. Obfuscated among the greenery was a door designed to keep at bay the bourgeois conformity lurking on the other side. Katja Augustin, Jörg Prinz, and Carsten Wieworra made it all the way to the final round with their proposed planting of 100 meters' worth of nonindigenous trees, in whose branches would be placed symbols of love and devotion alongside the names of well-known gays and lesbians from the period of Nazi persecution. Another suggestion was for a half circle of stone, playing off of the Eisenman design in a different way and serving as a formal space of reflection and repose from which to contemplate the history of persecution more broadly. This design might have functioned similarly to the memorial to Sinti and Roma which has since had a kind of "ambiguous productivity" in affording marginal groups a stage from which to voice intersectional, transtemporal opposition to contemporary debates.[84]

In Pretzel's estimation, the winning submission by Elmgreen and Dragset was careful to sidestep well-worn homophobic clichés while equally avoiding the all-too-familiar symbology of the now-ubiquitous pink triangle.[85] Operating on the level of abstraction, it seemed best suited to conjure up an emotional response from the imagined visitor through the proposed film's use of images of intimacy and desire, with a bit of voyeurism tacked on. Cruising and public sex were woven into the memorial, gestured toward if not made explicit. A possible problem with the design, Pretzel conceded, was its refusal to address the hierarchical nature of kinship through victimization, and it was here, he suggested, that the artists may have opened themselves up to criticism and scorn.[86] And scorn there was. In a final salvo reminiscent of gay liberation's denigration of cruising, Schwarzer called on Elmgreen and Dragset to rethink their "homage to toilet sex" (*Klappensex*) since it was a most unfitting contribution to Berlin's memorial landscape. "An abstract artistic design should be able to speak to both experiences," she argued, citing that over a thousand men and women—including members of Queer Nations, a newly formed LGBTQIA organization that had been working behind the scenes to try to find a third way out of the quagmire—now called for a "radical new conceptualization."[87]

Gendering Persecution

There was widespread worry among those in the heritage industry that the fissures of kinship between gays and lesbians and their respective organizations might grow in size and derail the project altogether. On its webpage, and then downloaded, annotated, and sent around to members of the LSVD and Queer Nations, the director of the Berlin-Brandenburg State Office of Memorials posted a statement in December 2006 outlining his organization's concern that the issue had gone so far as to "push the memorialization of homosexual victims of Nazi persecution into the background." Highlighting the shifting temporal context of commemoration through the course of this debate, Günter Morsch noted that, at the same time that Nazi-era persecution was falling out of sight, the memorial was quickly moving away from the temporal moorings of its original mandate. In embracing a "more contemporary and future-oriented perspective," it teetered dangerously toward a full-fledged "political instrumentalization of memory."[88] In order to avoid this, the LSVD pulled together several podium discussions to speak specifically to the issues of representation, space, and commemoration. On an evening in mid-January, at the so-called MANEO-Soirée in the ballroom of the Charlottenburg-Wilmersdorf district city hall, sponsored again by the antiviolence action group, Pretzel and Kroymann were joined by an SPD (Socialist Party of Germany) member of the federal parliament, the chairperson of the Left Party (die Linke), and the LSVD's Günter Dworek. Moderated by the *taz*'s Jan Feddersen—who had already voiced his displeasure at the inclusion of lesbians in this history and would in a few more years speak out against Butler's intervention at the Christopher Street Day event—this evening was designed to provide a public airing of a variety of issues, from the suitability of the Elmgreen and Dragset design to "a debate that never gets talked about, the possibility of a brotherly or sisterly understanding (*geschwisterliches Verstanden*) of homosexuality."[89] Nowhere on the agenda was there any talk of the links between homophobia and transphobia—this had not yet been taken up in earnest as a subject of discussion—although migrant homophobia was the obvious elephant in the room given the urgency of linking the memorial to contemporary concerns.

Although she had participated in a fact-finding colloquium in 2005 that helped launch the design competition, Claudia Schoppmann was unequivocal in condemning the memorial for failing to adequately represent lesbians as victims of historical violence. She cited examples from the research that had gone into her landmark publication *Days of Masquerade: Life Stories of Lesbians during the Third Reich*. Lesbians were persecuted by the Nazis, but not in the same manner as men. Nevertheless, they were frequently targeted as asocials and wore the black triangle in the camps. Because it didn't occur under Paragraph 175, and thus was not a focus of gay and lesbian organizing in the postwar period, it was overlooked and forgotten. This gendering of persecution was even further evidence of the pressing need to revamp the memorial and expand queer kinship through victimization to include women.[90]

As the treatment of gays and lesbians was put under the microscope in the quest to sort out whether the monument in its current iteration paid adequate tribute to the plight of those who suffered during the Third Reich, the LSVD, the artists themselves, and various activist scholars weighed in on the veracity of Schoppmann's claims. Part of the problem was the murky language of the original 2003 parliamentary decree, which stipulated that the proposed monument must do three things: "honor the persecuted and killed," "keep the memory of injustice alive," and serve as "an ongoing symbol against intolerance, enmity, and the marginalization of gays and lesbians." At the MANEO-Soirée, Andreas Pretzel drew attention to three myths circulating in the background. These included allegations that the Nazis were themselves gay, that the persecution of gay men represented a kind of "Homocaust," and that there was a systematic lesbian persecution on par with gay men. The monument in its current incarnation lent itself to the perpetuation of these myths, he averred. Opponents of the monument were already raising the specter of queer Nazis. For others, the way the single stele appears broken off from the Eisenman monument conjures up the idea of homosexual persecution as a derivative of the Holocaust. And the *EMMA* debate certainly traded on the notion of a systematic campaign against lesbians during the Third Reich. Pretzel suggested that these myths, however problematic, formed a core part of contemporary gay and lesbian consciousness. The monument needed to put an end to factionalism once and for all. A way forward might lie with the highly existential experience of viewing the film. Since it could only accommodate a single viewer at a time, it created the feeling of alienation to which both gay men and lesbians might relate. What was needed was an artistic intervention that might find "a way to remember lesbians (while) recognizing their specific fate. All this, without evoking the spirit of competition or a sense of equalization."[91] A suitable representational strategy could capture the shared but different experiences and emotional cost of marginalization, a queering of kinship as well as of place through a visual strategy that both encapsulated and went beyond the singularity of experience of persecution and victimhood. But, as we'll see, the identitarian impulses at the heart of commemoration proved difficult to overcome.

The Memorial as Media Event

The battle over queer commemorative kinship was never just a German affair. From the beginning of its conceptualization to its unveiling, the LGBTQIA memorial was always a media event. Owing to the symbolic importance of the city and Nazi persecution to Western queer subjectivities, it was almost inevitable that it would have resonance beyond borders. Feminist and lesbian activism had succeeded in opening up a space for greater visibility and, by the end of 2007, several prominent Social Democratic and Green Party politicians had joined members of the LSVD and Berlin's queer mayor Klaus Wowerweit to formally request that the artists reconceptualize the monument's design to speak in some way to lesbian experience. They conceded. The plan was to change the infinite loop of men kissing every two years and replace it with a lesbian kiss. For many journalists, to say nothing of commentators on blogs, wikis, and forums, the compromise was a concession not a long-term solution.[92] Indeed, journalists in the legacy press used the unveiling as an opportunity to revisit the dispute. In the *Berliner Zeitung*, the erstwhile daily of communist East Berlin, the columnist Gunnar Schupelius doubted very much that the "kissing men in black and white" would awaken people to remember the violent past. The Springer-owned *Welt* newspaper saw it differently. "The memorial, as a piece of public memorial culture, is another example that monuments can also be good art."[93] For the liberal *Die Zeit*, the question of whether a kiss was an appropriate symbol of persecution seemed most pressing. According to their reporter, more important still was the fact that this debate forced consideration of the relationship of monuments to the past. In their estimation, it was the interactive nature of the "Film-Monument" from Elmgreen and Dragset that rendered the past the subject of present and future disputation. Misogynistic nastiness continued to surface in print. Historian Götz Aly went so far as to proclaim as late as 2010 in the *Berliner Zeitung* that "organized lesbians" were still mobilizing for their own film of kissing women according to the motto "Unfair, we want to be victims too!"[94] In the conservative *Frankfurter Allgemeine Zeitung*, Matthias Hannemann reported it was "a victory for the lesbian lobby."[95]

At a cost of roughly 600,000 euros, the memorial was finally unveiled in the spring of 2008 after the intervention of federal minister of culture Bernd Neumann, who nudged the various groups toward a compromise. Günter Dworek of the LSVD reminded those in attendance that the struggle to realize a memorial was almost two decades long. Still, there were signs amid the celebration that all was not perfect with the commemorations. Despite efforts to hold up the memorial as a symbol of Western tolerance, the artists told the local scene magazine *Zitty* that the federal minister of culture had actually refused to allow invitations to be imprinted with images of "the Kiss"—the shorthand term for the infinite loop of kissing men. Other observers noted the absence of Germany's president Horst Köhler, who had been present at the unveiling of the Memorial to the Murdered Jews of Europe.[96] Israel Gutman of Yad Vashem voiced unease of his own to a reporter with *Deutsche Welle*, bringing back into view the argument that the Nazis had persecuted "exclusively German" homosexuals (which is not true), many of whom had fallen victim to "internal political battles within the NSDAP."[97] Queer suffering may have been legitimized through the building of the memorial, but it still was not embraced universally.

More certain was the meaning of the memorial for non-German queers. Both the controversy and the unveiling quickly entered the international queer mediascape through transnational subcultural networks and pathways. Already in 2007, the New York *Gay City News* had reported on the cavernous divide between gays and lesbians. In an article by Benjamin Weinthal, the acrimonious falling out was captured in infinite detail and translated for an English-speaking audience. A core feature of the story was the perspective of the expat American and Berlin-based activist Jim Baker, who reflected on the differences between queer organizing in the United States and Germany. "The lack of coalition building has affected gay and lesbian politics in

Germany" to the extent that advocacy is still very male centered there.[98] An article in the *Advocate* in 2006 titled "A Memorial of Our Own" underscored the importance of the Elmgreen and Dragset design to international queer identity politics, while a later article went a step further in placing the Berlin memorial in conversation with other transnational queer commemorative cultures, like those that have resulted in memorials in Amsterdam, Sydney, and Tel Aviv.[99] Similarly, positioned in the World News section of the *Gay and Lesbian Times* next to articles on Argentine efforts to legalize same-sex marriage and the Russian ban on blood donation, the memorial's location was described as having great symbolic purchase given its proximity to where decisions were made on the fate of a variety of social and racial outcasts.[100] Even blogs like *Gays without Borders* carried the story.[101] Queer kinship was a global mediatized affair with Germany occupying a special place in a shared cultural imaginary.

The queer media engagement with the memorial demonstrates how pivotal Nazi persecution remained to gays and lesbians abroad, although Anika Oettler has shown that actual visitor experience at the site was somewhat ambivalent and mixed.[102] Still, the memorial debate and actualization helped solidify a permanent place for queer memory in Berlin, even as it remained contentious. Indeed, almost every article cited its placement in close proximity to the Eisenman memorial as a sign that injustices against gays and lesbians had finally acquired legitimacy even if tensions between queer kin remained high. Along the same vein, it was important that the federal government had sanctioned its construction. What began as a testament to German subcultural public memory had entered the national orbit and was quickly taken up as a symbol of the historic mistreatment of gays and lesbians in many parts of the world. It also managed to earn the support of all the major parties, save the CDU, which had voted against the idea back in 2003. By 2008, it seemed SPD party member Johannes Kahrs was correct in recognizing that the discourse around the memorial was generative, "held great meaning and would bring awareness to the entire Republic about the experiences of the different victims groups."[103] Building the memorial was greeted as an important step forward in recognizing past wrongs while serving as a rallying cry for ongoing struggles. In this way, the memorial in Berlin aided in the materialization of queer memories of suffering, linking the German past to a transnational present. In cyberspace and among the readers of the subcultural media, the memorial also helped lend shape and form to a universalized set of common queer memories (if not trans* or queer of color). The events in Berlin conjured up German crime and trauma. In linking it symbolically to the ongoing battle against marginalization and homophobia worldwide, the memorial helped bind international queers emotionally across national and temporal divides. In queering place in Berlin, not just in the sense of creating space for a queer memorial but also in transcending state and nation, the memorial and the international reportage in the queer counterpublic sphere constructed an alternative kind of kinship based around the shared heritage and symbology of Nazi violence and its importance for contemporary queer identity.[104] The City of Berlin emerged as a "rainbow capital" in the truest sense, forged on diversity and toleration of difference.

Yet the memorial campaign's advocacy around policies of openness, equality, diversity, and toleration also turned on what Lisa Duggan calls "the recoding of key terms in gay politics." Equality in commemoration was still defined narrowly around gay men's experiences. Lesbians were included begrudgingly, and tensions around persecution would continue into the 2020s, with trans* victims still waiting for historical reckoning amid growing radical feminist backlash. As the plaque's logic also shows, certain populations were scrutinized ever more concretely for failing to uphold the supposedly race-blind affordances of the liberal democratic state.[105] Kinship for some was forged out of the marginalization of others, with the racialization of memory bridging some borders while creating other divides.

Once the dust had settled, the result was a compromise: the film would be changed out now and then to feature other members of the queer and trans* communities kissing, embracing, and sometimes frolicking on the U-Bahn, in city streets, all over Berlin.[106] While this seems to be a workable solution to the issue of representation (although it also unleashed opposition and further debate), it failed to rectify the assumptions around homophobia that undergirded the project's evolution into the present day. If anything it brought back into view the kiss-in motifs from MANEO, which similarly sought to ground activism in a respatialization of the capital, taking queer desire literally and now visually out of traditional gayborhoods into so-called no-gay areas where queers feared retribution from improperly assimilated migrants.[107] At the memorial site itself, a plaque would be placed in front of the monument explaining the intricacies of queer persecution under the Nazis. It reads: "Because of its history, Germany has a special responsibility to actively oppose the violation of gay men's and lesbians' human rights. In many parts of the world, people continue to be persecuted for their sexuality, homosexual love remains illegal and a kiss can be dangerous [referring to the film]. With this memorial, the Federal Republic of Germany intends to honor the victims of persecution and murder, to keep alive the memory of this injustice, and to create a lasting symbol of opposition to enmity, intolerance and the exclusion of gay men and lesbians." There can be no doubt that this was a hard-fought victory. The monument set in motion a process culminating in a formal apology for the criminalization of homosexuality after 1945 with remuneration for the few remaining men who could prove persecution. Naming sexual preference as a human right is also undeniably significant. But in opting for identity politics in lieu of intersectional forms of kinship around the issue of risk, hate, and outsider status broadly defined, this attempt to forge queer public memory remains piecemeal. When queer visibility is predicated on the supposition that homophobia is separate from transphobia (something I return to in the epilogue) and is located elsewhere in the world (i.e., outside Germany) where "people continue to be persecuted for their sexuality and homosexual love remains illegal," the memorial loses an opportunity to combat homophobia and transphobia as a German problem, with a homegrown history and legacy. Instead, it places it on the shoulders of improperly socialized "others" who will continue to be a problem unless they are suitably acculturated to Western ways, which, as this debate surely shows, are not always tolerant of difference. Worse still, these suppositions against migrant populations did not just come from the state and its institutions but were cultivated through mainstream gay and lesbian organizations that saw themselves as the "oppressed majority"—to echo back the response to Judith Butler's speech in 2010 ("You are not in the majority").[108] This failure to recognize the exclusionary underpinnings of queer entry into polite society through the politics of commemoration hampers coalitional efforts to deal honestly and thoroughly with homophobia and transphobia alongside other forms of racial and economic disparities that continue to affect those living within the boundaries of Germany today.

What does this struggle to queer victimhood and representation along the lines of race and gender—and the international interest in how this played out—tell us about the role of history in kinship and place making in Berlin? To get at this, we need to take seriously the divergent understandings of the past emanating out of the debate and the ways in which the struggle for representation forced a frank—if acrimonious—discussion of the rules, structures, and organization of city, rhetorical, and commemorative space. In bearing witness to past crimes as a way of focusing attention on current struggles, the memorial contributed to claims making in the present. These claims would not only help redraw the boundaries of community and belonging among queer-identified Berliners; they would be of direct importance for future struggles for legal recognition, a formal apology, and remuneration—even for civil union—as emblems of a time when rights to privacy, personality, and self-determination were systematically violated "in the name of the people," the English translation of "Im Namen des Volkes" which adorned every court case ledger during the Third Reich. In other words, history was used by these activists to create a coherent meaning of place amid the shifting terrain of identity politics and invented traditions. The fact that this battle was waged in cyberspace and in the international media as well as in the various subcultural and legacy newspapers tells us that what appears as a localized struggle for a national queer monument quickly breeched these boundaries. In other words, the struggle to realize a Homo-Monument, as it was called colloquially, was at once local and global, national and transnational, quotidian and mediatized. Berlin was no longer the building site for a unified German identity, but it quickly became a place of symbolic purchase for international human rights struggles.[109] If we are to truly appreciate the role and significance of the memorial in queer kinship making, we have to think of it as a site claimed by many and instrumentalized by some in the name of community and identity on a German, European, and global scale. Making space for queer place means looking at how the "past helps make the present." But, more importantly, it also means thinking seriously about the unique role played by the city of Berlin itself in crafting a cosmopolitan queer kinship on the backs of people who continue to be deemed improperly persecuted both in a historic and a contemporary sense.[110]

What purpose is served by thinking about the quest to build a monument to queer persecution, past and present, as an uneven, charged, and still unfolding process of claims making? Focusing in on the way disparate groups claim and make sense of certain city spaces and the emotions and memories they help call into being shines a light on the role of competing and sometimes overlapping practices and interactions that make up collective memory. Not only does this foreground the messiness of commemorative practices, but it also points to the high degree of emotionality involved in the politics of place making itself. As Nigel Thrift has argued, thinking about claims to space as an inherently relational process is not only methodologically more sound—allowing as it does a way to see place making as having a basis in overlapping, intersectional identities—but it might also make for a more progressive memory politics given the important social, sexual, gender, ethnic, and political orientations, inflections, and implications it makes visible at the core of the memorial process itself.[111] Given the way that collective memory is so often "used, misused, and exploited" by governments and the heritage industry and taken up by average people to give themselves "a coherent identity, a national narrative, (and) a place in the world," it is sometimes important to find ways of keeping it messy, so as to capture the contentiousness of claims making if only to undermine the power of localist, identitarian, and nationalist assertions of neutrality in suggestions that certain spaces bear essential or universal meaning.[112] Instead of reproducing neat yet myopic histories, perhaps a more responsible approach might tackle what Doreen Massey refers to as "the inevitable hybridities at work in the constitution of anywhere."[113]

Instead of thinking of this battle over definitions of persecution that pitted gays against feminists and lesbians over whose history should be encapsulated in the monument as an example of the corrosiveness of identity politics, I have argued that it might be more useful to see it as an exercise in kinship and place making—that is, as the process by which selective histories gel and become fixed in actual material space. Efforts to make the memorial speak to everyday oppressions, both in Germany and abroad, afforded it a more fixed (though no less problematic) meaning as a site of reflection, pilgrimage, and memory. But in not being able to speak honestly to the wide diversity of sexual practices, identities, and experiences in historical and present-day queer and trans* communities, including the myopic definition of toleration and the uncomfortable place of unlimited intimacies in the LGBTQIA scene, the monument is more a symbol of homogenization than a kinship more robustly defined.

QUEER KINSHIP IN
DANGEROUS TIMES

6

QUEER HISTORY HAS A PROBLEM with memory. As
we saw in chapters 4 and 5, the Nazi past galvanized
a sense of belonging for many people on both sides of
the Atlantic. But this quest for recognition, essential
to overcoming decades of homophobia and mistreatment, was also selective in terms of whose experiences
would be taken up as part of that past. Memory is often
folded into queer and trans* history in the search for
ancestors, collapsing real and tangible differences in
how we think about identity today with how our historical subjects may have characterized their lives in
the past.[1] As we've seen here too, some things are
just left out. We misremember the role of intergenerational desire in subcultural formation; race in the
queer gaze; the place of trauma, loss, and melancholy
in the wake of AIDS that helped birth queer theory;
and the different histories and experiences of violence
and marginalization inside queer kinship networks
themselves. This is not a matter of choice; it is baked
into the structure of memory making generally. As Pat
Gentile and Gary Kinsman have evocatively argued on
the clash between progressive and conformist politics
more generally, "the social organization of forgetting"
is a core feature of how governments rule in matters of
queer citizenship.[2] We seize on dates as turning points,
1968 or 1969 in East and West Germany, and forget the

struggle, losses, inequalities, and compromises that continued to mark queer life after decriminalization. In accepting state-driven narratives of becoming and integration, we forget the historical entanglements of radical queer worldmaking, including the uneasy but important coalitions that sometimes existed across difference. In the era of civil union and gay marriage, we forget too that there once were different notions of sexual and gender consciousness that stood in direct opposition to privatized, siloed, and heteronormative forms of relationality that seem the only way to think about rights and privileges today. That there once were alternative arguments for how to live one's life queerly seems almost inconceivable.

To reclaim these lost and forgotten memories, we need a kind of insurgent remembrance to rebuild our connection to and awareness of queer ancestry not in the biological sense of lineage or hagiography but of being-together-in-difference. If governance structures in late liberalism are bound to an "ahistorical sense of memory" as Alexis Shotwell suggests, celebrating turning points that failed to turn, then we need to reestablish our connection to these earlier radical traditions. This would allow us to rekindle a sense of Germany's productively fraught queer past to better appreciate how this has been reworked in public memory, writing out the richness of diversity and cosmopolitanism in the language of universalism.[3] It would require denaturalizing our investment in the exclusivity of identity as ontological ground in favor of a method that emphasizes how we might access multiple, intersectional ways "of being, feeling, and knowing in the world."[4]

Feelings serve as one way that we might tap into a more fulsome understanding between ourselves and others in the past. As we'll see here, artist interventions have a special power in creating opportunities to explore different structures of feeling, to gather a sense of being in relation to different affective sensibilities other than our own at different scales. This experience of together-in-difference, which I call queer kinship, is not flawless, but it does hold the potential to destabilize monocultural minoritarianism and to recollect the role of race, class, and gender nonconformity within the queer past. Doing so helps us imagine more capacious queer futures as well.

Thanks to queer of color and trans* historical critique, we've learned to recognize the way that cis white heteropatriarchal notions of normativity continue to mark hegemonic notions of identity that have accompanied queer/trans* entry into the mainstream. This chapter draws on these interventions to explore how we might connect with and remember queer ancestry productively in a way that unsettles both the assimilationist and siloed elements of identity politics in favor of an approach that recognizes collective, shared mappings of ourselves in relation to others. This approach is not to deny the structural reasons why different groups "feel differently and navigate the material world on a different emotional register."[5] Rather, it queries how an aesthetic-historical practice centered around desire might surface possibilities for a relational form of queer kinship—one that is "singular plural," to cite Jean-Luc Nancy—which breaches the confines of individualist and familial bonds as the foundation of queer worldmaking in the twenty-first century.[6] My goal is not to present conditions for a new universalism. Instead, the aim is to develop our faculties so we might "touch across time," to try to imagine our sources and our world otherwise than we have thus far, to be better able to see, listen to, and hear how communities of difference have for some time narrated themselves into the fabric of our shared world. First, I present the possibilities of ancestorship in a brief discussion of three pioneers of gay, lesbian, queer, and trans* worldmaking who helped create interest in the productive possibilities of intimacy and desire for imagining the world otherwise.[7] Then I turn to several artists living, working, and connected to Berlin whose work holds great potential for creating the affective ties that bind us all—together and apart—as queer kin.

Forebears

We are constantly surrounded by those who came before, those whose books, articles, and artifacts shape our thinking today. Sitting down at my desk, preparing to write my contribution to what in German is referred to as a *Festschrift*, a commemorative volume in honor of a scholar's legacy, I clicked on the URL for the University of Wisconsin oral history archive to listen to the five interviews Jim Steakley gave in 2010 at his former place of work.[8] This volume will appear in German, not English, a testament to the impact Steakley had in German studies on both sides of the Atlantic as one of the first to publish on the history of homophobia and gay persecution under the Nazis. Listening to the interviews, one thing became clear: Steakley was constantly on the move. He was also, remarkably, a witness to many of the key events of the era we might think of as forming part of the sexual revolution. He lived in Frankfurt during the 1968–69 student movement, where he muses he may have attended class with Angela Davis. He fought the draft with the help of Frank Kameny of the DC Mattachine Society and spent another year in the Federal Republic on a fellowship from Cornell

University where he found good company with activists in the fledgling Homosexual Action Group West Berlin. Returning to the United States, a chance meeting with some queers from Toronto at a gay dance in Upstate New York led him to leave the States for another year, this time for Canada, a surprising "hotbed of gay liberation." There, he would learn about "Canadian socialist-feminist perspectives" and pen five articles for the monthly gay and lesbian magazine the *Body Politic*,[9] the very first analysis in English on the two-fold history of liberation and repression that marked the lives of many gay people during the Weimar Republic and Nazi period.

These articles would have wide resonance. Indeed, the ties that bound transatlantic queers to this German past were stronger than anyone could have imagined. Christopher Isherwood sent a note of appreciation. David Thorstad, founder of the National Association of Man Boy Love, was a fan. The scholars Richard Plant and Jonathan Ned Katz urged Steakley to collaborate with them on related projects.[10] Buoyed by its reception, Steakley transposed some of these ideas into what would become his landmark 1974 book *The Homosexual Emancipation Movement in Germany*, which brought the pioneering work of Magnus Hirschfeld to a Western audience decades after he was forced to abandon Berlin, a target of the Nazis.

In a year away in East Germany to research the life and writing of the anarchist poet, playwright, and writer Erich Mühsam, Steakley became one of the few North Americans to live and love across the Berlin Wall. Put up in a dream apartment on the corner of the storied boulevard Unter den Linden and Friedrichstrasse, he forged lifelong friendships with members of the nascent and subterranean East German gay rights scene. He served as a conduit between activists in the East and the West, exchanging information about gay organizing, socialist feminism, and BDSM in Canada, the United States, and East and West Germany.

Ten years later, another itinerate American would find her way to Berlin and help ignite a movement. Audre Lorde, the self-described "black, lesbian, mother, warrior, poet," lived in the western half of the city from 1984 to her death from cancer in 1992. While there, she gave lectures and readings, held workshops, and perhaps most importantly, shared her infectious personality and time with scores of Black German women who gravitated to her as a sister, lover, mother figure, and friend.[11] Combing through her letters at Spelman College and the Lorde Archive at the Free University of Berlin, the historian Tiffany Florvil was able to reproduce the affective ties that bound Afro-German women to the enigmatic poet. And they were considerable, nurtured by conversation, sexuality, and the written word. Sensual, sometimes erotic, the bonds of love and friendship forged among these women helped create a foundation for a cultural flourishing that established the voices and perspectives of women across the African diaspora, who otherwise struggled to find acceptance in Germany. At the time, many Afro-Germans felt disconnected from any sense of home. Some had no connection or knowledge of their personal legacy or heritage. Others were scattered throughout East and West Germany, housed in orphanages, or with foster parents or white German families, far from major cities.[12] West Berlin, with its universities, activist networks, and luster as part of the Cold War frontier, drew students, scholars, and everyday people in search of something new. What they found in Lorde was incendiary. She ignited their passion for self-discovery, for community, for shared purpose and solidarity.

Chief among Lorde's gifts to the Berlin Afro-German community was the belief that every woman was a poet, an intellectual, a knowledge keeper and creator. Her friend Dagmar Schultz, a filmmaker, helped negotiate a visiting professorship for her at the Free University of Berlin, after meeting the poet at the 1980 UN Conference on Women. As Lorde herself wrote in her landmark 1984 collection of speeches and essays, *Sister Outsider*, "Each one of us holds an incredible reserve of creativity and power, of unexamined and unrecorded emotion and feeling" that is "neither white nor surface" but "dark," "ancient," and "deep."[13] These powers would help guide women in dealing with the burdens of misogyny, homophobia, and anti-Black racism; like the erotic, which Lorde opined carried political power, they were a salve against violent unbecoming, galvanizing mind, body, and spirit.[14] Lorde taught that writing and poetry in particular were the ultimate forms of resistance against erasure because all that art conjured up—love, intuition, desire, self-love, emotion, nonlinearity, storytelling, and oral traditions—were qualities devalued by Western ontologies.[15]

One of the outcomes of these encounters was the 1986 edited volume *Farbe Bekennen*, known in English as *Showing Our Colours: Afro-German Women Speak Out*. Edited by three members of Lorde's circle—the poet May Opitz (later Ayim), the historian Katharina Oguntoye, and the filmmaker Dagmar Schultz—it was a mix of autobiographical texts, interviews, poetry, and Opitz's own master's thesis, which she had been writing at the University of Regensburg. Like Steakley's *Homosexual Emancipation Movement in Germany*, this single text would galvanize an entire field of study, deepened by doctoral dissertations-turned-books by Opitz herself, Fatima El-Tayeb, then in Hamburg, and across the Atlantic in Michigan with Tina Campt, whose visionary analysis of Black diasporic vernacular photography was only a few years away. So fertile was this soil that it quickly breached the confines of literary/activist circles in Berlin. Scholar activists like the Afro-Surinamese Dutch scholar Gloria Wekker would go on to establish an influential node in the Afro-European women's movement in Amsterdam, creating a lesbian feminist group aptly named Sister Outsider in honor of the poet, before herself finishing a doctoral dissertation at UCLA. She returned to the Netherlands to occupy a chair in women's studies at the University of Utrecht, influencing policy on diversity and decolonization and training a new generation of scholar activists to continue the fight to address discrimination at home and abroad, part of the Black internationalist opposition to racism and sexism.[16]

Meanwhile, a few decades later, the world would be treated to Dough Wright's runaway hit play *I Am My Own Wife*, based around the 1992 memoirs of the celebrated trans* bon vivant Charlotte von Mahlsdorf, which the filmmaker Rosa von Praunheim simultaneously released that same year as a film.[17] Born in 1928 to an abusive father who believed in Prussian principles of sternness, Mahlsdorf was a fixture of the GDR queer activist scene for most of the 1970s and 1980s. For better but also for worse, Mahlsdorf's life is a mirror image of Germany's twentieth century. At age fifteen she purportedly read Magnus Hirschfeld's landmark study *The Transvestites* and drew inspiration from this text—and support from a lesbian aunt—to dress in women's clothes for the remainder of her life. She claims to have murdered her abusive father in 1944, somehow surviving capture by the SS and the onslaught of Soviet retribution in the final days of the war. From her family estate in a southeastern district of East Berlin, she managed to host meetings of the Homosexual Interest Group (Homosexuelle Interessengemeinschaft, or HIB) at her salon, which included among its curios the furniture from the celebrated gay and lesbian bar Mulackritze, once the watering hole of Bertolt Brecht, Magnus Hirschfeld, and Marlene Dietrich.[18]

Mahlsdorf had always been a kind of cause célèbre in East German gay, lesbian, and BDSM circles. Because she loaned period pieces from her museum to directors, she was featured in several films, including a documentary on The Other Love of queers in the late GDR.[19] She even had a bit part in the Heiner Carow queer drama *Coming Out* which was screened at the very same time that the Berlin Wall was breached by revelers on October 3, 1989. Although curiously absent from Wright's stage production, she was unrepentantly sexual well into her advanced age, refusing the terms transsexual and transgender in favor of a knowledge of the self that included maleness and femaleness.[20] Yet Mahlsdorf's story is not one of heroism unbound. Shortly after the success of her memoir, it was reported that like so many other citizens, she had served as an informant for the Stasi. Although no evidence ever surfaced that she had reported on her fellow HIB activists, her work for the secret police had landed a fellow antiques collector in prison.[21] Perhaps more distasteful still, some of her prized museum collection purportedly consisted of clothing and artifacts that she had acquired from Jewish Germans who had suffered deportation.[22] Hounded by these revelations and attacked by neo-Nazis, she fled for Sweden where she would spend her final days.

The Steakley interviews, Lorde's letters, and the Mahlsdorf memoir reveal traces of lives of influence that moved between worlds. Although unique in so many ways, with hints once again of the different social force of queer, lesbian, and trans* affective and temporal frames, these stories are also emblematic of the social, sexual, and intellectual meanderings of an entire generation of queer artists, writers, and scholars—not just in Madison and Berlin but also in Bremen, New York, London, Montreal, Ann Arbor, Paris, and Amsterdam—who went on to occupy the first professorships devoted to social justice themes. Steakley's, Lorde's, and Mahlsdorf's Berlin—as well as the transnational migrations of their ideas—form the outline of a complex and vibrant network that breached national boundaries and connected activists, scholars, and lovers through the circulation of ideas, intimate encounters, books, magazines, objects, and political endeavor. It forged, as I will explore in this chapter by way of the work of, among others, the Canadian-born, Paris-based, equally itinerate audiovisual artist Benny Nemer, a kind of queer kinship, a form of recognition and belonging nurtured by and through bonds of intimacy, love, politics, and longing. Like Steakley's histories of the German gay rights movement, Lorde's poetry, Mahlsdorf's irreverence, and the work of all those who read and circulated and added to this queer/lesbian/trans* canon, Nemer's art project *I Don't Know Where Paradise Is* (*Paradise* for short) is a testament to the kinship bonds of activists and lovers, elders and ancestors, whose work, passions, pickups, affairs, articles, and libraries went on to influence and shape how future generations would relate to the LGBTQIA past. The relational, sensorial, and participatory aspect of Nemer's art piece, an audio guide in several chapters steeped in song, storytelling, and voice, brings the listener into a relationship with this past in all its libidinous glory. Indeed, at the heart of this vision of queer kinship is a refusal of linear historicism, the boundedness of identity, and an embrace of the erotic in the Lordean sense—that is, as an at times irrational, bodily force built around shared experiences and desire. As she argues in "The Uses of the Erotic": "The sharing of joy, whether physical, emotional, psychic, or intellectual, forms a bridge between the sharers that can be the basis for understanding much of what is not shared between them, and lessens the threat of their difference."[23] Lorde was writing explicitly for women as a strategy of self-realization and empowerment over and against the racism and sexism in the wider society and also within feminist and queer circles; nevertheless, there is usefulness in allying with her to think more carefully about aesthetic practices of representation as holding the possibility of intersectional forms of kinship with each other in our collective (though differently rooted) relationship to each other and the past. When we look at, and read for, and listen to the stylized encounters Nemer makes possible with these stories of queer, lesbian, and trans* lives and elders, we find schemata for a shared experience of queer worldmaking in its broadest sense, one that moves beyond visibility politics and families of origin toward a world that "will always welcome lovers."[24]

In what follows, we will journey through ways we might explore this search for community and belonging as an aesthetic experience of relationality and kinship. The route we will take is circuitous. We will travel from where you are sitting reading this text to the red-light district in Amsterdam, to apartments visited and imagined in Paris, Berlin, London, and North Africa, and across the ocean to the old Jewish neighborhood of Montreal. It begins with an audio guide that caps off three years of research Nemer spent with the libraries, artifacts, and holdings of several queer elders. You may listen to it now, if you wish, before reading any further, or you might come back to it at the end.[25] Perhaps you won't listen at all. Whichever path you choose, in just reading these words, you are entering into conversation with queer ancestors, whose stories, like Steakley's and Lorde's and Mahlsdorf's, have much to tell us about the productive—if not always unproblematic—potential of affect, transgression, and desire for how to write and experience queer history, provided we learn how to listen.

Beginnings

As with all kinships, these are deeply personal. I first met Nemer—then based in Berlin—at the Alberta College of Art and Design in Calgary in the winter of 2011, an odd place for an art opening and conference on the legacy of sexology and the German gay rights movement. *PopSex!* was inspired by Rainer Herrn's own exhibition *Sex Brennt* (Sex Burns) at Berlin's Charité Hospital in 2008 commemorating the burning of books from Magnus Hirschfeld's Institute for Sexual Science. Curated by Annette Timm and Michael Taylor, prophetically, this event formed the beginning of a series of transatlantic collaborations between Herrn, Timm, and Taylor who would go on to produce the *TransTrans* exhibit tracing the migration of ideas and research around transsexual/transgender life and science.[26] It was also the beginning of conversations between Nemer and me, which led not just to friendship but to a deep affinity and intellectual partnership. Over the next several years, together and apart, we would explore the theme of queer kinship in our own registers.[27] Thanks to a grant from Canada's Social Science Humanities Research Council, we met in various city cafes, restaurants, and parks—as well as virtually over the internet. I would write articles about Nemer's craft; he would include me in the various happenings related to his practice-based doctorate in Edinburgh. We gave a performative keynote together at a gender conference in Gothenburg, Sweden, while I journeyed to meet him in Montreal, Paris, Amsterdam, and Berlin to work through various phases of his library project, which he ultimately showcased at my university art gallery during the COVID-19 pandemic in the fall of 2020.[28]

The *PopSex!* exhibition, where we met, included the work of twelve artists who had been asked to respond in their own ways to the archival legacy of Magnus Hirschfeld and the sex museum that formed part of his Institute for Sexual Science. Taking inspiration from Louis Pasteur's biological institute in Paris and the regimes of collection, spectatorship, and display long in evidence in Europe's anthropological museums, Hirschfeld used the exhibition spaces of the institute to showcase the frontiers of sex research as a place where art met science.[29] Patients coming to the institute for medical consultation and advice might pass by glass cases with birth control aids, fetish gear, and photographs of nude figures including intersex persons, inverts, and so-named transsexuals. In her analysis of Hirschfeld's archive, Heike Bauer notes the way "the objects of fantasy and desire gathered at the institute" prompted for the Berlin enthusiast and author Christopher Isherwood "an admission of queer kinship."[30] Despite the range of objects and identities on view that might create this sense of belonging in difference, each exhibit's musealization and display were explicitly staged to educate the general public and avoid titillation.[31] Every photograph and every object was positioned with research, treatment, and advocacy in mind and also to avoid attracting censorship by the authorities. The book burnings of May 1933 proved how symbolically relevant this material was to the anti-smut prurience of the Nazi Party. Yet these same images had the power to transcend their own emplotment. Sexologists may have intended for the images on display to affirm the legitimacy and respectability of their research as an objective science, but these objects and images retained a certain charge and frisson, giving a face to the faceless while also igniting the imagination in unintended ways. Taylor and Timm wanted to engage scholars and artists to take up this challenge of the musealization of sex and its role in straddling scientific knowledge production and collective memory making around utopian, reformist-oriented future imaginings rooted in the institute; Nemer and I wanted to retain a focus on the erotic underpinnings of queer spectatorship and the transformative potential of the illicit.[32]

In Calgary, I gave an animated presentation about Herbert Tobias's erotic photography that recentered the focus on the erotic/pornographic and performative place of images and cruising as sites of queer subject formation. Nemer later told me that his interest in my work was piqued by the way I channeled Tobias's erotic charge in my own analysis. As we saw in chapter 2, my interest in Tobias's work is indeed the way it creates an "erotohistoriography" that pushes against temporalities of pain and loss to bring back into view what Elizabeth Freeman calls "the value of surprise, of pleasurable interruptions and momentary fulfillments from elsewhere, other times."[33] To not linger over the eroticism that underlies Tobias's work is to neglect the generative place of desire in queer subcultures and how that is actualized through photography. As Jennifer Nash argues in her analysis of racialized pornography, *The Black Body in Ecstasy*, focusing solely on trauma, injury, and recovery takes away our ability to countenance and even see the agency of pleasure when it does surface in the historical register.[34] Instead of surfacing queerness, an overemphasis on loss as "the condition of community" has the effect of silencing other forms of subalternity.[35] These examples of eroticism unbound, of nonnormative bodies as imperfectly melancholy, of "failing," to put it in Jack Halberstam's term, do not deny trauma. Rather, they ask us to consider the implications of a politics based around a view of the past as a wounded attachment, as eternal suffering.[36] If suffering becomes the ground of queer kinship, especially if its mobilizing power leads to an uncritical assimilationist politics of acceptance, it confirms what Benjamin referred to in the "Theses on the Philosophy of History" as Left Melancholia, a view of the past as static and fixed, which inevitably privileges the victor.[37] In doing so, it also denies history the power of presenting alternative empathies. Seeing kinship more fulsomely is not to deny legacies of trauma; it means thinking about the ties that bind "minoritarian group identities" not just as "a particular set of physiological distinctions or cultural bonds" based in trauma but also as forged through vocabularies of queer pleasure—however fraught. It is less an affirmation of a utopian ideal than a recognition of a fuller spectrum of lived experience.[38]

Nemer's contribution to the Calgary exhibition and conference embraced this challenge of enlisting the erotic as a source of kinship in his audiovisual installation, *The Legacy*. This short film mixes the recitation of literary passages from "gay elders" with images of young men who are projected via a baroque cutout screen hanging in the middle of the galleryspace while cruising in the Grünewald forest in the southwest corner of Berlin.[39] The suspended screen acts as a portal into this other realm, where a seeker protagonist is seen speaking as though to an oracle, receiving words of wisdom from four ancestors. Some hold up mirrors to the viewer, while the seeker himself peers through a crownlike headpiece that covers his eyes, adorned with reflective squares. The elders tell their visitor about the perilousness of this world, of a society not yet prepared to countenance queer kinships. The stories all have as their origins the time of troubles in the mid-1980s when AIDS ravaged the transatlantic gay scene. One passage, from "An Englishman in New York," delivers the words of the immortal Quentin Crisp about the racialized boundaries of belonging via the Haitian-born, New York–trained, and Berlin-based artist Jean-Ulrick Désert: "You have the burden and the great joy of being outsiders. Every day you live is a kind of triumph. This you should cling onto. You should make no effort to try and join society. Stay right where you are . . . and wait for society to form itself around you."

In dream-like sequences like these with each of the four oracles, we hear stories of redemption, tragedy, and overcoming. But we also are reminded by the very nature of the mise-en-scène that this is first and perhaps foremost an erotic landscape, a space of cruising and encounter. *Legacy* culminates in a tribal scream as seeker and oracle join in an embrace of their quest and desire. The howl brings the audience into this communion as well, as an embodied act of curiosity and climax. Although it wasn't clear to me at the time, this mix of historicity and desire as the engine of queer sociality, blending past with future and involving the audience as participant as well as viewer is what drew me to Nemer's work, especially the way he combined fantasy and performance to bring out historical resonances albeit in a different form. This was history done differently, meaningfully, in a way I had never imagined. Over the course of the next several years, I made sure to check in with him, to see how his ideas were evolving. In 2015 we began our work together.

The Past Made Present

An exhibited artist in his native Canada, with pieces in the permanent collection of the National Gallery, by the time we began working together, Nemer had succeeded in creating a niche for himself as an artist working across media and genre. During short sojourns as artist in residence in several European cultural institutions, he started working with song and story to find new ways to tell visitors about collection pieces. He had just begun experimenting with the audio guide around the time I met him in Calgary. Typical museum audio guides impart curatorial expertise in plain language. Nemer wanted to explore the medium in a new way, to wrest it from its didactic elitism and draw out its more evocative, aesthetic potential. He toyed with ways one might explicitly mediate a listener's experience with artworks, public monuments, and the gallery or museum space through interventions in the sensory world, to open up a more multivalent, empathically driven history, one that would lend a sense of urgency, depth, and dignity to the historical subjects under examination without universalizing their experiences in the process.[40] Nemer's audio works do this through the use of choreographic cues that buoy the listener from each object and scenario to the next, or in the case of guides to items in actual collections, from room to room. These immersive renderings weave their way between the factual, the mythical, the musical, and the poetic. Despite a grounding in the history of art and visual culture, at their core these vignettes consist of stories, by turns solemn and exultant, that conjure up a range of subjectivities out of the social, cultural, and material traces animated in texts, objects, and images. The appeal of the audio guide is its ability to create opportunities for deeper, more empathic ways of seeing beyond the objectified, observational mode of the museum, which Nemer feels limits which stories—historically as well as contemporary—might be seen, felt, identified with, and heard.[41] As much as this enterprise is an aesthetic one, drawing on the tools of historical craftsmanship, it is also eminently queer insofar as it makes good on Carla Freccero's argument, among others, that different methods of reading and engaging with past worlds are needed to render visible alternative timelines and nonnormative ways of being.[42] It recalls, too, Lorde's suggestion that the aesthetic register, in her case poetry, houses a particular ability to sharpen the senses to queer life. Nemer's practice not only provides a useful heuristic to think about how historical work happens in alternative spaces, places, modes, and registers but also suggests that this more sentimental, empathic way of making and experiencing history is vital to rendering marginality visible and thus better understood.

This somatic approach to history is also a deeply personal one. Born into a Jewish Canadian family with a keen interest in classical music and the fine arts, and nurtured by his beloved grandmother Rosalie, Nemer was always fascinated by the human voice. Classically trained himself, he wondered at the voice's "ability to transcend the body and occupy the interstitial spaces between maleness and femaleness, human, child, animal and machine."[43] As audiologists will tell us, the voice holds great power and prosodic cues like pitch, contour, and speed help awaken emotion, imagination, and nostalgia as conduits to knowledge.[44] For these reasons, it has emerged as Nemer's chief artistic material. It also has allowed him to craft what I have called a "queer art of history"—that is, a relational, sensorially driven art practice that constructs as well as communicates diverse, overlapping, intersecting pasts through sound, empathetic listening, and voice.[45] Some of these pasts are similar to the ones outlined by Steakley and Lorde, a past of radicalism, of discovery, of cross-border intimacies, of a queer activism and culture based on networks of intellectual exchange and also of sex. But the search for new ways of being in the world fully and completely, beyond the confines of marriage and state institutions, is enabled by re-creating a world of encounter, of imagining, of desire.

Cruising as Method

After several museum residencies, Nemer embarked on the various events that would culminate in the *Paradise* project. Originally imagined as something usable in any setting, the audio project soon evolved into a gallery piece for the Carleton University Art Gallery consisting of an audio guide and a series of sculpted installations extrapolated from the libraries visited, although this would have to be altered with the onset of COVID-19. Much like a historian, who presents conference papers so as to shape an idea, an artist hones their vision through performance pieces, workshops, and smaller staged events. In the early part of our work together, Nemer gained acceptance into the practice-based PhD program at the University of Edinburgh, where he began to craft dedicated workshops and art happenings with this project in mind. At the center of this program of research was the idea of kinship, of the ties that bind us to those in our midst and to those who came before us. Interestingly, it was through kinship networks in Edinburgh, and with the members of the Cruising the 70s Project (CRUSEV) specifically that Nemer learned of the work of another contemporary queer Jewish artist based in Berlin, who shared an interest in cruising as method.[46] Since the 2000s, the New York performance artist and filmmaker Liz Rosenfeld has explored the ways in which memory is queered, using cruising methodologies to illuminate how people enact their desire, take up space, and express the excessive abundance—and multidimensionality—of desire. In collaboration with the filmmaker Marit Östberg in 2015, Liz made the film *When We Are Together We Can Be Everywhere*, an erotic representation of cruising, friendship, and intimacy as shared commensurabilities within the eroticism of bodily desire. As Östberg put it in a podcast interview with Rosenfeld, "it was a way of exploring the world through your body."[47] Audre Lorde's embrace of the generative place of erotics is never far away from the pleasure activism of artists like Rosenfeld and Östberg, who, drawing inspiration from Black feminist models articulated by the scholar activist Adrienne Maree Brown, endeavor to center care, trust, and intimacy as a queer kinship practice. The intimacy of cruising as kinship extends to the audience of viewers in Rosenfeld's own performance art, which acts as a "duet of breath and flesh. Of giving my body to many bodies. Of allowing them to look at me. To be with me. To be with them." For Rosenfeld, cruising is an intersectional, nonbinary "practice, an art form, a need, a feeling, a glimpse into bodies, needs, uncomplicated while also intensely entangled in conflicting, mostly silent, emotions."[48] And it is a way to connect with Berlin's multivalent queer histories, across differences of gender comportment, sexuality, and desire. In connecting back to social and erotic interactions as a form of radical queer worldmaking and historicity, Liz's practice becomes part of what Fiona Anderson and Glyn Davies of CRUSEV have called a desire revolution (see plate 6).[49]

In *Paradise*, Nemer similarly takes up these ideas of erotic perambulations, of curiosity, cruising, and intellectual and metaphysical coming together amid gendered expectations, orientations, and performances, while moving through and beyond texts, encountering objects, fashioning lifeworlds, and exploring new as well as old ways of being together and sometimes apart.

What it became, this set of stories evocatively rendered, was a blueprint for a kind of kinship, one that moves beyond the heteronormative framework of family to include bonds of emotional and sometimes physical intimacy, rituals of togetherness, shared confessions and symbols, common associations, love, lust, and ideas. Using voice, song, touch, imagination, reading, and the books and material items found in the home libraries of these scholar/ancestors, it is an art piece that moves backward and forward through time, surfacing, reconstructing, and creating anew the emotional, social, intellectual, and sometimes sexual bonds that help us forge our various entries into the history, present, and possible futurities of LGBTQIA communities.

The contents of these home libraries are not the sole focus—and indeed, among the libraries visited, some are no longer in their original state, as in the case of the photographer and writer Hervé Guibert, who tragically died, at the age of thirty-six, of complications from a suicide attempt while living with AIDS. Indeed, it is what these libraries and their holdings open up and enable, whether as a literal archive of past lives or of what Ann Cvetkovich has called an archive of feeling, a real or imagined repository of shifting thoughts, sentiments, memories, and emotions that make up what it means to enter into queer relation with the past.[50] These libraries and archives tell their own stories of queerness, sometimes as identity but also, in Carolyn Dinshaw's sense, as a kind of slippage between norms and lack of fit.[51] It is in this space, too, that queer kinship resides, unlocked by experimental aesthetic practices of recovery and reanimation. The remnants of Jürgen Baldiga's estate, housed in the cellar of the Schwules Museum,* had that same resonance for the Black, queer/trans* filmmaker and theater director Jasco Viefhues, who decided to make a film about the scene photographer's life and death to AIDS. *Rescue the Fire/Rettet das Feuer* (2019), Viefhues's intimate portrayal of Baldiga's life and loves, rooted in the collective trauma of the AIDS crisis, was a conduit for his own exploration of the world of queer ancestors and what connects him personally to a queer community and history that does not always embrace people like him.[52] Yet Baldiga's life resonated for him for a host of reasons. Living in Berlin, he found one was always stumbling on a remnant of Baldiga in a cafe or bar, or at a friend's house; he was everywhere and nowhere at the same time all these years since his death in 1993. Another reason was his photography of the Tunte scene, discussed in chapter 3, and the sheer enormity of his artistic output, which included hundreds of photographs, forty diaries, and even Super 8 film—"a living archive of memory." As Viefhues recalls in conversation with the Brazilian German trans* performance artist Sanni Est

PLATE 1 SO36 of DJ
Ipek Ipekçioglu.
© Schwules Museum*
Berlin.

PLATE 2 Gayhana.
© Schwules Museum*
Berlin.

PLATE 3 Still frame from *It's Not the Homosexual That Is Perverse but the Situation in Which He Lives.* © Rosa von Praunheim.

PLATE 4 Gedenkkügel for Ravensbrück, Initiative for Autonomous Feminist Women and Lesbians from Germany and Austria. Designed by Petra Abel.

PLATE 5 Homo-Monument Berlin. © Christiane Wilke.

PLATE 6 From Liz Rosenfeld's *Tremble*, 2021, video installation. Still taken by Christa Holka. © Liz Rosenfeld.

PLATE 7 *The Rosa Song*, 2011. © Benny Nemer.

PLATE 8 *Bastien Partout, Epistolary Collage (A Letter to Elizabeth Lebovici)*, 2019. © Benny Nemer.

PLATE 9 *Gert and Mattias's Library*, 2017.
© Benny Nemer.

PLATE 10 *The World Will Always Welcome Lovers*, 2017. © Benny Nemer.

PLATE 11 *The World Will Always Welcome Lovers*, 2017. © Benny Nemer.

PLATE 12 *Playfair Library, Old College, University of Edinburgh*, 2019. © Benny Nemer.

PLATE 13 Benny Nemer exhibition, *I Don't Know Where Paradise Is*, Carleton University Art Gallery, 2020. © Olivia Johnston.

in her *Tea Talk* podcast series, archival collections like those in the Schwules Museum* are abundant. What we need is a way to renarrate them, to "unbox them" in such a way as to to expose what is already there—that is, intersections of Black, trans*, and queer lives and histories.[53] The way to unearth these kinships is by encouraging new ways of imagining historical work.[54] Kinship, like the queer art of history, is of limitless possibility provided it is grounded in recognition of difference and how that shapes and sometimes limits how people are able to narrate the story of their lives.

Nemer's sound pieces offer just such an opportunity to make manifest the various entry points into queer ancestry. They entreat their listener to respond on impulse and conjure up for themselves, through their senses, the shape and contours of complex and countervailing queer ecologies.[55] In privileging listening and sound as subjectivity's vector, the guide narrates an encounter with queerness as a polyvalent "space of entrances, exits, unsystematized lines of acquaintance, projecting horizons, typifying examples, alternate routes, blockages, (and) incommensurate geographies."[56] The world thus revealed relationally is a series of encounters between our own bodies in the present and the intimacies of the past unmasked through story and voice. Just as it materializes a whiff of what once was, there is always a slant, an untidy affordance that disrupts the possibility of scripted conventions and heteronormative alignments.[57] That slant is the sumptuousness of queer desire.

Each chapter of *Paradise* unfolds in a narrative read by different voices, with different cadences, and is focused around an object, a passage in a book or several books in a bathroom, a clock, a plant, or a mirror, creating what the artist refers to as "a touch across time." This way of evoking pastness through objects and story links the history of bathrooms and urinals and bathhouses to reading, cruising, and collecting as part of the search for queer selfhood in the present. But it is not about eliding time and collapsing difference. It is better aligned with what Dinshaw argues is a search for sameness while recognizing essential differences, one that counters simple "mimetic identification with the past or blanket alteritism" to make plain the "never-perfect aspect of identification" with "incommensurate lives and phenomena."[58] This approach holds great power. For those typically written out of history, memory is "a valuable historical resource, and ephemeral and personal collections of objects stand alongside the documents of the dominant culture in order to offer alternative modes of knowledge."[59] Indeed, this "will to remember," whether in history writing or in building community archives, has played a guiding role in LGBTQIA consciousness these last few decades.[60] As Heather Love says in *Feeling Backward*, knowledge of the "the losses of the past motivate us and give meaning to our current experience." It galvanizes a sense of imperative to continue fighting for rights and representation. Because successes can always be unmade, Love argues, "we are bound to memorialize" losses. Remembering the past as tragedy acts as a call to arms against present-day mistreatment, creating a shared struggle as a stand-in for lineage, an origin story, in the quest to "overcome that past, to escape its legacy," and never go back."[61] But pinned to this notion of the past as trauma are two things that are countered in Nemer's project: a nostalgia for a history told solely through suffering and the use of this narrative in stabilizing a vision of the present as a process of continual overcoming. There is something else too, an effort to move beyond the "wounded attachments" of identity politics in honor of hope, struggle, love, loss, and possibility.[62]

Told through short sonic vignettes downloaded to a personal device as an app or accessible via desktop, each story shuffles randomly with each new hearing. In this way, *Paradise* reveals different pathways through the various collections. No single experience dominates. From fleeting encounters with flowers, collections, and ephemera, to the ex libris stamp on a frontispiece, a glance in a hallway mirror, a moment alone with a book on a bathroom shelf, and an errant hand on an inner thigh, the audio-guide stories unlock a world of literature, poetry, lost love, of faraway magical places, of people in bondage as well as liberation, of lives lived—some feted—and others fully lost. In conjuring up these pasts, these library stories create moments of what Eve Sedgwick called queer identification, experiences at once subjective as well as shared, relational yet mediated through an earpiece or computer and a description of a plant, object, or book. As she had written in her 1993 essay "Queer and Now" in response to the growing number of queer suicides (already an issue in the early 1990s), things both real and imagined help concretize these conflicting emotions: "We needed an ability to attach intently to a few cultural objects, objects of high or popular culture or both, objects whose meaning seemed mysterious or oblique in relation to the codes most readily available to us, which became a prime source of survival. We needed there to be sites where meanings didn't line up tidily with each other, and we learnt to invest these sites with fascination and love." Prophetically, given the dangerous times we live in today, Sedgwick realized the importance of recognizing ourselves in these differences, especially when "institutions are speaking with one voice," when "religion, state, capital, ideology, domesticity, the discourses of power and legitimacy unite as a monolith around one word like 'family' or 'nation.'"[63] Queer performance and identification, Jennifer Doyle reminds us—whether through art actions, books, films, or stories—serve as "user's manuals for finding pleasure in a world more often than not organized around that pleasure's annihilation."[64]

But performing queerness should not be confused with looking to the past for icons and iconographies of fixed and firm sexual and gender identities. Already in that other moment of crisis in the 1990s—in the shadow of AIDS and Don't Ask, Don't Tell—scholars from Douglas Crimp to Jennifer Doyle, José Muñoz to Michael Warner had cautioned against an art practice bent on producing discrete and palatable subjects.[65] These criticisms mirrored those going on in the larger gay and lesbian movement, at least in North America, between anti-identitarians who wanted to keep the focus on the transformative role of desire and the assimilationists who argued that rights and representation meant working with the system. While rights-driven activists like Larry Kramer went so far as to blame the AIDS epidemic on queer promiscuity, Michael Warner affirmed the place of desire in *The Trouble with Normal*, claiming that "only when the indignity of sex is spread about the room, and in fact leaving no one out, does it begin to resemble the dignity of the human."[66] The art we need and deserve, Crimp argued, should be one that "defies the coherence and stability of all sexuality."[67]

This is not always what we got. In the quest to open up the notion of kinship to those previously outside of the system, the radicalism of libidinous queer sexuality somehow lost its edge. In some instances, it was co-opted by homonationalist valorizations of progress and diversity, positioning the West as best, on the backs of racialized and colonialized subjects, whom Jin Haritaworn has argued were at once pathologized as excessively queer and also not queer friendly enough.[68] It was confined to ever more private spaces with rampant gentrification and the closure of bars, bookstores, and cinemas.[69] And it was both mediatized and spectacularized through cruising apps and TV shows. As Lisa Duggan had argued in 2003, legal challenges and hard-won victories seemed to reinforce privilege instead of unmaking it.[70] So, the question becomes, how might an art practice open up a space for a genealogy of queer lives and history that moves beyond siloed identities; that retains an element of sex radicalism, beauty, and camp; that breaks down hierarchies of class, race, and gender; and that honors where we've come from and the battles waged; all while retaining an air of openness and fluidity and guiding us toward our uncertain future? One way is by taking what Nemer calls queer paths into queer libraries.[71]

Through circuitous routes of diverse beginnings and endings, *Paradise* lays this foundation for a new kind of history telling, one that proposes a relational, sensorially driven mode of making and communicating diverse stories. Nemer's use of voice, storytelling, gesture, movement, and sound helps create conditions for empathic listening, widening the spectrum of possibilities for ways to think about the relationship of the past to the present. This mix of aesthetic and historical registers, the blending of fact with fiction, stresses multivalence and possibility over a singular narrative truth. The act of listening to an audio guide outside of the gallery or museum space promotes shared subjective commensurabilities that challenge the exclusionary function of traditional museum displays, which turn on objective, documentary claims, while often reflecting a hegemonic vision of the past. In this way, Nemer offers a queer historical practice for how we might (re)present and engage with the diversity of past pasts, regardless of where we are positioned on the spectrum of identity. His multisensorial approach conjures up "new relations . . . with past figures who elude resemblance to us but with whom we can be connected partially by virtue of shared marginality, queer positionality."[72] Placing emphasis instead on the nodes and networks that bind us all in our own unique ways to this earlier time, it offers up a critical nostalgia instead of a redemptive one, focused around our shared connectedness to queer ancestors, whose lessons will help us navigate the road ahead.

"O Ancestors, What Was That Time Like?"

Like Viefhues, who was similarly drawn by the siren call of the archive and nostalgia for what once was, Nemer undertook countless visits to the homes of queer elders to step into the lost world of collections and the spaces and places of longing, comfort, community, lust, and sometimes, perhaps often, of sex.[73] It began with a series of encounters in 2014 in the library of the long-time lovers and collaborators Gert Hekma and Mattias Duyves. Hekma was a retired sociologist and anthropologist who founded gay and lesbian studies at the University of Amsterdam, where Duyves also taught as a sociologist. They had already encountered Nemer's *I Am a Boy Band* video installation from 2002, while conducting research for a course on masculinity. Hearing from mutual friends that he was in town, they invited him to their home four stories up a narrow staircase in an old building in the red-light district. The very same day, they received a book, *Rosa Radikale: Die Schwu-*

lenbewegung der 1970er Jahre (Pink Radicals: The Gay Movement in the 1970s), in which Simon Schultz von Dratzig speaks with the editors Andreas Pretzel and Volker Weiß about Nemer's 2011 community-led remake of the filmmaker Rosa von Praunheim's iconic *It Is Not the Homosexual Who Is Perverse but the World in Which He Lives*, which updates the iconic boudoir scene to include trans* and BIPOC performers and explicit mention of a queer politics and sociability that includes lesbians, migrants, and desire.[74] It is networks such as these, at once academic, social, intellectual, and artistic as well as activist, that Nemer hoped to surface in his audio guide (see plate 7).

Although Nemer's initial forays into the library project began with tea and flowers in Gert and Mattias's rooftop home, it quickly breached these boundaries. It would soon take Nemer to the libraries of the writer and photographer Hervé Guibert (Paris), the film scholars Adrian Rifkin (London) and Thomas Waugh (Montreal), the philosopher René Schérer (Paris), the RoSa Library for Gender Equality and Feminism (Brussels) as well as to sites, spaces, and projects that served as counterarchives for generations of queer and trans* people. These included the Thielska Galleriet (Stockholm), the cruising ground at the Hampstead Heath (London), and the Schwules Museum* (Berlin). The libraries of the trans* journalist Hélène Hazera, the art historian Elisabeth Lebovici, and the Morroccan filmmaker Abdellah Taïa, all in Paris, also figured in Nemer's artistic creation, although ultimately he was unable to gain access to them. Hinting at the fact that the ties of kinship are not always easy, he found alternative ways of incorporating them into his audio-guide installation on their terms through postcards and letters (see plate 8).

From that very first moment in Gert and Mattias's home, when his eyes darted from book to book, Nemer moved through the rows and stacks of books and ephemera pushed along by impulse. Like cruising for sex, opening oneself to that feeling of sexual charge and frisson and how it orients a person, a body, with a mix of curiosity and pleasure, Nemer encountered these holdings through a similar kind of sensory arousal. He decided to incorporate this sense of frisson and community into the project itself.

Moving this way and that, from one book spine to another, he allowed impulse to serve as navigation so much so that he decided to make cruising part of the art practice itself, with touch and sound orienting him, in Sara Ahmed's sense, through a series of sensual encounters that might disorient as much as they seemed to give direction.[75] These deviant directionalities, as Nemer calls them, unveil hidden perspectives, revealing the "minor histories" that make up queer kinship.[76] Moving sideways, to quote Ahmed directly, "puts one in contact with different bodies and worlds. This contact involves following rather different lines of connection, association, and even exchange, as these lines are often invisible to others."[77] Cruising the queer library and then reproducing these thoughts, impulses, and sentiments in the intimacy of the audio-guide encounter allowed Nemer to center erotic curiosity as a core feature of queer nostalgia and worldmaking.

Perched atop a pale blue stepladder in a corner of Gert and Mattias's library during one of twenty visits in total over several years, Nemer began one such journey. In his lap, he held "The Young and the Evil," a 1933 story by Charles Henri Ford and Parker Tyler, which Gert had located for him in his double-rowed bedroom bookcase. The artist had already met Ford in an anthology from a small shelf in Gert and Mattias's hallway toilet, in which Ford reminisces about his beloved Paris, where he met the surrealist René Crevel at one of Gertrude Stein's salons and the poet Edith Sitwell introduced him to the love of his life, the painter Pavel Tchelitchew. Ford tells this story while conjuring up an image of Djuna Barnes in faraway Tangier, in the flat they had shared for a time. Nemer's describes how at the time his eyes moved to the publisher of the anthology, *Gay Sunshine Interviews*, Winston Leyland, a British-American priest, author, and publisher whom the beat poet Allen Ginsberg credited with bringing gay-themed Asian and European literature to a wider audience at a time when even academics failed to appreciate its literary contribution.[78] Surprisingly, Leyland's name would be strewn throughout Gert and Mattias's collection. Simon Karlinsky, professor emeritus of Slavic languages at the University of California, Berkeley, put it this way: Leyland was part of a generation of "wonderful young people energetically asserting their identity and their rights to revolution" through the creation of a truly queer canon.[79] Nemer noticed this too. He noted in his Edinburgh dissertation that in the Hekma/Duyves collection Leyland "appears as the publisher of a book about consent in sadomasochism called *The Kiss of the Whip*; he is credited as the editor of a book of gay Latin American fiction entitled *My Deep Dark Pain Is Love*; and he is thanked in the translator's notes of a collection of homoerotic poetry by the eighth-century Persian poet Abu Nuwas." His connection to the library is even more personal still. When an errant letter addressed to Gert falls from one of the books, Nemer reads how Leyland himself thanked his host for helping him find an apartment in Amsterdam. Closing the circle that linked Paris to North Africa to the Global South and back to Amsterdam, Leyland signed off cordially with "yours in affectionate comradeship in gay liberation."[80] But the journey didn't end there, for beside the toilet anthology was a book of photography by the Nigerian-born photographer Rotimi Fani-Kayode, who died of AIDS in 1989, and another book, *Oceanic Homosexualities*, with a chapter, Nemer notes, "about a shaman from an indigenous Siberian community—a "woman transformed into a man"—who fastens the gastrocnemius from the leg of a deer to himself with a leather belt, using it as a strap-on dildo with which to penetrate his wife."[81] Cruising the library unearths a past more indecorous and diverse than first meets the eye.

In the audio guide to Gert and Mattias's library, first tested as part of a tour of their apartment in *The World Will Always Welcome Lovers* in 2017, Nemer explored these alternative ways we might overlay aesthetic, sonic, erotic, haptic, and historical registers to construct new ways of experiencing and appreciating the queer archive and queer lineage. He did this in two ways: by creating conditions for a series of sensorial, embodied encounters with queer legacies; and by revivifying these queer social, intellectual, and sometimes sexual networks of queer kinship. Here, Nemer presents us with a practice for honoring past relations while forging new possibilities for solidarity across difference. As Michael Warner argues, "Queer scenes are the true *salon des refusés*, where the most heterogeneous people are brought into great intimacy by their common experience of being despised and rejected in a world of norms that they now recognize as false morality."[82] Nemer extends this into the audio-guide encounter through an erotohistorical art practice centering kinship as a lived experience, as a relation or set of relations, instead of a category of belonging and being.

All My Relations

Kinship is not the same thing as family formation. Unlike the fight for civil union which reconfigures the queer family as a repository of rights and recognition, Nemer's art piece engages in another kind of kinship making, beyond the heteronormative underpinnings of social and legal categories. This mobile, relational, socially and intellectually libidinous queer sociability has existed as long as cruising and companionship, overshadowed and forgotten in the meanwhile in the long battle for acceptance. Fighting erasure of an explicitly violent sort, Indigenous studies scholars have pushed us to think past "kinship as family" as an apolitical, assimilationist model of being in the world, one that buttresses a modernist ontology and subject formation that has served settler colonialism and genocide. Instead of focusing on identity claims around visibility—who is represented and who is absent—she asks, What if we were to look instead for relationality or, in Kim TallBear's words, ways we might live "in good relation" with the world around us?[83] These relations would include honoring what came before us, critiquing it when necessary, and emphasizing what connects us to the world around us, including the social, physical, animate and inanimate, emotional communities in which we circulate and live. It would mean taking seriously how networks of ideas, impulses, and emotions orient us toward each other, how the shared experience of reading certain texts, collecting certain images, and holding artifacts and totems in our hands bind us in unique ways to vestiges of queer worlds. Not unlike Nancy's notion of "being singular plural," to live mindfully "in good relation" to ongoing pasts—sharing in these embodied acts of remembering together and alone by listening to storytellers and hearing the human voice—creates entry points into community, and in the case of these library collections of LGBTQIA elders, invisible, diverse, intricate, submerged, and forgotten worlds. In other words, it is about recognizing a kind of kinship that isn't hierarchical and progress driven, based on codifying difference and seeking inclusion. It is, as Katie Sutton argues, "an ethics of attentiveness" that seeks out and nurtures the fabulous as well as fraught ways we might already be living "in good relation" with those in our midst, harnessing the radical potential to dismantle and transform the siloed world in which we often find ourselves today.[84] Artistic creation like Nemer's is well poised to do this, perhaps in a way that history writing and museum curation is unable to do.[85]

Nemer's project traces the ties that bind us to queer and trans* communities historically as well as today, not eschewing the fissures that sometimes test our bonds. He re-creates a lost world of ideas and interactions, of traces and observances both ephemeral and real, linked together in an inchoate yet discernible way of being in the world together and sometimes apart. We are all, in a sense, networked via a series of interactions and encounters connecting actors, objects, and ideas on a continuum. These networks render legible the sometimes disconnected, and they help make the invisible seen. Nemer and I met through similarly circuitous kinship networks culminating in an art show/conference in Calgary. We realized, despite our differences, that we were living "in good relation" to the same kinds of issues and debates. So I became a bit of a participant observer to Nemer's art practice, attending some of the earlier ambulatory experiments with rendering the library stories discernible to an audience of listeners both in the space itself and in several other locations.

These same kinds of kinship networks are reconstituted in *Paradise*, workshopped in art actions in Berlin, Paris, and Amsterdam, first displayed in 2019 at the Playfair Library, Old College, University of Edinburgh, in September 2019, and then radically reconceived during the pandemic fall of 2020 in Ottawa.[86] In the Edinburgh variation, through story and recitation and musical interludes, Nemer enlists the listener in the journey to materialize encounters past. Although inspired by actual spaces, a home library in Amsterdam or across the street from the Bain Coloniale bathhouse in Montreal, the audio-guide vignettes are to some extent also untethered. They move across time and space, backward and forward, at once ethnographic and also historical (see plate 12).

These sonic circulations nudge the listener into a world of rituals, performances, and cues like the shared practice of collecting, touching, or citing from books. Words connect the audience/visitor across time and space just as the same book or photograph might be in Gert and Mattias's library as in Tom's or Elizabeth's or Adrian's or mine because we read the same work, cite the same sources, and consume the same images. Of course, this exchange is uneven and varied. As the fallout over Gert's participation in the Sexual Nationalism conference in Amsterdam in 2011 makes searingly plain, one person's diasporic is another person's homonationalism.[87] The traffic in thoughts and ideas, objects and collectables, however, is porous. It replicates our multiple affiliations while pointing to the limits of boundaries of identity. Nemer's evocations wrestle with this simultaneity, at once honoring the rarefied and at times exclusionary literary and visual iconographies of cruising, intergenerational sex, race, and beauty while opening up moments of reflection around the very politics of visibility itself, including the eroticization of a whole host of others. This is not homo-nostalgia, as Gloria Wekker rightfully calls out in *White Innocence*, recalling Lorde's intimate circle and its postcolonial critique; it is an aesthetic appeal for a more embodied, intersectional memory.[88]

But the ties that bind here go beyond what is found in the libraries themselves and the connections between the books and their authors, readers, owners, and users. They are also found in what is not represented in the library. As Nemer says in the opening sequence of the audio guide, drawing on Tina Campt, it is the soft hum of the not yet known or unrepresentable pushing its way back into our frame.[89] Or as Nemer puts it: "A vibration comes from the library: a hum. Is it the hum of the books? The murmur of characters and diagrams and photographs tightly pressed between pages, rubbing up against each other? Is it the hum of the things that for one reason or another did not find their ways into the library, humming, calling out for a reader?" These traces of lost, subterranean lives materialize in our ears and minds through the encounters offered up to the listener through ambulatory, improvisational, and scripted paths into and through these libraries, highlighting the recursive power that dwells in a queerness that emphasizes "the open mesh of possibilities, gaps, overlaps, dissonances and resonances, lapses and excesses of meaning."[90] Just as it is impossible to know the entirety of the contents of the library, so too is it impossible to reproduce the complexity of queer kinship. However, it is the hum that holds out the ever-present promise of possibility, of connection, of imagining the queer past anew.

Pandemic Pleasures, Plants,
and the Bonds of Community

When it became clear that COVID-19 was going to make an immersive in-person gallery experience impossible, Nemer, together with Carleton University Art Gallery curator Heather Anderson, began to chart out alternatives. The art project was always conceived as locative, connecting the audience to place through objects; now, the trick was to find new ways to orient participants listening from afar, to stimulate reflection and the attachments of kinship. Nemer did this with a mix of audio-guide story and art action, making floral arrangements with select members of the Ottawa-Gatineau LGBTQIA and Two Spirit community. Each week, participants would listen to a chapter of the audio guide and together with the expat East Berliner Kat Kost, owner of the Blumenstudio floral shop, craft their own interpellations with the libraries, gardens, and homes of these queer elders. Often integrating their own objects into their arrangements, from photographs to torn pages of books—even a whip and cock ring—respondents generated a series of personalized responses to the audio-guide chapters, extending the network of kinship outward in unanticipated ways. Through flowers and sculptural elements, these mediated encounters became moments of co-curation of the queer and now trans* and two-spirit past combining gesture, imagination, intimacy, and tactility with the aural experience of orientation facilitated by

Nemer. As Heather Anderson put it, the arrangements became "a poignant gesture amidst all the uncertainty, restrictions, anxiety; holding a space for the desire for normalcy, connection, and beauty. They served as a conduit for an array of emotions from sorrow and grief, loneliness and depression, to joy and wonder and on and on."[91] Nemer titled it *If You Have a Garden and a Library, Nothing Will Fail* after a passage from the Roman poet Cicero cited in the audio-guide chapter "A *Ficus Drupacea Pubescens*," which at once celebrates gardens and mocks the writer for his steadfast homophobia. The usurpation of his words within the generative framing of the plant installation and audio guide is a playful act of resistance against the duplicitousness of the Western canon, at once promoting homosociality while denigrating acts of same-sex love (see plate 13).

In the section of the audio guide named for the ficus, we hear about the constellations of potted plants and flowers on display in several of the libraries. In the Amsterdam collection, viewable from the sitting room, there is a giant ficus, a *Ficus Drupacea pubescens*, as the audio-guide voice instructs us. Its teardrop-shaped leaves reach out in every direction, touching shelves and furniture, expanding into the space while not dominating it. "Like the library, the ficus is a plural entity," a kind of fecundity unbound. This particular ficus, we are told, is robust, living, spreading, and reproducing while the actual species is now extinct in Europe. Mattias gives clippings to visitors, "offspring and disciples." The plants live on in the homes of friends as offspring in a vast floral network of hope and futurity. Plants and florals emerge in several aspects of Nemer's work. In the audio guide, they are "constellations that cluster and accumulate" even in the face of death. The artist juxtaposes the vivaciousness of a plant's longevity to that of the stories housed in the library, with comparisons between the legacies captured between the book covers to the preciousness of a preserved peony, its flowers and leaves pressed between the pages of a book. Breaking the divide between the human and nonhuman world, death and life, past and future, the ficus segment, like many others in the audio guide, evokes this alternative model of kinship as a polysemous set of relations both within and outside of time, to be nurtured, treasured, and shared even as they go on in multiple, sometimes simultaneous directions.

A section of the audio guide entitled "an octagonal mirror" tells this story of multiplicity and desire. The segment begins with a visual image of a sideways reflection in a curious curio, an octagonal mirror hung in the hallway of Gert and Mattias's library. It is announced by a female declarative voice before transitioning to a series of interlocutors young and old—although we can't know for sure—who speak to us in variously accented English, their words bouncing through our ears, painting pictures in our minds as we move with and against their instructions to look, see, and smell what they are describing. This vocal scaffolding mirrors the diversity of glances and gazes and viewpoints housed in and also obscured by the library.

The story soon diverges from the mirror into a meditation on the immensity of the library and the inability of the visitor to take it all in. "Seven thousand books in total," Mattias says, "far as the eye can see." There are books in the kitchen, in Dutch and French and German, "books on music stands, on armoires, on desks, behind the curtains, in boxes upstairs." There are books in the basement, behind other, hidden rows of books, behind tracksuits and clothes and the stuff of life. Just as the library's unending diversity breaches the boundary of what is thinkable, so too do the books blur together with the potted plants parked along the stacks, on stands, leading out to the veranda garden or the back yard. The cultural world of books bleeds into the natural world of plants. These stories have a life. They continue to grow even as they can no longer be contained. Nemer meditates on this in his discussion of the ficus.

No two audio encounters, even with the same listener, will be the same. Like the ficus, the audio-guide story is a living and growing thing; it is scripted in such a way that it could be augmented at a later time by other objects and stories from other libraries and new encounters. It may be listened to in situ, in a gallery setting, as when *Paradise* opened in September 2020, or in one's own library or living room from remote via the app and URL. The act of listening to these voices together and apart is a bodily experience that is at once subjective and connective. Its open-ended, transitory, participatory nature challenges contemporary museological and representational strategies of production and display. Queer paths into queer libraries require queer forms of listening.

In "Two Clocks," which refers to objects in Adrian Rifkin's London flat, we learn of the presence of two clocks with two different chimes, each marking, in effect, a different temporality. The storytellers in this segment, including Rifkin himself, remind us that the histories and characters brought together in these libraries live lives both out of time and in a kind of disjunct simultaneity. There is the time chronicled by the era in which the books themselves were penned, there are the stories that never made it into print, and there is the hum of those voices whose histories can never be read. Sound and also listening open up the potential to hear and feel and see this multiplicity of stories, of temporalities, of life courses. It is in connecting sound and movement and story that *Paradise* offers an entry into a new way of experiencing queer worldmaking, by enlisting the help of the audience to sort these images in their mind as they listen.

These vignettes create conditions for a relational, sensorially driven mode of making, communicating, and experiencing diverse histories. The use of voice, storytelling, gesture, movement, and sound, lends shape to a kind of empathic listening, bridging the past and present and widening the spectrum of possibilities for new and diverse knowledge formations and solidarities. This use of aesthetic and historical registers—the blending of fact with fantasy, the movement backward and forward in time and across space—stresses multivalence and possibility over a singular narrative truth. Listening queerly helps create an erotohistorical practice around shared affinities, allowing for new ways to experience the diversity of past pasts and imagine possible futures.

Queer Practices

What is the queer potential of such an art practice both for addressing the fullness of queer worldmaking and as a possibility of solidarity across difference? The audio guide is a nonsequential, open-ended act of artistic creation that forges a palimpsest of impressions, each washing over the listener. When thought of as an art and museum piece, these sonorous embellishments provide a more broadened spectrum of historical experience by disrupting traditional forms of documentation and display, which recenters hegemonic tellings, devoid of emotion, subjectivity, and pathos. Seeking to capture the sumptuousness of life, love, and desire in a multiplicity of forms, *Paradise*'s embodied interactions manifest a plurality of ways of being in relation to the queer past. In conjuring up forgotten associations within collective queer history, it enacts a social experience of radical remembrance. If memory is a social and political process of relating to the past, queering kinship implicates us in this history, holding out the possibility of emboldening action in the present and "remembering for the future."[92]

How should we think about Nemer's mix of truth and fantasy in his plurivocal recasting of historical artifacts and events? For one, this immersive, participatory experience, guided by at least the perception if not the attainment of truth and a search for the real, affords meaningful opportunities to unsettle hegemonic sources and narratives to better see, feel, and identify with a multivalent, nonnormative, queer past. Nemer manipulates form and content in ways that disrupt traditional historical narrative practice. Yet his audio guides are deeply historical, the product of archival and secondary source research. Each vignette unfolds out of the next, collapsing time and historical distance. When combined with instructions for how to move about the space, it reinforces a shared, empathic historical experience as the interplay of voice, movement, and listening displace what the cultural theorist Adriana Cavarero has argued is the detached documentary impulse that marks much of the Western tradition with its attendant privileging of the mind over the body.[93] According to Nancy, the phenomenological, bodily experience of listening empathically affords a better opportunity to understand alternative cadences, "accents, timbres, and resonances" typically absent from the historical record.[94] Unlike the fears Carolyn Dean cites regarding traditional narrative accounts and their tendency to universalize suffering in the service of meaning making, the sensory nature of these audio-guide story- and soundscapes allows for a measure of multivalence, of multiple possible tellings coexisting in one overarching narrative.[95] We see this in the way that Nemer purposely avoids synthesis; nowhere does he fuse together disparate elements into a single narrative. Instead, his stories are open-ended, circuitous, and diffuse. At the same time, each is deeply personal or rather personalized as his polyphonic sounds and stories call on listeners to imagine a world of relationships and experiences beyond the dialogue and musical cues.[96]

Audio-guide storytelling roots such knowledge in the body, in its impulses, desires, and emotions. It emphasizes listening and imagining over seeing, in contradistinction to Western sensory modernity which privileges texts, vision, and visuality. *Paradise* orients us toward objects, spaces, and places—the urinal, the bathhouse, the garden—and opens up new orientations for how to think about them as part of a shared imaginary with multiple points of entry. In the urinal segment, which begins with a glance out the window to the red-light district, only to build into a nuanced cultural history of urban transgression, cruising, spectatorship, and female prostitution, its broadened narrative creates conditions of empathy across difference, among improperly queer, wayward, unruly subjects.[97] Nemer unlocks affective affinities as a basis for communing and communicating with the queer/trans* past as a form of kinship similar to TallBear's notion of "being in relation"—an imaginative yet deeply felt kind of kinship and solidarity based around vulnerability and marginalization but also around the "shifting intensities between nastiness and lovingness."[98] In creating ways we might imagine ourselves as connected each in our own way through affinities, desires, solidarities, and "shared horizons of struggle," this relational kinship does not hinge on a preformed, neatly delineated queer subject.[99] Rather, kinship is always already imperfect. And because it is also material, insofar as it is not just a performance, kinship also houses within it possibilities for a critique of locatedness in recognition that these relations are not the same. Just as TallBear's concept of relationality is land-derived, drawing attention to the very material, ongoing emergency of Indigenous erasure, so too does *Paradise* materialize possibilities for thinking critically about whose stories comprise the erotohistorical canon. It does this by situating sex itself alongside histories of love, loss, community, and mutual aid, decentering cis and reproductive temporalities while likewise refusing to fix new, revolutionary, queer/trans* ones. In this way, Nemer's art piece honors the radical though sometimes problematic worldmaking of queer elders while opening up possibilities for new, connective, bodily histories of desire to challenge the staid conventionalism of today's dangerously changing world.

In an age of antigender campaigns, and populist and far right mobilizations against queer, trans*, feminist, and antiracist places, policies, and people, it is especially important to develop ways we might organize in good relation and across difference. A way to do this is to unearth the historical ties that have bound our various communities across race, across borders, through different gender performances, spaces, times, and place. These ties are not identifications in the sense of sameness or wholeness. They are not without power imbalances that desperately need addressing. We can never lose our critical lens. Rather, kinship asks us to reconsider, as our ancestors did, whether there isn't power in a kind of queer worldmaking that rebukes the urge to affirm, align, or assimilate with the dominant culture. A way there is with a radical rethink of genre, one that merges the aesthetic with the historical—a queer art of history.

EPILOGUE

Either we share the world with everyone, or we lose
it with everyone.

—Sabine Hark, *Gemeinschaft der Ungewählten*

THIS BOOK has made the argument that kinship serves
as a better conceptual model than identity for how we
might think more capaciously about queer and trans*
lives, loves, struggles, and journeys in the past and the
experiences that might be possible in the future. It asks
us to look for the embodied, sensorial, and relational
ways in which people have navigated homophobia and
persecution, often in very different ways, considering
the diverse and sometimes strained coalitions that
have evolved out of individual and collective responses
to injustice and invisibility. Kinship is a useful analytic
because it pushes back at the teleological assumptions
at work in the narrative of queer and trans* becoming
that has come to dominate much of the twentieth-
and early twenty-first-century story of LGBTQIA activism and politics, papering over a richer, if no less
complex—and not always happy—history. Among
the wrinkles ironed out in the dominant telling is an
uncritical embrace of toleration as the cornerstone
of German liberal democracy, without subjecting to
scrutiny which bodies, selves, practices, and ways of

being in the world have challenged recognition and full citizenship, paraphrasing Fatima El-Tayeb, as the gays who could not properly be gay.[1] Kinship directs our attention to the fraught and sometimes contingent alliances and associations born of struggle. Drawing on transdisciplinary frameworks allows us to see the elaborate interlacing of difference, while situating ourselves in the process of discovery and interpretation. Queer kinship challenges us to think beyond the artificially drawn and contingent boundaries that often denote our scholarly practice while at the same time questioning claims to knowledge that purport to speak for the whole without thinking through differences of experience, scale, status, marginality, and power.[2] It is at once a politics of radical alterity and a method.

The answer to this problem of how to write a more capacious history of LGBTQIA life after fascism is not, in other words, to find new ways to silo experiences. Rather, it is to develop a robust methodology that allows us to think intersectionally, across difference, to open the frame to new and diverse ways people have come together historically, to truly queer how history in fact happens and how we make sense of it. Viewing queer relationality, as messy, ambiguous, fraught, and also fabulous as it can and sometimes has been, allows us a space to tease out the multiple and different ways in which queer- and trans*-identified people have imagined their pasts and futures, sometimes within the bounds of marriage, family, normative gender presentation, and reproductive citizenship, and at other times with and beyond them. It offers more than a wedge in the narrative of queer futurity, one that bears a strange resemblance to hegemonic, heteronormative institutions and experience. It renders thinkable the unthought, the histories that have fallen by the wayside in our quest to narrate the successes of social and legal recognition. Here, a huge debt is owed to Black feminist and queer of color critique for insisting on history's role in crafting not just a recuperative kinship but one imbued with the possibility of rupture itself. As Saidiya Hartman had contended in 2003, cultural histories of power and liberation must do more than recount "the desire for inclusion within the limited set of possibilities that the national project provides." What is necessary is a radical rethinking of what emancipatory politics means when the language of freedom, choice, and rights simply reinforces, in a new form, the essence of alterity in the first place, transposed onto other citizens.[3]

Queer kinship understood as a kind of radical relationality can do this work because it is more nuanced and more encompassing than identity. It speaks to the intellectual and emotional attachments that link people across difference to the struggles of everyday life. Kinship affords us insight into the affective affinities that bind gays, lesbians, and trans*-identified people—and their allies—in a personal quest for greater emotional and sexual fulfilment and connection. This radical form of relationality across difference questions how that might drive but also inhibit emancipatory politics, especially around matters of race.[4] Kinship entreats us to consider different points of emphasis in our history writing, to linger over ambivalences and silences, as we think about paths not taken or immediately revealed through the sources. Relationality is unbearable, as Berlant and Edelman write, for the way it productively disturbs pretenses of cohesiveness and the fixity of identity.[5] Instead of writing a narrative of persecution and overcoming, as an example, which in the German context has privileged white gay male experience, kinship broadens the scope to include countervailing impulses within LGBTQIA activisms that unveil the different temporalities of experience around visibility, community, and subjectivity that emerged out of the tensions, fissures, exclusions, and oppositions in queer memory and worldmaking. Instead of taking for granted the teleology of liberation and its more assimilationist outcomes, a focus on partnerships, parallels, and even untenable allegiances makes the journey toward legal recognition strange. Disturbing the practice of writing queer and trans* history as a genealogy of becoming, in other words, of looking for ancestors and tracing back aspects of what is taken for granted now as fixed and firm, kinship nudges us to ponder other usable pasts, sometimes overlapping ones, and the tensions, discontinuities, and pluralisms that marked them along the way, sometimes even propping up dominant tellings.[6]

Viewed from the first decades of the twenty-first century, queer life after fascism has come quite far. Queer exhibitions have secured state funding, the Schwules Museum* has transformed from a small community archive into a center of research and museological innovation (while retaining its roots as a place of activism), and queer victims have earned a space in national memory, if not always in a value-neutral way. Some small, activist-driven organizations have grown into independent foundations, like the Magnus Hirschfeld Foundation, which advances a robust research agenda while still serving an important role in archiving the stories and memories of queer and trans* kin. In almost every mid- to large-size city from Kiel to Konstanz, there are local-level groups meeting the needs of their constituents, be that in health and welfare provision, migration-related outreach, and simple but important community building. These civil society organizations are the lifeblood of queer, trans*, and migrant activism, community, and memory work. Some groups have mobilized intersectionally around antiracist initiatives to remember the victims of the National Socialist Underground (NSU) murderers and the Hanau shootings, to draw out connections between antisemitism, white supremacy, and homophobia, while other activists work within the panoply of federal foundations associated with the various parties to develop queer-feminist analysis of economic precarity, climate change, global antitrans* and antigender campaigns, health, human rights, law, and social justice.[7] Others, like the artist Moshtari Hilal and the geographer Sinthujan Varantharajah have taken different tacks, using social media to direct attention to what in the spring of 2021 they saw as the inability of mainstream German society to see how race continues to undergird all aspects of everyday life. In protesting the gentrification of the erstwhile immigrant and working-class neighborhood of Neukölln in Berlin through the establishment of a posh lesbian feminist bookstore, financed, they argued, by family money tarnished by Nazi connections, the artists drew attention to the inconsistencies of progressivism, especially one wrapped in the rainbow flag.[8] That this work consistently falls on the shoulders of "persons with a migration background," as the inelegant German phrasing goes, is itself telling.

In other words, as we have seen here, as certain LGBTQIA lives have been mainstreamed as part of the fabric of the liberal state, others continue to challenge the universalist impulses that govern how these normalized queer identities take shape. Despite the critical interventions of queer, queer of color, Black feminist, and trans* approaches, identity has reemerged as both the question and the answer for how to recognize queer lives in the past. As Michel Foucault put it in an interview in the *Advocate* from 1984, a sexual politics of experimentation, fluidity, and flux has given way to one of recognition in which "identity becomes the law, the principle, the code of (one's) existence." Suddenly, one's place in the world today is secured by a past that confirms how we got here. This leaves very little room for bad gays, difficult histories, and internecine struggles, in essence for a productively fraught politics of difference.[9] It also masks the coalitional successes amid these charged moments of shared struggle that may not have elided differences completely but held forth the prospect of actuating relationships "of differentiation, of creation, of innovation," in a word *kinship*.[10]

Another benefit of a heuristic-like queer kinship is its malleability, the way it is able to take on many different hues across different traditions. When deployed mindfully, self-critically, it can explore the broad range and potential of anti-identitarian historical critique while putting forward ways to theorize intersectional experiences. There is an ethical component as well, as the writer/researcher and student of history self-consciously examines the past with multivocality in mind, listening for the "hum" of buried lives amid the cacophony of noises from the past.[11] In this way, looking and listening for historical kinship means keeping the door open for what Michael O'Rourke has called "queer insists"—that is, the as-yet illusory but not quite unimaginable prospect of a different future.[12] In other words, an attentiveness to the messiness of meaning in the past makes possible new and different ways forward. Viewing queer coalitional activism as running across local, national, and transnational spaces holds the potential for seeing queer and trans* citizenship in places and spaces that are not always recognized as sites of political action and belonging.

Thinking about the queer past relationally, both across identity and in relation to outcomes, real and imagined, reveals the paradoxes on which queer claims making is founded, nudging us to think about the societal investments in and around particular historical projects and protocols. But while some historians are committed to genealogical critique, we still tend to frame LGBTQIA historical developments in law, justice, and society as owing to the power of pluralism and the embrace of transgressive identities that are "taken as the referential sign of a fixed set of customs, practices, and meanings, an enduring heritage, a readily identifiable sociological category, a set of shared traits and/or experiences."[13] When pluralism is accepted uncritically as the outcome of shared struggle without subjecting the different investments in diversity of experience to questioning, we fail to grasp the slippages around whose behavior, thoughts, and actions have challenged these new, supposedly progressive norms. The perceived universalism of identity then—even when rooted in emancipatory politics—simply reinforces the normalization of certain social formations over others, and mostly, as we've seen here, those closest to white heteronormative ideals.

In recent years, Germany has become fertile ground for conversations around identity politics. Some of this is the result of a resurgent Far Right populism, which has seized on academic feminism, queer and trans* theory, and postcolonialism in the service of attracting adherents. Other parts of the debate are owed to shifts in memory culture more generally around the place of colonial violence and structural racism and how, for some, this challenges the singular place of the Holocaust in how Germans come to terms with past crimes. Debates around postcoloniality and race have taken different forms, from disagreements about the BDS movement to the Achille Mbembe controversy more specifically and the scholar's comparison of Israeli occupation policy to apartheid.[14] At the heart of these conversations around violence, citizenship, and remembering are questions of implication and responsibility for a history writing and memory that may be used to cement and protect human rights.[15] Those who critique the liberal paradigm and call for greater attention to the ways in which we remain implicated in and sometimes inadvertently supportive of structures of oppression have incurred all sorts of opposition from charges of antisemitism to cultural relativism. These positions transcend left and right and have seeped into the wider queer counterpublic sphere, with a good bit of vitriol directed at intersectionality, queer of color, postcolonial, and academic feminist and trans* approaches within and outside the LGBTQIA community.[16] Challenges to intersectional organizing have a long history, with several different flashpoints, including divisions between the reformist and radical wings of the homosexual action groups, the challenge posed by intergenerational sex, lesbian separatism, the primacy of gay male persecution in the memory politics of the twentieth century, and the role of race and transsexuality in lesbian and queer activism. As with all social movements, queer, lesbian, feminist, and trans* organizing has always been productively contentious and multidimensional.[17] But there is something particularly pernicious about the form such criticisms have taken since the mid-2000s. Unlike the height of the culture wars, when conservatives were among the most vocal critics of identity politics, academic feminism, multiculturalism, and queer theory, now it is the liberal middle that has intersectionality in its sights, and in Germany this poses a great challenge to postfascist kinship.

Critics argue that identity politics threatens to undermine the hard-won gains made over the course of the last decades and century. Forcing attention toward the inequalities within mainstream LGBTQIA organizations around race, immigration status, gender presentation, and the different experiences of cisgendered same-sex-desiring men, women, and transpersons—so the argument goes—has a silencing effect and takes away from the successes of the movement. Worse still, according to Jan Feddersen, the editor of the left-leaning Berlin daily newspaper *taz*, it is a form of "Queergida." Not unlike the Far Right anti-immigration "rightwing mob (Pegida) that threatens the liberal republic," those "members of the smart as shit insider club (Klugscheisser*innensekte)" espouse a politics of moralism, sanctioning all those who don't toe the ideological line.[18] Weaned on the writing of "the academic high priestess," Judith Butler, Feddersen argued that they are worse than a cult, waging a war against cis white men and lesbians. Recriminations to this particular phrasing were swift. Jörg Litwinschuh-Bartel, then executive director of the Magnus Hirschfeld Foundation, wasted no time calling Feddersen out for normalizing Pegida, "discrediting LGBTQIA emancipatory and activist work [*Emanzipations- und Bildungsarbeit*] and creating gay victims where they don't exist," but the damage was already done.[19]

What comments like these really do is expose the fault lines and fissures within the various queer communities, even in an era of greater acceptance. To some extent this is a generational shift, brought about by changes in Germany's memory culture as it grapples with how to think about the history of race and racism beyond the tragedy of the Shoah. But it is also a clash of approaches, ideologies, and traditions, each laying claim to queer insouciance. At the center are disagreements over the place of queer, queer-feminist, and trans* modes of critique, especially when they force progressives to take an unwelcome look in the mirror at their own foibles and frailties and the way that they themselves may perpetuate and benefit from structural injustices disrupting the unifying claims of community. In the hands of these critics—part of a queer counterpublic sphere that includes journalists, writers, and lay and public historians, some with large platforms and wide reach—this criticism pushes back against academic debates originating to a certain extent in the English-speaking world, a sign of the provincialism of queer and trans* history as a field with a small but dedicated presence in the German university. But there is more here too. These criticisms are also a sign of the normalization of populist discourses around queer, feminist, and intersectional criticism within the mainstream. And this is worrying.

The charge of identity politics—once the domain of the right—has become the clarion call of parts of the liberal and left center, with gendered language, racial inequality, and gender nonconformism the new battleground. Not infrequently, history itself is at the center of debate, with the past weaponized in the service of argument. As this book has shown, this is a process that has been underway for some time. It bubbled up again at the time of writing and is worth lingering over by way of conclusion because it shows us how urgently needed a queer art of history and kinship is in these troubled times.

The argument most often launched by critics of intersectional, antiracist, queer/trans* critique is that it is political, polarizing, against history and truth. We saw this in evidence in the spring of 2021, when the former SPD federal president Wolfgang Thierse went on record in the *Frankfurter Allgemeine Zeitung* asking, "How much identity can society handle?" His concern was that "ethnic, gender, and sexual identity discussions are dominating" the national conversation through an increasingly aggressive set of claims making, choking out political discourse with assertions of structural racism, sexism, homophobia, and transphobia that are so polarizing that they threaten to undermine the common good.[20] Thierse went so far as to claim in successive follow-up interviews that "normal members of the SPD" agreed with his take, which *Tagesspiegel* columnist Sidney Gennies suggested was as good as saying white men stand in agreement with him, that gender, sexuality, and race are divisive issues that don't represent the party's base.[21] This was followed up by another op-ed in the *FAZ*, the same newspaper that had published Thierse, this one by Alexander Zinn, the former opponent of including lesbians in the Homo-Monument, now a research associate at the Fritz Bauer Institute (named after the closeted judge and prosecutor who helped bring down Adolf Eichmann). In the time since the monument debate, Zinn has made the minimization of lesbian persecution his stock in trade, claiming that attempts to write women into the story of Third Reich abuses threatens to "clear a path for a new form of historical falsification."[22] In the *FAZ* article, he made the outrageous claim that diversity-driven projects, like those that shine a light on Islamophobia within the queer movement, are not just divisive; they are akin to the government of Iran's heinous treatment of queers by throwing them off of rooftops.[23] Even Sahra Wagenknecht, leader of the Left Party, took a page from the right-wing AfD Party's playbook on the coercive role of gender studies and queer theory with her comments that "ever more curious minorities" (*skurille Minoritäten*) and so-called lifestyle leftists are self-entitled and morally righteous, a blight on the movement.[24]

Although adherents would suggest that this is a form of "left fascism," the overheated discussion of identity politics and cancel culture shares many of the same talking points as the global Far Right. As Roman Kuhar and David Paternotte have shown, in the last years similar tropes have surfaced in different national contexts, all united by the vitriolic hatred of gender and queer studies.[25] Indeed, in 2017, the AfD made this one of the main pillars of their federal parliamentary bid.[26] But this is more than a simple example of the power of the Vatican to shape debates around the family, or the platform of Far Right parties and regimes against the future of difference.[27] It is a reflection of the crisis of democratic liberalism generally, a reactionary effort to construct a new universalism, which threatens to normalize regimes of power based around the hierarchization of identity with real-world implications for immigration policy, human rights standards, and everyday life.

What sociologists have labeled antigenderism has already motivated the closure of gender studies programs in Hungary; has placed academic feminism, queer theory, critical race theory, and postcolonialism in the crosshairs in France and Germany; and has armed pundits with a vernacular language with which to besmirch opponents—widely and openly in legacy, scene, and niche media.[28] It has united older so-called 1968ers (the generation of student activists associated with the New Left) with a new crop of social critics, many of whom have struggled to find their footing in the precarious aftermath of the 2008 financial crisis. Like the Far Right, they have leveled their criticism at the expertise of scholars and the terms of intellectual debate, which they see as veering away from the course of equality-based mobilizations.[29] They purport to be the voice of truth and reason while advancing arguments steeped in the language of culture wars and entrenchment against what they see as the shrill, guilt-inducing narratives of structural racism.[30] Their language betrays a deep-seated animosity toward third-wave feminism, postcolonial thinking, and the transatlantic exchange in ideas. Sometimes it is as though the manosphere's Jordan Peterson himself has penned the copy. As former student of gender studies turned anti–queer theory polemicist Vojin Saša Vukadinović puts it, "The queerfeminist next generation pummels on campus, in the streets and in the internet 'white cis men' . . . incessantly denounces the 'privileges' of others, demands gender neutral pronouns, and ponders with whiny verve about vulnerability. Personal pain has been made a theme of academic discussion, and guilt for one's own shortcomings cast outward on someone else."[31] The fact that it is voices like those of Feddersen, Zinn, and Vukadinović that get platformed in mainstream press is troubling.

The ultimate goal is unmistakable: to roll back the influence of academic feminism, queer theory, and postcolonial theory for their supposed lack of scholarly rigor, for perpetuating an us-versus-them mentality, for insisting on the study of racism and social inequality within progressive causes, and for supposedly emboldening an entire generation of adherents to shout down naysayers. With the 2017 publication of the book *Beißreflexe* (Bite Reflex) and follow-up volumes edited by Vukadinović and the political cabarettist and Tunte (Sissy) Patsy l'Amour laLove, these linkages made their way into the queer community as well. These volumes—published in the deliberately polemical Kreisch-Reihe (Shout Out Loud) series of the LGBTQIA scene Querverlag with a fleet of essayists—are self-styled polemics on what contributors see as a form of queer-feminist groupthink perpetuated by gender studies professors and their underlings. What for Feddersen was the almost cult-like stance of adherents of Judith Butler, in the hands of Vojin Saša Vukadinović is the narcissism of a generation that can't think for itself.[32] Although it is tempting to see this as just another manifestation of internecine battles within and among adherents of the splintered left, sprinkled among these statements are deeply concerning comments on the almost inherent violence of Islam, the danger of gender nonconformism to the feminist cause, and the propensity not only for language policing but violence itself, often, against an unsuspecting middle that doesn't see it coming.[33]

This deeply pessimistic criticism of queer and gender theory takes aim at intersectionality and what critics see as a hierarchization of oppression, which leaves no space for legitimate critique of real-world issues affecting everyday citizens: violence against women, structural racism, and economic precarity. Yet, in the service of polemics, it is a deliberate misreading of the central tenets of intersectionality, that no axis of identity is wholly insepa-rable from others, and that certain configurations of class, gender, sexuality, ethnicity, and nation are better represented in politics, memory, and social institutions to the privilege of some and the detriment of others. Hegemonic identities, indifferent to contrasting degrees of status and power within and across social groups and movements, put pressure on other members of the community to see themselves in a single way too, reacting against those who dare to question the singularity of identity and the continuation of structural forms of inequality.

Although critics of hierarchies within the queer counterpublic sphere are often charged with undermining the universalism of the movement tout court by (in their logic) overemphasizing the persistence of inequality as a kind of "wounded attachment" or ressentiment without end, at its core, the project of queer liberation was by definition an intersectional politics of refusal.[34] To argue that now-intersectional approaches are undermining the power of coalitional politics and universalism is not only a display of extreme igno-rance but a misreading of the multidimensional history of queer organizing in the 1960s and 1970s that serves as an antecedent to the present day.[35] In effect, the mainstreaming of gay liberation has separated us from this rich and productively fraught history of discord. What we really need to be ask-ing is how this legacy of queer activism has turned into an endorsement of the status quo, which in today's landscape is littered with fears of feminist, gender, and trans* critique bordering on anti-intellectualism. What should truly puzzle us is how a once radical political movement has become so defanged that it rests on a vision of queerness that endorses monolithic logics as the epitome of progress and reason.

Polemics like Feddersen's and Vukadinović's point to the limits of toleration, one of liberal democracy's most central virtues. They would be just another stand-alone relic of generational anxiety and turnover within the movement if not for the fact that both writers hold considerable sway in the mainstream and subcultural media. Both have taken particularly firm stances on freedom of expression, Feddersen on the side of gender-critical feminists like the former Sussex professor Kathleen Stock, a victim of what he termed "Wokistan" to connote the "anti-freedom mob in a state of self-intoxication," and Vukadinović as a member of the Network of Freedom of Academic Expression, which has mobilized against perceived threats to research and teaching from "ideologically motivated restrictions" to language conventions and the Trans* Self ID Law.[36]

As this book has shown, Feddersen's vitriol against intersectional queer and trans* scholarship has a long history. It surfaced again in late 2019 around an effort to build a new queer cultural center. Named after Johanna Eberskirchen and Magnus Hirschfeld, as a nod to the entangled histories of feminism and sexology, the Eberskirchen-Hirschfeld-Haus, or E2H project, was imagined as a central archive and cultural space in central Berlin.[37] This queer cultural house, the brainchild of Initiative Queer Nations e.V., hoped to open its doors in 2020 in the former location of the *taz* newspaper offices near Checkpoint Charlie, the former boundary between East Berlin and West Berlin. Funded by Berlin state money, with an academic council of prominent historians, it would gather under a single roof many of the city's smaller gay, lesbian, trans*, and intersex libraries, archives, and cultural centers including the lesbian archive Spinnboden, the Magnus Hirschfeld Society, the feminist archive FFBIZ, and the Research Unit of Cultural History of Sexuality at the Humboldt University of Berlin.[38] The goal was to bring these groups together in solidarity while respecting each organization's rich history and autonomy, providing a space for research, outreach, and learning steeped in the historical importance of sexology to the human rights struggle around sexuality and gender nonconformism.[39] There were bound to be hiccups figuring out how to proceed, especially in an already charged atmosphere with Feddersen not only a guiding force within the project but one of the two chairpersons of the board. Indeed, when the organization offered a platform to a known transphobic radical feminist in the name of "free speech," things boiled over. Letters to the editor of major newspapers ensued, and one by one the archives and libraries pulled out of the initiative. Lost was a real opportunity here for kinship across difference. But there were also real lines in the sand. An earlier version of the talk was to take the name "Transkrake," or Trans Octopus, an image evoking the multiple tentacles and reach of trans* activism that treads a wee bit too closely to the widely circulated antisemitic canard. As I wrote in the *Tagesspiegel*, in kinship with US, UK, Australian, Israeli, and German academics, "a queer institution that is transphobic is worth nothing."[40]

That this noxious brew of racism and transphobia has been somehow rendered *salonfähig* in Germany should give us pause. How can it be that it continues to mark queer life after fascism? As I have argued here, not only are these arguments and platforms frequently based on a misrepresentation of the present, but they also rest on a misrepresentation of the past, a past that has given ample evidence of the productively fraught nature of queer kinships over time. Although often told as a single-issue quest for sexual freedom, gay liberation (as it was once called) was always—if awkwardly— intersectional, emerging out of a variety of progressive struggles around race, gender equity, class, colonialism, and sexuality. Indeed, the early histories of the Homosexual Action Group in West Germany and the Homosexuelle Interessengemeinschaft in the East were not just multidimensional; they were transnational, incorporating ideas from those united in struggle from other countries. These groups mobilized around analyses of interlocking oppressions. Peopled by gay, lesbian, and gender variant activists—not always in easy alliance—they endeavored to find ways to transform society and improve the human condition.

These early groups demonstrated the capacity to mobilize around an intersectional platform that in theory at least linked the question of sexual liberation to antiracist, anticapitalist, and anti-imperialist rebellion, although not all members of these groups necessarily saw eye to eye. Tiffany Florvil has shown that queer Black Germans stood in uneasy alliance with their lesbian and feminist sisters despite their common goals. And the Pfingsttreffen of 1973 and the so-called *Tuntenstreit* exposed huge chasms within the HAW along the lines of gender presentation, which ultimately divided the move- ment between reformists who saw change as achievable through the system with allies from mainstream parties and organizations, and radicals who opted to stick to some vestige of the revolutionary tradition.

With time, this multipronged radical agenda ceded territory to a single- issue politics of rights, respectability, and national belonging in support of the free market. To quote Roderick Ferguson, the queer of color theorist and professor at Yale University, who draws from Herbert Marcuse, queer politics became "a one-dimensional affair" delinked from these parallel projects for racial, gender, and class justice and focused instead, exclusively, on the matter of individual rights. Sexuality was made a private matter, no longer a catalyst for widespread social change. This was not just a kind of realpolitik; it was a form of backlash to the multi-issue character of the radical queer project. Now those who wish to draw attention to long-standing tensions around ethnicity, race, gender, transgender equality, and class inequalities that once drove the movement are deemed divisive or, worse, they are blamed for threatening to undermine the gains so hard won, losing the hearts and minds of the middle, or even worse, embracing a kind of nihilist cultural relativism that threatens the democratic project itself.[41]

What is the way forward? A better use of our time and collective energy than calling out leftists and feminists and trans* and queer of color activists for supposedly silencing debate, reading Butler, and undermining democracy as we know it would be to look at queer history for those moments of coalitional activism and falling out, so as to question the myths of universal progress and tolerance that have overlooked an even grander and sometimes problematic tradition of refusal, discord, and debate. We have witnessed important gains. As queerness made its way into the political and economic mainstream, it has produced opportunities that were unthinkable decades ago. Yet many of those same gains have been made by institutions that benefit some more than others, canceling out the intersectional and multidimensional past that helped make the movement in the first place. Kinship asks us to consider lessons from feminist antiracist formations of positionality, to account for the differently legible, visible, and accepted and how we might find new ways to relate those experiences to community, and on what terms. Thinking about the cost of inclusion asks us to look for more ethical, mindful, varied, self-reflexive histories by thinking about how we might live "in good relations" with the world around us. This means honoring what came before, recognizing the friction, violence, and messiness, so as to tap instead into the emotions, temporalities, hums, sights, and sounds of belonging. Such a model of kinship isn't about seeking inclusion in the state but about transforming it, which in an age where centrist antigender studies campaigns look an awful lot like populist and Far Right attacks on queer, trans*, feminist, and antiracist spaces, places, policies, and people, it is that much more crucial and necessary.

Notes

Introduction

1 Tobias, "Ein nostalgischer Ausflug."

2 Isherwood, *Christopher and His Kind*, 2. The age of consent was 21 for same-sex activity among men and 16 for heterosexual couples. In 1973 the age of consent was lowered from 21 to 18. See Moeller, "Private Acts."

3 Fischel, *Screw Consent*; Rubin, "Thinking Sex."

4 Halperin and Hoppe, *War on Sex*.

5 Stanley, *Atmospheres of Violence*, 3; Hobson, *Lavender and Red*.

6 W. Brown, *In the Ruins of Neoliberalism*; Reddy, *Freedom with Violence*.

7 J. Butler, "Critically Queer," 20.

8 Scott, "Evidence of Experience"; Toews, "Intellectual History."

9 Doan, *Disturbing Practices*; Haritaworn, "Shifting Positionalities."

10 Howard Chiang has provided a useful critique of the salience of identity-based medical models, arguing instead for more fluidity in how we think and write about experience and identities. See Chiang, *Transtopia*.

11 Hanhardt, "Radical Potential of Queer Political History?"

12 Cohen, "Punks, Bulldaggers, and Welfare Queens."

13 Gentile and Kinsman, *Canadian War on Queers*; Halperin and Hoppe, *War on Sex*.

14 B. Smith, *Home Girls*.

15 The list is long here, but central to my own thinking is the work again of Cathy J. Cohen, "Punks, Bulldaggers, and Welfare Queens," but also the challenge posed by Sharon Holland to Judith Butler and to queer theory in general: to take stock of systemic racism in how we theorize the radical potential of queer worldmaking as an alternative form of kinship. Holland, *Erotic Life of Racism*. See also Ferguson, *Aberrations in Black*; and Gill-Peterson, *Histories of the Transgender Child*.

16 Eng, *Feeling of Kinship*.

17   Cook, *Queer Domesticities*; Allen, "Black/Queer/Diaspora"; Gill-Peterson, "Trans* of Color Critique."

18   J. Butler, "Critically Queer"; Heintz, "Crisis of Kinship."

19   Spillers, "Mama's Baby, Papa's Maybe."

20   Freeman, "Queer Belongings," 305.

21   Garde, "Provincializing Trans* Modernity."

22   Haritaworn et al., "Obligation, Social Projects and Queer Politics."

23   Beachy, *Gay Berlin*.

24   Aviv, "German Experiment"; S. C. Huneke, "'Do Not Ask Me.'"

25   Nay and Steinbock, "Critical Trans* Studies."

26   Marhoefer, "Queer Fascism and the End of Gay History."

27   El-Tayeb, "'Gays Who Cannot Properly Be Gay.'"

28   Paul, *Perverse Assemblages*.

29   TallBear, "Caretaker Relations"; LaDuke, *Recovering the Sacred*; Bernardin, "Intergenerational Memory."

30   On the need for alternative methods for getting at those written out of the archive, see Hartman, "Venus in Two Acts"; and Sharpe, *In the Wake*.

31   Traub, *Thinking Sex*.

32   Rose, *Politics of Life Itself*.

33   Ahmed, *Queer Phenomenology*; Evans, "Seeing Subjectivity"; Gammerl, *Anders fühlen*.

34   Halperin, *How to Do the History*.

35   Aizura et al., "Thinking with Trans* Now," 127.

36   Amin, "Genealogies of Queer Theory"; Doan, *Disturbing Practices*.

37   Chakrabarty, "History and the Politics of Recognition."

38   Doan, *Disturbing Practices*.

39   Smith-Rosenberg, "Female World of Love and Ritual."

40   Dinshaw et al., "Theorizing Queer Temporalities," 179.

41   Harsin Drager and Platero, "At the Margins."

42   Campt, *Listening to Images*; Muñoz, *Cruising Utopia*.

43   Duggan, "Discipline Problem"; Herzog, "Sexuelle Revolution"; Herzog, *Sex after Fascism*.

44   In the German case, much of this important story has only recently become available in English. See Griffiths, *Ambivalence of Gay Liberation*; S. C. Huneke, *States of Liberation*; and Newsome, *Pink Triangle Legacies*. An excellent beginning analysis of homoeroticism in Far Right imaginaries is Tobin, "Evolian Imagination."

45   Puar, *Terrorist Assemblages*; Haritaworn, "Shifting Positionalities."

46   Thanks to Laura Horak for drawing my attention to this. See also Haritaworn, "Queer Injuries"; Haritaworn, *Queer Lovers*; and Stryker, "My Words to Victor Frankenstein."

47 Gopinath, *Impossible Desires*.

48 Wiegman, *Object Lessons*.

49 Jin Haritaworn reflects on queer methodologies as a form of orienting oneself toward the past in Sara Ahmed's sense in "Shifting Positionalities," a wonderfully rich and prescient call for an ethics of care when conducting queer research.

50 An interesting exception to this is Benno Gammerl, *Anders fühlen*.

51 Garde, "Provincializing Trans* Modernity."

52 Fischel, *Sex and Harm*.

53 Miller and Lemmey, *Bad Gays*; Haritaworn, *Queer Lovers*; Stryker, "My Words to Victor Frankenstein."

54 Ferguson, "Of Our Normative Strivings"; Stryker, "Interview."

55 Chitty, *Sexual Hegemony*; H. Lewis, *Politics of Everybody*.

56 Rubin, "Thinking Sex."

57 Sedgwick, *Epistemology of the Closet*.

58 Warner, *Fear of a Queer Planet*, xviii.

59 J. Butler, "Lesbian S&M."

60 Weinberg, "Pleasure and Danger."

61 For a collection of photographs from the series *Schwule Ladys*, 1986, see *Love at First Fight!* exhibition, Schwules Museum*, Berlin, accessed July 17, 2021, https://www.schwulesmuseum.de/ausstellung/love-at-first-fight-english/.

62 Martin, *Femininity Played Straight*, 84; Holland, *Erotic Life of Racism*, especially her chapter on desire.

63 Edelman, *No Future*, 3.

64 Hennessy, *Profit and Pleasure*.

65 Garcia, "Can Queer Theory Be Critical Theory?"

66 Holland, *Erotic Life of Racism*, 3.

67 Ferguson, *Aberrations in Black*; Muñoz, *Disidentifications*.

68 Puar, *Terrorist Assemblages*.

69 Halberstam, "Straight Eye for the Queer Theorist."

70 Halberstam, *In a Queer Time and Place*.

71 Dinshaw et al., "Theorizing Queer Temporalities," 178.

72 Ahmed, "Affective Economies"; see also Kai Pyle's notion of transtemporal kinship in "Naming and Claiming."

73 TallBear, "Caretaker Relations."

74 Muñoz, *Disidentifications*.

75 Alexander, *Pedagogies of Crossing*, 308.

76 Lorde, "Uses of the Erotic," 57; E. P. Johnson, "Revelatory Distillation," 313.

77 Moten and Harney, *Undercommons*, 30.

78 Ahmed, *Living a Feminist Life*, 15.

79 Cohen, "Radical Potential of Queer?," 142.

1. Entangled Histories

Parts of chapter 1 appeared in *Life among the Ruins: Cityscape and Sexuality in Cold War Berlin* (Basingstoke, UK: Palgrave Macmillan, 2011).

1 Rubin, "Thinking Sex"; Weston, *Families We Choose*.

2 Dinshaw et al., "Theorizing Queer Temporalities"; Freeman, *Time Binds*.

3 Sedgwick, *Epistemology of the Closet*; Ferguson, *Aberrations in Black*; Halberstam, "Forgetting Family."

4 Cohen, "Radical Potential of Queer?"; Stryker, "Time Has Come."

5 Ferguson, *Aberrations in Black*, 4, 17.

6 Berlant, "Starved," 435.

7 Love, *Feeling Backward*.

8 Grossmann, "Question of Silence."

9 Stryker, *Transgender History*, 1.

10 Micheler, Michelsen, Terfloth, "Archivalische Entsorgung der deutschen Geschichte?"; Ruddat, "Geschredderte NS-Dokumente."

11 Schoppmann, *Zeit der Maskierung*; Marhoefer, "Lesbianism, Transvestitism"; Dennert, Leidinger, and Rauchut, *In Bewegung bleiben*.

12 Jellonnek, *Homosexuelle unter dem Hakenkreuz*; Micheler, *Selbstbilder und Fremdbilder*; Pretzel, *NS-Opfer unter Vorbehalt*; Pretzel and Roßbach, *Wegen der zu erwartenden hohen Strafe*.

13 Florvil, *Mobilizing Black Germany*.

14 See especially the chapters by Ingeborg Boxhammer and Christiane Leidinger, Rainer Herrn, and Ulrike Klöppel in Schwartz, *Homosexuelle im Nationalsozialismus*.

15 Tomberger, "Homosexuellen-Geschichtsschreibung."

16 Micheler, "Homophobic Propaganda," 195.

17 Espagne, *Transferts*; Osterhammel, *Geschichtswissenschaft jenseits des Nationalstaats*.

18 Conrad, Randeria, and Sutterlüty, *Jenseits des Eurozentrismus*.

19 Evans, *Life among the Ruins*.

20 Stryker, Currah, and Moore, "Introduction: Trans-, Trans, or Transgender?," 14.

21 Judith Butler, "Merely Cultural," 265; N. J. Smith, *Capitalism's Sexual History*; Therborn, "Entangled Modernities."

22 Stockton, *Queer Child*; Gill-Peterson, *Histories of the Transgender Child*.

23 Sedgwick, *Tendencies*, 8.

24 Kruse, *Bomben, Trümmer, Lucky Strikes*, 12.

25 Knopp, "Sexuality and Urban Space," 149.

26 Hoffmann, "Gazing at Ruins."

27 Evans, "Bahnhof Boys."

28 Ciesla, "'Über alle Sektorengrenzen hinweg . . .'"; Major, *Behind the Iron Curtain?*, 28.

29 Bader, *Soziologie der Deutschen Nachkriegskriminalität*; Thurnwald, *Gegenwartsprobleme Berliner Familien*.

30 Von Rönn, "Politische und psychiatrische Homosexualitäts-Konstruktionen."

31 Harsch, *Revenge of the Domestic*; Timm, *Politics of Fertility*; Heineman, *What Difference Does a Husband Make?*

32 Riechers, "Freundschaft und Anständigkeit"; Balser et al., *Himmel und Hölle*; Pretzel and Roßbach, *Wegen der zu erwartenden hohen Strafe*.

33 Dobler, *Polizei*; Bollé, *Eldorado*.

34 Kammergericht Berlin, "Urteil v. 21.2.1950."

35 Grau, "Im Auftrag der Partei"; Grau, "Sozialistische Moral und Homosexualität."

36 Klemens, *Die kriminelle Belastung*, 15.

37 Amtsgericht Tiergarten, 274 Ds 100/55, June 1, 1955.

38 Landesarchiv Berlin (hereafter LAB), B Rep 013 Senatverwaltung für Jugend und Familie. Nr. 502 letter from Der Senator für Jugend und Sport, Hauptpflegeamt, Berlin-Reinickendorf, July 21, 1955, to Frau Kay regarding a newspaper article in *Der Abend* from July 2, 1955, entitled "Arbeitshaus für Strichjungen."

39 LAB, C Rep 303/9 Polizeipräsident in Berlin, Nr. 248 Tätigkeitsbuch MII/I—Aussendienst—, May 8, 1948–April 23, 1949, 10.

40 LAB, C Rep 341 Stadtbezirksgericht Mitte, Nr. 4743 case against Hans. L. 18 Ju Js 585.50—99 Ds 100.50.

41 Roos, *Weimar*.

42 Bessel, *Germany 1945*, 225.

43 Heineman, "Hour of the Woman"; Heineman, *What Difference Does a Husband Make?*

44 Biess, "Survivors of Totalitarianism"; Moeller, "Last Soldiers of the 'Great War.'"

45 Weeks, *World We Have Won*.

46 Evans and Mailänder, "Cross-Dressing."

47 See Kriminalhauptkommissar Schramm, "Das Strichjungenunwesen," 90.

48 LAB, B Rep 051 Amtsgericht Tiergarten #10685.

49 See the court case files from LAB, B Rep 051 Amtsgericht Tiergarten.

50 LAB, C Rep 303/9 Polizeipräsident in Berlin 1945–48, Nr. 259.

51 LAB, C Rep 303/9 Ministerium des Innern, Der Polizeipräsident in Berlin. Nr. 249 Weibliche Kriminalpolizei 1945–48, 6–12.

52 LAB, C Rep 303/9 Polizeipräsident in Berlin 1945–48, Nr. 243 Abteilung V. Meldungen und Berichte 1945–48. See also the "Survey of Juvenile Delinquency in Berlin" from the Office of the Military Government of the US Sector (OMGUS), Berlin Sector dated August–October 1946, US National Archives and Records

Administration (NARA), College Park, Maryland, RG 260 OMGUS Berlin Sector, Public Welfare Branch, box 192.

53   LAB, C Rep 303/9 Polizeipräsident in Berlin 1945–48, Nr. 259, 310. Raid report, Bunker Schlesischer Bahnhof dated February 11, 1946.

54   Whisnant, "Styles of Masculinity."

55   LAB, B Rep 051 Amtsgericht Tiergarten, Acc. 1687 #100685. Statement of Jugendamt to Bezirksjugendgericht Belin-Schöneberg by social worker overseeing the case.

56   Evans, "Decriminalization."

57   E. Butler, *City Divided*, 80.

58   Middleton, *Where Has Last July Gone?*, 148.

59   Moreck, *Führer durch das 'lasterhafte' Berlin*, see especially 564.

60   Prickett, "'We Will Show You Berlin,'" 165.

61   Moreck, "Wir zeigen Ihnen Berlin," 564.

62   Brett-Smith, *Berlin '45*, 103.

63   Gasser, *Erinnerungen und Berichte*, 129.

64   Brett-Smith, *Berlin '45*, 106.

65   E. Butler, *City Divided*, 72.

66   Brett-Smith, *Berlin '45*, 105.

67   Brett-Smith, *Berlin '45*, 106.

68   Akantha [Werner Becker], "Berlin tanzt!"

69   Dobler, *Von anderen Ufern*, 112–13.

70   Dobler, *Von anderen Ufern*, 110.

71   LAB, B Rep 20 Acc. 993, Nr. 6975.

72   Dobler, *Von anderen Ufern*, 252.

73   Schlüter, Steinle, and Sternweiler, *Eberthardt Brucks*, 158.

74   "We're All in This Together," research project by Markues, supported by the Schwules Museum* in Berlin, accessed July 17, 2021, http://wereinthistogether.de/.

75   Schlüter, Steinle, and Sternweiler, *Eberthardt Brucks*, 158.

76   Meeker, *Contacts Desired*.

77   On this, see Andrea Rottmann's fabulous dissertation, "Queer Home Berlin," where she uncovered previously unseen police reports on night raids in the city's queer bars. This will be published as a monograph in 2023 as *Queer Lives across the Wall*.

78   Timo Glamor, interview by Karl-Heinz Steinle.

79   Schoppmann, *Days of Masquerade*; Lybeck, *Desiring Emancipation*.

80   On the Nazi history of these establishments, see Dobler, *Von anderen Ufern*, 182–90.

81   Rottmann, "Queer Home Berlin," 142–44.

82 Rottmann, "Queer Home Berlin," 144; "Kampf dem Laster: Razzia in Kreuz-berg," *7 Uhr Blatt am Sonntag Abend*, November 10, 1957.

83 Dobler, *Von anderen Ufern*, 254.

84 See discussion of the court case in Dobler, *Von anderen Ufern*, 254.

85 Pulver, *"Das war janz doll!,"* 99–100.

86 Dobler, *Von anderen Ufern*, 232–34.

87 Dobler, *Von anderen Ufern*, 236.

88 See the *Queer as German Folk* exhibition, a joint offering of the Schwules Museum* and Goethe Institut North America, accessed July 15, 2021, http://queerexhibition.org/en/before/ellis-bierbar.

89 Mahlsdorf, *I Am My Own Woman*, 110.

90 Mahlsdorf, *I Am My Own Woman*, 110.

91 McCormick, *Gender and Sexuality*, 6.

92 Von Praunheim, *Sex und Karriere*, 51.

93 Muñoz, *Disidentifications*.

94 Erel et al., "On the Depoliticisation."

95 Puar, *Terrorist Assemblages*, 212.

2. The Optics of Desire

Parts of chapter 2 were published in "Seeing Subjectivity: Erotic Photography and the Optics of Desire," *American Historical Revi*ew 118, no. 2 (2013): 430–62.

1   Domröse, *Herbert Tobias*, 241.

2   Bauer and Cook, introduction to *Queer 1950s*, 6.

3   Asibong, *"Nouveau Désordre"*; Littauer, "'Someone to Love.'"

4   Nash, *Black Body*; Steinbock, *Shimmering Images*.

5   Shimizu, *Hypersexuality of Race*, 5.

6   Fischel, *Screw Consent*.

7   Mercer, "Reading Racial Fetishism"; Mercer, "Just Looking for Trouble." This notion of "feeling at home" is from Lorde, "Uses of the Erotic."

8   Mercer, "Reading Racial Fetishism," 194.

9   Passerini, *Europe in Love*; and the contributions to Passerini, Ellena, and Geppert, *New Dangerous Liaisons*.

10 Williams, *Hard Core*.

11 Heartfelt thanks to Elspeth Brown for nudging me in this direction.

12 Muñoz, *Cruising Utopia*, 2009, 42.

13 E. Robinson, "Touching the Void."

14 Thomas, "Evidence of Sight."

15 Edwards, "Thinking Photography," 33.

16 Attwood, "Reading Porn"; F. Jackson, *Strategies of Deviance*; Ahmed, *Cultural Politics of Emotion*; Clark, *Desire*; Stoler, *Carnal Knowledge and Imperial Power*.

17 Apel and Smith, *Lynching Photographs*; Tucker, *Nature Exposed*; Trachtenberg, *Reading American Photographs*; Barriault, "Hard to Dismiss," 222–23.

18 Wells, *Photography*, 59.

19 Burke, *Eyewitnessing*, 10.

20 Auslander, "Beyond Words"; Hunt and Schwartz, "Capturing the Moment," 269.

21 Waugh, "Third Body"; Evans, "Queer Beauty."

22 Barthes, *Camera Lucida*, 27–28.

23 Gell, *Art and Agency*.

24 Benjamin, "Work of Art"; Crew, "Visual Power?"

25 Sontag, "On Photography," 351.

26 An important exception to this is McLellan, "Visual Dangers."

27 Tagg, "Neither Fish nor Flesh."

28 Sekula, "On the Invention," 87.

29 Halberstam, *Queer Art of Failure*, 147–72; Herzog, *Sex after Fascism*; Whisnant, *Male Homosexuality*.

30 Cvetkovich, *Archive of Feelings*; Halberstam, *In a Queer Time and Place*; Love, *Feeling Backward*; Dinshaw et al., "Theorizing Queer Temporalities."

31 Moeller, "Private Acts."

32 Scott, "Evidence of Experience."

33 Herzog, "Syncopated Sex."

34 Tobias, "Die Erinnerung ist das einzige Paradies," 6–9.

35 Tobias, "Leben zu Protokoll," 8–13.

36 Hoffmann, "Gazing at Ruins."

37 Domröse, *Herbert Tobias*, 12–14.

38 Tobias, "Geschichte mit Manfred," 21. On cruising across the German-German boundary, see Evans, "Bahnhof Boys."

39 Azoulay, *Civil Contract*.

40 Warner, *Publics and Counterpublics*.

41 Beccalossi, "'Italian Vice,'" 188–90.

42 Barthes, "Wilhelm von Gloeden," 204–6.

43 Vendrell, *Seduction of Youth*, 81.

44 Samper Vendrell makes this point in new work on von Gloeden.

45 Amin, *Queer Attachments*.

46 Shepard, "'Something Notably Erotic.'"

47 Vendrell, *Seduction of Youth*, 82.

48 Crane, *Fashion and Its Social Agendas*, 193; Sender, *Business and the Making of a Gay Market*, 28.

49 Ellenzweig and Stambolian, *Homoerotic Photograph*; Gardiner, *Who's a Pretty Boy, Then?*; Weiermair and Nielander, *Hidden Image*.

50 Boone, "Vacation Cruises"; Mulvey, "Visual Pleasure and Narrative Cinema."

51 Waugh, *Hard to Imagine*; Katz and Ward, *Hide/Seek*.

52 Wittdorf, *Lieblinge*.

53 Waugh, *Hard to Imagine*, 99; Turner, *Backward Glances*.

54 Waugh, "Posing and Performance"; E. H. Brown, "Queering Glamour."

55 Goldin et al., *Ballad of Sexual Dependency*.

56 Ellenzweig and Stambolian, *Homoerotic Photograph*, 113; Hall, *Minor White*.

57 Waugh, *Hard to Imagine*, 406; Hanson, *Bob's World*.

58 Knappett, "Photographs"; Pinney, "Things Happen."

59 Domröse, *Herbert Tobias*, 265.

60 Pretzel, *Homosexuellenpolitik*; Kennedy, *Ideal Gay Man*; Meeker, "Behind the Mask."

61 Kaye, "Male Prostitution," 5.

62 Hoven, *Der unaufhaltsame Selbstmord*.

63 Baseler et al., *Himmel und Hölle*, 136; Laserstein, *Strichjunge Karl*, 54; Micheler, "Homophobic Propaganda," 125.

64 Dannecker and Reiche, *Der gewöhnliche Homosexuelle*.

65 Schmidt-Relenberg, Kärner, and Pieper, *Strichjungen-Gespräche*; Schickedanz, *Homosexuelle Prostitution*.

66 Churchill, "Transnationalism"; Julian Jackson, "Arcadie"; Rizzo, "Ideal Friend."

67 Cook, "Families of Choice?"; Hornsey, *Spiv and the Architect*.

68 Sternweiler, "Poesie of a Gay Everyday," 42.

69 Castiglia and Reed, *If Memory Serves*.

70 This negative is one of the 46,000 bequeathed to the Berlinische Galerie and transported there in one of three deposits, as per his wishes, from the Hamburg apartment of his executor and friend Pali Meller Marcovicz. Domröse, *Herbert Tobias*, 8.

71 Dyer, *Heavenly Bodies*.

72 Friedlander and Szarkowski, *E. J. Bellocq*.

73 Borhan, *Men for Men*, 73.

74 S. M. Smith, *Photography on the Color Line*, 6.

75 Tobias, "Ein nostalgischer Ausflug," 24–25; Escoffier, *Bigger Than Life*.

76 Pultz, *Body and the Lens*, 11.

77 Mercer, "Reading Racial Fetishism," 177.

78 Mercer, "Reading Racial Fetishism," 177.

79 Mercer, "Reading Racial Fetishism," 181.

80 Nash, *Black Body*.

81 Evans, "Long 1950s."

82 Tobias, "Leben zu Protokoll," 9.

83 Tobias, "Ein nostalgischer Ausflug," 24–25.

84 Borhan, *Men for Men*.

85 Heineman, *Before Porn Was Legal*.

86 Escoffier, *Bigger Than Life*; Regener "Amateure"; Frackman, "Homemade Pornography."

87 Stratton, *Desirable Body*, 179.

88 Ahmed, "Affective Economies."

89 Mort, *Cultures of Consumption*.

90 Borhan, *Men for Men*, 256; Liddiard, "Changing Histories," 23.

91 Clarke, *Photograph*.

3. Imagining Trans*gression

Portions of chapter 3 appeared in "Cross-Dressing, Male Intimacy and the Violence of Transgression in Third Reich Photography," *German History* 39, no. 1 (March 2021): 54–77, which I cowrote with Elissa Mailänder.

1 Steinbock, "Photographic Flashes," 254.

2 Sedgwick, *Tendencies*, xii.

3 Steinbock, "Wavering Line."

4 Benjamin, "Work of Art."

5 Drager and Platero, "At the Margins."

6 Silverman, *Miracle of Analogy*.

7 Keegan, "Getting Disciplined."

8 Tourmaline, Stanley, and Burton, *Trap Door*.

9 Mbembe, *Necropolitics*. For examples of this, see Tourmaline, Stanley, and Burton, *Trap Door*. An example of trans* portraiture in the hands of trans* and nonbinary artists is the *Radical Tenderness: Trans for Trans Portraiture* exhibition at Alice Austin House, accessed July 21, 2021, https://aliceausten .org/radical-tenderness/.

10 Berlant, *Cruel Optimism*; Steinbock, "Puncture Wounds."

11 Halberstam, *Trans**.

12 Barad, "TransMaterialities," 401.

13 Bosold, Brill, and Weitz, *Homosexuality_ies*, 3.

14 Regener, *Visuelle Gewalt*.

15 E. H. Brown and Phu, *Feeling Photography*; Köppert, *Queer Pain*; Meyer, "Mapplethorpe's Living Room."

16 Hirschfeld and Tilke, *Der erotische Verkleidungstrieb*, 1–2.

17 Sutton, "Sexology's Photographic Turn." See also Herrn, *Das 3. Geschlecht*.

18 Herrn, *Das 3. Geschlecht*.

19 Halberstam, *In a Queer Time and Place*, 107.

20 Sutton, "'We Too Deserve a Place.'"

21 Herrn, "Transvestitismus in der NS-Zeit"; Herrn, "In der heutigen Staatsführung"; Schwartz, *Homosexuelle im Nationalsozialismus*, 101–6.

22 Marhoefer, "Lesbianism, Transvestitism"; Marhoefer, *Sex and the Weimar Republic*, 59–60. See also Sutton, "'We Too Deserve a Place.'"

23 Sternweiler, "Er ging mit ihm alsbald," 59–63.

24 Whisnant, *Queer Identities and Politics*, 231.

25 Baer, *Spectral Evidence*.

26 Appadurai, *Social Life of Things*.

27 Roos, "Backlash," 81; Schnorr, "Jenseits der 'Volksgemeinschaft'?"

28 Le Schäfer, "Neue Gesetzgebung."

29 Landesarchiv Berlin (hereafter LAB), A Pr.Br.Rep. 030-02-05–169, 1935–1938 Police Investigation Department, punitive action Kitzing, Fritz (*December 28, 1905).

30 See Herrn, *Schnittmuster des Geschlechts*; Rosenkranz, Bollmann, and Lorenz have explored the experiences of gay transvestites in *Homosexuellenverfolgung in Hamburg 1919–1969*, 63–69.

31 Roos, *Weimar*; Timm, "Sex with a Purpose."

32 Caplan, "Administration of Gender Identity"; Herrn, "In der heutigen Staatsführung"; Sternweiler, "Er ging mit ihm alsbald."

33 B. Grünheid, "Fritz Kitzing," accessed June 21, 2021, https://rosawinkel .kulturring.berlin/?biografie=fritz-kitzing, which draws on Sternweiler, "Er ging mit ihm alsbald."

34 Report dated June 11, 1935, LAB, A Pr.Br.Rep. 030-02-05–169.

35 Marhoefer, "Lesbianism, Transvestitism."

36 Boxhammer and Leidinger, "Sexismus, Heteronormativität," 96.

37 Berlin Gestapo protective custody report, March 4, 1936, LAB, A Pr.Br.Rep. 030-02-05–169.

38 Taylor and Herrn, "Hirschfeld's 'Female Transvestites,'" 137.

39 Sekula, "On the Invention"; Fischer, *Sozialanthropologie*.

40 Regener, *Visuelle Gewalt*, 95.

41 Barthes, *Camera Lucida*.

42 It is not insignificant that the best theorization of refusal comes from critical race theory. See Fanon, *Wretched of the Earth*. See also Campt, *Image Matters*, 80.

43 Stryker and Chaudhry, "Ask a Feminist."

44 Steinbock, "Photographic Flashes," 260.

45 Haritaworn, Moussa, and Ware, *Marvelous Grounds*, 5; Stryker, "(De)Subjugated Knowledges."

46 Letter from Hans Joachim Kitzing to Fritz Kitzing in police custody, March 3, 1936, LAB, A Pr.Br.Rep. 030-02-05–169, Polizeipräsidium Berlin-Kriminalpolizeileitstelle.

47 Rottmann, "Queer Home Berlin?"; Pretzel, *Homosexuellenpolitik*; Pretzel, *NS-Opfer*; Neiden, "'. . . Er ist §175 (warmer Bruder)'"; S. C. Huneke, *States of Liberation*.

48 S. C. Huneke, "Morality."

49 Bakker et al., *Others of My Kind*.

50 Halberstam, *Trans**, 24.

51 Taylor, "Visual Medical Rhetorics of Transgender Histories," 210.

52 Steinbock, "Wavering Line."

53 Stein, "Next," 405–6. See also Ades, "Duchamp's Masquerades"; and Jones, "'Women' in Dada."

54 D. Johnson, "R(r)ose Sélavy," 84.

55 Blessing, *Rrose Is a Rrose*.

56 Namaste, *Invisible Lives*.

57 J. H. Jackson, *Paper Bullets*.

58 Evans, "Seeing Subjectivity."

59 Prosser, *Second Skins*, 11.

60 Spector, "Note on Photography," 159.

61 Berger, *Ways of Seeing*.

62 Spector, "Note on Photography," 173.

63 Kaiser, "8. Zusammenfassung und Ausblick," 8.

64 Jürgen Klauke, *Physiognomies*, Art Institute of Chicago, accessed July 15, 2021, https://www.artic.edu/artists/70741/jurgen-klauke.

65 Cahan, *Mounting Frustration*.

66 Frackman, "Homemade Pornography."

67 S. C. Huneke, "Gay Liberation behind the Iron Curtain."

68 McLellan, "Visual Dangers."

69 Zuromskis, *Snapshot Photography*.

70 Rottmann, *Queer Lives across the Wall*.

71 From Thomas's stated biography—as encapsulated in the archives of the FFBIZ, the Feminist Archive, the Schwules Museum*, and in interviews conducted by the Hirschfeld Foundation as part of their Archive of Other Memories project—we'd learn she identified then as now as a "Bubi" (a German euphemism for lesbian).

72 Rottmann, "Queer Home Berlin?," 153–54; Steinle and Leffers, "Mittenmang."

73 Halberstam, *Trans**, 50.

74 Sutton draws on Breger, *Making Worlds*.

75 Muñoz, *Cruising Utopia*, 2009, 22.

76 Maria Sabine Augstein, interview by Ulrike Klöppel, Konstanze Plett, and Daniel Hübner, January 22, 2017; excerpts are available at https://mh-stiftung.de/interviews/?cookie-state-change=1615996184805#Filme.

77 Augstein, *Transsexuellengesetz*.

78 Armer, "Ein ganz normales Leben." This catalog, self-published by Inea Gukema-Augstein, accompanied the exhibition by the same name at her mother's gallery, Galerie Anna Augstein Fine Arts Berlin.

79 Miller, *Turkish Guest Workers*; Stokes, "Permanent Refugee Crisis"; Nay and Steinbock, "Critical Trans* Studies."

80 Schumann, "Zu den Fotografien," 16, 20.

81 Umbach, "Selfhood," esp. images 16, 17, and 18.

82 Schumann, "Zu den Fotografien."

83 Ferree, *Varieties of Feminism*; Florvil, *Mobilizing Black Germany*; Freeland, *Feminist Transformations*.

84 Kiliç and Petzen, "Culture of Multiculturalism."

85 Ramalingam, "Fixing Transience," 4.

86 Benjamin, "Little History," 512.

87 Eckert, *Wie Alle*, 84, 116–23.

88 Eckert, "Trans Transatlantic," 248.

89 "Object of the Month February," Schwules Museum*, accessed November 25, 2021, https://www.schwulesmuseum.de/bibliothek-archiv/objekt-des-monats -februar-nadja-schallenbergs-coming-out-album-1990/?lang=en.

90 "Zeitzeug*innen-Interview mit Nadja Schallenberg im Rahmen des Projektes Zeitzeuginnengespräche—1989/90 aus lesbisch/feministischer Perspektive," FFBIZ—das feministische Archiv e.V. M Rept. Berlin 20.1, accessed November 25, 2021, https://www.meta-katalog.eu/Record/36553ffbiz.

91 Felten and Kahn, "Unboxed."

92 Schrödl and Wittrock, *Theater* in queerem Alltag und Aktivismus*.

93 Markues, "We're in This Together," accessed July 19, 2021, http:// wereinthistogether.de/#about.

94 "Zeitzeug*innen-Interview mit Nadja Schallenberg."

95 W. Müller, *Subkultur Westberlin*.

96 Fürst, *Flowers through Concrete*.

97 Uhlig, "Failing Gender."

98 Reichert, "Begehren ist nicht rassistisch"; l'Amour LaLove, *Beißreflexe*. On the Tuntenszene more generally, see S. C. Huneke, *States of Liberation*; Griffiths, "Konkurrierende Pfade"; S. Tremblay, "Proudest Symbol"; and Newsome, *Pink Triangle Legacies*.

99 *Fuck Gender—Photos by Annette Frick 1995–2003*, February 26, 2003–May 26, 2003, Schwules Museum*, accessed July 21, 2021, https://www.schwulesmuseum .de/ausstellung/fuck-gender-fotos-von-anette-frick-1995-2003/?lang=en.

100 "Press Information," *Camera Austria*, accessed March 22, 2021, https:// camera-austria.at/en/presse/133-2016-3/.

101 Steinbock, *Shimmering Images*.

102 Steinbock, *Shimmering Images*, 11.

103 Miller, *Turkish Guest Workers*; Petzen, "Home or Homelike?"

104 Soysal, "Diversity of Experience."

105 Schlober, "Blick über Tellerrand," 38–40.

106 Kulish, "Gay Muslims Pack a Dance Floor of Their Own"; Hartmann, "Queeres Jubiläum im SO36."

107 Hartman, *Wayward Lives*.

108 Bosold, Brill, and Weitz, *Homosexualität_en*, 191; Olesen, *Some Faggy Gestures*.

109 Steinmetz, "Material Enactments."

110 Rottmann and Hacke, "Homosexualität_en."

111 Prosser, "Judith Butler."

4. Pathways to Liberation

Parts of chapter 4 appeared in "The Long 1950s as Radical In-Between," in *Queer 1950s*, ed. Heike Bauer and Matt Cook (Basingstoke: Palgrave Macmillan, 2012), 13–28.

1 Lugones, *Pilgrimages/Peregrinajes*, 5; Haver, *Body of This Death*.

2 Marhoefer, "Queer Fascism and the End of Gay History."

3 Ferguson, *One-Dimensional Queer*, 48–49.

4 W. Brown, *States of Injury*, 65.

5 Schwartz, *Homosexuelle im Nationalsozialismus*; Farges et al., "Forum"; Hájková, "Introduction"; Marhoefer, "Lesbianism, Transvestitism," 1167–95.

6 Evans, "Bahnhof Boys"; Grau, "Im Auftrag der Partei"; Whisnant, *Male Homosexuality*.

7 Curt Röbel, Mecklenburgisches Landeshauptarchiv, Landtag Mecklenburg 1946–1952 Nr. 144, not numbered. See also Grau, "Strafrechtliche Verfolgung," 48.

8 Giles, "Legislating Homophobia"; Grau, "Im Auftrag der Partei."

9 Marhoefer, *Sex and the Weimar Republic*.

10 Evans, "Decriminalization"; Thinius, "Erfahrungen schwuler Männer."

11 Moeller, "Germans as Victims?," 162; Neiden, "Als 'Opfer des Faschismus,'" 8.

12 McLellan, *Love in the Time*, 116–18; S. C. Huneke, *States of Liberation*.

13 Fehrenbach, *Cinema*.

14 Biess and Eckert, "Introduction." On the insufficiencies of liberalization on matters of race, see Chin, "Thinking Difference."

15 Evans, "Bahnhof Boys."

16 Biess, "'Everybody Has a Chance,'" 3; see also Moeller, *War Stories*; and Whisnant, "Styles of Masculinity."

17 Vendrell, "Case of a German-Jewish Lesbian."

18 Lugones, *Pilgrimages/Peregrinajes*, 84.

19 Borowski, "Erste Erkenntnisse"; Sillge, *Un-Sichtbare Frauen*.

20 Spurlin, *Lost Intimacies*.

21 Sharp, "Sexual Unification."

22 Moeller, "Private Acts."

23 B. Lewis, *Wolfenden's Witnesses*; Bauer and Cook, *Queer 1950s*; Steinbacher, *Wie der Sex*.

24 Grau, "Im Auftrag der Partei," 118; McLellan, "State Socialist Bodies," 55; Evans, "Moral State"; T. Smith, *Comrades in Arms*; Minning, "Who Is the 'I'?"

25 S. C. Huneke, "Morality."

26 Heineman, *Before Porn Was Legal*.

27 Herzog, *Sex after Fascism*, 143–44; Heineman, "Economic Miracle"; Buske, *Fräulein Mutter*; Frevert, "Umbruch der Geschlechterverhältnisse?"

28 Herzog, *Sexuality in Europe*, 170.

29 Adorno, "Sexualtabus," 533–54. See also Herzog, *Sex after Fascism*, 308–9. Giese, "Geschlechtsunterschiede," 876–77; and Giese, *Der homosexuelle Mann*.

30 Herzog, "Sexuelle Revolution."

31 McLellan, *Love in the Time*, 117.

32 Canaday, "Thinking Sex."

33 Herzog, "Sexuelle Revolution."

34 Hillhouse, "Out of the Closet."

35 Hirsch, *Generation of Postmemory*.

36 Grau, "Ein Leben im Kampf," 62; Steakley, "Gays under Socialism."

37 Hans Zauner, interview by Llew Gardner, *Sunday Express*, 1960, quoted in Albert Knoll, *Totgeschlagen—totgeschwiegen*, 101.

38 Oral History Interview: James Steakley, UW-Madison Oral History Program, Summer 2010. Second Interview 2010, timestamp 00:56:05. Accessed July 21, 2021, http://digital.library.wisc.edu/1793/60843.

39 McLellan, "Glad to Be Gay," 105. See also Peter Rausch's interview with the Third Generation Ost project, accessed July 15, 2021, http://thirdgenerationost .com/projects/symposium-30-jahre-mauerfall/peter-rausch/.

40 Dobler, *Verzaubert in Nord-Ost*, 169–73.

41 Oral History Interview: James Steakley, Second Interview.

42 McLellan, *Love in the Time*, 121.

43 Brühl, "Sozialistisch und Schwul," 109.

44 Fürst and McLellan, *Dropping Out*.

45 McLellan, "Glad to Be Gay," 115.

46 Yurchak, *Everything Was Forever*, 132.

47 Betts, *Within Walls*.

48 See Hingst, *Goodbye to Berlin?*, 97–98; Evans, *Life among the Ruins*; and Whisnant, *Male Homosexuality*.

49 McLellan, "From Private Photography," 415.

50 Stryker, *Transgender History*; Cvetkovich, *Archive of Feelings*.

51 McLellan, *Love in the Time.*

52 Stapel, *Warme Brüder*, 80.

53 McLellan, "Lesbians," 95.

54 Bühner, "[W]ir haben einen Zustand."

55 McLellan, "Lesbians"; Bühner, "Lesbe, Lesbe, Lesbe."

56 Rottmann, "Zeitzeug*innen-Interview mit Nadja Schallenberg."

57 Herzog, *Sex after Fascism.*

58 Holy, "Einige Daten."

59 Heger, *Die Männer.*

60 "28 Activists Remember," accessed June 24, 2021, https://feministberlin1968ff
    .de/berlin-wird-feministisch/.

61 "28 Activists Remember."

62 "Aufbruch! Die Anfänge der Homosexuellen-Bewegung in Münster," ac-
    cessed July 23, 2021, https://www.stadt-muenster.de/museum/ausstellungen
    /aufbruch-die-anfaenge-der-homosexuellen-bewegung-in-muenster.html.

63 Craig Griffiths provides an excellent overview of these schisms in *The Ambiva-
    lence of Gay Liberation*, 100–101, as does Jens Dobler in "Schwule Lesben" in
    Pretzel and Weiss, *Rosa Radikale*, 120. For a firsthand account of this struggle,
    see Kuckuc [pseud.], *Der Kampf gegen Unterdrückung.*

64 Beljan, *Rosa Zeiten?* See also Gammerl, "Ist frei sein Normal?"

65 Moeller, *War Stories*; Chin et al., *After the Nazi Racial State*; Fehrenbach, *Race
    after Hitler*; Höhn, *GIs and Fräuleins*; El-Tayeb, *European Others.*

66 Pretzel, *Homosexuellenpolitik.*

67 Ewing, "'Color Him Black'"; Steinle, "Die 'Kameradschaft.'"

68 Ewing, "'Color Him Black'"; Boovy, "Belonging."

69 Evans, "Long 1950s."

70 Beachy, "German Invention"; Tobin, *Peripheral Desires.*

71 "Das Ergebnis der Abonnentenumfrage für den Bilderteil unserer Zeitschrift,"
    Der Kreis 3 (1958): 14.

72 Shepard, "'Something Notably Erotic.'"

73 Griffiths, *Ambivalence of Gay Liberation.*

74 "Die schwule Sau," *Du & Ich* 1 (1970): 4.

75 "Integration—für wen und warum?," *Du & Ich* 4 (1971): 4.

76 Ewing, "Color Him Black," 399.

77 *Du & Ich* 1 (1973): 16.

78 Griffiths, "Sex, Shame," 450.

79 Dannecker and Reiche, *Der gewöhnliche Homosexuelle*, 204.

80 Dennert, Leidinger, and Rauchut, *In Bewegung bleiben*; Kuckuc [pseud.], *Der
    Kampf.*

81 "Gibt es Sex nach dem Tode? Thesen zum Thema AIDS," *Der Spiegel* 48
    (1984): 228.

82   Love, *Feeling Backward*, 204.

83   Evans, "Streiten, Verstehen und Zusammenstehen."

84   Griffiths, "Konkurrierende Pfade."

85   Afken and Wolf, *Sexual Culture*, 102–3.

86   Hamilton, "Very Quintessence."

87   Stryker, *Transgender History*.

88   In her article, "The Very Quintessence of Persecution," Hamilton suggested that Tunten were part of the transgender and gender-nonconforming impulse of early 1970s anticapitalism.

89   "Vorwort," in *Tuntenstreit*, 2.

90   *Tuntenstreit*, 6–8.

91   *Tuntenstreit*, 18.

92   Newton, *Mother Camp*, 56.

93   *Tuntenstreit*, 26.

94   Haritaworn, "Wounded Subjects."

95   Whisnant, "Styles of Masculinity."

96   "Männer lasst das Knollen sein kommt herauf und reiht euch ein!," *HAW Info* 20 (1975): 60–62.

97   Claire [pseud.], "Zur SM-Diskussion: Thesen zur Funny," *HAW Info* 22 (1976): 18–19. This is also discussed in Griffiths, "Sex, Shame," 460.

98   Jensen, "Pink Triangle," 326; Hanshew, "'Sympathy for the Devil?'"

99   Hamilton, "Very Quintessence." See also Braunthal, *Political Loyalty*.

100 Plastargias, *RotZSchwul*.

101 Schwules Museum*, Berlin, HAW Feministengruppe "Rosa Winkel," November 1973, SL HAW 16–29, folder 25; Holy, "Der entliehene rosa Winkel"; Jensen, "Pink Triangle."

102 Newsome, *Pink Triangle Legacies*.

103 Holy, "Der entliehene rosa Winkel," 83. See also Griffiths, "Gay Activism," 64.

104 Griffiths, "Gay Activism," 65.

105 Steakley, "Homosexuals and the Third Reich."

106 Rothberg, *Multidirectional Memory*.

107 Hamilton, "Very Quintessence," 69.

108 Newsome, *Pink Triangle Legacies*; S. Tremblay, "The Proudest Symbol."

109 "AIDS: Eine Epidemie, die erst beginnt," *Der Spiegel* 23 (1983): 144–63.

110 Bartholomae, "Klappentexte: Verlage, Buchläden und Zeitschriften"; Dobler, "Staat im Aufbruch."

111 Ewing, "Archives in Europe."

112 Gammerl, *Anders fühlen*.

113 Griffiths, "Sex, Shame," 58.

114 Griffiths, "Gay Activism."

115 NARGS, *Schwule gegen Unterdrückung und Faschismus*.

116 "Die Freiburger Thesen der FDP," 35; Wahlprogramm der FDP zur Bund-estagswahl 1980, Friedrich Naumann Stiftung, accessed July 21, 2022, https://www.freiheit.org/de/deutschland/wahlprogramme-der-fdp-zu-den -bundestagswahlen; S. C. Huneke, *States of Liberation*, 20.

117 Dannecker and Reichelt, *Der gewöhnliche Homosexuelle*, 370–71.

118 "Begegnung in Köln," 2. See also Könne, "Homosexuelle und die Bundesrepub-lik Deutschland."

119 Selitsch, Talis, and Reichelt, "Aktion '80 der deutschen Homophilen-Presse," 14.

120 AHA, "Entwurf eines Antidiskrimminerungsgesetzes der AG Juristen."

121 Samuel Clowes Huneke gives a fascinating account of this event in *States of Liberation* and comes to the conclusion that the 1980s were a moment of pos-sibility for queers. Craig Griffiths on the other hand is more circumspect.

122 Beier-Herzog, "Anmerkungen zur Veranstaltung."

123 Schädlich and Bachnick, . . . *Alle Schwestern werden Brüder* . . .

124 "Die Spitzel sind unter uns! Von der Praktiken der Polizei in der Homoszene," *Du & Ich* (October 1985), 18; S. C. Huneke, *States of Liberation*; Griffiths, *Ambivalence*.

125 For examples of the wide array of opportunities listed, see the section labeled "Gruppen" in *Du & Ich*.

126 Koshar, *From Monuments*, 230. See also Moeller, *War Stories*.

127 Lupu, "Memory Vanished," 30.

128 Könne, "Gleichberechtigte Mitmenschen?"

129 McLellan, *Love in the Time*; see also Bryant, "Queering."

130 Samirah Kenawi, "Gespräch mit Frau Anni Sindermann Vorsitzende des nationalen Ravensbrückkomitees der DDR—am 3.5.1985 in ihrer Wohnung," reproduced in Kenawi, *Frauengruppen in der DDR*, 393–94.

131 Hájková, "Introduction"; Hájková, *Menschen ohne Geschichte sind Staub*.

132 Samirah Kenawi, "Bericht der 'Lesben in der Kirche,'" in Kenawi, *Frauen-gruppen in der DDR*, 389–90.

133 Gedenkkügel—Lesbian Commemorative Orb, accessed June 12, 2022, https:// europeanlesbianconference.org/gedenkkugel-lesbian-commemorative-orb -ravensbruck/.

134 Zinn, "Zwischen Opfermythos und historischer Präzision," 14.

135 Adorno, *Aspekte*, 9.

5. The Boundaries of Toleration

Portions of chapter 5 were published as "Harmless Kisses and Infinite Loops: Making Space for Queer Place in Twenty-First Century Berlin," in *Queer Cities, Queer Cultures: Europe since 1945*, coedited with Matt Cook (London: Blooms-bury, 2014), 75–94.

1   Rothberg, *Multidirectional Memory*.

2   Oettler, *Das Berliner Denkmal*.

3   "Mal wieder die Frauen vergessen!," *EMMA*, September 1, 2006, accessed April 14, 2014, https://www.emma.de/artikel/homo-mahnmal-mal-wieder-die -frauen-vergessen-263541.

4   Heimrod, Schlusche, and Seferens, *Der Denkmalstreit—das Denkmal?*, 73.

5   H. W. Smith, *Germany: A Nation in Its Time*, 462–63.

6   Thompson and Zablotsky, "Nationalismen der Anerkennung," 162.

7   Evans, "Harmless Kisses."

8   This is the language of the signboard at the memorial site.

9   Haritaworn, "Queer Injuries."

10 Marhoefer, "Was the Homosexual Made White?"; Puar, "Celebrating Re-fusal"; Tobin, "Was Judith Butler Right?"; Petzen, "Queer Trouble." For some of the local coverage, see "Judith Butler lehnt Berlin CSD Zivilcouragepreis ab! Presseerklärung von SUSPECT zum 19. Juni," June 21, 2010, http:// nohomonationalism.blogspot.com/2010/06/judith-butler-lehnt-berlin -csd.html; Duman, "Eine Minderheit unter vielen"; LesMigraS (Lesbische Migrantinnen und Schwarze Lesben)—Antigewalt und Antidiskriminierungs-bereich der Lesbenberatung Berlin e.V., "Klares Signal gegen Rassismus," June 22, 2010, http://lesmigras.de/tl_files/lesmigras/pressemitteilungen /Stellungnahme_LB_Butler.pdf; Böger, "Die Vorwürfe sind einfach grotesk"; K. Ludwig, "Hello, Mrs. Butler, Nice to Meet You." The transcript of Butler's speech is documented in Butler, '"Ich muss mich von dieser Komplizenschaft mit Rassismus distanzieren."

11 For a more fulsome discussion of the speech itself, see Marhoefer, "Homo-sexuality," 265–67.

12 Feddersen, "War die Absage von Judith Butler das richtige Signal?"; Petzen, "Queer Trouble," 298.

13 Bauer, *Hirschfeld Archives*, 2.

14 Haritaworn, "Women's Rights"; El-Tayeb, *European Others*.

15 Haritaworn, "Women's Rights."

16 McRuer, *Crip Theory*, 2.

17 Wilke, "Remembering Complexity?"

18 Halberstam, *Queer Art of Failure*; Edelman, *No Future*; Love, *Feeling Back-ward*; Rubin, "Thinking Sex."

19 Chiang, *Transtopia*.

20 Scott, *Sex and Secularism*.

21 Paternotte and Kuhar, "Disentangling and Locating"; Kuhar, "Playing with Science."

22 Kuhar and Paternotte, *Anti-gender Campaigns*.

23 Lavers, "Poland's Anti-LGBTQ President Reelected"; Soguel and Rebala, "As Poland's Election Heats Up"; Barát, "Revoking the MA in Gender Studies."

24 Herzog, *Sexuality in Europe*.

25 El-Tayeb, *European Others*; Scott, *Sex and Secularism*; Wekker, *White Innocence*.

26 W. Brown, *Regulating Aversion*; W. Brown and Forst, *Power of Tolerance*.

27 W. Brown, *Regulating Aversion*, 4.

28 Marhoefer, "Was the Homosexual Made White?"

29 Bauer, *Hirschfeld Archives*; Feuchtner, "Indians, Jews, and Sex"; Funke, "Navigating the Past."

30 Haritaworn, "Queer Injuries."

31 Bundnis 90/Die Grunen 2008 Berliner Aktionsplan gegen die Homophobie. Abgeordnetenhaus Berlin, Drucksache 16/1966 (December 1), 16th legislative period.

32 SPD/Die Linke 2009 Initiative Berlin tritt ein fur Selbstbestimmung und Akzeptanz sexueller Vielfalt. Motion of the Faction SPD and the Left Faction in the Berlin Parliament (March 11).

33 Huyssen, "Voids of Berlin."

34 Evans, *Life among the Ruins*.

35 Massey, *For Space*, 9.

36 Lefebvre, *Production of Space*.

37 Till, "Artistic and Activist Memory-Work."

38 Reed, "Imminent Domain."

39 Freccero, "Queer Spectrality."

40 Jensen, "Pink Triangle."

41 Ladd, *Ghosts of Berlin*; Halbwachs, *Collective Memory*; Huyssen, *Present Pasts*; Jordan, *Structures of Memory*; Till, *New Berlin*; Ward, *Post-Wall Berlin*; Young, *At Memory's Edge*.

42 Wilke, "Remembering Complexity?"

43 King, "Architecture," 404.

44 Molnar, "Cultural Production."

45 Young, "Berlin's Holocaust Memorial," 56.

46 Bryant, "Queering."

47 Cowell, "Challenge Is Raised to Plan for a Holocaust Monument in Berlin."

48 Olick and Levy, "Collective Memory."

49 Jordan, *Structures of Memory*, 220. See also Markovitz and Reich, *German Predicament*.

50 "Beschluss der Deutschen Bundestages," June 25, 1999, https:// www.holocaust -denkmal-berlin.de/index.php?id=44; Christiane Wilke makes the important point that there is an intersectional relationship between victims' groups and their efforts to secure national commemoration of their struggles. Wilke, "Remembering Complexity?"

51 Initiative Homo-Monument, "Homo-Monument," 11.

52 Senatsverwaltung für Wissenschaft, Forschung und Kultur Kunst im Stadtraum und am Bau, "Entwurf der Auslobung: Gedenkort für die im Nationalsozialismus verfolgten Homosexuellen," May 5, 2005, accessed April 20, 2012, http://www.gedenkort.de/ files/GedO_Auslobung_dt_engl.pdf.

53 Lautmann, "Pink Triangle."

54 Freccero, "Queer Spectrality," 194–214.

55 Rothberg, *Multidirectional Memory*.

56 Bisky, "Küssende Jungs."

57 El-Tayeb, "Begrenzte Horizonte."

58 Haritaworn, "Wounded Subjects," 140.

59 Haritaworn, "Colorful Bodies," 14.

60 Ewing, "Color of Desire," 177.

61 Grassmann, "Migrantenkinder gegen Schwule." On this, see Haritaworn, "Wounded Subjects."

62 Eicker, "Küssen verboten?," 16. Haritaworn has done the most comprehensive work on this; see "Queer Injuries."

63 Haritaworn, Tauqir, and Erdem, "Gay Imperialism."

64 Haritaworn, "Queer Injuries," 76.

65 Haritaworn and Petzen, "Invented Traditions."

66 For a detailed account of the scandal, see Tomberger, "Das Homosexuellen-Denkmal seit seiner Übergabe 2008."

67 "Mal wieder die Frauen vergessen!"

68 Kroymann, "Verschwundene Minderheit."

69 Stellungnahme der Künstler, "Ein Porträt ist keine Representation," September 20, 2006, accessed April 14, 2014, http://www.berlin.lsvd.de/cms/index.php?option=com_content&task=view&id =191&Itemid=175.

70 Gerides, "Why Was the Video to the Memorial of Gay Holocaust Victims Changed?"

71 Muñoz, *Disidentifications*. On the history of queer aesthetic traditions, see Evans, "Seeing Subjectivity."

72 Stellungnahme der Künstler, "Ein Porträt ist keine Representation."

73 Anna Hájková's online bibliography of resources is the most up-to-date resource on this material: "Bibliography on Lesbian and Trans Women in Nazi Germany," accessed September 8, 2022, https://sexualityandholocaust.com/blog/bibliography/.

74 Ilse Kokula, in Senatsverwaltung für Jugend und Familie, *Der homosexuellen NS-Opfer gedenken*, 13.

75 Feddersen, "Falsche Opferpolitik."

76 "Resolution—Denkmal für die im Nationalsozialismus verfolgten Homosexuellen—Den preisgekrönten Entwurf verwirklichen," October 28, 2006, https://berlin.lsvd.de/neuigkeiten/lsvd-berlin-resolution-zum-denkmal

-fur-die-im-nationalsozialismus-verfolgten-homosexuellen/; Tomberger, "'Der homosexuellen NS-Opfer gedenken'"; Tomberger, "Wessen Gedenken?" See also S. C. Huneke, "Heterogeneous Persecution."

77 "Stoppt das Homo-Mahnmal," *EMMA*, June 1, 2006, https://www.emma.de /artikel/noch-nicht-zu-spaet-stoppt-das-homo-mahnmal-263098.

78 "Stein des Anstoßes: Um das Homo-Mahnmal ist eine Diskussion entbrannt, weil Lesben sich vom Entwurf nicht repräsentiert fühlen; Die Siegessäule gibt Meinungen Raum," *Siegessäule* 11 (2006): 8–9.

79 Letter from Member of European Parliament Lissy Gröner to the Representative of the Cultural Committee in the Federal Parliament Monika Griefahn, November 23, 2006. Reproduced by Queer Nations e.V online as "Ein Mahmal nur für schwule NS-Opfer?," November 22, 2006, https://www.queer.de/detail .php?article_id=5984.

80 S. Tremblay, "Solidarity Means Shifting Categories."

81 Pretzel, "Ein 'Mahnmal Homosexuellenverfolgung,'" 30.

82 Baedeker, *Berlin and Its Environs*; Moreck, *Führer durch das 'lasterhafte' Berlin*.

83 Pretzel and Roßbach, *Wegen der zu erwartenden hohen Strafe*.

84 Romsics, "Meaning of Occupation."

85 Pretzel, "Ein 'Mahnmal Homosxuellenverfolgung,'" 30.

86 Pretzel, "Ein 'Mahnmal Homosxuellenverfolgung,'" 30.

87 Schwarzer, "Im Getto des Kitsches."

88 Morsch, "Erklärung des Arbeitskreises I der Berlin-Brandenburgischen Gedenkstätten"; Cotten, *Transgender Migrations*.

89 *MANEO-Soirée—die Talkrunde: Ein Mahnmal nur für Schwule?* 11.1.07, 20 Uhr, Festsaal des Rathaus Charlottenburg-Wilmersdorf, accessed June 12, 2015, http://www.maneo.de/news/maneo-news07.html. See the discussion by Tomberger, "Das Berliner Homosexuellen-Denkmal"; and Tomberger, "Wessen Gedenken?"

90 Schoppmann, "Im Schatten der Verfolgung"; Schoppmann, *Days of Masquerade*. See also *MANEO-Soirée—die Talkrunde: Ein Mahnmal nur für Schwule?*

91 Pretzel, "Eine Debattenbeitrag zum Streit um den Gedenkort für die im Nationalsozialismus verfolgten Homosexuellen."

92 Hannemann, "Szenelokalverbot gleich Konzentrationslager?"

93 Schupelius, "Mein Ärger"; Luehrs-Kaiser, "Zwei Männer und ein schwules Denkmal."

94 Aly, "Homosexuelle im Tiergarten."

95 Hannemann, "Szenelokalverbot gleich Konzenstrationslager?"

96 "Remembering Different Histories: Monument to Homosexual Holocaust Victims Opens in Berlin," *Der Spiegel*, May 27, 2009, https://www.spiegel .de/international/germany/remembering-different-histories-monument-to -homosexual-holocaust-victims-opens-in-berlin-a-555665.html.

97 "Holocaust Academic Pans Monument to Nazis' Gay Victims," *Deutsche Welle*, May 29, 2008, https://www.dw.com/en/holocaust-academic-pans-monument -to-nazis-gay-victims/a-3368183.

98 Weinthal, "Berlin's Harshly Felt Divide."

99 "A Memorial of Our Own," *Advocate*, February 28, 2006, 957.

100 Wocker and Kelly, "Holocaust Gay Memorial Unveiled in Berlin," 8.

101 "Gay Holocaust Memorial Unveiled in Berlin," *Gays without Borders*, accessed June 21, 2021, https://gayswithoutborders.wordpress.com/2008/05/28/ gay-holocaust-memorial-unveiled-in-berlin/.

102 Oettler, "Berlin Memorial to the Homosexuals Persecuted under the National Socialist Regime."

103 Speech of Johannes Kahrs, accessed June 15, 2015, http://www.gedenkort.de /hin-bt03-aussprache-lengsfeld.htm.

104 A similar point is made by Nguyen Tan Hoang in "Theorizing Queer Temporalities," 6–7.

105 Duggan, *Twilight of Equality?*; G. Ludwig, "Desiring Neoliberalism."

106 Endlich, "Das Berliner Homosexuellen-Denkmal."

107 The MANEO antiviolence initiative logs may be found at http://www.maneo.de /ueber-maneo.html (accessed September 9, 2022). Jin Haritaworn and Jennifer Petzen have documented this phenomenon of anti–hate crime activism, kiss-ins, and the racial coding of queer neighborhoods. See Haritaworn, *Queer Lovers and Hateful Others*; Petzen, "Queer Trouble."

108 El-Tayeb, "Oppressed Majority."

109 Cochrane, "Making Up Meanings," 24.

110 Massey, "Places and Their Pasts," 187.

111 Thrift, "Intensities of Feeling"; Wilke, "Remembering Complexity?"; Crenshaw, "Mapping the Margins."

112 Said, "Invention, Memory, and Place," 179. James Young makes the point that "the surest engagement with memory lies in its perpetual irresolution . . . simply the never-to-be-resolved debate over which kind of memory to preserve, how to do it, in whose name, and to what end." Young, *Texture of Memory*, 21.

113 Massey, "Geographies of Responsibility," 7.

6. Queer Kinship in Dangerous Times

Parts of chapter 6 appeared as "Queer Life in Dangerous Times," in *Dies- und jenseits des Großen Teichs: Festschrift für James Steakley zum 75. Geburtstag* [On This Side and the Other of the Big Pond: Commemorative Volume for James Steakley on his 75th Birthday], ed. Florian Mildenberger and Wolfram Setz (Berlin: Bibliothek rosa Winkel, 2021).

1 Doan, "Queer History/Queer Memory."

2 Gentile and Kinsman, *Canadian War on Queers*, 21.

3   Shotwell, *Against Purity*, 39.

4   Muñoz, *Sense of Brown*, xi.

5   Muñoz, *Sense of Brown*, 12.

6   Nancy, *Being Singular Plural*, xiii.

7   Campt, *Image Matters*; Campt, *Listening to Images*.

8   Oral History Interview: James Steakley, UW-Madison Oral History Program, Summer 2010. Second Interview 2010, http://digital.library.wisc.edu/1793/60843.

9   Oral History Interview: James Steakley, Second Interview, 2010, timestamp 00:47:30.

10 Oral History Interview: James Steakley, Second Interview, 2010, timestamp 00:56:05.

11 Florvil, review of *Audre Lorde*; Florvil, *Mobilizing Black Germany*.

12 Höhn, *GIs and Fräuleins*; Höhn and Klimke, *Breath of Freedom*.

13 Lorde, *Sister Outsider*, 36.

14 Lorde, *Sister Outsider*, 53–59.

15 El-Tayeb, *European Others*, 47.

16 Florvil, *Mobilizing Black Germany*.

17 Mahlsdorf, *I Am My Own Woman*.

18 Giersdorf, "Why Does Charlotte von Mahlsdorf Curtsy?," 191.

19 *Die Andere Liebe*, dir. Axel Otten and Helmut Kißling (DEFA 1988).

20 Giersdorf, "Why Does Charlotte von Mahlsdorf Curtsy?," 180.

21 McLellan, "Glad to Be Gay." See also Schiavi, "Tease of Truth."

22 Wright, *I Am My Own Wife*, 12; "Die Geschichte des Hauses" [The History of the House], Gründerzeit Museum in the Gutshaus Mahlsdorf, accessed July 21, 2021, http://www.gruenderzeitmuseum-mahlsdorf.de/geschichte.html.

23 Lorde, *Sister Outsider*, 89.

24 Muñoz, *Cruising Utopia*, 2009, 1. *The World Will Always Welcome Lovers* is the title of one of the earlier art experiments and audio guides to the home library of Gert Hekma and Mattias Duyves in Amsterdam, chronicled at https://Nemer.be/The-World-Will-Always-Welcome-Lovers (accessed June 10, 2021).

25 Benny Nemer, *I Don't Know Where Paradise Is*, Carleton University Art Gallery exhibition, September 24–December 12, 2020, https://where-paradise-is.eu/.

26 Bakker et al., *Others of My Kind*.

27 Bakker et al., *Others of My Kind*.

28 *Benny Nemerofsky Ramsay: I Don't Know Where Paradise Is*, Calgary University Art Gallery exhibition, September 24–December 12, 2020, https://cuag.ca/exhibition/benny-Nemerofsky-ramsay-i-dont-know-where-paradise-is/.

29 Zimmerman, *Anthropology*.

30 Bauer, *Hirschfeld Archives*, 91.

31 Taylor and Timm, "Sex on Display," 236.

32 Taylor and Timm, "Sex on Display."

33 Freeman, "Theorizing Queer Temporalities," 59.

34 Nash, *Black Body*.

35 J. Butler, "Afterword: After Loss What Then?," 467.

36 W. Brown, "Wounded Attachments"; Cho, "Future Perfect Loss."

37 Benjamin, "Theses," 255.

38 Eng, "Melancholia," 1276.

39 Kriebel, "Sexology's Beholders."

40 C. Dean, *Fragility of Empathy*, 60.

41 Berger, *Ways of Seeing*.

42 Dinshaw et al., "Theorizing Queer Temporalities."

43 Benny Nemer artist site, https://Nemer.be/Voices.

44 Canadian Academy of Audiology, "Emotion, Speech, and Music."

45 Evans, "Sound."

46 Cruising the Seventies, June 15, 2020, https://www.crusev.ed.ac.uk/about-2/.

47 Östberg, "Liz Rosenfeld."

48 Rosenfeld, "This Should Happen Here More Often," 33, 27

49 Anderson, Davis, and Raha, "Desire Revolution."

50 Cvetkovich, *Archive of Feelings*.

51 Dinshaw, *Getting Medieval*, 39.

52 Östberg, "Jasco Viefhues."

53 Felten and Kahn, "Unboxed: Transgender in a Gay Museum?"

54 Est, "Jasco Viefhues und die Suche nach neuen Narrativen."

55 Ahmed, *Queer Phenomenology*.

56 Berlant and Warner, "Sex in Public," 198.

57 Halberstam, *In a Queer Time and Place*, 9.

58 Dinshaw, *Getting Medieval*, 21.

59 Cvetkovich, *Archive of Feelings*, 8.

60 Nestle, "Will to Remember."

61 Love, *Feeling Backward*, 1.

62 W. Brown, *States of Injury*.

63 Sedgwick, *Tendencies*, 3, 35.

64 Doyle, *Sex Objects*, xxxi.

65 Crimp, "Getting the Warhol," 65; Doyle, *Sex Objects*; Muñoz, *Disidentifications*; Warner, *Trouble with Normal*.

66 Warner, *Trouble with Normal*, 35.

67 Crimp, "Getting the Warhol," 65.

68 Schotmiller, "Reading *RuPaul's Drag Race*"; Hall-Araujo, "Ambivalence"; Heller, "RuPaul Realness."

69 Druschel, "Evolution."

70 Duggan, *Twilight of Equality?* See also Marhoefer, "Was the Homosexual Made White?"; and Gomes Pereira, "Reflecting."

71 Nemer, "I Don't Know Where Paradise Is."

72 Dinshaw, *Getting Medieval*, 21.

73 "O Ancestors, What Was That Time Like?" is featured in Nemer, "I Don't Know Where Paradise Is," 14.

74 Nemer, "I Don't Know Where Paradise Is," 16; "Schwule und queere Visionäre."

75 Nemer, "I Don't Know Where Paradise Is," 77.

76 Benny Nemer, *I Don't Know Where Paradise Is?*, Carleton University Art Gallery exhibition opening, September 23, 2020.

77 Ahmed, *Queer Phenomenology*, 564.

78 Kirtley, "Let the Sunshine In."

79 Karlinsky is quoted in Kirtley, "Let the Sunshine In."

80 Nemer, "I Don't Know Where Paradise Is," 13.

81 Murray, *Oceanic Homosexualities*, 14.

82 Warner, *Trouble with Normal*, 35–36.

83 TallBear, "Caretaker Relations."

84 Sutton, "Cultivating an Ethical Gaze."

85 Cvetkovich, "Kent Monkman's *Shame and Prejudice*."

86 *I Don't Know Where Paradise Is*, postlude, accessed June 15, 2020, https://files.cargocollective.com/c715319/POSTLUDE2.pdf.

87 Gert Hekma was at the center of controversy at the 2011 conference for his deeply troubling essentialist, Islamophobic claims around Muslims, queers of color, and BDSM. His comments, which were called out repeatedly during the event itself as well as in publications after the fact, may be read as part of the generational struggle between gay liberationist discourse and queer of color, postcolonial critique. See Tauqir et al., "Queer Anti-racist Activism." See also the reflections and comments on a local activist group blog: "Start with Amsterdam!," *Queerin-Amsterdam*, February 16, 2011, https://queerintersectional.wordpress.com/.

88 Wekker, *White Innocence*.

89 Campt, *Listening to Images*.

90 Sedgwick, *Tendencies*, 8.

91 Benny Nemer, *If You Have a Garden in Your Library*, accessed June 10, 2020, https://Nemer.be/If-you-have-a-garden-in-your-library.

92 Shotwell, *Against Purity*, 43.

93 Cavarero, *For More Than One Voice*.

94 Jay, *Downcast Eyes*, 3.

95 C. Dean, *Fragility of Empathy*, 60.

96 Fiumara, *Other Side of Language*; C. Robinson, "Listening Art"; Small, *Musicking*.

97 Hartman, *Wayward Lives*; Seitz, *House of Prayer*.

98 Steinbock, *Shimmering Images*, 96.

99 Stryker, "Interview."

Epilogue

1   El-Tayeb, "'Gays Who Cannot Properly Be Gay.'"

2   Dölling and Hark, "She Who Speaks Shadow Speaks Truth."

3   Hartman and Wilderson III, "Position of the Unthought," 185.

4   Gammerl, *Anders fühlen*.

5   Berlant, *Sex, or the Unbearable*.

6   Doan, *Disturbing Practices*.

7   For two examples, from the Green Party–sponsored Heinrich-Böll Stiftung and the left-leaning Die Partei–associated Rosa-Luxemburg-Stiftung, see "International Gender Policy & LGBTI | Heinrich Böll Stiftung," *Heinrich-Böll-Stiftung*, accessed April 15, 2021, https://www.boell.de/en/international -gender-policy-lgbti; and "Queer-Feminismus—Rosa-Luxemburg-Stiftung," accessed April 15, 2021, https://www.rosalux.de/veranstaltung/es_detail /ZCI42/queer-feminismus/.

8   Hauenstein, "Nazi-Hintergrund, NS-Erbe und materielle Kontinuität."

9   Miller and Lemmy, *Bad Gays*.

10 Foucault, "Sex, Power," 166.

11 Campt, *Listening to Images*.

12 O'Rourke, *Queer Insists*.

13 Scott, "Multiculturalism," 14.

14 "Comparing Comparisons: From the 'Historikerstreit' to the Mbembe Affair— Rosa-Luxemburg-Stiftung," Rosa Luxemburg Foundation, accessed April 19, 2021, https://www.rosalux.de/en/news/id/43395/comparing-comparisons -from-the-historikerstreit-to-the-mbembe-affair.

15 Rothberg, *Implicated Subject*.

16 Zinn, "Einfalt Statt Vierfalt."

17 Evans, "Streiten, Verstehen und Zusammenstehen."

18 Feddersen, "Unsere Queergida."

19 Kowalski, "Queergida."

20 Thierse, "Grabenkämpfe gegen Gemeinsinn."

21 Gennies, "Die Identitätspolitik des Wolfgang Thierse."

22 Zinn, "Abschied von der Opferperspektive."

23 Zinn, "Einfalt Statt Vierfalt."

24 Kuhar and Paternotte, *Anti-gender Campaigns*; "Sahra Wagenknecht macht 'skurrile Minderheiten' verächtlich," *Mannschaft Magazin*, April 14, 2021, https://mannschaft.com/sahra-wagenknecht-widerlich-nicht-nur-vorm -hintergrund-zunehmender-gewalt-gegen-queers/.

25 Paternotte and Kuhar, "Disentangling and Locating."

26 Pilarczyk, "Drecksäcke Aller Länder."

27 Hark and Villa, *Future of Difference*.

28 Korolczuk and Graff, "Gender as 'Ebola.'"

29 Vukadinović, "Butler erhebt 'Rassismus'-Vorwurf."

30 Villa, "The Sargnagel Talks Back."

31 "Der queerfeministische Nachwuchs pöbelt auf dem Campus, in den Straßen und im Internet gegen 'weiße Cis-Männer,' gegen 'TERFS' (trans*-exclusionary radical feminists, also radikale Feministin, die Trans*menschen ausschließt) oder 'SWERFS' (sex worker exclusionary radical feminist, also radikale Feministin, die Sexarbeiterinnen ausschließt), prangert unentwegt 'Privilegien' anderer an, fordert geschlechtsneutrale Pronomen ein und sinniert mit weinerlicher Verve über 'Verletzbarkeit.' Das persönliche Leiden an der Welt wird zum wissenschaftlichen Thema verklärt, Schuld für das eigene Befinden als Dritte personifiziert." Vukadinović, "Butler erhebt 'Rassismus'-Vorwurf."

32 Rehberg, "Kritik vs. Selbstkritik."

33 Pilarczyk, "Drecksäcke aller Länder."

34 Evans, "Streiten, Verstehen und Zusammenstehen."

35 Zinn, "Wie LGBTI-Verbände Ins Linksidentitäre Fahrwasser Abdriften."

36 Feddersen, "Antifreiheitliches Wokistan." See the Manifesto of the Network at https://www.netzwerk-wissenschaftsfreiheit.de/ueber-uns/manifest/ (accessed June 21, 2022). See Simon Strick on anti-trans* media debates in "Warum die trans*feindliche Debatte einfach nicht verstummt."

37 Reicherdt, "Die Namensgebung des Elberskirchen-Hirschfeld-Hauses."

38 Gammerl, "Das Elberskirchen-Hirschfeld-Haus (E2H)."

39 Gammerl and Kiupel, "Wir bauen ein Haus!"

40 Evans et al., "Eine queere Institution, die Trans*feindlichkeit unterstutzt, ist nichts wert."

41 See the important edited collection *Eure Heimat ist unser Albtraum*, edited by Fatma Aydemir and Hengameh Yaghoobfarah, translated into English in the journal *Transit*: "Your Homeland Is Our Nightmare," accessed December 15, 2022, https://transit.berkeley.edu/archives/your-homeland-is-our-nightmare/.

Bibliography

Ades, Dawn. "Duchamp's Masquerades." In *The Portrait in Photography*, edited by Graham Clarke, 94–114. Seattle: Reaktion, 1992.

Adorno, Theodor W. *Aspekte des neuen Rechtsradikalismus: Ein Vortrag*. Berlin: Suhrkamp Verlag AG, 1967.

Adorno, Theodor W. "Sexualtabus und Recht heute." In *Kulturkritik und Gesellschaft II* (Gesammelte Schriften 10.2), 533–54. Frankfurt: Suhrkamp, 1963.

Afken, Janin, and Benedikt Wolf. *Sexual Culture in Germany in the 1970s: A Golden Age for Queers?* Berlin: Springer Nature, 2019.

AHA. "Entwurf eines Antidiskriminerungsgesetzes der AG Juristen." Schwules Museum* Archive, AHA Sammlung.

Ahmed, Sara. "Affective Economies." *Social Text* 79, no. 2 (2004): 117–39.

Ahmed, Sara. *The Cultural Politics of Emotion*. New York: Routledge, 2004.

Ahmed, Sara. *Living a Feminist Life*. Durham, NC: Duke University Press, 2017.

Ahmed, Sara. *Queer Phenomenology: Orientations, Objects, Others*. Durham, NC: Duke University Press, 2006.

Aizura, Aren Z., with Marquis Bey, Toby Beauchamp, Treva Ellison, Jules Gill-Peterson, and Eliza Steinbock. "Thinking with Trans Now: Left of Queer." *Social Text* 38, no. 4 (145) (2020): 125–47.

Akantha [Werner Becker]. "Berlin tanzt!" *Der Kreis* 17, no. 9 (1949).

Alexander, M. Jacqui. *Pedagogies of Crossing: Meditations on Feminism, Sexual Politics, Memory, and the Sacred*. Durham, NC: Duke University Press, 2006.

Allen, Jafari S. "Black/Queer/Diaspora at the Current Conjuncture." *GLQ: A Journal of Lesbian and Gay Studies* 18, nos. 2–3 (2012): 211–48.

Aly, Götz. "Homosexuelle im Tiergarten." *Berliner Zeitung*, March 30, 2010.

Amin, Kadji. "Genealogies of Queer Theory." In *The Cambridge Companion to Queer Studies*, edited by Siobhan B. Somerville, 17–29. Cambridge: Cambridge University Press, 2020.

Amin, Kadji. *Queer Attachments: Genet, Modern Pederasty, and Queer Theory*. Durham, NC: Duke University Press, 2017.

Anderson, Fiona, Glyn Davis, and Nat Raha. "Desire Revolution: Imaging Queer Europe." *Third Text* 35, no. 1 (2021): 1–9.

Apel, Dora, and Shawn Michelle Smith. *Lynching Photographs*. Berkeley: University of California Press, 2008.

Appadurai, Arjun. *The Social Life of Things*. Cambridge: Cambridge University Press, 1998.

Armer, Karl Michael. "Ein ganz normales Leben." In *Der Intime Blick: Maria Sabine Augstein; Fotografien von Inea Gukema-Augstein 1985–1988*, edited by Inea Gukema-Augstein, 23–26. Tutzing, Altet Forsthaus: Gukema-Augstein, 2008.

Asibong, Andrew. "*Nouveau Désordre*: Diabolical Queerness in 1950s French Cinema." In *Queer 1950s: Rethinking Sexuality in the Postwar Years*, edited by Heike Bauer and Matt Cook, 29–41. Basingstoke, UK: Palgrave Macmillan, 2012.

Attwood, Feona. "Reading Porn: The Paradigm Shift in Pornography Research." *Sexualities* 1, no. 1 (February 2002): 91–105.

Augstein, Maria Sabine. *Transsexuellengesetz*. Baden-Baden: Nomos, 2012.

Auslander, Leora. "Beyond Words." *American Historical Review* 110, no. 4 (October 2005): 1015–45.

Aviv, Rachel. "The German Experiment That Placed Foster Children with Pedophiles." *New Yorker*, July 16, 2021.

Aydemir, Fatma, and Hengameh Yaghoobifarah, eds. *Eure Heimat ist unser Albtraum*. Berlin: Ullstein, 2019.

Azoulay, Ariela. *The Civil Contract of Photography*. Princeton, NJ: Princeton University Press, 2008.

Bader, Karl. *Soziologie der Deutschen Nachkriegskriminalität*. Tübingen: JCB Mohr, 1949.

Baedeker, Karl. *Berlin and Its Environs: A Guide for Travellers*. Leipzig: Baedeker Verlag, 1923.

Baer, Ulrich. *Spectral Evidence: The Photography of Trauma*. Cambridge, MA: MIT Press, 2002.

Bakker, Alex, Rainer Herrn, Michael Thomas Taylor, and Annette F. Timm, eds. *Others of My Kind: Transatlantic Transgender Histories*. Calgary: University of Calgary Press, 2020.

Balser, Kristof, Mario Kramp, Jürgen Müller, and Joanna Gotzmann. *Himmel und Hölle: Das Leben der Kölner Homosexuellen, 1945–69*. Cologne: Emons, 1994.

Barad, K. "TransMaterialities: Trans*/Matter/Realities and Queer Political Imaginings." *GLQ: A Journal of Lesbian and Gay Studies* 21, nos. 2–3 (2015): 387–422.

Barát, Erzsébet. "Revoking the MA in Gender Studies." *Eurozine*, January 10, 2020.

Barriault, Marcel. "Hard to Dismiss: The Archival Value of Gay Male Erotica and Pornography." *Archivaria* 68 (Fall 2009): 222–23.

Barthes, Roland. *Camera Lucida*. Translated by Richard Howard. New York: Hill and Wang, 1981.

Barthes, Roland. "Wilhelm von Gloeden." In *Der entgegenkommende und der stumpfe Sinn: Kritische Essays*, vol. 3, translated by Dieter Hornig, 204–6. Frankfurt: Suhrkamp, 1990.

Bartholomae, Joachim. "Klappentexte: Verlage, Buchläden und Zeitschriften." In *Zwischen Autonomie und Integration*, edited by Andreas Pretzel and Volker Weiss, 69–90. Hamburg: Männerschwarm Verlag, 2013.

Bauer, Heike. *The Hirschfeld Archives: Violence, Death, and Modern Queer Culture*. Philadelphia: Temple University Press, 2017.

Bauer, Heike, and Matt Cook. Introduction to *Queer 1950s: Rethinking Sexuality in the Postwar Years*, 1–10. Basingstoke, UK: Palgrave Macmillan, 2012.

Bauer, Heike, and Matt Cook, eds. *Queer 1950s: Rethinking Sexuality in the Postwar Years*. Basingstoke, UK: Palgrave Macmillan, 2012.

Beachy, Robert. *Gay Berlin: Birthplace of a Modern Identity*. New York: Alfred A. Knopf, 2014.

Beachy, Robert. "The German Invention of Homosexuality." *Journal of Modern History* 82, no. 4 (2010): 801–38.

Beccalossi, Chiara. "The 'Italian Vice': Male Homosexuality and British Tourism in Southern Italy." In *Italian Sexualities Uncovered, 1789–1914*, edited by Valeria Babini, Chiara Beccalossi, and Lucy Riall, 185–206. New York: Palgrave Macmillan, 2015.

"Begegnung in Köln: Zwischen Homo-Gruppen und Parteien." *Gay Journal* 11 (1979): n.p.

Beier-Herzog, Gerhard. "Anmerkungen zur Veranstaltung in der Beethovenhalle." *AHA Info* (July/August 1980): 19–25.

Beljan, Magdalena. *Rosa Zeiten? Eine Geschichte der Subjektivierung männlicher Homosexualität in den 1970er und 1980er Jahren der BRD*. Bielefeld: transcript Verlag, 2014.

Benjamin, Walter. "Little History of Photography." In *Selected Writings*, vol. 3, *1935–1938*, edited by Michael W. Jennings, Howard Eiland, and Gary Smith, 507–30. Cambridge, MA: Harvard University Press, 2002.

Benjamin, Walter. "Theses on the Philosophy of History." In *Illuminations: Essays and Reflections*, translated by Harry Zohn, edited by Hannah Arendt, 253–64. New York: Schocken Books, 1969.

Benjamin, Walter. "The Work of Art in the Age of Mechanical Reproduction." In *Illuminations: Essays and Reflections*, translated by Harry Zohn, edited by Hannah Arendt, 217–55. New York: Schocken, 1969.

Berger, John. *Ways of Seeing*. London: British Broadcasting Corporation, 1972.

Berlant, Lauren. *Cruel Optimism*. Durham, NC: Duke University Press, 2011.

Berlant, Lauren. *Sex, or the Unbearable*. Durham, NC: Duke University Press, 2014.

Berlant, Lauren. "Starved." *South Atlantic Quarterly* 106, no. 3 (2007): 433–44.

Berlant, Lauren, and Michael Warner. "Sex in Public." In *Publics and Counterpublics*, edited by Michael Warner, 187–208. New York: Zone Books, 2005.

Bernardin, Susan. "Intergenerational Memory and the Making of Indigenous Literary Kinships." In *Gender in American Literature and Culture*, edited by Jean Lutes and Jennifer Travis, 142–59. Cambridge: Cambridge University Press, 2021.

Bessel, Richard. *Germany 1945: From War to Peace*. New York: HarperCollins, 2009.

Betts, Paul. *Within Walls: Private Life in the German Democratic Republic*. Oxford: Oxford University Press, 2010.

Biess, Frank. "'Everybody Has a Chance': Nuclear Angst, Civil Defence, and the History of Emotions in Postwar West Germany." *German History* 27, no. 2 (2009): 215–43.

Biess, Frank. "Survivors of Totalitarianism: Returning POWs and the Reconstruction of Masculine Citizenship in West Germany, 1945–55." In *The Miracle Years: A Cultural History of West Germany, 1949–68*, edited by Hanna Schissler, 57–82. Princeton, NJ: Princeton University Press, 2001.

Biess, Frank, and Astrid M. Eckert. "Introduction: Why Do We Need New Narratives for the History of the Federal Republic?" *Central European History* 52, no. 1 (March 2019): 1–18.

Bisky, Jan. "Küssende Jungs." *Süddeutsche Zeitung*, May 17, 2010. https://www.sueddeutsche.de/kultur/mahnmal-fuer-verfolgte-homosexuelle-kuessende-jungs-1.192688.

Blessing, Jennifer. *Rrose Is a Rrose Is a Rrose: Gender Performance in Photography*. New York: Guggenheim Museum, 1997.

Böger, Frauke. "Die Vorwürfe sind einfach grotesk." *taz*, August 3, 2010.

Bollé, Michael, ed. *Eldorado: Homosexuelle Frauen und Männer in Berlin 1850–1950: Geschichte, Alltag und Kultur*. For the Verein der Freunde eines schwulen Museums Berlin e.V. Berlin: Edition Hentrich, 1992.

Boone, Joseph A. "Vacation Cruises; or, The Homoerotics of Orientalism." *PMLA* 110, no. 1 (1995): 89–107.

Boovy, Bradley. "Belonging in Black and White: Race, Photography, and the Allure of Heimat in West German Gay Magazines from the 1950s." *Seminar: A Journal of Germanic Studies* 54, no. 4 (2018): 428–41.

Borhan, Pierre. *Men for Men: Homoeroticism and Homosexuality in the History of Photography since 1840*. New York: Jonathan Cape, 2007.

Borowski, Maria. "Erste Erkenntnisse zum lesbischen und schwulen Alltagsleben in der DDR." In *Konformitäten und Konfrontationen: Homosexuelle in der DDR*, edited by Rainer Marbach and Volker Weiss, 51–63. Hamburg: Männerschwarm Verlag, 2017.

Bosold, Birgit, Dorotheé Brill, and Betlef Weitz, eds. *Homosexualität_en*. Berlin: Sandstein Verlag, 2015. Exhibition catalog.

Boxhammer, Ingeborg, and Christiane Leidinger. "Sexismus, Heteronormativität und (staatliche) Öffentlichkeit im Nationalsozialismus: Eine queer-feministische Perspektive auf die Verfolgung von Lesben und/oder Trans* in (straf-)rechtlichen Kontexten." In *Homosexuelle im Nationalsozialismus: Neue Forschungsperspektiven zu Lebenssituationen von lesbischen, schwulen, bi-, trans*- und intersexuellen Menschen 1933 bis 1945*, edited by Michael Schwartz, 93–100. Berlin: De Gruyter Oldenbourg, 2014.

Braunthal, Gerard. *Political Loyalty and Public Service in West Germany: The 1972 Degree against Radicals and Its Consequences*. Amherst: University of Massachusetts Press, 1990.

Breger, Claudia. *Making Worlds: Affect and Collectivity in Contemporary European Cinema*. New York: Columbia University Press, 2020.

Brett-Smith, Richard. *Berlin '45: The Grey City*. New York: Macmillan, 1966.

Brown, Elspeth H. "Queering Glamour in Interwar Fashion Photography: The 'Amorous Regard' of George Platt Lynes." *GLQ: A Journal of Lesbian and Gay Studies* 23, no. 3 (2017): 289–326.

Brown, Elspeth H., and Thy Phu, eds. *Feeling Photography*. Durham, NC: Duke University Press, 2014.

Brown, Wendy. *In the Ruins of Neoliberalism: The Rise of Antidemocratic Politics in the West*. New York: Columbia University Press, 2019.

Brown, Wendy. *Regulating Aversion: Tolerance in the Age of Identity and Empire*. Princeton, NJ: Princeton University Press, 2006.

Brown, Wendy. *States of Injury: Power and Freedom in Late Modernity*. Princeton, NJ: Princeton University Press, 2020.

Brown, Wendy. "Wounded Attachments." *Political Theory* 21, no. 3 (August 1993): 390–410.

Brown, Wendy, and Rainer Forst. *The Power of Tolerance: A Debate*. Edited by Luca Di Blasi and Christoph F. E. Holzhey. New York: Columbia University Press, 2014.

Brühl, Olaf. "Sozialistisch und Schwul: Eine subjektive Chronologie." In *Homosexualität in der DDR: Materialien und Meinungen*, edited by Wolfram Setz, 89–152. Hamburg: Männerschwarm Verlag, 2006.

Bryant, Dara. "Queering the Antifascist State: Ravensbrück as a Site of Lesbian Resistance." *Edinburgh German Yearbook 3. Contested Legacies: Constructions of Cultural Heritage in the GDR* (2009): 76–89.

Bühner, Maria. "'Lesbe, Lesbe, Lesbe: Ein Wort mit Kampfpotential, mit Stachel, mit Courage'; Lesbische Leben in der DDR zwischen Unsichtbarkeit und Bewegung." *In Lesben raus! Für mehr lesbische Sichtbarkeit*, edited by Stephanie Kuhnen, 104–15. Berlin: Querverlag, 2017.

Bühner, Maria. "'[W]ir haben einen Zustand zu analysieren, der uns zu Außenseitern macht': Lesbischer Aktivismus in Ost-Berlin in den 1980er-Jahren." *Themenportal Europäische Geschichte*, April 7, 2017. https://www.europa.clio-online.de/Portals/_Europa/documents/B2017/E_Buehner_LiK.pdf.

Burke, Peter. *Eyewitnessing: The Uses of Images as Historical Evidence*. Ithaca, NY: Cornell University Press, 2001.

Buske, Sibylle. *Fräulein Mutter und ihr Bastard: Eine Geschichte der Unehelichkeit in Deutschland 1900–1970*. Göttingen: Wallstein Verlag, 2004.

Butler, Ewan. *City Divided: Berlin 1955*. New York: Frederick A. Praeger, 1955.

Butler, Judith. "Afterword: After Loss, What Then?" In *Loss: The Politics of Mourning*, edited by David Kazanjian and David L. Eng, 467–74. Berkeley: University of California Press, 2002.

Butler, Judith. "Critically Queer." *GLQ: A Journal of Lesbian and Gay Studies* 1, no. 1 (1993): 17–32.

Butler, Judith. "Ich muss mich von dieser Komplizenschaft mit Rassismus distanzieren." Civil Courage Prize Refusal Speech, Christopher Street Day, June 19, 2010, European Graduate School. http://www.egs.edu/faculty/judith-butler/articles/ich-muss-mich-distanzieren/ and http://www.egs.edu/faculty/judith-butler/articles/i-must-distance-myself/.

Butler, Judith. "Lesbian S&M: The Politics of Dis-illusion." In *Against Sadomasochism: A Radical Feminist Analysis*, edited by Robin Ruth Lindon, Darlene R. Pagano,

Diana E. H. Russell, and Susan Leigh Star, 169–74. East Palo Alto, CA: Frog in the Well, 1982.

Butler, Judith. "Merely Cultural." *Social Text* 15, nos. 3–4 (1997): 265–77.

Bychowski, M. W., Howard Chiang, Jack Halberstam, Jacob Lau, Kathleen P. Long, Marcia Ochoa, C. Riley Snorton, Leah DeVun, and Zeb Tortorici. "Transhistoricities: A Roundtable Discussion." *Transgender Studies Quarterly* 5, no. 4 (2018): 658–85.

Cahan, Susan. *Mounting Frustration: The Art Museum in the Age of Black Power*. Durham, NC: Duke University Press, 2016.

Campt, Tina. *Image Matters: Archive, Photography, and the African Diaspora in Europe*. Durham, NC: Duke University Press, 2012.

Campt, Tina. *Listening to Images*. Durham, NC: Duke University Press, 2017.

Canaday, Margot. "Thinking Sex in the Transnational Turn: An Introduction." *American Historical Review* 114, no. 5 (2009): 1250–57.

Caplan, Jane. "The Administration of Gender Identity in Nazi Germany." *History Workshop Journal* 72, no. 1 (2011): 171–80.

Castiglia, Christopher, and Christopher Reed. *If Memory Serves: Gay Men, AIDS, and the Promise of the Queer Past*. Minneapolis: University of Minnesota Press, 2011.

Cavarero, Adriana. *For More Than One Voice: Toward a Philosophy of Vocal Expression*. Stanford: University of California Press, 2005.

Chakrabarty, Dipesh. "History and the Politics of Recognition." In *Manifestos for History*, edited by Keith Jenkins, Sue Morgan, and Alun Munslow, 77–87. New York: Routledge, 2007.

Chiang, Howard. *Transtopia in the Sinophone Pacific*. New York: Columbia University Press, 2021.

Chin, Rita. "Thinking Difference in Postwar Germany: Some Epistemological Obstacles around 'Race.'" In *Migration, Memory, and Diversity: Germany from 1945 to the Present*, edited by Cornelia Wilhelm, 206–29. New York: Berghahn Books, 2016.

Chin, Rita, Heide Fehrenbach, Geoff Eley, and Atina Grossmann. *After the Nazi Racial State: Difference and Democracy in Germany and Europe*. Ann Arbor: University of Michigan Press, 2010.

Chitty, Christopher. *Sexual Hegemony: Statecraft, Sodomy, and Capital in the Rise of the World System*. Durham, NC: Duke University Press, 2020.

Cho, Lily. "Future Perfect Loss: Richard Fung's *Sea in the Blood*." *Screen* 49, no. 4 (December 2008): 426–39.

Churchill, David S. "Transnationalism and Homophile Political Culture in the Postwar Decades." *GLQ: A Journal of Lesbian and Gay Studies* 15, no. 1 (2009): 31–66.

Ciesla, Burghard. "'Über alle Sektorengrenzen hinweg . . .': Die Deutsche Reichsbahn und die Berlinkrisen (1945–1958)." In *Sterben für Berlin? Die Berliner Krisen 1948–1958*, edited by Burghard Ciesla, Michael Lemki, and Thomas Lindenberger, 133–52. Berlin: Metropol Verlag, 2000.

Clark, Anna. *Desire: A History of European Sexuality*. New York: Routledge, 2008.

Clarke, Graham. *The Photograph*. Oxford: Oxford University Press, 1997.

Cochrane, Allan. "Making Up Meanings in a Capital City: Power, Memory and Monuments in Berlin." *European Urban and Regional Studies* 13, no. 1 (January 2006): 5–24.

Cohen, Cathy J. "Punks, Bulldaggers, and Welfare Queens: The Radical Potential of Queer Politics?" *GLQ: A Journal of Lesbian and Gay Studies* 3, no. 4 (1997): 437–65.

Cohen, Cathy J. "The Radical Potential of Queer? Twenty Years Later." *GLQ: A Journal of Lesbian and Gay Studies* 25, no. 1 (2019): 140–44.

Conrad, Sebastian, Shalini Randeria, and Beate Sutterlüty. *Jenseits des Eurozentrismus: Postkoloniale Perspektiven in den Geschichts- und Kulturwissenschaften.* Frankfurt am Main: Campus, 2002.

Cook, Matt. "Families of Choice? George Ives, Queer Lives and the Family in Early Twentieth-Century Britain." *Gender and History* 22, no. 1 (2010): 1–20.

Cook, Matt. *Queer Domesticities: Homosexuality and Home Life in Twentieth-Century London.* Basingstoke, UK: Palgrave Macmillan, 2014.

Cotten, Trystan, ed. *Transgender Migrations: The Bodies, Borders, and Politics of Transition.* New York: Routledge, 2011.

Cowell, Alan. "Challenge Is Raised to Plan for a Holocaust Monument in Berlin." *New York Times*, February 5, 1998.

Crane, Diana. *Fashion and Its Social Agendas: Class, Gender, and Identity in Clothing.* Chicago: University of Chicago Press, 2000.

Crenshaw, Kimberlé. "Mapping the Margins: Intersectionality, Identity Politics, and Violence against Women of Color." *Stanford Law Review* 43, no. 6 (1991): 1241–99.

Crew, David F. "Visual Power? The Politics of Images in Twentieth-Century Germany and Austria-Hungary." *German History* 27, no. 2 (April 2009): 271–85.

Crimp, Douglas. "Getting the Warhol We Deserve." *Social Text* 59 (Summer 1999): 49–66.

Cvetkovich, Ann. *An Archive of Feelings: Trauma, Sexuality, and Lesbian Public Cultures.* Durham, NC: Duke University Press, 2003.

Cvetkovich, Ann. "Kent Monkman's *Shame and Prejudice*: Artist Curation as Queer and Decolonial Museum Practice." In *Museums, Sexuality, and Gender Activism*, edited by Joshua G. Adair and Amy K. Levin, 133–44. New York: Routledge, 2020.

Dannecker, Martin, and Reimut Reiche. *Der gewöhnliche Homosexuelle.* Frankfurt: S. Fischer Verlag, 1984.

Dean, Carolyn Janice. *The Fragility of Empathy after the Holocaust.* Ithaca, NY: Cornell University Press, 2004.

Dennert, Gabriele, Christiane Leidinger, and Franziska Rauchut. *In Bewegung bleiben: 100 Jahre Politik, Kultur und Geschichte von Lesben.* Berlin: Querverlag, 2007.

"Die Freiburger Thesen der FDP" [The Freiburg Theses of the FDP]. In *Bilanz der sozialliberalen Koalition: Documentation*, edited by Wolfram Bickerich, 190–201. Reinbek bei Hamburg: Rowohlt, 1982.

Dinshaw, Carolyn. *Getting Medieval: Sexualities and Communities, Pre- and Postmodern.* Durham, NC: Duke University Press, 1999.

Dinshaw, C., L. Edelman, R. A. Ferguson, C. Freccero, E. Freeman, J. Halberstam, A. Jagose, C. Nealon, and N. T. Hoang. "Theorizing Queer Temporalities: A Roundtable Discussion." *GLQ: A Journal of Lesbian and Gay Studies* 13, nos. 2–3 (2007): 177–95.

Doan, Laura L. *Disturbing Practices: History, Sexuality, and Women's Experience of Modern War.* Chicago: University of Chicago Press, 2013.

Dobler, Jens. *Polizei: Vom Zwangsverhältnis zur Zweckehe?* Berlin: Verlag rosa Winkel, 1996.

Dobler, Jens. "Staat im Aufbruch: Der Sonntags-Club." In *Homosexuelle in Deutschland 1933–1969*, edited by Alexander Zinn, 102–7. Göttingen: V&R Unipress, 2020.

Dobler, Jens. *Verzaubert im Nord-Ost.* Berlin: Gmünder, 2009.

Dobler, Jens. *Von anderen Ufern: Geschichte der Berliner Lesben und Schwulen in Kreuzberg und Friedrichshain.* Berlin: Gmünder, 2003.

Dölling, Irene, and Sabine Hark. "She Who Speaks Shadow Speaks Truth: Transdisciplinarity in Women's and Gender Studies." *Signs* 25, no. 4 (2000): 1195–98.

Domröse, Ulrich, ed. *Herbert Tobias, 1924–1982: Blicke und Begehren.* Hamburg: Steidl Göttingen, 2008.

Doyle, Jennifer. *Sex Objects: Art and the Dialectics of Desire.* Minneapolis: University of Minnesota Press, 2006.

Druschel, Bruce E. "The Evolution Will Not Be Broadcast (or Published): Social Capital, Assimilation, and the Changing Queer Community." *Journal of Homosexuality: Of Acceptance and Celebration* 66, no. 12 (2019): 1756–68.

Duggan, Lisa. "The Discipline Problem: Queer Theory Meets Lesbian and Gay History." *GLQ: A Journal of Lesbian and Gay Studies* 2, no. 3 (1995): 179–91.

Duggan, Lisa. *The Twilight of Equality? Neoliberalism, Cultural Politics, and the Attack on Democracy.* Boston: Beacon, 2003.

Duman, Tülin. "Eine Minderheit unter vielen." *taz*, July 3, 2010.

Dyer, Richard. *Heavenly Bodies: Film Stars and Society.* New York: St. Martin's, 2003.

Eckert, Nora. "Trans Transatlantic." Translated by Michael Thomas Taylor and Annette F. Timm. In *Others of My Kind: Transatlantic Transgender Histories*, edited by Alex Bakker, Rainer Herrn, Michael Thomas Taylor, and Annette F. Timm, 247–50. Calgary: University of Calgary Press, 2020.

Eckert, Nora. *Wie Alle, Nur Anders: Ein Transsexuelles Leben in Berlin.* Munich: C. H. Beck, 2021.

Edelman, Lee. *No Future: Queer Theory and the Death Drive.* Durham, NC: Duke University Press, 2004.

Edwards, Elizabeth. "Thinking Photography beyond the Visual?" In *Photography: Theoretical Snapshots*, edited by J. J. Long, Andrea Noble, and Edward Welch, 31–48. New York: Routledge, 2009.

Eicker, Philip. "Küssen verboten?" *Hinnerk* 4 (2007): n.p.

Endlich, Stefanie. "Das Berliner Homosexuellen-Denkmal: Kontext, Erwartungen und die Debatte um den Videofilm." In *Homophobie und Devianz: Weibliche und männliche Homosexualität im Nationalsozialismus*, edited by Insa Eschebach, 167–86. Berlin: Metropole, 2016.

Ellenzweig, Allen, and George Stambolian. *The Homoerotic Photograph: Male Images from Durieu/Delacroix to Mapplethorpe.* New York: Columbia University Press, 1992.

El-Tayeb, Fatima. "Begrenzte Horizonte: Queer Identity in der Festung Europa." In *Spricht die Subalterne deutsch? Migration und postkoloniale Kritik*, edited by Encarnación Gutiérrez Rodríguez and Hito Steyerl, 129–45. Münster: Unrast, 2003.

El-Tayeb, Fatima. *European Others: Queering Ethnicity in Postnational Europe*. Minneapolis: University of Minnesota Press, 2011.

El-Tayeb, Fatima. "'Gays Who Cannot Properly Be Gay': Queer Muslims in the Neoliberal European City." *European Journal of Women's Studies* 19, no. 1 (2012): 79–95.

El-Tayeb, Fatima. "Oppressed Majority: Violence and Muslim Communities in Multicultural Europe." In *With Stones in Our Hands: Writings on Muslims, Racism, and Empire*, edited by Sohail Daulatzai and Junaid Rana, 83–100. Minneapolis: University of Minnesota Press, 2018.

Eng, David. *The Feeling of Kinship: Queer Liberalism and the Racialization of Intimacy*. Durham, NC: Duke University Press, 2010.

Eng, David. "Melancholia in the Late-Twentieth Century." *Signs* 25, no. 4 (2000): 1275–81.

Erel, Umut, Jin Haritaworn, Encarnación Gutiérrez Rodríguez, and Christian Klesse. "On the Depoliticisation of Intersectionality Talk: Conceptualising Multiple Oppressions in Critical Sexuality Studies." In *Theorizing Intersectionality and Sexuality*, edited by Yvette Taylor, Sally Hines, and Mark E. Casey, 56–77. London: Palgrave Macmillan, 2010.

Escoffier, Jeffrey. *Bigger Than Life: The History of Gay Porn Cinema from Beefcake to Hardcore*. New York: Running Press, 2009.

Espagne, Michel. *Transferts: Les relations interculturelles dans l'espace franco-allemand (XVIIIe et XIXe siècles)*. Paris: Éditions recherche sur les civilisations, 1988.

Est, Sanni. "Jasco Viefhues und die Suche nach neuen Narrativen." *The Tea Talk*. Accessed June 21, 2021. https://open.spotify.com/episode/48avXXiphyRkHCQr RVAYJz?si=SoqnyCuQTECKVv5M0SD8ig.

Evans, Jennifer V. "Bahnhof Boys: Policing Male Prostitution in Post-Nazi Berlin." *Journal of the History of Sexuality* 12, no. 4 (2003): 605–36.

Evans, Jennifer V. "Decriminalization, Seduction, and 'Unnatural Desire' in the German Democratic Republic." *Feminist Studies* 36, no. 3 (2010): 553–77.

Evans, Jennifer V. "Harmless Kisses and Infinite Loops: Making Space for Queer Place in Twenty-First Century Berlin." In *Queer Cities, Queer Cultures: Europe since 1945*, edited by Jennifer Evans and Matt Cook, 75–94. London: Bloomsbury, 2014.

Evans, Jennifer V. *Life among the Ruins: Cityscape and Sexuality in Cold War Berlin*. Basingstoke, UK: Palgrave Macmillan, 2011.

Evans, Jennifer V. "The Long 1950s as Radical In-Between: The Photography of Herbert Tobias." In *Queer 1950s: Rethinking Sexuality in the Postwar Years*, edited by Heike Bauer and Matt Cook, 13–28. London: Palgrave Macmillan, 2012.

Evans, Jennifer V. "The Moral State: Men, Mining, and Masculinity in the Early GDR." *German History* 23, no. 3 (2005): 355–70.

Evans, Jennifer V. "Queer Beauty: Image and Acceptance in the Expanded Public Sphere." In *Globalizing Beauty: Consumerism and Body Aesthetics in the Twentieth Century*, edited by Hartmut Berghoff and Thomas Kühne, 91–107. Basingstoke, UK: Palgrave Macmillan, 2013.

Evans, Jennifer V. "Seeing Subjectivity: Erotic Photography and the Optics of Desire." *American Historical Review* 118, no. 2 (2013): 430–62.

Evans, Jennifer V. "Sound, Listening, and the Queer Art of History." *Rethinking History* 22, no. 1 (2018): 25–43.

Evans, Jennifer V. "Streiten, Verstehen und Zusammenstehen: Die Queere Bewegung in Deutschland—Eine Vielstimmige Geschichte." *Tagesspiegel*, April 16, 2021. https://www.tagesspiegel.de/gesellschaft/queerspiegel/streiten-verstehen-und -zusammenstehen-die-queere-bewegung-in-deutschland-eine-vielstimmige -geschichte/27098002.html.

Evans, Jennifer, Anna Hájková, Sabine Hark, Ervin Malakaj, Iris Rachamimov, Laurie Marhoefer, and Katie Sutton. "Eine queere Institution, die Transfeindlichkeit unterstutzt, ist nichts wert." *Tagesspiegel*, March 2, 2020. https://www.tagesspiegel .de/gesellschaft/queerspiegel/diskussion-um-das-queere-kulturhaus-in-berlin -eine-queere-institution-die-transfeindlichkeit-unterstuetzt-ist-nichts-wert /25601858.html.

Evans, Jennifer, and Elissa Mailänder. "Cross-Dressing, Male Intimacy and the Violence of Transgression in Third Reich Photography." *German History* 39, no. 1 (March 2021): 54–77.

Ewing, Christopher B. "Archives in Europe." In *Global Encyclopedia of Lesbian, Gay, Bisexual, Transgender, and Queer (LGBTQ) History*, vol. 1, edited by Howard Chiang and Anjali R. Arondekar, 103–6. New York: Charles Scribner's Sons, 2019.

Ewing, Christopher B. "The Color of Desire: Contradictions of Race, Sex, and Gay Rights in the Federal Republic of Germany." PhD diss., City University of New York, 2018.

Ewing, Christopher B. "'Color Him Black': Erotic Representations and the Politics of Race in West German Homosexual Magazines, 1949–1974." *Sexuality and Culture* 21, no. 2 (June 2017): 382–404.

Fanon, Frantz. *The Wretched of the Earth*. New York: Grove, 1963.

Farges, Patrick, Doris Bergen, Anna Hàjkovà, Elissa Mailänder, and Atina Grossmann. "Forum: Holocaust and the History of Gender and Sexuality." *German History* 36, no. 1 (2018): 78–100.

Feddersen, Jan. "Antifreiheitliches Wokistan." *taz*, January 1, 2011. https://taz.de /Professorin-tritt-nach-trans-Eklat-ab/!5809038/.

Feddersen, Jan. "Falsche Opferpolitik." *taz*, August 28, 2006. http://www.taz.de/pt /2006/08/28/a0116.1/text.

Feddersen, Jan. "Unsere Queergida: So wird 'cis, weiss, männlich' diffamiert." *Mannschaft Magazin*, April 6, 2019. https://mannschaft.com/unsere-queergida-so -wird-cis-weiss-maennlich-diffamiert/.

Feddersen, Jan. "War die Absage von Judith Butler das richtige Signal?" *taz*, June 20, 2010. http://www.taz.de/1/debatte/kommentar/artikel/1/war-die-absage-von -butler-das-richtige-signal/.

Fehrenbach, Heide. *Cinema in Democratizing Germany: National Identity after Hitler*. Chapel Hill: University of North Carolina Press, 1995.

Fehrenbach, Heide. *Race after Hitler: Black Occupation Children in Postwar Germany and America*. Princeton, NJ: Princeton University Press, 2005.

Felten, Sebastian, and Rebecca Kahn. "Unboxed: Transgender in a Gay Museum? A Field Report by the Curators." *TSQ: Transgender Studies Quarterly* 8, no. 2 (May 2021): 257–64.

Ferguson, Roderick A. *Aberrations in Black: Toward a Queer of Color Critique*. Minneapolis: University of Minnesota Press, 2004.

Ferguson, Roderick A. "Of Our Normative Strivings: African American Studies and the Histories of Sexuality." *Social Text*, nos. 84–85 (2005): 85–100.

Ferguson, Roderick A. *One-Dimensional Queer*. Cambridge, UK: Polity, 2018.

Ferree, Myra. *Varieties of Feminism: German Gender Politics in Global Perspective*. Stanford, CA: Stanford University Press, 2012.

Feuchtner, Veronika. "Indians, Jews, and Sex: Magnus Hirschfeld and Indian Sexology." In *Imagining Germany Imagining Asia: Essays in Asian-German Studies*, edited by Veronika Fuechtner and Mary Rhiel, 111–30. Rochester, NY: Camden House, 2013.

Fischel, Joseph J. *Screw Consent: A Better Politics of Sexual Justice*. Berkeley: University of California Press, 2019.

Fischel, Joseph J. *Sex and Harm in the Age of Consent*. Minneapolis: University of Minnesota Press, 2016.

Fischer, Eugen. *Sozialanthropologie und ihre Bedeutung für den Staat: Vortrag gehalten in der Naturforschenden Gesellschaft zu Freiburg i.Br. am 8. Juni 1910*. Freiburg i.B.: Speyer and Kaerner, 1910.

Fiumara, G. Corradi. *The Other Side of Language: A Philosophy of Listening*. New York: Routledge, 1990.

Florvil, Tiffany N. Review of *Audre Lorde: The Berlin Years, 1984–1992*, by Dagmar Schultz. *Black Camera: The Newsletter of the Black Film Center/Archives* 5, no. 2 (2014): 201–3.

Florvil, Tiffany N. *Mobilizing Black Germany: Afro-German Women and the Making of a Transnational Movement*. Champaign: University of Illinois Press, 2020.

Foucault, Michel. "Sex, Power, and the Politics of Identity." In *Ethics: Subjectivity and Truth*, edited by Paul Rabinow, 163–74. New York: New Press, 1997.

Frackman, Kyle. "Homemade Pornography and the Proliferation of Queer Pleasure in East Germany." *Radical History Review* 2022, no. 142 (January 2022): 93–109.

Freccero, Carla. "Queer Spectrality: Haunting the Past." In *A Companion to Lesbian, Gay, Bisexual, Transgender, and Queer Studies*, edited by George E. Haggerty and Molly McGarry, 194–214. Malden, MA: Blackwell, 2007.

Freeland, Jane. *Feminist Transformations: Domestic Violence Activism in Divided Berlin, 1968–2002*. Oxford: Oxford University Press, 2022.

Freeman, Elizabeth. "Queer Belongings: Kinship Theory and Queer Theory." In *A Companion to Lesbian, Gay, Bisexual, Transgender, and Queer Studies*, edited by George E. Haggerty and Molly McGarry, 293–314. Malden, MA: Blackwell, 2007.

Freeman, Elizabeth. "Theorizing Queer Temporalities: A Roundtable Discussion." *GLQ: A Journal of Lesbian and Gay Studies* 13, nos. 2–3 (2007): 177–92.

Freeman, Elizabeth. *Time Binds: Queer Temporalities, Queer Histories*. Durham, NC: Duke University Press, 2010.

Frevert, Ute. "Umbruch der Geschlechterverhältnisse? Die 60er Jahre als geschlechterpolitischer Experimentierraum." In *Dynamische Zeiten: Die 60er Jahre in den beiden deutschen Gesellschaften*, edited by Axel Schildt, Detlef Siegfried, and Karl Christian Lammers, 642–60. Hamburg: Christians Verlag, 2000.

Friedlander, Lee, and John Szarkowski. *E. J. Bellocq: Storyville Portraits*. New York: Little Brown, 1970.

Funke, Jana. "Navigating the Past: Sexuality, Race, and the Uses of the Primitive in Magnus Hirschfeld's *The World Journey of a Sexologist*." In *Sex, Knowledge, and Receptions of the Past*, edited by Kate Fisher and Rebecca Langlands, 111–34. Oxford: Oxford University Press, 2015.

Fürst, Juliane. *Flowers through Concrete: Explorations in Soviet Hippieland*. New York: Oxford University Press, 2021.

Fürst, Juliane, and Josie McLellan, eds. *Dropping Out of Socialism: The Creation of Alternative Spheres in the Soviet Bloc*. Lanham, MD: Lexington Books, 2017.

Gammerl, Benno. *Anders fühlen: Schwules und lesbisches Leben in der Bundesrepublik; Eine Emotionsgeschichte*. Munich: Carl Hanser Verlag, 2021.

Gammerl, Benno. "Das Elberskirchen-Hirschfeld-Haus (E2H): Queeres Kulturhaus in Berlin." *L'Homme: Europäische Zeitschrift für Feministische Geschichtswissenschaft* 29, no. 2 (2018): 127–33.

Gammerl, Benno. "Ist frei sein Normal? Männliche Homosexualitäten seit den 1960er Jahren zwischen Emanzipation und Normalisierung." In *Sexuelle Revolution? Zur Geschichte der Sexualität im deutschsprachigen Raum seit den 1960er Jahren*, edited by Peter-Paul Bänziger, Magdalena Beljan, Franz X. Eder, and Pascal Eitler, 223–43. Bielefeld: transcript Verlag, 2015.

Gammerl, Benno, and Birgit Kiupel. "Wir bauen ein Haus! E2H—das Elberskirchen-Hirschfeld-Haus. Ein konkreter Vorschlag." *Blog der Iniative Queer Nations e.V*, June 4, 2013. https://queernations.blogspot.com/2013/06/wir-bauen-ein-haus.html?fbclid=IwAR3v8Q8-k3lBgnljkm_jRHps8ABVlEwdoPZJiJd9EsjnPrs4HjoPTggqLAI.

Garcia, Michael-Hames. "Can Queer Theory Be Critical Theory?" In *New Critical Theory: Essays on Liberation*, 201–22. Lanham, MD: Rowman and Littlefield, 2001.

Garde, Jonah I. "Provincializing Trans* Modernity: Asterisked Histories and Multiple Horizons in *Der Steinachfilm*." *TSQ: Transgender Studies Quarterly* 8, no. 2 (May 2021): 207–22.

Gardiner, James. *Who's a Pretty Boy, Then? One Hundred and Fifty Years of Gay Life in Pictures*. London: Serpent's Tail, 1998.

Gasser, Manuel. *Erinnerungen und Berichte*. Zürich: Verlag der Arsch, 1981.

Gell, Alfred. *Art and Agency: An Anthropological Theory*. Oxford: Clarendon, 1998.

Gennies, Sidney. "Die Identitätspolitik des Wolfgang Thierse: 'Normalität' ist die Cancel Culture des alten weißen Mannes." *Tagesspiegel*, March 11, 2021. https://www.tagesspiegel.de/gesellschaft/die-identitaetspolitik-des-wolfgang-thierse-normalitaet-ist-die-cancel-culture-des-alten-weissen-mannes/26996920.html.

Gentile, Patrizia, and Gary Kinsman. *The Canadian War on Queers: National Security as Sexual Regulation*. Vancouver: UBC Press, 2010.

Gerides, Stefanie. "Why Was the Video to the Memorial of Gay Holocaust Victims Changed?" *Gay Star News*, January 11, 2017. https://www.gaystarnews.com/article/video-berlins-memorial-gay-holocaust-victims-changed/.

Giersdorf, Jens. "Why Does Charlotte von Mahlsdorf Curtsy? Representations of National Queerness in a Transvestite Hero." *GLQ: A Journal of Lesbian and Gay Studies* 12, no. 2 (2006): 171–96.

Giese, Hans. *Der homosexuelle Mann in der Welt*. Stuttgart: Ferdinand Enke, 1964.

Giese, Hans. "Geschlechtsunterschiede im homosexuellen Verhalten." In *Mensch, Geschlecht, Gesellschaft: Das Geschlechtsleben unserer Zeit gemeinverständlich dargestellt*, edited by Hans Giese, 876–77. Baden-Baden: Verlag für angewandte Wissenschaften, 1961.

Giles, Geoffrey J. "Legislating Homophobia in the Third Reich: The Radicalization of Prosecution against Homosexuality by the Legal Profession." *German History* 23, no. 3 (2005): 339–54.

Gill-Peterson, Jules. *Histories of the Transgender Child*. Minneapolis: University of Minnesota Press, 2020.

Gill-Peterson, Jules. "Trans of Color Critique before Transsexuality." *TSQ: Transgender Studies Quarterly* 5, no. 4 (November 2018): 606–20.

Glamor, Timo. Interview by Karl-Heinz Steinle. "Lockmittel und Versprechen: Sammlerkolumne von Tina Glamor." *ReVu: Magazin für Fotografie und Wahrnehmung*, August 21, 2021. https://www.re-vue.org/beitrag/sammlerkolumne-tina-glamor.

Goldin, Nan, Marvin Heiferman, Mark Holborn, and Suzanne Fletcher. *The Ballad of Sexual Dependency*. New York: Aperture, 1986.

Gomes Pereira, Pedro Paulo. "Reflecting on Decolonial Queer." *GLQ: A Journal of Lesbian and Gay Studies* 25, no. 3 (2019): 403–29.

Gopinath, Gayatri. *Impossible Desires: Queer Diasporas and South Asian Public Cultures*. Durham, NC: Duke University Press, 2005.

Grassmann, Philip. "Migrantenkinder gegen Schwule: Homophobes Berlin." *Süddeutsche Zeitung*, May 17, 2010. https://www.sueddeutsche.de/panorama/migrantenkinder-gegen-schwule-homophobes-berlin-1.335341.

Grau, Günter. "Ein Leben im Kampf gegen den Paragraphen 175: Zum Wirken des Dresdener Arztes Rudolf Klimmer 1905–1977." In *100 Jahre Schwulenbewegung*, edited by Manfred Herzer, 46–64. Berlin: Verlag rosa Winkel, 1998.

Grau, Günter. "Im Auftrag der Partei: Versuch einer Reform der strafrechtlichen Bestimmungen zur Homosexualität in der DDR 1952." *Zeitschrift für Sexualforschung* 9 (1996): 109–30.

Grau, Günter. "Sozialistische Moral und Homosexualität: Die Politik der SED und das Homosexuellenstrafrecht 1945 bis 1989—Ein Rückblick." In *Die Linke und das Laster: Schwule Emanzipation und linke Vorurteile*, edited by Detlef Grumbach, 85–141. Hamburg: Männerschwarm Skript-Verlag, 1995.

Grau, Günter. "Strafrechtliche Verfolgung der Homosexualität in der DDR." In *§175 StGB Rehabilitierung der nach 1945 verurteilten homosexuellen Männer*, edited by Senatsverwaltung für Arbeit, Integration und Frauen Berlin, 44–58. Berlin: Pressestelle der Senatsverwaltung, 2012.

Griffiths, Craig. *The Ambivalence of Gay Liberation: Male Homosexual Politics in 1970s West Germany*. Oxford: Oxford University Press, 2021.

Griffiths, Craig. "Gay Activism in *Modell Deutschland.*" *European Review of History: Revue européenne d'histoire* 22, no. 1 (2015): 60–76.

Griffiths, Craig. "Konkurrierende Pfade der Emanzipation: Der Tuntenstreit (1973–1975) und die Frage des 'respektablen Auftretens.'" In *Rosa Radikale: Die Schwulenbewegung der 1970er Jahre*, edited by Andreas Pretzel and Volker Weiss, 143–59. Hamburg: Männerschwarm Verlag, 2012.

Griffiths, Craig. "Sex, Shame and West German Gay Liberation*." *German History* 34, no. 3 (September 2016): 445–67.

Grossmann, Atina. "A Question of Silence: The Rape of German Women by Occupation Soldiers." *October* 72 (1995): 43–63.

Hájková, Anna. "Introduction: Sexuality, Holocaust, Stigma." *German History* 39, no. 1 (2021): 1–14.

Hájková, Anna. *Menschen ohne Geschichte sind Staub: Homophobie und Holocaust*. Munich: Wallstein Verlag GmbH, 2021.

Halberstam, Jack. "Forgetting Family: Queer Alternatives to Oedipal Relations." In *A Companion to Lesbian, Gay, Bisexual, Transgender, and Queer Studies*, edited by George E. Haggerty and Molly McGarry, 315–24. Malden, MA: Blackwell, 2007.

Halberstam, Jack. *In a Queer Time and Place: Transgender Bodies, Subcultural Lives*. New York: New York University Press, 2005.

Halberstam, Jack. *The Queer Art of Failure*. Durham, NC: Duke University Press, 2011.

Halberstam, Jack. "Straight Eye for the Queer Theorist—a Review of 'Queer Theory without Antinormativity.'" *BullyBloggers*, September 12, 2015. https://bullybloggers.wordpress.com/2015/09/12/straight-eye-for-the-queer-theorist-a-review-of-queer-theory-without-antinormativity-by-jack-halberstam/.

Halberstam, Jack. *Trans*: A Quick and Quirky Account of Gender Variability*. Berkeley: University of California Press, 2017.

Halbwachs, Maurice. *The Collective Memory, 1950*. New York: Harper Colophon Books, 1980.

Hall, James Baker. *Minor White: Rights and Passages*. New York: Aperture, 2005.

Hall-Araujo, Lori. "Ambivalence and the 'American Dream' on RuPaul's Drag Race." *Film, Fashion and Consumption* 5, no. 2 (2016): 233–41.

Halperin, David M. *How to Do the History of Homosexuality*. Chicago: University of Chicago Press, 2002.

Halperin, David M., and Trevor Hoppe. *The War on Sex*. Durham, NC: Duke University Press, 2017.

Hamilton, Rosa. "A Clarification." *Radical History Review* 2021, no. 141 (October 2021): 221–23.

Hamilton, Rosa. "The Very Quintessence of Persecution: Queer Anti-fascism in 1970s Western Europe." *Radical History Review* 2020, no. 138 (October 2020): 60–81.

Hanhardt, Christina B. "The Radical Potential of Queer Political History?" *GLQ: A Journal of Lesbian and Gay Studies* 25, no. 1 (2019): 145–50.

Hannemann, Matthias. "Szenelokalverbot gleich Konzentrationslager? Streit ums Homosexuellen-Mahnmal." *Frankfurter Allgemeine Zeitung*, June 24, 2006. https://www.faz.net/aktuell/feuilleton/streit-ums-homosexuellen-mahnmal -szenelokalverbot-gleich-konzentrationslager-1547365.html.

Hanshew, Karrin. "'Sympathy for the Devil?': The West German Left and the Challenge of Terrorism." *Contemporary European History* 21, no. 4 (2012): 511–32.

Hanson, Dian. *Bob's World: The Life and Boys of AMG's Bob Mizer*. Cologne: Taschen, 2009.

Haritaworn, Jin. "Colorful Bodies in the Multikulti Metropolis: Vitality, Victimology and Transgressive Citizenship in Berlin." In *Transgender Migrations: The Bodies, Borders, and Politics of Transition*, edited by Trysten Cotton, 11–31. New York: Routledge, 2011.

Haritaworn, Jin. "Queer Injuries: The Racial Politics of 'Homophobic Hate Crime' in Germany." *Social Justice* 37, no. 1 (119) (2010): 69–89.

Haritaworn, Jin. *Queer Lovers and Hateful Others: Regenerating Violent Times and Places*. Chicago: Pluto, 2015.

Haritaworn, Jin. "Shifting Positionalities: Empirical Reflections on a Queer/Trans of Colour Methodology." *Sociological Research Online* 13, no. 1 (March 21, 2008). https://www.socresonline.org.uk/13/1/13.html.015.

Haritaworn, Jin. "Women's Rights, Gay Rights and Anti-Muslim Racism in Europe: Introduction." *European Journal of Women's Studies* 19, no. 1 (2012): 73–78.

Haritaworn, Jin. "Wounded Subjects: Sexual Exceptionalism and the Moral Panic on 'Migrant Homophobia' in Germany." In *Decolonizing European Sociology: Trans-disciplinary Approaches*, edited by Encarnación Gutiérrez Rodriguez, Manuela Boatcă, and Sérgio Costa, 135–52. New York: Routledge, 2016.

Haritaworn, Jin, Adi Kuntsman, Silvia Posocco, and Elizabeth Povinelli. "Obligation, Social Projects and Queer Politics." *International Feminist Journal of Politics* 15, no. 4 (2013): 554–64.

Haritaworn, Jin, Gaida Moussa, and Syrus Marcus Ware. *Marvelous Grounds: Queer of Colour Histories of Toronto*. Toronto: Between the Lines, 2018.

Haritaworn, Jin, and Jennifer Petzen, "Invented Traditions, New Intimate Publics: Tracing the German 'Muslim Homophobia' Discourse." In *Islam in Its International Context: Comparative Perspectives*, edited by C. Flood, S. Hutchings, Galina Miazhevich, and Henri Nickels, 48–64. Cambridge: Cambridge Scholars Press, 2014.

Haritaworn, Jin, Tamsila Tauqir, and Esra Erdem. "Gay Imperialism: The Role of Gender and Sexuality Discourses in the 'War on Terror.'" In *Out of Place: Silences in Queerness/Raciality*, edited by E. Miyake and A. Kuntsman, 9–33. York: Raw Nerve Books, 2008.

Hark, Sabine, and Paula-Irene Villa. *The Future of Difference: Beyond the Toxic Entanglement of Racism, Sexism, and Feminism*. London: Verso, 2019.

Harris, Victoria. *Selling Sex in the Reich: Prostitutes in German Society, 1914–1945*. Oxford: Oxford University Press, 2010.

Harsch, Donna. *Revenge of the Domestic: Women, the Family, and Communism in the German Democratic Republic*. Princeton, NJ: Princeton University Press, 2008.

Harsin Drager, Emmett, and Lucas Platero. "At the Margins of Time and Place: Trans-sexuals and the Transvestites in Trans Studies." *TSQ: Transgender Studies Quarterly* 8, no. 4 (November 2021): 417–25.

Hartman, Saidiya V. "Venus in Two Acts." *Small Axe* 12, no. 2 (2008): 1–14.

Hartman, Saidiya V. *Wayward Lives, Beautiful Experiments: Intimate Histories of Social Upheaval*. New York: W. W. Norton, 2019.

Hartman, Saidiya V., and Frank B. Wilderson III. "The Position of the Unthought." *Qui Parle* 13, no. 2 (December 2003): 183–201.

Hartmann, Andreas. "Queeres Jubiläum im SO36: 'Gayhane heißt Schwulenhaus.'" *taz*, January 25, 2019, sec. Berlin. https://taz.de/!5565083/.

Harvey, David. *Paris, Capital of Modernity*. New York: Routledge, 2003.

Hauenstein, Hanno. "Nazi-Hintergrund, NS-Erbe und materielle Kontinuität: Das Sch-weigen brechen." *Berliner Zeitung*, April 10, 2021. https://www.berliner-zeitung.de/wochenende/nazi-hintergrund-ns-erbe-und-materielle-kontinuitaet-das-schweigen-brechen-li.150838.

Haver, William. *The Body of This Death: Historicity and Sociality in the Time of AIDS*. Stanford, CA: Stanford University Press, 1996.

Heger, Heinz. *Die Männer mit dem rosa Winkel: Der Bericht eines Homosexuellen über seine KZ-Haft von 1939–1945*. Hamburg: Merlin Verlag, 1972.

Heimrod, Ute, Günter Schlusche, and Horst Seferens, eds. *Der Denkmalstreit–das Denkmal? Die Debatte um das "Denkmal für die ermordeten Juden Europas." Eine Dokumentation*. Berlin: Philo, 1999.

Heineman, Elizabeth D. *Before Porn Was Legal: The Erotica Empire of Beate Uhse*. Chicago: University of Chicago Press, 2011.

Heineman, Elizabeth D. "The Economic Miracle in the Bedroom: Big Business and Sexual Consumption in Reconstruction West Germany." *Journal of Modern History* 78, no. 4 (2006): 846–77.

Heineman, Elizabeth D. "The Hour of the Woman: Memories of Germany's 'Crisis Years' and West German National Identity." *American Historical Review* 101, no. 2 (April 1996): 354–96.

Heineman, Elizabeth D. *What Difference Does a Husband Make? Women and Marital Status in Nazi and Postwar Germany*. Berkeley: University of California Press, 1999.

Heintz, Lauren. "The Crisis of Kinship: Queer Affiliations in the Sexual Economy of Slavery." *GLQ: A Journal of Lesbian and Gay Studies* 23, no. 2 (2017): 221–46.

Heller, Meredith. "RuPaul Realness: The Neoliberal Resignification of Ballroom Dis-course." *Social Semiotics* 30, no. 1 (2020): 133–47.

Hennessy, Rosemary. *Profit and Pleasure: Sexual Identities in Late Capitalism*. New York: Routledge, 2000.

Herrn, Rainer, ed. *Das 3. Geschlecht*. Hamburg: Männerschwarm Verlag, 2016.

Herrn, Rainer. "'In der heutigen Staatsführung kann es nicht angehen, daß sich Män-ner in Frauenkleidung frei auf der Straße bewegen': Über den Forschungsstand zum Transvestitismus in der NSZeit." In *Homosexuelle im Nationalsozialismus: Neue Forschungsperspektiven zu Lebenssituationen von lesbischen, schwulen, bi-, trans- und intersexuellen Menschen 1933 bis 1945*, edited by Michael Schwartz, 101–6. Munich: De Gruyter Oldenbourg, 2014.

Herrn, Rainer. *Schnittmuster des Geschlechts: Transvestitismus und Transsexualität in der frühen Sexualwissenschaft*. Gießen: Psychosozial-Verlag, 2005.

Herrn, Rainer. "Transvestitismus in der NS-Zeit: Ein Forschungsdesiderat." *Zeitschrift für Sexualforschung* 27, no. 4 (2013): 330–71.

Herzog, Dagmar. *Sex after Fascism: Memory and Morality in Twentieth-Century Germany*. Princeton, NJ: Princeton University Press, 2007.

Herzog, Dagmar. *Sexuality in Europe: A Twentieth-Century History*. Cambridge: Cambridge University Press, 2011.

Herzog, Dagmar. "Sexuelle Revolution und Vergangenheitsbewältigung." *Zeitschrift für Sexualforschung* 13, no. 2 (2000): 87–103.

Herzog, Dagmar. "Syncopated Sex: Transforming European Sexual Cultures." *American Historical Review* 114, no. 5 (2009): 1287–308.

Hillhouse, Raelynn J. "Out of the Closet behind the Wall: Sexual Politics and Social Change in the GDR." *Slavic Review* 49, no. 4 (1990): 585–96.

Hingst, Monika, ed. *Goodbye to Berlin? 100 Jahre Schwulenbewegung*. Berlin: Verlag rosa Winkel, 1997.

Hirsch, Marianne. *The Generation of Postmemory: Writing and Visual Culture after the Holocaust*. New York: Columbia University Press, 2012.

Hirschfeld, Magnus, and Max Tilke. *Der erotische Verkleidungstrieb (Die Transvestiten): Illustrierter Teil*, vol. 2. 2nd ed. Berlin: Alfred Pulvermacher, 1912.

Hoang, Nguyen Tan. "Theorizing Queer Temporalities: A Roundtable Discussion." *GLQ: A Journal of Lesbian and Gay Studies* 13, nos. 2–3 (2007): 6–7.

Hobson, Emily K. *Lavender and Red: Liberation and Solidarity in the Gay and Lesbian Left*. Berkeley: University of California Press, 2016.

Hoffmann, Stefan-Ludwig. "Gazing at Ruins: German Defeat as Visual Experience." In *The Ethics of Seeing: Photography and Twentieth-Century German History*, edited by Jennifer V. Evans, Paul Betts, and Stefan-Ludwig Hoffmann, 138–56. New York: Berghahn Books, 2018.

Höhn, Maria. *GIs and Fräuleins: The German-American Encounter in 1950s West Germany*. Chapel Hill: University of North Carolina Press, 2002.

Höhn, Maria, and Martin Klimke. *A Breath of Freedom: The Civil Rights Struggle, African American GIs, and Germany*. Basingstoke, UK: Palgrave Macmillan, 2010.

Holland, Sharon Patricia. *The Erotic Life of Racism*. Durham, NC: Duke University Press, 2012.

Holy, Michael. "Der entliehene rosa Winkel." In *Der Frankfurter Engel, Mahnmal Homosexuellenverfolgung: Ein Lesebuch*, edited by Initiative Mahnmal Homosexuellenverfolgung, 74–87. Frankfurt am Main: Eichborn, 1997.

Holy, Michael. "Einige Daten zur zweiten deutschen Homosexuellenbewegung (1969–1983)." In *Schwule Regungen—schwule Bewegungen*, edited by Willi Frieling, 183–94. Berlin: Verlag rosa Winkel, 1985.

Hornsey, Richard. *Spiv and the Architect: Unruly Life in Postwar London*. Minneapolis: University of Minnesota Press, 2010.

Hottle, Rachel. "Emotion, Speech, and Music." *Canadian Audiologist* 4, no. 5 (September 2017). https://canadianaudiologist.ca/emotion-speech-music-feature/.

Hoven, Herbert, ed. *Der unaufhaltsame Selbstmord des Botho Laserstein: Ein deutscher Lebenslauf.* Frankfurt: Luchterhand, 1991.

Huneke, Erik G. "Morality, Law, and the Socialist Sexual Self in the German Democratic Republic, 1945–1972." PhD diss., University of Michigan, 2013.

Huneke, Samuel Clowes. "'Do Not Ask Me Who I Am.'" *Point Magazine*, June 2, 2021.

Huneke, Samuel Clowes. "Gay Liberation behind the Iron Curtain." *Boston Review*, April 17, 2019. http://bostonreview.net/gender-sexuality/samuel-clowes-huneke -gay-liberation-behind-iron-curtain.

Huneke, Samuel Clowes. "Heterogeneous Persecution: Lesbianism and the Nazi State." *Central European History* 54 (2021): 297–325.

Huneke, Samuel Clowes. *States of Liberation: Gay Men between Dictatorship and Democracy in Cold War Germany.* Toronto: University of Toronto Press, 2022.

Hunt, Lynn, and Vanessa R. Schwartz. "Capturing the Moment: Images and Eyewitnessing in History." *Journal of Visual Culture* 9, no. 3 (2009): 259–71.

Huyssen, Andreas. *Present Pasts: Urban Palimpsests and the Politics of Memory.* Stanford, CA: Stanford University Press, 2003.

Huyssen, Andreas. "The Voids of Berlin." *Critical Inquiry* 24, no. 1 (1997): 57–81.

Initiative Homo-Monument. "Homo-Monument: Eine Republik auf eine selbstgestellte Frage." In *Der homosexuellen NS-Opfer gedenken*, edited by Heinrich Böll Stiftung. Berlin: Heinrich Böll Stiftung, 1999.

Isherwood, Christopher. *Christopher and His Kind.* New York: Farrar, Straus and Giroux, 1975.

Jackson, Earl, Jr. *Strategies of Deviance: Studies in Gay Male Representation.* Bloomington: Indiana University Press, 1995.

Jackson, Jeffrey H. *Paper Bullets: Two Artists Who Risked Their Lives to Defy the Nazis.* Chapel Hill, NC: Algonquin Books, 2020.

Jackson, Julian. "Arcadie: Sense and Issues of the 'Homophile' in France, 1954–82." *Revue d'Histoire Moderne et Contemporaine* 53, no. 4 (2006): 150–74.

Jay, Martin. *Downcast Eyes: The Denigration of Vision in Twentieth-Century French Thought.* Berkeley: University of California Press, 1994.

Jellonnek, Burkhard. *Homosexuelle unter dem Hakenkreuz: Die Verfolgung von Homosexuellen im Dritten Reich.* Paderborn: Ferdinand Schöningh Verlag, 1990.

Jensen, Erik N. "The Pink Triangle and Political Consciousness: Gays, Lesbians, and the Memory of Nazi Persecution." *Journal of the History of Sexuality* 11, nos. 1–2 (2002): 319–51.

Johnson, Deborah. "R(r)ose Sélavy as Man Ray: Reconsidering the Alter Ego of Marcel Duchamp." *Art Journal* 72, no. 1 (2013): 80–94.

Johnson, E. Patrick. "A Revelatory Distillation of Experience." *Women's Studies Quarterly* 40, no. 3 (2012): 311–14.

Jones, Amelia. "'Women' in Dada: Elsa, Rrose, and Charlie." In *Women in Dada: Essays on Sex, Gender, and Identity*, edited by Naomi Sawelson-Gorse, 142–72. Cambridge, MA: MIT Press, 2001.

Jordan, Jennifer A. *Structures of Memory: Understanding Urban Change in Berlin and Beyond*. Stanford, CA: Stanford University Press, 2006.

Kaiser, Monika. "8. Zusammenfassung und Ausblick." In *Neubesetzungen des Kunst-Raumes*, 277–86. Bielefeld: transcript Verlag, 2014.

Kammergericht Berlin. "Urteil v. 21.2.1950." *Neue Justiz* 4 (1950): 129.

Katz, Jonathan D., and David C. Ward, eds. *Hide/Seek: Difference and Desire in American Portraiture*. Washington, DC: Smithsonian, 2011.

Kaye, Kerwin. "Male Prostitution in the Twentieth Century: Pseudohomosexuals, Hoodlum Homosexuals, and Exploited Teens." *Journal of Homosexuality* 46, nos. 1–2 (2003): 1–77.

Keegan, Cáel M. "Getting Disciplined: What's Trans* about Queer Studies Now?" *Journal of Homosexuality* 67, no. 3 (2020): 384–97.

Kenawi, Samirah. *Frauengruppen in der DDR: Eine Dokumentation*. Berlin: Dokumentationszelle GrauZone, 1995.

Kennedy, Hubert C. *The Ideal Gay Man: The Story of "Der Kreis."* Binghamton: Routledge, 1999.

Kiliç, Zeynep, and Jennifer Petzen. "The Culture of Multiculturalism and Racialized Art." *German Politics and Society* 31, no. 2 (2013): 49–65.

King A. D. "Architecture, Capital and the Globalization of Culture." *Theory, Culture and Society* 7 (1990): 397–411.

Kirtley, Charles. "LET THE SUNSHINE IN: The Pioneering Role of Winston Leyland in Gay Publishing." *Lesbian and Gay New York* (Spring 1998). http://www.leylandpublications.com/article_leyland.html.

Klemens, Klaus Ulrich. *Die kriminelle Belastung der männlichen Prostituierten: Zugleich ein Beitrag zur Rückfallsprognose*. Berlin: Duncker und Humblot, 1967.

Knappett, Carl. "Photographs, Skeuomorphs and Marionettes: Some Thoughts on Mind, Agency and Object." *Journal of Material Culture* 7, no. 1 (2001): 97–117.

Knoll, Albert. *Totgeschlagen—totgeschwiegen: Die homosexuellen Häftlinge im KZ Dachau*. Munich: Forum Queeres Archiv München e.V, 2000.

Knopp, Lawrence. "Sexuality and Space: A Framework for Analysis." In *Mapping Desire*, edited by David Bell and Gill Valentine, 137–49. New York: Routledge, 1995.

Könne, Christian. "Gleichberechtigte Mitmenschen? Homosexuelle und die Bundesrepublik Deutschland." Bundeszentrale für Politische Buildung, September 7, 2018. https://www.bpb.de/geschichte/zeitgeschichte/deutschlandarchiv/275113/homosexuelle-und-die-bundesrepublik-deutschland.

Könne, Christian. "Homosexuelle und die Bundesrepublik Deutschland. Gleichberechtigte Mitmenschen?" *Deutschland Archiv,* September 7, 2018. http://www.bpb.de/275113.

Köppert, Katrin. *Queer Pain: Schmerz als Solidarisierung, Fotografie als Affizierung; Zu den Fotografien von Albrecht Becker aus den 1920er bis 1990er Jahren*. Berlin: Neofelis Verlag, 2021.

Korolczuk, Elżbieta, and Agnieszka Graff. "Gender as 'Ebola from Brussels': The Anticolonial Frame and the Rise of Illiberal Populism." *Signs: Journal of Women in Culture and Society* 43, no. 4 (2018): 797–821.

Koshar, Rudy. *From Monuments to Traces: Artifacts of German Memory, 1870–1990*. Berkeley: University of California Press, 2000.

Kowalski, Markus. "'Queergida': Jan Feddersen provoziert einen Shitstorm." *Queer.de*, April 8, 2019. https://www.queer.de/detail.php?article_id=33349.

Kricbel, Sabine. "Sexology's Beholders: The Exhibition *Popsex!* in Calgary." In *Not Straight from Germany: Sexual Publics and Sexual Citizenship since Magnus Hirschfeld*, edited by Michael Thomas Taylor, Annette F. Timm, and Rainer Herrn, 80–102. Ann Arbor: University of Michigan Press, 2017.

Kriminalhauptkommissar Schramm. "Das Strichjungenunwesen." In *Sittlichkeitsdelikte: Arbeitstagung im Bundeskriminalamt Wiesbaden vom 20. April bis 25. April 1959 über Bekämpfung der Sittlichkeitsdelikte*, 89–104. Wiesbaden: Bundeskriminalamt, 1959.

Kroymann, Maren. "Verschwundene Minderheit." *taz*, August 28, 2006. https://taz.de/Verschwundene-Minderheit/!385588/.

Kruse, Peter, ed. *Bomben, Trümmer, Lucky Strikes: Die Stunde Null in bisher unbekannten Manuskripten*. Berlin: wjs-Verlag, 2004.

Kuckuc, Ina [pseud.]. *Der Kampf gegen Unterdrückung: Materialien aus der deutschen Lesbierinnenbewegung*. Munich: Verlag Frauenoffensive, 1975.

Kuhar, Roman. "Playing with Science: Sexual Citizenship and the Roman Catholic Church Counter-narratives in Slovenia and Croatia." *Women's Studies International Forum* 49 (2015): 84–92.

Kuhar, Roman, and David Paternotte, eds. *Anti-gender Campaigns in Europe: Mobilizing against Equality*. New York: Rowman and Littlefield, 2017.

Kulish, Nicholas. "Gay Muslims Pack a Dance Floor of Their Own." *New York Times*, January 1, 2008. https://www.nytimes.com/2008/01/01/world/europe/01berlin.html.

Ladd, Brian. *The Ghosts of Berlin: Confronting German History in the Urban Landscape*. Chicago: University of Chicago Press, 1997.

LaDuke, Winona. *Recovering the Sacred: The Power of Naming and Claiming*. Toronto: Between the Lines, 2005.

l'Amour LaLove, Patsy, ed. *Beißreflexe: Kritik an queerem Aktivismus, autoritären Sehnsüchten, Sprechverboten*. Berlin: Quer Verlag, 2017.

Laserstein, Botho. *Strichjunge Karl: Ein kriminalistischer Tatsachenbericht*. Hamburg: Janssen Verlag, 1954.

Lautmann, Rüdiger. "The Pink Triangle: The Homosexual Males in Concentration Camps in Nazi Germany." *Journal of Homosexuality* 6 (1981): 141–60.

Lavers, Michael. "Poland's Anti-LGBTQ President Reelected." *PrideSource*, July 14, 2020. https://pridesource.com/article/polands-anti-lgbtq-president-reelected/.

Lefebvre, Henri. *The Production of Space*. New York: Wiley, 1992.

Lewis, Brian. *Wolfenden's Witnesses: Homosexuality in Postwar Britain*. Basingstoke, UK: Palgrave Macmillan, 2016.

Lewis, Holly. *The Politics of Everybody: Feminism, Queer Theory, and Marxism at the Intersection*. London: Zed Books, 2016.

Liddiard, Mark. "Changing Histories: Museums, Sexualities, and the Future of the Past." *Museum and Society* 2, no. 1 (2004): 15–29.

Littauer, Amanda. "'Someone to Love': Teen Girls' Same-Sex Desire in the 1950s United States." In *Queer 1950s: Rethinking Sexuality in the Postwar Years*, edited by Heike Bauer and Matt Cook, 61–76. Basingstoke, UK: Palgrave Macmillan, 2012.

Lorde, Audre. *Sister Outsider: Essays and Speeches*. Trumansburg, NY: Crossing Press, 1984.

Lorde, Audre. "The Uses of the Erotic." In *Sister Outsider: Essays and Speeches*. New York: Crossing Press, 1984.

Love, Heather. *Feeling Backward: Loss and the Politics of Queer History*. Cambridge, MA: Harvard University Press, 2009.

Ludwig, Gundula. "Desiring Neoliberalism." *Sexuality Research and Social Policy* 13, no. 4 (2016): 417–27.

Ludwig, Katharina. "Hello, Mrs. Butler, Nice to Meet You." *Migrazine* 2 (2010). http://www.migrazine.at/artikel/hello-mrs-butler-nice-meet-you.

Luehrs-Kaiser, Kai. "Zwei Männer und ein Schwules Denkmal." *Welt*, May 27, 2008. https://www.welt.de/regionales/berlin/article2040221/Zwei-Maenner-und-ein-schwules-Denkmal.html.

Lugones, María. *Pilgrimages/Peregrinajes: Theorizing Coalition against Multiple Oppressions*. Lanham, MD: Rowman and Littlefield, 2003.

Lupu, Noam. "Memory Vanished, Absent, and Confined: The Countermemorial Project in 1980s and 1990s Germany." *History and Memory: Studies in Representation of the Past* 15, no. 2 (September 2003): 130–65.

Lybeck, Marti. *Desiring Emancipation: New Women and Homosexuality in Germany, 1890–1933*. Albany: SUNY Press, 2014.

Mahlsdorf, Charlotte von. *I Am My Own Woman: The Outlaw Life of Charlotte von Mahlsdorf, Berlin's Most Distinguished Transvestite*. San Francisco: Cleis, 1995.

Major, Patrick. *Behind the Iron Curtain? East Germany and the Frontiers of Power*. Oxford: Oxford University Press, 2011.

Marhoefer, Laurie. "Homosexuality and Theories of Culture." In *Was ist Homosexualität? Forschungsgeschichte, gesellschaftliche Entwicklungen und Perspektiven*, edited by Jennifer V. Evans, Florian Mildenberger, Rüdiger Lautmann, and Jakob Pastötter, 255–69. Hamburg: Männerschwarm Verlag, 2014.

Marhoefer, Laurie. "Lesbianism, Transvestitism, and the Nazi State: A Microhistory of a Gestapo Investigation, 1939–1943." *American Historical Review* 121, no. 4 (2016): 1167–95.

Marhoefer, Laurie. "Queer Fascism and the End of Gay History." *NOTCHES*, June 19, 2018. https://notchesblog.com/2018/06/19/queer-fascism-and-the-end-of-gay-history/.

Marhoefer, Laurie. *Sex and the Weimar Republic: German Homosexual Emancipation and the Rise of the Nazis*. Toronto: University of Toronto Press, 2015.

Marhoefer, Laurie. "Was the Homosexual Made White? Race, Empire, and Analogy in Gay and Trans Thought in Twentieth-Century Germany." *Gender and History* 31, no. 1 (2019): 91–114.

Markovitz, Andrei S., and Simon Reich. *The German Predicament: Memory and Power in the New Europe*. Ithaca, NY: Cornell University Press, 1997.

Martin, Biddy. *Femininity Played Straight: The Significance of Being Lesbian*. New York: Routledge, 1996.

Massey, Doreen. *For Space*. London: Sage, 2005.

Massey, Doreen. "Geographies of Responsibility." *Geografiska Annaler* 86B, no. 1 (2004): 5–18.

Massey, Doreen. "Places and Their Pasts." *History Workshop Journal* 39, no. 1 (1995): 182–92.

Mbembe, Achille. *Necropolitics*. Durham, NC: Duke University Press, 2019.

McCormick, Richard W. *Gender and Sexuality in Weimar Modernity: Film, Literature, and "New Objectivity."* New York: Palgrave Macmillan, 2001.

McLellan, Josie. "From Private Photography to Mass Circulation: The Queering of East German Visual Culture, 1968–1989." *Central European History* 48, no. 3 (September 2015): 405–23.

McLellan, Josie. "Glad to Be Gay behind the Wall: Gay and Lesbian Activism in 1970s East Germany." *History Workshop Journal*, no. 74 (2012): 105–30.

McLellan, Josie. "Lesbians, Gay Men and the Production of Scale in East Germany." *Cultural and Social History* 14, no. 1 (2017): 89–105.

McLellan, Josie. *Love in the Time of Communism: Intimacy and Sexuality in the GDR*. Cambridge: Cambridge University Press, 2011.

McLellan, Josie. "State Socialist Bodies: East German Nudism from Ban to Boom." *Journal of Modern History* 79, no. 1 (2007): 48–79.

McLellan, Josie. "Visual Dangers and Delights: Nude Photography in East Germany." *Past and Present*, no. 205 (2009): 143–74.

McRuer, Robert. *Crip Theory: Cultural Signs of Queerness and Disability*. New York: Oxford University Press, 2006.

Meeker, Martin. "Behind the Mask of Respectability: Reconsidering the Mattachine Society and Male Homophile Practice, 1950s and 1960s." *Journal of the History of Sexuality* 10, no. 1 (2001): 78–116.

Meeker, Martin. *Contacts Desired: Gay and Lesbian Communications and Community, 1940s–1970s*. Chicago: University of Chicago Press, 2005.

Mercer, Kobena. "Just Looking for Trouble: Robert Mapplethorpe and Fantasies of Race." In *Dangerous Liaisons: Gender, Nation, and Postcolonial Perspectives*, edited by Anne McClintock, Aaimir Mufti, and Ella Shohat, 240–52. Minneapolis: University of Minnesota Press, 1997.

Mercer, Kobena. "Reading Racial Fetishism: The Photographs of Robert Mapplethorpe." In *Welcome to the Jungle: New Positions in Black Cultural Studies*, 174–219. London: Routledge, 1994.

Meyer, Richard. "Mapplethorpe's Living Room: Photography and the Furnishing of Desire." *Art History* 24, no. 2 (2001): 292–311.

Micheler, Stefan. "Homophobic Propaganda and the Denunciation of Same-Sex-Desiring Men under National Socialism." *Journal of the History of Sexuality* 11, nos. 1–2 (2002): 95–130.

Micheler, Stefan. *Selbstbilder und Fremdbilder der "Anderen": Eine Geschichte Männer begehrender Männer in der Weimarer Republik und der NS-Zeit*. Konstanz: Universität Verlagsgesellschaft, 2005.

Micheler, Stefan, Jakob Michelsen, and Moritz Terfloth. "Archivalische Entsorgung der deutschen Geschichte? Historiker fordern die vollständige Aufbewahrung wichtiger Gerichtsakten aus der NS-Zeit." *Zeitschrift für Sozialgeschichte des 20. und 21. Jahrhunderts* 3, no. 96 (1999): 138–45.

Middleton, Drew. *Where Has Last July Gone? Memoirs*. New York: Quadrangle, 1973.

Miller, Ben, and Huy Lemmey. *Bad Gays: A Homosexual History*. London: Verso, 2022.

Miller, Jennifer A. *Turkish Guest Workers in Germany: Hidden Lives and Contested Borders, 1960s to 1980s*. Toronto: University of Toronto Press, 2018.

Minning, Heidi. "Who Is the 'I' in 'I Love You'? The Negotiation of Gay and Lesbian Identities in Former East Berlin, Germany." *Anthropology of East Europe Review* 18, no. 2 (2000): 103–14.

Moeller, Robert G. "Germans as Victims? Thoughts on a Post–Cold War History of World War II's Legacies." *History and Memory* 17, nos. 1–2 (2005): 145–94.

Moeller, Robert G. "The Last Soldiers of the 'Great War' and Tales of Family Reunions in the Federal Republic of Germany." *Signs: Journal of Women in Culture and Society* 24, no. 1 (1998): 129–45.

Moeller, Robert G. "Private Acts, Public Anxieties, and the Fight to Decriminalize Male Homosexuality in West Germany." *Feminist Studies* 36, no. 3 (2010): 528–52.

Moeller, Robert G. *War Stories: The Search for a Usable Past in the Federal Republic of Germany*. Berkeley: University of California Press, 2001.

Molnar, Virag. "The Cultural Production of Locality: Reclaiming the 'European City' in Post-Wall Berlin." *International Journal of Urban and Regional Research* 34, no. 2 (June 2010): 281–309.

Moreck, Curt. *Führer durch das 'lasterhafte' Berlin*. Leipzig: Verlag moderner Stadtführer, 1931.

Moreck, Curt. "Wir zeigen Ihnen Berlin." In *The Weimar Republic Sourcebook*, edited by Anton Kaes, Martin Jay, and Edward Dimendberg, 563–64. Berkeley: University of California Press, 1995. First published in *Führer durch das 'lasterhafte' Berlin* (Leipzig: Verlag moderner Stadtführer, 1930).

Morris, Robert J. "Same-Sex Friendships in Hawaiian Lore: Constructing the Canon." In *Oceanic Homosexualities*, edited by Stephen O. Murray, 71–102. New York: Garland, 1992.

Morsch, Günter. "Erklärung des Arbeitskreises I der Berlin-Brandenburgischen Gedenkstätten." *Der Lesben- und Schwulenverband in Deutschland*, December 15, 2006. http://www.gedenkort.de/psbbg151206.htm.

Mort, Frank. *Cultures of Consumption: Masculinities and Social Space*. London: Psychology Press, 1996.

Moten, Frank, and Stefano Harney. *The Undercommons: Fugitive Planning and Black Study*. Wivenhoe: Minor Compositions, 2013.

Müller, Joachim, and Andreas Sternweiler. *Homosexuelle Männer im KZ Sachsenhausen*. Berlin: Verlag rosa Winkel, 2000.

Müller, Wolfgang. *Subkultur Westberlin 1979–1989—Freizeit*. Hamburg: Philo Fine Arts, 2012.

Mulvey, Laura. "Visual Pleasure and Narrative Cinema." *Screen* 16, no. 3 (October 1975): 6–18.

Muñoz, José Esteban. *Cruising Utopia: The Then and There of Queer Futurity*. New York: New York University Press, 2009.

Muñoz, José Esteban. *Cruising Utopia, 10th Anniversary Edition*. New York: New York University Press, 2019.

Muñoz, José Esteban. *Disidentifications: Queers of Color and the Performance of Politics*. Minneapolis: University of Minnesota Press, 1999.

Muñoz, José Esteban. *The Sense of Brown: Ethnicity, Affect, and Performance*. Durham, NC: Duke University Press, 2020.

Murray, Stephen O. *Oceanic Homosexualities*. New York: Garland, 1992.

Namaste, Vivienne. *Invisible Lives: The Erasure of Transsexual and Transgendered People*. Chicago: University of Chicago Press, 2000.

Nancy, Jean-Luc. *Being Singular Plural*. Translated by Robert Richardson and Anne O'Byrne. Stanford, CA: Stanford University Press, 2000.

NARGS. *Schwule gegen Unterdrückung und Faschismus*. Berlin: SMB, 1977.

Nash, Jennifer C. *The Black Body in Ecstasy: Reading Race, Reading Pornography*. Durham, NC: Duke University Press, 2014.

Nay, Yv E., and Eliza Steinbock. "Critical Trans Studies in and beyond Europe: Histories, Methods, and Institutions." *TSQ: Transgender Studies Quarterly* 8, no. 2 (May 2021): 145–57.

Neiden, Susanne zur. "Als 'Opfer des Faschismus' nicht tragbar: Über den Umgang mit verfolgten Homosexuellen im Berlin der ersten Nachkriegsjahre." In *Homosexuelle in Deutschland 1933–1969: Beiträge zu Alltag, Stigmatisierung und Verfolgung*, edited by Alexander Zinn, 131–48. Göttingen: V&R Unipress, 2020.

Neiden, Susanne zur. "'. . . Er ist §175 (warmer Bruder)': Ausgrenzungen verfolgter Homosexueller in Berlin 1945 bis 1949." In *Verfolgung homosexueller Männer 1933–1945*, edited by Joachim Müller and Andreas Sternweiler, 338–53. Berlin: Schwules Museum, 2000.

Nemer, Benny. "I Don't Know Where Paradise Is: Queer Paths through Museums and Libraries." PhD diss., Edinburgh College of Art, 2020.

Nestle, Joan. "The Will to Remember: The Lesbian Herstory Archives of New York." *Feminist Review* 34, no. 1 (March 1990): 86–94.

Newsome, W. Jake. "Homosexuals after the Holocaust: Sexual Citizenship and the Politics of Memory in Germany and the United States, 1945–2008." PhD diss., University of Buffalo, 2016.

Newsome, W. Jake. *Pink Triangle Legacies: Coming Out in the Shadow of the Holocaust*. Ithaca, NY: Cornell University Press, 2022.

Newton, Esther. *Mother Camp: Female Impersonators in America*. Englewood Cliffs, NJ: Prentice-Hall, 1972.

Oettler, Anika. "The Berlin Memorial to the Homosexuals Persecuted under the National Socialist Regime: Ambivalent Responses to Homosexual Visibility." *Memory Studies* 14, no. 2 (2021): 333–47.

Oettler, Anika, ed. *Das Berliner Denkmal für die im Nationalsozialismus verfolgten Homosexuellen: Entstehung, Verortung, Wirkung*. Bielefeld: transcript Verlag, 2017.

Oleson, Henrik. *Some Faggy Gestures*. Zürich: Museum für Gegenwartskunst, 2008.

Olick, Jeffrey, and David Levy. "Collective Memory and Cultural Constraint: Holocaust Myth and Rationality in German Politics." *American Sociological Review* 62, no. 6 (December 1997): 921–36.

O'Rourke, Michael. *Queer Insists (for José Esteban Muñoz)*. Brooklyn, NY: punctum books, 2014.

Östberg, Marit. "Jasco Viefhues." *Film School* (podcast), Episode 2. Accessed June 21, 2021. https://soundcloud.com/marit-oestberg/episode-2-jasco-viefhues.

Östberg, Marit. "Liz Rosenfeld." *Film School* (podcast), Episode 1. Accessed July 15, 2021. https://soundcloud.com/marit-oestberg/filmschool-with-liz-rosenfeld?si=27 a461069f7c49858445bb04554eb888.

Osterhammel, Jürgen. *Geschichtswissenschaft jenseits des Nationalstaats: Studien zu Beziehungsgeschichte und Zivilisationsvergleich*. Göttingen: Vandenhoeck und Ruprecht, 2000.

Otten, Axel, and Helmut Kißling, dirs. *Die andere Liebe*. Potsdam: DEFA, 1988.

Passerini, Luisa. *Europe in Love, Love in Europe: Imagination and Politics between the Wars*. New York: New York University Press, 1999.

Passerini, Luisa. *Women and Men in Love: European Identities in the Twentieth Century*. Translated by Juliet Haydock with Allan Cameron. New York: Berghahn Books, 2012.

Passerini, Luisa, Liliana Ellena, and Alexander C. T. Geppert, eds. *New Dangerous Liaisons: Discourses on Europe and Love in the Twentieth Century*. New York: Berghahn Books, 2010.

Paternotte, David, and Roman Kuhar. "Disentangling and Locating the 'Global Right': Anti-gender Campaigns in Europe." *Politics and Governance* 6, no. 3 (2018): 6–19.

Paul, Barbara, Josch Hoenes, Atlanta Ina Beyer, Natascha Frankenberg, and Rena Onat, eds. *Perverse Assemblages: Queering Heteronormativity Inter/Medially*. Berlin: Revolver, 2017.

Petzen, Jennifer. "Home or Homelike? Turkish Queers Manage Space in Berlin." *Space and Culture* 7, no. 1 (February 2004): 20–32.

Petzen, Jennifer. "Queer Trouble: Centring Race in Queer and Feminist Politics." *Journal of Intercultural Studies* 33, no. 3 (June 2012): 289–302.

Pilarczyk, Hannah. "Drecksäcke aller Länder." Bundestagswahl 2017: Linke Debattenkultur. *Der Spiegel*, July 30, 2017. https://www.spiegel.de/kultur/gesellschaft /bundestagswahl-2017-linke-debattenkultur-drecksaecke-aller-laender-a -1158594.html.

Pinney, Christopher. "Things Happen: Or, From Which Moment Does That Object Come?" In *Materiality*, edited by Daniel Miller, 256–72. Durham, NC: Duke University Press, 2005.

Plastargias, Jannis. *RotZSchwul: Der Beginn einer Bewegung (1971–1975)*. Berlin: Querverlag, 2015.

Pretzel, Andreas. "Eine Debattenbeitrag zum Streit um den Gedenkort für die im Nationalsozialismus verfolgten Homosexuellen." Text from MANEO-Soiree event, January 11, 2007. From author.

Pretzel, Andreas. "Ein 'Mahnmal Homosexuellenverfolgung.'" *Kunststadt Stadtkunst* 53 (2006): 30–31. https://docplayer.org/54128174-Kunststadt-stadtkunst.html.

Pretzel, Andreas. *Homosexuellenpolitik in der frühen Bundesrepublik: 3. Jahrgang, Heft 8*. Hamburg: Männerschwarm Verlag, 2010.

Pretzel, Andreas. *NS-Opfer unter Vorbehalt: Homosexuelle Männer in Berlin nach 1945*. Münster: Lit, 2002.

Pretzel, Andreas, and Gabriele Roßbach, eds. *Wegen der zu erwartenden hohen Strafe: Homosexuellenverfolgung in Berlin 1933–1945*. Berlin: Verlag rosa Winkel, 2000.

Pretzel, Andreas, and Volker Weiss. *Rosa Radikale: Die Schwulenbewegung der 1970er Jahre*. Hamburg: Männerschwarm Verlag, 2012.

Prickett, David James. "'We Will Show You Berlin': Space, Leisure, Flânerie and Sexuality." *Leisure Studies* 30, no. 2 (2011): 157–77.

Prosser, Jay. "Judith Butler: Queer Feminism, Transgender, and the Transubstantiation of Sex." In *The Transgender Studies Reader*, edited by Susan Stryker and Stephen Whittle, 257–80. New York: Routledge, 2006.

Prosser, Jay. *Second Skins: The Body Narratives of Trans*sexuality*. New York: Columbia University Press, 1993.

Puar, Jasbir K. "Celebrating Refusal: The Complexities of Saying No." *Bully Bloggers*, June 23, 2010. https://bullybloggers.wordpress.com/2010/06/23/celebrating-refusal-the-complexities-of-saying-no/.

Puar, Jasbir K. *Terrorist Assemblages: Homonationalism in Queer Times*. Durham, NC: Duke University Press, 2007.

Pultz, John. *The Body and the Lens: Photography 1839 to the Present*. New York: H. N. Abrams, 1995.

Pulver, Marco, ed. *"Das war janz doll!": Gottfried Stechers Memoiren; Eine schwule Biographie*. Berlin: Books on Demand, 2001.

Pyle, Kai. "Naming and Claiming: Recovering Ojibwe and Plains Cree Two-Spirit Language." *TSQ: Transgender Studies Quarterly* 5, no. 4 (November 2018): 574–88.

Queer Nations e.V. "Ein Mahmal nur für schwule NS-Opfer?" *Queer.de*, November 22, 2006. https://www.queer.de/detail.php?article_id=5984.

Ramalingam, Chitra. "Fixing Transience: Photography and Other Images of Time in 1830s London." In *Time and Photography*, edited by Jan Baetens, Alexander Streitberger, and Hilde Van Gelder, 3–26. Leuven: Leuven University Press, 2010.

Reddy, Chandan. *Freedom with Violence: Race, Sexuality, and the US State*. Durham, NC: Duke University Press, 2011.

Reed, Christopher. "Imminent Domain: Queer Space in the Built Environment." *Art Journal* 55, no. 4 (Winter 1996): 64–70.

Regener, Susanne. "Amateure: Laien verändern die visuelle Kultur." *Photogeschichte: Beiträge zur Geschichte und Aesthetik der Photographie* 29, no. 111 (2009): 5–10.

Regener, Susanne. *Visuelle Gewalt: Menschenbilder aus der Psychiatrie des 20. Jahrhunderts*. Bielefeld: transcript Verlag, 2016.

Rehberg, Peter. "Kritik vs. Selbstkritik." *SissyMag*, March 21, 2021. https://www
.sissymag.de/vojin-sasa-vukadinovic-hg-zugzwaenge/.

Reicherdt, Babette. "Die Namensgebung des Elberskirchen-Hirschfeld-Hauses: Über
Benennungspraxen und die Suche nach historischen Vorbildern in der LSBTI-
Geschichte." *Jahrbuch Sexualitäten* 2 (2017): 159–66.

Riechers, Burckhardt. "Freundschaft und Anständigkeit: Leitbilder im Selbstverständ-
nis männlicher Homosexueller in der frühen Bundesrepublik." *Invertito: Jahrbuch
für die Geschichte der Homosexualitäten* (1999): 12–46.

Reichert, Martin. "Begehren ist nicht rassistisch." *taz*, July 7, 2018. https://taz.de
/Patsy-lAmour-laLove-ueber-Hass-in-Berlin/!5512805.

Rizzo, Domenico. "The Ideal Friend: The Homophile Canon and 'Market' of Relations
in the 1950s." *Revue d'Histoire Moderne et Contemporaine* 53, no. 4 (2006): 53–73.

Robinson, C. "Listening Art: Making Sonic Artworks That Critique Listening." PhD
diss., University of Melbourne, 2016.

Robinson, Emily. "Touching the Void: Affective History and the Impossible." *Rethinking History: The Journal of Theory and Practice* 14, no. 4 (2010): 503–20.

Romsics, Gergely. "The Meaning of Occupation: The Ambiguous Productivity of the
Memorial to the Sinti and Roma Victims of National Socialism in Berlin." *Intersections* 6, no. 1 (2020): 84–114.

Rönn, Peter von. "Politische und psychiatrische Homosexualitäts-Konstruktionen im
NS-Staat." *Zeitschrift für Sexualforschung* 11, no. 2 (1998): 99–129.

Roos, Julia. "Backlash against Prostitutes' Rights: Origins and Dynamics of Nazi Prostitution Policies." *Journal of the History of Sexuality* 11, nos. 1–2 (2002): 67–94.

Roos, Julia. *Weimar through the Lens of Gender: Prostitution Reform, Woman's Emancipation, and German Democracy, 1919–1933*. Ann Arbor: University of Michigan
Press, 2010.

Rose, Nikolas. *The Politics of Life Itself: Biomedicine, Power, and Subjectivity in the
Twenty-First Century*. Princeton, NJ: Princeton University Press, 2009.

Rosenfeld, Liz. "This Should Happen Here More Often: All My (W)Holes and All My
Folds of Cruising." *Third Text* 35, no. 1 (2021): 25–36.

Rosenkranz, Bernhard, Ulf Bollmann, and Gottfried Lorenz. *Homosexuellen-
Verfolgung in Hamburg, 1919–1969*. Hamburg: Lambda, 2009.

Rothberg, Michael. *The Implicated Subject: Beyond Victims and Perpetrators*. Stanford, CA: Stanford University Press, 2019.

Rothberg, Michael. *Multidirectional Memory: Remembering the Holocaust in the Age
of Decolonization*. Stanford, CA: Stanford University Press, 2009.

Rottmann, Andrea. "Queer Home Berlin? Making Queer Selves and Spaces in the
Divided City, 1945–1970." PhD diss., University of Michigan, 2019.

Rottmann, Andrea. *Queer Lives across the Wall: A Different History of Divided Berlin,
1945–1970*. Toronto: University of Toronto Press, 2023.

Rottmann, Andrea. "Zeitzeug*innen-Interview mit Nadja Schallenberg." Digi-
tales Deutsches Frauenarchiv, FFBIZ, June 12, 2020. https://www.digitales

-deutsches-frauenarchiv.de/meta-objekt/zeitzeuginnen-interview-mit-nadja
-schallenberg-im-rahmen-des-projektes-zeitzeuginnengespraeche-198990-aus
-lesbischfeministischer-perspektive/36553ffbiz.

Rottmann, Andrea, and Hannes Hacke. "Homosexualität_en: Exhibiting a Contested History in Germany in 2015." *Social History in Museums* 41 (2017): 63–72.

Rubin, Gayle S. "Thinking Sex: Notes for a Radical Theory of the Politics of Sexuality." In *Deviations: A Gayle Rubin Reader*, 137–81. Durham, NC: Duke University Press, 2012.

Ruddat, Martha. "Geschredderte NS-Dokumente: Staatsarchiv räumt Fehler ein." *taz*, September 4, 2018. https://taz.de/!5529873/.

Said, Edward W. "Invention, Memory, and Place." *Critical Inquiry* 26, no. 2 (2000): 175–92.

Schädlich, Rainer, and Dieter Bachnick. *. . . Alle Schwestern werden Brüder . . . Zusammenarbeit zwischen den vielfältigen Gruppen homosexueller Männer und Frauen—geht das überhaupt? Ist gar die Gründung eines Dachverbandes möglich?* Berlin: Trifolium, 1986.

Schäfer, Leopold. "Neue Gesetzgebung und Rechtsprechung zur Prostitutionsfrage." *Deutsche Zeitschrift für Wohlfahrtspflege* 9 (1933): 157–65.

Schiavi, Michael R. "The Tease of Truth: Seduction, Verisimilitude (?), and Spectatorship in *I Am My Own Wife*." *Theatre Journal* 58, no. 2 (2006): 195–220.

Schickedanz, Hans-Joachim. *Homosexuelle Prostitution: Eine empirische Untersuchung über sozial diskriminiertes Verhalten bei Strichjungen und Call-Boys*. Frankfurt: Campus Verlag, 1979.

Schlober, C. "Blick über Tellerrand: Selman Arikboga und die 'Schwule International.'" *Männer-aktuell*, December 1991, 38–40.

Schlüter, Bastian, Karl-Heinz Steinle, and Andreas Sternweiler. *Eberthardt Brucks: Ein Grafiker in Berlin; Herausgegeben anlässlich der Ausstellung zum 90. Geburtstag des Berliner Grafikers Eberhardt Brucks, 11. April bis 11. August 2008*. Berlin: Schwules Museum, 2008.

Schmidt-Relenberg, Norbert, Hartmut Kärner, and Richard Pieper. *Strichjungen-Gespräche: Zur Soziologie jugendlicher Homosexuellen-Prostitution*. Darmstadt: Luchterhand, 1975.

Schnorr, Miriam. "Jenseits der 'Volksgemeinschaft'? Von Prostituierten und Zuhältern." In *Geschlechterbeziehungen und "Volksgemeinschaft,"* edited by Klaus Latzel, Elissa Mailänder, and Franka Maubach, 109–31. Göttingen: Wallstein, 2018.

Schoppmann, Claudia. *Days of Masquerade: Life Stories of Lesbians during the Third Reich*. New York: Columbia University Press, 1996.

Schoppmann, Claudia. "Im Schatten der Verfolgung: Lesbische Frauen im Nationalsozialismus." Dokumentation des Auftakt-Kolloquiums zum Kunstwettbewerb "Gedenkort für die im Nationalsozialismus verfolgten Homosexuellen," Berliner Forum für Geschichte und Gegenwart e.V. im Auftrag der Senatsverwaltung für Wissenschaft, Forschung und Kultur, 35–43. Berlin, 2005.

Schoppmann, Claudia. *Zeit der Maskierung: Lebensgeschichten lesbischer Frauen im "Dritten Reich."* Berlin: Orlanda Frauenverlag, 1993.

Schotmiller, Carl. "Reading *RuPaul's Drag Race*: Queer Memory, Camp Capitalism, and RuPaul's Drag Empire." PhD diss., UCLA, 2017.

Schrödl, Jenny, and Eike Wittrock. *Theater* in queerem Alltag und Aktivismus der 1970er und 1980er Jahre*. Berlin: Neofelis Verlag, 2022.

Schumann, Sarah. "Zu den Fotografien von Inea Gukema-Augstein." In *Der Intime Blick: Maria Sabine Augstein; Fotografien von Inea Gukema-Augstein 1985–1988*, edited by Inea Gukema-Augstein. Tutzing, Altet Forsthaus: Gukema-Augstein, 2008.

Schupelius, Gunnar. "Mein Ärger." *Berliner Zeitung*, June 13, 2008.

Schwartz, Michael, ed. *Homosexuelle im Nationalsozialismus: Neue Forschungsperspektiven zu Lebenssituationen von lesbischen, schwulen, bi-, trans- und intersexuellen Menschen 1933 bis 1945*. Berlin: De Gruyter Oldenbourg, 2014.

Schwarzer, Alice. "Im Getto des Kitsches: Warum der Entwurf für das in Berlin geplante Homo-Mahnmal nicht nur politisch ein Skandal ist, sondern auch künstlerisch." *EMMA*, January 2007.

"Schwule und queere Visionäre: Zwei Filme von Rosa v. Praunheim und Benny Nemerofsky Ramsay. Simon Schultz von Dratzig im Gespräch mit Andreas Pretzel und Volker Weiß." In *Rosa Radikale: Die Schwulenbewegung der 1970er Jahre*, edited by Andreas Pretzel and Volker Weiss, 239–58. Hamburg: Männerschwarm Verlag, 2012.

Scott, Joan W. "The Evidence of Experience." *Critical Inquiry* 17, no. 4 (1991): 773–97.

Scott, Joan W. "Multiculturalism and the Politics of Identity." *October* 61 (1992): 12–19.

Scott, Joan W. *Sex and Secularism*. Princeton, NJ: Princeton University Press, 2018.

Sedgwick, Eve Kosofsky. *Epistemology of the Closet*. Durham, NC: Duke University Press, 1990.

Sedgwick, Eve Kosofsky. *Tendencies*. New York: Routledge, 1994.

Seitz, David. *A House of Prayer for All*. Minneapolis: University of Minnesota Press, 2019.

Sekula, Allan. "On the Invention of Photographic Meaning." In *Thinking Photography*, edited by Victor Burgin, 84–109. New York: Macmillan Education, 1982.

Selitsch, Wolfgang, Gerd Talis, and Hans-Peter Reichelt. "Aktion '80 der deutschen Homophilen-Presse." *Du & Ich* 7 (1980): 14.

Senatsverwaltung für Jugend und Familie, Fachbereich für gleichgeschlechtliche Lebensweisen, ed. *Der homosexuellen NS-Opfer gedenken: Denkschrift*. Berlin: Senatsverwaltung für Jugend und Familie, Fachbereich für gleichgeschlechtliche Lebensweisen, 1995.

Sender, Katherine. *Business and the Making of a Gay Market*. New York: Columbia University Press, 2005.

Sharp, Ingrid. "The Sexual Unification of Germany." *Journal of the History of Sexuality* 13, no. 3 (2004): 348–65.

Sharpe, Christina. *In the Wake: On Blackness and Being*. Chapel Hill: University of North Carolina Press, 2018.

Shepard, Todd. "'Something Notably Erotic': Politics, 'Arab Men,' and Sexual Revolution in Post-decolonization France, 1962–1974." *Journal of Modern History* 84, no. 1 (2012): 80–115.

Shimizu, Celine Parreñas. *The Hypersexuality of Race: Performing Asian/American Women on Screen and Scene*. Durham, NC: Duke University Press, 2007.

Shotwell, Alexis. *Against Purity: Living Ethically in Compromised Times*. Minneapo lis: University of Minnesota Press, 2016.

Sillge, Ursula. *Un-Sichtbare Frauen: Lesben und ihre Emanzipation in der DDR*. Berlin: Links Verlag, 1991.

Silverman, Kaja. *The Miracle of Analogy, or The History of Photography, Part 1*. Stanford, CA: Stanford University Press, 2015.

Small, C. *Musicking: The Meanings of Performing and Listening*. Hanover, NH: University Press of New England, 1998.

Smith, Barbara, ed. *Home Girls: A Black Feminist Anthology*. ACLS Humanities E-Book. New Brunswick, NJ: Rutgers University Press, 2000.

Smith, Helmut Walser. *Germany: A Nation in Its Time*. New York: W. W. Norton, 2020.

Smith, Nicola J. *Capitalism's Sexual History*. Oxford: Oxford University Press, 2020.

Smith, Shawn Michelle. *Photography on the Color Line: W. E. B. Du Bois, Race, and Visual Culture*. Durham, NC: Duke University Press, 2004.

Smith, Tom. *Comrades in Arms: Military Masculinities in East German Culture*. New York: Berghahn Books, 2020.

Smith-Rosenberg, Carroll. "The Female World of Love and Ritual: Relations between Women in Nineteenth-Century America." *Signs: Journal of Women in Culture and Society* 1, no. 1 (1975): 1–29.

Soguel, Dominique, and Monika Rebala. "As Poland's Election Heats Up, So Does Anti-LGBTQ Rhetoric. Why?" *Christian Science Monitor*, October 2, 2019. https://www.csmonitor.com/World/Europe/2019/1002/As-Poland-s-election-heats-up-so-does-anti-LGBTQ-rhetoric.-Why.

Sontag, Susan. "On Photography." In *A Susan Sontag Reader*. New York: Farrar, Straus and Giroux, 1982.

Soysal, Levent. "Diversity of Experience, Experience of Diversity: Turkish Migrant Youth Culture in Berlin." *Cultural Dynamics* 13, no. 1 (2001): 5–28.

Spector, Nancy. "A Note on Photography: Documentation as Art Form in the 1970s." In *Rrose Is a Rose Is a Rose: Gender Performance in Photography*, edited by Jennifer Blessing, 156–75. New York: Guggenheim Museum, 1997.

Spillers, Hortense J. "Mama's Baby, Papa's Maybe: An American Grammar Book." *Diacritics* 17, no. 2 (1987): 65–81.

Spurlin, William J. *Lost Intimacies: Rethinking Homosexuality under National Socialism*. New York: Peter Lang, 2009.

Stanley, Eric E. *Atmospheres of Violence: Structuring Antagonism and the Trans/Queer Ungovernable*. Durham, NC: Duke University Press, 2021.

Stapel, Eduard. *Warme Brüder gegen kalte Krieger: Schwulenbewegung in der DDR im Visier der Staatssicherheit*. Magdeburg: Landesbeauftragte für die Unterlagen des Staatssicherheitsdienstes der Ehemaligen DDR Sachsen-Anhalt, 1999.

Steakley, James D. "Gays under Socialism: Male Homosexuality in the German Democratic Republic." *Body Politic* 29 (1976/1977): 15–18.

Steakley, James D. "Homosexuals and the Third Reich." *Body Politic*, no. 11 (January/February 1974): 1–3.

Stein, Gertrude. "Next: Life and Letters of Marcel Duchamp." In *Geography and Plays*, 405–6. Madison: University of Wisconsin Press, 2012.

Steinbacher, Sybille. *Wie der Sex nach Deutschland kam: Der Kampf um Sittlichkeit und Anstand in der frühen Bundesrepublik*. Munich: Siedler Verlag, 2011.

Steinbock, Eliza. "Photographic Flashes: On Imaging Trans Violence in Heather Cassils' Durational Art." *Photography and Culture* 7, no. 3 (2014): 253–68.

Steinbock, Eliza. "Puncture Wounds: Sensing Stigmata in the Gender Nonconforming Portrait." In *Perverse Assemblages: Queering Heteronormativity Inter/Medially*, edited by Barbara Paul, Josch Hoenes, Atlanta Ina Beyer, Natascha Frankenberg, and Rena Onat, 33–44. Berlin: Revolver, 2017.

Steinbock, Eliza. *Shimmering Images: Trans Cinema, Embodiment, and the Aesthetics of Change*. Durham, NC: Duke University Press, 2019.

Steinbock, Eliza. "The Wavering Line of Foreground and Background: A Proposal for the Schematic Analysis of Trans Visual Culture." *Journal of Visual Culture* 19, no. 2 (2020): 171–83.

Steinle, Karl-Heinz. "Die 'Kameradschaft die runde' und ihr Kampf gegen den Homosexuellenparagrafen 175." *Schwäbische Heimat* 72, no. 3 (September 2021): 21–27.

Steinle, Karl-Heinz, and Maika Leffers. "Mittenmang: Homosexuelle Frauen und Männer in Berlin 1945–1969." Schwules Museum*. Accessed July 14, 2021. http://www.schwulesmuseum.de/ausstellungen/archives/2003/view/mittenmang-homosexuelle-frauen-und-maenner-in-berlin-1945-1969/.

Steinmetz, Julia. "Material Enactments: The Transformational Aesthetics of Cassils and Yishay Garbasz." *Transgender Studies Quarterly* 5, no. 2 (2018): 268–74.

Sternweiler, Andreas. "Er ging mit ihm alsbald ein sogenanntes 'Festes Verhältnis' ein." In *Homosexuelle Männer im KZ Sachsenhausen*, edited by Joachim Müller and Andreas Sternweiler, 58–78. Berlin: Verlag rosa Winkel, 2000.

Sternweiler, Andreas. "Poesie of a Gay Everyday." *Herbert Tobias, 1924–1982: Blicke und Begehren*, edited by Ulrich Domröse, 42–48. Hamburg: Haus der Photographie Directorhallen Hamburg, 2008.

Stockton, Kathryn Bond. *The Queer Child, or Growing Sideways in the Twentieth Century*. Durham, NC: Duke University Press, 2009.

Stokes, Lauren. "The Permanent Refugee Crisis in the Federal Republic of Germany, 1949." *Central European History* 52, no. 1 (2019): 19–44.

Stoler, Ann Laura. *Carnal Knowledge and Imperial Power: Race and the Intimate in Colonial Rule*. Berkeley: University of California Press, 2010.

Stratton, Jon. *The Desirable Body: Cultural Festishism and the Erotics of Consumption*. Champaign: University of Illinois Press, 1996.

Strick, Simon. "Warum die transfeindliche Debatte einfach nicht verstummt." *Der Spiegel*, August 14, 2022. https://www.spiegel.de/kultur/geschlechter-identitaet-warum-die-transfeindliche-debatte-einfach-nicht-verstummt-a-83f1a47f-e800-46bf-b5ed-252afb213310.

Stryker, Susan. "(De)Subjugated Knowledges." In *The Transgender Studies Reader*, edited by Susan Stryker and Stephen Whittle, 1–19. New York: Routledge, 2006.

Stryker, Susan. "Interview: Thinking about 'Gender in Spatial Terms' by Justin Time." In *Trans *homo: Differences—Alliances—Contradictions*, edited by Jannik Franzen and Justin Time, 247–60. Berlin: NoNo Verlag, 2012.

Stryker, Susan. "My Words to Victor Frankenstein above the Village of Chamounix: Performing Transgender Rage." *GLQ: A Journal of Lesbian and Gay Studies* 1, no. 3 (1994): 237–54.

Stryker, Susan. "The Time Has Come to Think about Gayle Rubin." *GLQ: A Journal of Lesbian and Gay Studies* 17, no. 1 (2011): 79–83.

Stryker, Susan. *Transgender History: The Roots of Today's Revolution*. 2nd ed. New York: Seal, 2017.

Stryker, Susan, Paisley Currah, and Lisa Jean Moore. "Introduction: Trans-, Trans, or Transgender?" *Women's Studies Quarterly* 36, nos. 3–4 (2008): 11–22.

Stryker, Susan, and V Varun Chaudhry. "Ask a Feminist: Susan Stryker Discusses Trans Studies, Trans Feminism, and a More Trans Future with V Varun Chaudhry." *Signs: Journal of Women in Culture and Society* (blog), February 2021. http://signsjournal.org/stryker/.

Sutton, Katie. "Cultivating an Ethical Gaze: Thinking with and beyond Identity in Queer and Trans German Pasts and Presents." UBC Ziegler Lecture, April 24, 2020.

Sutton, Katie. "Sexology's Photographic Turn: Visualizing Trans Identity in Interwar Germany." *Journal of the History of Sexuality* 27, no. 3 (2018): 442–79.

Sutton, Katie. "'We Too Deserve a Place in the Sun': The Politics of Transvestite Identity in Weimar Germany." *German Studies Review* 35, no. 2 (2012): 335–54.

Tagg, John. "Neither Fish nor Flesh." *History and Theory* 48, no. 4 (2009): 77–81.

TallBear, Kim. "Caretaker Relations Not American Dreaming." *Kalfou: A Journal of Comparative and Relational Ethnic Studies* 6, no. 1 (2019): 24–41.

Tauqir, Tamsila, Jennifer Petzen, Jin Haritaworn, Sokari Ekine, Sarah Bracke, Sarah Lamble, Suhraiya Jivraj, and Stacy Douglas. "Queer Anti-racist Activism and Strategies of Critique: A Roundtable Discussion." *Feminist Legal Studies* 19, no. 2 (2011): 169–91.

Taylor, Michael Thomas. "Visual Medical Rhetorics of Trans*gender Histories." In *Others of My Kind: Transatlantic Transgender Histories*, edited by Alex Bakker, Rainer Herrn, Michael Thomas Taylor, and Annette F. Timm, 177–217. Calgary: University of Calgary Press, 2020.

Taylor, Michael Thomas, and Rainer Herrn. "Hirschfeld's 'Female Transvestites.'" In *Others of My Kind: Transatlantic Transgender Histories*, edited by Alex Bakker, Rainer Herrn, Michael Thomas Taylor, and Annette F. Timm, 136–37. Calgary: University of Calgary Press, 2020.

Taylor, Michael Thomas, and Annette F. Timm. "Sex on Display: Sexual Science and the Exhibition PopSex!" In *Exhibiting the German Past: Museums, Film, and Musealization*, edited by Peter M. McIsaac and Gabriele Mueller, 227–47. Toronto: University of Toronto Press, 2015.

Therborn, Göran. "Entangled Modernities." *European Journal of Social Theory* 6, no. 3 (2003): 293–305.

Thierse, Wolfgang. "Grabenkämpfe gegen Gemeinsinn: Wie viel Identität verträgt die Gesellschaft?" *Frankfurter Allgemeine Zeitung*, February 21, 2021. https://www.faz.net/aktuell/feuilleton/debatten/wolfgang-thierse-wie-viel-identitaet-vertraegt-die-gesellschaft-17209407.html.

Thinius, Bert. "Erfahrungen schwuler Männer in der DDR und in Deutschland Ost." In *Homosexualität in der DDR: Materialien und Meinungen*, edited by Wolfram Setz, 9–88. Hamburg: Männerschwarm Verlag, 2006.

Thomas, Julia Adeney. "The Evidence of Sight." *History and Theory* 48, no. 4 (2009): 151–68.

Thompson, Vanessa E., and Veronika Zablotsky. "Nationalisen der Anerkennung: Gedenken, Differenz und die Idee einer 'europäischen Kultur der Erinnerung.'" In *Decolonize the City! Zur Kolonialität der Stadt: Gespräche/Aushandlungen/Perspektiven*, edited by Zwischenraum Kollektiv, 154–78. Münster: UNRAST-Verlag, 1999.

Thrift, Nigel. "Intensities of Feeling: Towards a Spatial Politics of Affect." *Geografiska Annaler* 86B (2004): 57–78.

Thurnwald, Hilde. *Gegenwartsprobleme Berliner Familien: Eine soziologische Untersuchung an 498 Familien*. Berlin: Weidmann, 1948.

Till, Karen E. "Artistic and Activist Memory-Work: Approaching Place-Based Practice." *Memory Studies* 1, no. 1 (2008): 99–113.

Till, Karen E. *The New Berlin: Memory, Politics, Place*. Minneapolis: University of Minnesota Press, 2005.

Timm, Annette F. *The Politics of Fertility in Twentieth-Century Berlin*. Cambridge: Cambridge University Press, 2010.

Timm, Annette F. "Sex with a Purpose: Prostitution, Venereal Disease and Militarized Masculinity in the Third Reich." *Journal of the History of Sexuality* 11, nos. 1–2 (2002): 223–55.

Tobias, Herbert. "Die Erinnerung ist das einzige Paradies." In *Herbert Tobias, 1924–1982: Blicke und Begehren*, edited by Ulrich Domröse, 6–9. Hamburg: Steidl Göttingen, 2008.

Tobias, Herbert. "Ein nostalgischer Ausflug in die Vergangenheit." In *Herbert Tobias, 1924–1982: Blicke und Begehren*, edited by Ulrich Domröse, 24–25. Hamburg: Steidl Göttingen, 2008.

Tobias, Herbert. "Leben zu Protokoll." In *Herbert Tobias, 1924–1982: Blicke und Begehren*, edited by Ulrich Domröse, 8–13. Hamburg: Steidl Göttingen, 2008.

Tobias, Herbert. "Geschichte mit Manfred." *him* 12 (December 1974): 20–23.

Tobin, Robert Deam. "The Evolian Imagination: Gender, Race, and Class from Fascism to the New Right." *Journal of Holocaust Research* 35, no. 2 (April 2021): 75–90.

Tobin, Robert Deam. *Peripheral Desires: The German Discovery of Sex*. Philadelphia: University of Pennsylvania Press, 2015.

Tobin, Robert Deam. "Was Judith Butler Right to Refuse Berlin Award?" *Gay and Lesbian Review* 17, no. 5 (2010): 6.

Toews, John. "Intellectual History after the Linguistic Turn: The Autonomy of Meaning and the Irreducibility of Experience." *American Historical Review* 92 (1987): 879–907.

Tomberger, Corinna. "Das Berliner Homosexuellen-Denkmal: Ein Denkmal für Schwule und Lesben?" In *Homophobie und Devianz: Weibliche und männliche Homosexualität im Nationalsozialismus*, edited by Insa Eschebach, 187–207. Berlin: Metropol, 2012.

Tomberger, Corinna. "Das Homosexuellen-Denkmal seit seiner Übergabe 2008. Nachtrag zum Text 'Wessen Gedenken? Geschlechterkritische Fragen an das geplante Homosexuellen-Mahnmal.'" Berlin, 2010. https://www.lesbengeschichte.org/ns_mahnmal_berlin_d.html.

Tomberger, Corinna. "'Der homosexuellen ns-Opfer gedenken'—Anmerkungen zu einer Denkmalinitiative." *Zeitschrift für Sozialgeschichte des 20. und 21. Jahrhunderts* 13, no. 1 (1998): 227–30.

Tomberger, Corinna. "Homosexuellen-Geschichtsschreibung und Subkultur: Geschlechtstheoretische und heternormativitätskritische Perspektiven." In *Homosexuelle im Nationalsozialismus*, edited by Michael Schwartz, 19–26. Berlin: De Gruyter Oldenbourg, 2014.

Tomberger, Corinna. "Wessen Gedenken? Geschlechterkritische Fragen an das geplante Homosexuellen-Mahnmal." *Invertito: Jahrbuch für Geschichte der Homosexualitäten* 9 (2007): 136–55.

Tourmaline, Eric A. Stanley, and Johanna Burton. *Trap Door: Trans Cultural Production and the Politics of Visibility*. Cambridge, MA: MIT Press, 2017.

Trachtenberg, Alan. *Reading American Photographs: Images as History; Mathew Brady to Walker Evans*. New York: Farrar, Straus and Giroux, 1990.

Traub, Valerie. *Thinking Sex with the Early Moderns*. Philadelphia: University of Pennsylvania Press, 2015.

Tremblay, Jean-Thomas. "Diagnostic Spectatorship: Modern Physical Culture and White Masculinity." *Modernism/Modernity Print Plus* 6, no. 2 (June 2021). https://modernismmodernity.org/forums/posts/tremblay-diagnostic-spectatorship-modern-physical-culture-and-white-masculinity.

Tremblay, Sébastien. "The Proudest Symbol We Could Put Forward: The Pink Triangle as Transatlantic Symbol of Gay and Lesbian Identities from the 1970s to the 1990s." Ph.D diss., Freie Universität Berlin, 2020.

Tremblay, Sébastien. "Solidarity Means Shifting Categories: Queer Victimhood and the National Socialist Past." *German Historical Institute London Bulletin* 44, no. 2 (November 2022): 57–65.

Tucker, Jennifer. *Nature Exposed: Photography as Eyewitness in Victorian Science*. Baltimore, MD: Johns Hopkins University Press, 2008.

Tuntenstreit: Theoriediskussion der Homosexuellen Aktion Westberlin. West Berlin: Verlag rosa Winkel, 1975.

Turner, Mark W. *Backward Glances: Cruising Queer Streets in New York and London*. London: Reaktion, 2009.

Uhlig, Tija. "Failing Gender, Failing the West: The Monstrous (Un)Becoming of a Genderqueer Clown in a Post-Soviet Borderland." *TSQ: Transgender Studies Quarterly* 8, no. 2 (2021): 223–37.

Umbach, Maiken. "Selfhood, Place, and Ideology in German Photo Albums, 1933–1945." *Central European History* 48, no. 3 (2015): 335–65.

Vendrell, Javier Samper. "The Case of a German-Jewish Lesbian Woman: Martha Mosse and the Danger of Standing Out." *German Studies Review* 41, no. 2 (2018): 335–53.

Vendrell, Javier Samper. *Seduction of Youth: Homosexual Rights in the Weimar Republic.* Toronto: University of Toronto Press, 2020.

Villa, Paula-Irene. "The Sargnagel Talks Back: Eine Replik auf die 'EMMA.'" *Missy Magazine*, July 12, 2017. https://missy-magazine.de/blog/2017/07/12/the -sargnagel-talks-back-eine-replik-auf-die-emma/.

von Praunheim, Rosa. *Sex und Karriere*. Munich: Rogner und Bernhard, 1976.

Vukadinović, Vojin Saša. "Butler erhebt 'Rassismus'-Vorwurf." *EMMA*, June 28, 2017. https://www.emma.de/artikel/gender-studies-sargnaegel-des-feminismus-334569.

Ward, Janet. *Post-Wall Berlin: Borders, Space, and Identity*. Basingstoke, UK: Palgrave Macmillan, 2011.

Warner, Michael. *Fear of a Queer Planet: Queer Politics and Social Theory*. Minneapolis: University of Minnesota Press, 1993.

Warner, Michael. *Publics and Counterpublics*. New York: Zone Books, 2005.

Warner, Michael. *The Trouble with Normal: Sex, Politics, and the Ethics of Queer Life*. New York: Free Press, 1999.

Waugh, Thomas. *Hard to Imagine: Gay Male Eroticism in Photography and Film from Their Beginnings to Stonewall*. New York: Columbia University Press, 1996.

Waugh, Thomas. "Posing and Performance: Glamour and Desire in Homoerotic Art Photography, 1920–1945." In *The Passionate Camera: Photography and Bodies of Desire*, edited by Deborah Bright, 58–77. New York: Routledge, 1998.

Waugh, Thomas. "The Third Body: Patterns in the Construction of the Subject in Gay Male Narrative Film." In *The Visual Culture Reader*, edited by Nicholas Mirzoeff, 636–53. New York: Routledge, 2004.

Weeks, Jeffrey. *The World We Have Won: The Remaking of Erotic and Intimate Life*. New York: Routledge Press, 2007.

Weiermair, Peter. *Hidden Image: Photographs of the Male Nude in the 19th and 20th Centuries*. Translated by Claus Nielander. Cambridge, MA: MIT Press, 1988.

Weinberg, Lorenz. "Pleasure and Danger: Butch/Femme und die Sex Wars." In *Femme/ Butch: Dynamik von Gender und Begehren*, edited by Sabine Fuchs, 273–30. Berlin: Querverlag, 2020.

Weinthal, Benjamin. "Berlin's Harshly Felt Divide." *Gay City News*, March 15, 2007.

Wekker, Gloria. *White Innocence: Paradoxes of Colonialism and Race*. Durham, NC: Duke University Press, 2016.

Wells, Liz, ed. *Photography: A Critical Introduction*. 3rd ed. New York: Routledge, 2003.

Weston, Kath. *Families We Choose: Lesbians, Gays, Kinship*. New York: Columbia University Press, 1991.

Whisnant, Clayton. *Male Homosexuality in West Germany: Between Persecution and Freedom*. Basingstoke, UK: Palgrave Macmillan, 2012.

Whisnant, Clayton. *Queer Identities and Politics in Germany: A History, 1880–1945*. New York: Harrington Park, 2016.

Whisnant, Clayton. "Styles of Masculinity in the West German Gay Scene." *Central European History* 39, no. 3 (2006): 359–93.

Wiegman, Robyn. *Object Lessons*. Durham, NC: Duke University Press, 2012.

Wilke, Christiane. "Remembering Complexity? Memorials for Nazi Victims in Berlin." *International Journal of Transitional Justice* 7, no. 1 (2013): 136–56.

Williams, Linda. *Hard Core: Power, Pleasure, and the "Frenzy of the Visible."* Berkeley: University of California Press, 1999.

Wittdorf, Jürgen. *Lieblinge: Arbeiten von 1952–2003: Sammlung Linkersdorf, Kvost*. Berlin: Distanz Verlag, 2020.

Wocker, Rex, and Billy Kelly. "Holocaust Gay Memorial Unveiled in Berlin." *Gay and Lesbian Times* 30, no. 12 (June 13–June 27, 2008).

Wright, Doug. *I Am My Own Wife*. New York: Farrar, Straus and Giroux, 2004.

Young, James. *At Memory's Edge: After-Images of the Holocaust in Contemporary Art and Architecture*. New Haven, CT: Yale University Press, 2000.

Young, James. "Berlin's Holocaust Memorial: A Report to the Bundestag Committee on Media and Culture, 3 March 1999." *German Politics and Society* 17, no. 3 (1999): 54–70.

Young, James. *The Texture of Memory: Holocaust Memorials and Meaning*. New Haven, CT: Yale University Press, 1993.

Yurchak, Alexei. *Everything Was Forever, Until It Was No More: The Last Soviet Generation*. Princeton, NJ: Princeton University Press, 2006.

Zimmerman, Andrew. *Anthropology and Antihumanism in Imperial Germany*. Chicago: University of Chicago Press, 2001.

Zinn, Alexander. "Abschied von der Opferperspektive: Plädoyer für einen Paradigmenwechsel in der schwulen und lesbischen Geschichtsschreibung." *Zeitschrift für Geschichtswissenschaft* 67 (2019): 935.

Zinn, Alexander. "Einfalt Statt Vierfalt: Wie LGBTI-Verbände ins Linksidentitäre Fahrwasser abdriften." *Franfurter Allgemeiner Zeitung*, March 16, 2021. https://www.faz.net/aktuell/feuilleton/debatten/wie-lgbti-verbaende-ins-linksidentitaere-fahrwasser-abdriften-17246497.html.

Zinn, Alexander. "Zwischen Opfermythos und historischer Präzision." *Berliner Zeitung*, April 7, 2021.

Zuromskis, Catherine. *Snapshot Photography: The Lives of Images*. Cambridge, MA: MIT Press, 2013.

Index